RESEARCH ON ROMAN BRITAIN:
1960–89

RESEARCH ON ROMAN BRITAIN: 1960–89

EDITED BY

Malcolm Todd

with contributions by T.F.C. Blagg, D.J. Breeze, C. Daniels, S. Esmonde Cleary, M. Fulford, A. Grant, C. Haselgrove, M. Henig, M. Jones, L.J.F. Keppie, V.A. Maxfield, D. Miles, T.W. Potter, M. Todd, J. Wacher, J.J. Wilkes.

Britannia Monograph Series
No. 11

Published by the Society for the Promotion of Roman Studies
31 GORDON SQUARE LONDON WC1H OPP

1989

BRITANNIA MONOGRAPH SERIES NO. 11

Published by the Society for the Promotion of Roman Studies
31–34 Gordon Square, London WC1H 0PP

Copies may be obtained from the Secretary of the Roman Society

British Library Cataloguing in Publication Data

Research on Roman Britain, 1960–89. – (Britannia monograph series, ISSN 0953-542X; v.11).
1. Great Britain. Social life, 43–410. Archaeological sources
I. Todd, Malcolm *1939–* II. Blagg, T.F.C. (Tom F.C.) III. Series
936.1'04

ISBN 0 907764 13 4

Front Cover: Detail of mosaic from Fishbourne
Back Cover: Gilded Bronze Head of Minerva, Bath

Produced by Alan Sutton Publishing Ltd, Gloucester
Printed in Great Britain

CONTENTS

LIST OF ILLUSTRATIONS

SHEPPARD FRERE

OB RES PROSPERE GESTAS IN BRITANNIA

PREFACE

The past thirty years have witnessed an extraordinary outpouring of work on Roman Britain. In 1960, the base-line for this collection of studies, a mere handful of general books existed on the subject; now they are legion and still they appear. It is now difficult to believe that the first full-scale history of Roman Britain, Sheppard Frere's *Britannia*, did not appear until 1967, while we still await the completion of the project to publish the Roman inscriptions of this small province, first formulated by the father of modern Romano-British studies Francis Haverfield. Only in the past few years have major treatments of many aspects of Roman Britain been made available. All this serves as a salutary reminder that although much is now known about this part of the Empire of Rome, we are closer to the beginning of work upon it than to the end, if there ever could be such a thing. Within the three decades covered by this volume discoveries of immense importance have been made. In 1960 no-one would have predicted the recovery of an archive of documents like those from Vindolanda, or the discovery of the earliest cache of Christian silver anywhere in the Roman Empire at Water Newton. It is occasionally suggested that our knowledge of Britannia is substantially complete and that mere in-filling is required to round off the edifice. How far this is from the truth is clear from the papers collected here and the changing pattern of research objectives which they outline. It will be clear that many subjects relating to Roman Britain are not treated in this volume, while others are less than fully covered. Any process of selection is bound to lead to such casualties. All that can be hoped for is agreement that most of the principal themes receive attention here.

Throughout the period under review, no single contribution has been greater than that of Sheppard Frere. Aside from his major excavations at Canterbury, Verulamium, Dorchester on Thames, Bignor, Longthorpe, Brandon Camp and Strageath, and his enduring *Britannia*, he was the founder-editor of this Society's journal *Britannia*, serving from 1970 to 1980, and the creator of *Britannia Monographs* and their trenchant editor for the first ten issues. The debt this Society owes to him is immense and can only be repaid in part, but a part he will appreciate, by maintaining the exacting standards he has set in the publication and dissemination of learning.

THE LATER IRON AGE IN SOUTHERN BRITAIN AND BEYOND*

By Colin Haselgrove

INTRODUCTION

In recent years, the nature of Iron Age societies in Britain in the century and a half preceding the Claudian invasion has received welcome reappraisal by several authors. Without denying the resulting advances in our knowledge, it is noticeable that this literature is still conceived largely in the context of two long-standing debates: the extent of the indigenous contribution to Romano-British developments[1] and the degree of Continental, including Roman, influence on late Iron Age communities.[2] Consequently, attention is directed primarily at southern England, where pre-Conquest influence is most evident in the archaeological record and the centre of gravity of the subsequent Roman province. Equally, discussions are often polarised around a series of well-worn 'great divides'.[3] Had late Iron Age society in various areas managed the critical transition to, for example, urbanism or political statehood, or to a market economy?[4]

Arguably, these preoccupations have deflected too much attention away from other, equally important issues. One such question is the formative role of the middle Iron Age (c.400–100 B.C.) in subsequent developments. The late Iron Age undeniably saw widespread agricultural, cultural and technological changes, along with apparently novel settlement types, increasing coin-use and an upsurge in visible long-distance trade.[5] Nevertheless, in focusing on these processes without due regard to earlier patterns, we run two risks. We may fail to recognise the extent to which

* I am very grateful to Martin Millett, Niall Sharples, Steve Trow and Greg Woolf for permission to refer to their unpublished work and to Pamela Lowther for her invaluable assistance in the preparation of the text and footnotes.

1. See e.g. C.C. Haselgrove, 'Romanisation before the conquest: Gaulish precedents and British consequences' in T.F.C. Blagg and A.C. King (eds.), *Military and civilian in Roman Britain* BAR 136 (1984), 5– 63; M.J. Millett, *The Romanization of Britain* (Cambridge, forthcoming); and S. Trow, 'By the northern shores of Ocean. Some observations on acculturation process at the edge of the Roman world', in T.F.C. Blagg and M.J. Millett (eds.) *The early Roman Empire in the West* (forthcoming).
2. See e.g. W.J. Rodwell, 'Coinage, oppida and the rise of Belgic power in south-west Britain,' in B.W. Cunliffe and R.T. Rowley (eds.), *Oppida: the beginnings of urbanisation in barbarian Europe* BAR S 11 (1976), 184–367; C.C. Haselgrove, 'Wealth, prestige and power: the dynamics of late Iron Age political centralisation in south-east England', in C. Renfrew and S. Shennan (eds.), *Ranking, Resource and Exchange* (Cambridge, 1982), 79–88; B.W. Cunliffe, 'Relations between Britain and Gaul in the first century BC and early 1st century AD' in S. Macready and F.H. Thompson (eds.), *Cross-channel trade between Gaul and Britain in the pre-Roman Iron Age* Soc Antiq Occ Paper 4 (London, 1984), 3–23; D. Nash, 'The basis of contact between Britain and Gaul in the late pre-Roman Iron Age', ibid, 92–107.
3. This point is made forcibly by G. Woolf, 'Assessing social complexity in the final Iron Age of central France' Paper given to First Millennium BC Seminar, (Cambridge, 1987).
4. See, for example, various papers in B.C. Burnham and H.B. Johnson (eds.), *Invasion and response: the case of Roman Britain* BAR 73 (1979).
5. Haselgrove, op. cit. (note 2).

these changes are merely an outgrowth of earlier trends and we may end up assuming quite wrongly that their cause lies in the other visible changes of the period. Not all commentators, of course, take a narrow view. In Jones' survey of agricultural developments, the late Iron Age emerges as a more significant period of change than those immediately before and afterwards.[6] Similarly, Bradley's overriding concern is the recurrent appearance and disappearance of particular kinds of archaeological patterns and what these tell us of social changes in the longer-term.[7] These exceptions merely underline how imposing artificial chronological divisions between periods frequently distorts our perception of change, just as conceptualising complex developments in terms of 'great divides' does little for our understanding of the processes involved.

Another question is how extensively regions other than southern England – the north, the west, the upland areas – shared in wider geographical processes. Equally, what variations were there between the different zones and when is there evidence of contact or conformity? Darvill's recent survey of late Iron Age Britain underlines the broad similarities between often widely separated areas.[8] In general, it has taken us far too long to realise that many supposed differences relate to variable patterns of regional research and archaeological survival rather than to fundamental cultural or geographical divisions. This is partly because the southern Iron Age continues to exert disproportionate influence on our thinking, while, in its own way, the English-Scottish border is now a more formidable demarcation line for fieldwork and research than the Channel. The work of George Jobey is the exception that proves the rule.[9]

Wider chronological and geographical perspectives are required. In particular, the middle Iron Age saw the start of many processes that continued to affect Britain in the following centuries and cannot be treated merely as the background to the more visible changes after 100–50 B.C.[10] Moreover, many of the distinctions used to divide off the late Iron Age from what went before are virtually restricted to southern England. These include the abandonment of many Wessex hillforts and the introduction of wheel-made pottery.[11] Yet 'developed hillforts' have a relatively restricted distribution and half of Britain was virtually aceramic at this period.[12] In many regions, cultural continuity is, if anything, the dominant theme of the 300 years leading up to the Conquest, e.g. in Dorset,[13] East Sussex and the East Midlands. Indeed, as far as ceramic traditions, coin distributions and settlement patterns each, in their separate ways, indicate shared group-identities, Millett[14] argues that the cultural or ethnic groupings on which the administrative division of Britain into *civitates* was based, are already a feature of the archaeological record as early as the second century B.C., albeit comprising numerous sub-units.[15]

There are other difficulties; in parts of the South-East, supposedly middle Iron Age ceramic traditions persist until close to the Conquest. In central southern England, too, a starting date as early as 100 B.C. for the appearance of characteristic late Iron Age wheelmade pottery[16] can be questioned, since on several sites imported amphorae are associated with middle Iron Age

6. M.K. Jones 'The development of crop husbandry', in M.K. Jones and G.W. Dimbleby (eds.), *The environment of man: the Iron Age to the Anglo-Saxon period* BAR 87 (1981), 95–127.
7. R.J. Bradley, *The social foundations of prehistoric Britain* (London, 1984).
8. See T. Darvill, *Prehistoric Britain* (London, 1987), Chapters 6 and 7.
9. Cf. R. Miket and C. Burgess (eds.), *Between and beyond the walls: essays in honour of George Jobey* (Newcastle, 1984).
10. Cf. the recent review article by T.C. Champion, 'The European Iron Age: assessing the state of the art', *Scottish Arch. Rev.* iv (1987), 98–107.
11. B.W. Cunliffe, 'Iron Age Wessex; continuity and change', in B.W. Cunliffe and D. Miles (eds.), *Aspects of the Iron Age in Central Southern Britain* (Oxford, 1984), 12–45.
12. B.W. Cunliffe, *Iron Age Communities in Britain* (London, 1978).
13. N. Sharples, 'Later Iron Age society and continental trade in Dorset', Paper given to A.F.E.A.F. (Quimper, 1988).
14. Millett, op. cit (note 1), Chapter 2.
15. Cf. G. Lambrick, 'Pitfalls and possibilities in Iron Age pottery studies – experiences in the Upper Thames Valley', in Cunliffe and Miles, op. cit. (note 11), 162–177.
16. B.W. Cunliffe, *Danebury: an Iron Age hillfort in Hampshire* CBA Res Rep 52 (London, 1984).

pottery.[17] So too can the idea that the inception of the late Iron Age coincides with Britain's reintegration into the wider European system, in contrast to her previous relative isolation.[18] As we shall see, this view perhaps both minimises the extent of earlier contacts and overemphasises the quantity and importance of later imports. Most regions, moreover, have no direct evidence of contact with the Roman world until the Conquest. However we view it, the current division between the middle and late Iron Ages masks a more complex pattern of continuity and change, and is better discarded; this paper will, therefore, address the later Iron Age as a whole, from the second and third centuries B.C. to the later first century A.D..

AGRICULTURAL DEVELOPMENT AND ECONOMIC SPECIALISATION

By the later Iron Age, mixed farming was the principal agricultural strategy throughout most of Britain. Caesar's perception of an uncivilised interior, where pastoralism predominated[19] is erroneous, compounded until very recently by the serious imbalance of evidence towards the south.[20] The underlying rationale for earlier views, Fox's classic division of the country into lowland and highland zones,[21] is now generally accepted as obscuring a much more complex picture in the different regions.[22] Arable activity was intensive in many highland areas, e.g. north-east England and eastern Scotland.[23] Conversely, some lowland sites in marginal environments specialised in stock raising, e.g. Farmoor on the Thames floodplain and Fengate.[24] At local level, climate (especially rainfall and temperature), altitude, soils and drainage were all important in determining the actual balance between arable and pastoral strategies. If anything, the most useful general distinction is probably that between east and west, Atlantic Britain enduring a somewhat wetter and less favourable climate. In areas of higher altitude, settlement was mainly focused around the fringes and in sheltered valleys, as with the well-known field systems at Grassington, West Yorkshire.[25]

From about 400 B.C., the climate was improving from the previous recession, possibly with a temporary return to colder conditions around 200 B.C.; by the end of the millennium it was probably similar to today.[26] This improvement can only have facilitated the widespread agricultural changes of the later Iron Age. By the third century B.C., there were important changes in the range of crops grown and soon afterwards Wessex chalkland sites started

17.   This and other difficulties with the chronology are discussed in more detail, in C.C. Haselgrove, 'An Iron Age community and its hillfort: the excavations at Danebury, Hampshire, 1969–79' *Arch. Journ.* cxliii (1986), 363–368; and by N. Sharples in *PPS* liii (1987), 507–509, in his review of B.W. Cunliffe, *Hengistbury Head Dorset Vol I: the prehistoric and Roman settlements 3500 BC-AD 500* O.U.C.A. Monograph 13 (Oxford, 1987).

18.   For example, Bradley, op. cit. (note 7).

19.   *De Bello Gallico* V, 14.

20.   op. cit. (note 6), fig. 6.1.

21.   C.F. Fox, *The personality of Britain* (Cardiff, 1932).

22.   See J. Evans and H. Cleere (eds.), *The effect of man on the landscape: the highland zone* CBA Res Rep 11 (London, 1975) and S. Limbrey and J. Evans (eds.), *The effect of man on the lowland zone* CBA Res Rep 21 (London, 1978).

23.   See for example, M. Van der Veen, 'Evidence for crop plants from north-east England: an interim overview with discussion of new results' in N.R.J. Fieller, D.D. Gilbertson and N.G.A. Ralph (eds.), *Palaeobiological Investigations* BAR S 266 (1985), 197–219 and L. MacInnes, 'Pattern and purpose: the settlement evidence', in D.W. Harding (ed.), *Later prehistoric settlement in south-east Scotland* Univ Edinburgh Occ Paper 8 (Edinburgh, 1982), 57–73.

24.   G. Lambrick and M. Robinson, *Iron Age and Roman riverside settlement at Farmoor, Oxfordshire* CBA Res Rep 32 (London, 1979) and F. Pryor and D. Cranstone, 'An interim report on excavations at Fengate, Peterborough 1975–77', *Northants Arch.* xiii (1978), 9–27.

25.   A. Raistrick, 'Prehistoric cultivation at Grassington, West Yorkshire', *Yorks. Arch. Journ.* xxxiii (1938), 166–174.

26.   See for example, H.H. Lamb, 'Climate from 1000 BC – 1000 AD', in Jones and Dimbleby, op. cit. (note 6), 53–67; J. Turner, 'The Iron Age', in I. Simmons and M. Tooley (eds.), *The environment in British prehistory*, (London, 1981), 250–81; and M. Robinson, 'Landscape and environment of central southern Britain in the Iron Age', in Cunliffe and Miles, op. cit. (note 11), 1–11.

specialising in different crops.[27] Broadly contemporary innovations include the iron tipping of ard shares, increasing use of rotary querns, and greater use of drainage ditches to facilitate the cultivation of damper ground and of manuring and crop rotation to maintain soil fertility.[28]

A common factor of these new techniques is that they required greater investment of limited resources like human labour and animal traction, as well as raw materials and thus imply a genuine intensification of agricultural activity. Although these innovations occur earliest in the south, they appear to have spread to other regions relatively rapidly. Rotary querns were present at Thorpe Thewles in Cleveland by the second century B.C.,[29] while the dominance of spelt wheat there and at other north-eastern sites contradicts Jones' previous suggestion that emmer remained the commonest wheat in northern Britain throughout the Iron Age.[30] The Upper Thames Valley is another region where the evidence suggests crop specialisation, innovatory sites like Bierton and Barton Court Farm growing substantial amounts of bread wheat, in contrast to established farms like nearby Ashville where it is absent.[31] (below, p. 132)

Animal husbandry also became increasingly specialised around this time. Chalkland sites like Winnall Down and Danebury show a greater emphasis on sheep, lower-lying sites like Ashville and Odell on cattle.[32] Alternatively, this pattern partially reflects seasonal differences with the developed hillforts like Danebury only being fully occupied during the winter.[33] Similar patterns of integration between upland and lowland sites can be cited elsewhere, e.g. in East Yorkshire and the North–East.[34] The suggestion that new site types like the banjo enclosure reflect increasing pastoral specialisation in some regions now needs revision, given the demonstration that some of them were settlements on agricultural land rather than stock enclosures.[35]

The landscape provides many other indications of agricultural intensification during the later Iron Age. Sites required access to a wide range of resources. The defended enclosure at Tattershall Thorpe, Lincolnshire, for example, was surrounded by a mixture of wetland, woodland, grassland, heathland and cultivated terrain.[36] In several cases, all the available land was clearly in use, e.g. at Ashville and Micheldever Wood, in Wessex.[37] In north–west Essex, settlement was well established by the end of the Iron Age on even the flattest and most poorly

27. P.J. Green, 'Iron Age, Roman and Saxon crops: the archaeological evidence from Wessex', in Jones and Dimbleby, op. cit. (note 6), 129–54.

28. Jones, op. cit., (note 6).

29. D.H. Heslop, *The excavation of an Iron Age settlement at Thorpe Thewles, Cleveland, 1980–82* CBA Res Rep 65 (London, 1987).

30. See M. Van der Veen, 'The plant remains', in Heslop, op. cit. (note 29), 93–9 and fiche 5E, *contra* Jones, op. cit. (note 6).

31. M.K. Jones, 'Regional patterns in crop production', in Cunliffe and Miles, op. cit. (note 11), 120–5. For the excavation reports on these sites, see D. Allen, 'Excavations in Bierton 1979', *Rec. Bucks.* xxviii (1986), 1–120; D. Miles (ed.), *Archaeology at Barton Court Farm, Abingdon, Oxon.* CBA Res Rep 50 (London, 1984) and M. Parrington, *The excavation of an Iron Age settlement, Bronze Age ring ditches and Roman features at Ashville Trading Estate, Abingdon, Oxfordshire 1974–76* CBA Res Rep 28 (London, 1978).

32. M. Maltby, 'Iron Age, Romano-British and Anglo-Saxon animal husbandry: a review of the faunal evidence', in Jones and Dimbleby, op. cit. (note 6), 155–204; and A. Grant, 'Animal husbandry in Wessex and the Thames Valley', in Cunliffe and Miles, op. cit. (note 11), 102–119. For the excavation reports, see P.J. Fasham, *The prehistoric settlement at Winnall Down Winchester*, (Gloucester, 1985); B. Dix, 'Excavations at Harold Pit, Odell 1974–78', *Beds. Arch. Journ.* xiv (1980), 15–18; Cunliffe, op. cit. (note 16); and Parrington, op. cit. (note 31).

33. J. Stopford, 'Danebury: an alternative view', *Scot. Arch. Rev.* iv (1987), 70–75.

34. C.C. Haselgrove, 'The later pre-Roman Iron Age between the Humber and the Tyne', in P.R. Wilson, R.F. Jones and D.M. Evans (eds.), *Settlement and society in the Roman North* (Bradford, 1984), 9–25 and A. King, 'Animal bones and the dietary identity of military and civilian groups in Roman Britain, Germany and Gaul', in Blagg and King, op. cit. (note 1), 187–218.

35. B.T. Perry, 'Excavations at Bramdean, Hampshire, 1983 and 1984, with some further discussion of the 'banjo' syndrome', *Proc Hants. Field Club Arch. Soc.* xlii (1986), 35–42.

36. P. Chowne, M. Girling and J. Greig, 'Excavations of an Iron Age defended enclosure at Tattershall Thorpe, Lincolnshire', *PPS* lii (1986), 159–188.

37. P.J. Fasham, *A banjo enclosure in Micheldever Wood, Hampshire*, (Gloucester, 1987); see also Jones, op. cit. (note 31).

drained parts of the plateau, soils which were once thought not to have been cleared until the post-Roman period.[38]　In other areas, such as Bedfordshire and Northamptonshire, settlement density rose markedly on a whole range of subsoils including the heavy clays by at least the third century B.C.[39] Other indicators for increasingly widespread exploitation of heavier soils and damp ground include new settlement types being established on the Sussex coastal plain; damp ground species in carbonised plant assemblages; late-first-millennium B.C. cultivation marks on heavy clay in the lower Severn valley, at Almonsbury, Avon; and pollen evidence of intensive later Iron Age clearance in north-east England.[40]

Agricultural expansion at the expense of forest and other marginal land is evident in many other areas during the same period, e.g. the Vale of York.[41] In the Cheviots, a series of small, remote sites with hand-hoed ridges suggesting farming units too small to maintain a plough team, e.g. at Snear Hill, gives every impression of a wave of pioneer settlers, although the dating evidence is slight and the episode could belong to the second millennium B.C.[42] The rise in water-table of the Thames floodplain during the Iron Age probably reflects the deforestation of much of the river's catchment, and colluviation in dry valley bottoms consequent on ploughing reached a maximum during the Iron Age.[43] The building of large-scale land boundaries also resumed at this period in areas as far apart as Wessex, Lincolnshire and East Yorkshire.[44] Elsewhere, field systems were established on long cleared but previously uncultivated land, e.g. in the Isles of Scilly,[45] and new large-scale organised landscapes were laid out: the co-axial field systems of East Anglia and the brickwork fields on the Bunter Sandstone of Nottinghamshire and South Yorkshire.[46] Other parallel field systems, e.g. in Essex, may be of similar date, while pre-existing field systems also saw extensive use at this period.[47] We should not, however, overlook the possibility that these new large-scale field systems were sometimes connected with stock raising rather than with arable cultivation. Either way, these and earlier developments must have provided the basic structure of the Roman landscape. Even in areas where the settlement forms, e.g. in the South-West, or palaeo-ecological evidence, e.g. in the Wear lowlands, County Durham and central Scotland, suggest greater emphasis on pastoral strategies,[48] we may assume that the landscape was already highly managed and subdivided.

The agricultural changes of the later Iron Age, were accompanied by changes in the organisation and scale of production. Signs of increasing economic specialisation include the

38. T. Williamson, 'The development of settlement in north-west Essex. The results of a recent field survey', *Essex Arch. Hist.* xvii (1986), 120–32.
39. D. Knight, *Late Bronze Age and Iron Age settlement in the Nene and Great Ouse basins* BAR 80 (1984).
40. O. Bedwin, 'Aspects of Iron Age settlement in Sussex', in Cunliffe and Miles, op. cit. (note 11), 46–51; Jones, op. cit. (note 6); Darvill, op. cit. (note 8); P.A.G. Clack, 'The northern frontier: farmers in the military zone', in D. Miles (ed.), *The Romano-British countryside* BAR 103 (1982), 377–402; D. Wilson, 'Pollen analysis and settlement archaeology of the first millennium BC from north-east England', in J.C. Chapman and H.C. Mytum (eds.), *Settlement in North Britain* BAR 118 (1983), 29–54.
41. M.J. Millett and S. McGrail, 'The archaeology of the Hasholme logboat', *Arch. Journ.* cxliv (1987), 69–155.
42. M.K. Jones, *England before Domesday* (London, 1987). For these Cheviot sites, see T. Gates, 'Unenclosed settlement in Northumberland', in Chapman and Mytum, op. cit. (note 40), 103–48.
43. See Robinson, op. cit. (note 26) and M. Bell, 'The effects of land-use and climate on valley sedimentation' in A.F. Harding (ed.), *Climatic change in later prehistory* (Edinburgh, 1982), 127–42.
44. J. Pickering, 'The Jurassic Spine', *Current Arch.* vi no. 64 (1978), 140–143; J. Dent, 'Cemeteries and settlement patterns of the Iron Age on the Yorkshire Wolds', *PPS* xlviii (1982), 437–458. For Wessex, see Bradley, op. cit. (note 7).
45. J. Evans, 'Excavations at Bar Point, St Marys, Isles of Scilly 1979–80', *Cornish Studies* xi (1983), 7–32.
46. T. Williamson, 'Early co-axial field systems on the East Anglian boulder clays', *PPS* liii (1987), 419–431; and D. Riley, *Early landscape from the air* (Sheffield, 1980).
47. W.J. Rodwell, 'Relict landscapes in Essex', in H.C. Bowen and P.J. Fowler (eds.), *Early land allotment* BAR 48 (1978), 89–98. See, more generally, P.J. Fowler, *The farming of prehistoric Britain* (Cambridge, 1983).
48. e.g. Darvill, op. cit. (note 8). For the specific cases, see A. Donaldson and J. Turner, 'A pollen diagram from Hallowell Moss near Durham City', *UK Journal of Biogeography* iv (1977), 25–33; and W.E. Boyd, 'Environmental change and Iron Age land management in the area of the Antonine Wall, Central Scotland: a summary', *Glasgow Arch. Journ.* xi (1984), 74–81.

standardisation of a range of products such as pottery, salt cakes and iron bars, and the development of a system of weights.[49] Against this and compared even with the meagre Continental evidence for industrial zones within some of the largest settlements there is little to imply the growth of a class of full-time producers, or that they were independent of their elite patrons.[50] Many developments, indeed, could easily be accommodated by part-time specialisation within the seasonal constraints of the agricultural cycle, such as coastal salt production[51] or the southern shale and northern jet industries. Others appear to be directly related to the agricultural changes of the period. The latter include the growth of industries based on the increasingly specialised environments which were now being colonised, such as textile production in the Somerset Levels, where we now recognise the role of sites like Glastonbury and Meare in facilitating the seasonal exploitation of local resources.[52] Meare, it is suggested, acted as a periodic meeting place for several separate communities.[53] Another example is quern production. The rotary querns from Lodsworth, West Sussex, were distributed over much greater distances than previously, production at the quarry reaching its peak during the first century A.D.[54] Conversely, in northern England, the increased utilisation of rotary querns apparently necessitated greater exploitation of local sources at the expense of high-quality products distributed over longer distances.[55]

The degree of specialisation behind the production and distribution of various finewares, including Glastonbury ware, in south-west England and the Welsh Marches is still unresolved.[56] Late in the Iron Age, however, the scale on which standardised wheel-made pottery was being mass-produced in various regions, including Dorset and the South-East, certainly implies specialised production.[57] The Upchurch ware industry operating in Kent from the start of the first century A.D. is one such enterprise.[58] The expanding distribution of salt produced at inland sources at Droitwich and in south-east Cheshire[59] also implies a specialist occupation. Droitwich, in particular, has yielded a massive quantity of the standardised containers used for the drying and long-distance transport of salt. Metalworking, too, shows signs of increasing specialisation: large-scale exploitation of iron sources in areas such as the Weald or Northamptonshire is reflected in increasing consumption on sites, e.g. at Danebury.[60] Bradley suggests that the move onto heavier clay soils allowed the greater use of iron ores in these and other areas, and by the end of the Iron Age there was smelting at all the major sources.[61]

49. J.V.S. Megaw and D.D.A. Simpson (eds.), *Introduction to British prehistory* (Leicester, 1979), Chapter 6, 'The Iron Age c 600BC – AD200 A: Southern Britain and Ireland', 345–421.
50. Woolf, op. cit. (note 3); cf. J. Collis, *Oppida: earliest towns north of the Alps* (Sheffield, 1984).
51. R.J. Bradley, 'Salt and settlement in the Hampshire-Sussex borderland', in K. de Brisay and K. Evans (eds.), *Salt – the study of an ancient industry* (Colchester, 1975), 20–25.
52. J. Barrett, 'The Glastonbury lake village: models and source criticism', *Arch. Journ.* cxliv (1987), 409–423.
53. B. and J.M. Coles, *Sweet Track to Glastonbury* (London, 1986).
54. D.P.S. Peacock, 'Iron Age and Roman quern production at Lodsworth, West Sussex', *Antiq. Journ.* xvii (1987), 61–85.
55. R.H. Hayes, J.E. Hemingway and D.A. Spratt, 'The distribution and lithology of beehive querns in north-east Yorkshire', *Journ. Arch. Science* vii (1980), 297–324; and D.H. Heslop, 'The study of the Beehive quern', *Scot. Arch. Rev.* v (1988), 59–65.
56. D.P.S. Peacock, 'A petrological study of certain Iron Age pottery from western England', *PPS* xxxiv (1968), 414–27; and 'A contribution to the study of Glastonbury ware from south-western Britain', *Antiq. Journ.* xlix (1969), 41–61.
57. e.g. Sharples, op. cit. (note 13); and I. Thompson, *Grog-tempered 'Belgic' pottery of south-eastern England* BAR 108 (1982).
58. J. Monaghan, *Upchurch and Thameside Roman pottery: a ceramic typology for northern Kent, 1st to 3rd centuries AD* BAR 173 (1987).
59. E. Morris, 'Prehistoric salt distributions: two case studies from Western Britain', *Bull Board Celtic Studies* xxxii (1985), 336–379; J. Sawle, 'Ceramic salt-making debris from Droitwich', *Bull Exper. Firing Group* ii (1984), 5–12; and H. Rees, 'Ceramic salt working debris from Droitwich', *Trans. Worcs. Arch. Soc.*[3] x (1986), 47–54.
60. C. Salter and R.M. Ehrenreich, 'Iron Age metallurgy in Central Southern Britain', in Cunliffe and Miles, op. cit. (note 11), 146–161.
61. Bradley, op. cit. (note 8); R.M. Ehrenreich, *Trade, technology and the iron working community of southern Britain in the Iron Age* BAR 144 (1985).

Particular tool types were increasingly manufactured from selected kinds of iron: high-phosphorous for adzes, ploughshares and large sickles – again the link with agricultural intensification is evident – and high-carbon for chisels.[62] It now seems increasingly probable that the so-called iron currency bars[63] were, in fact, iron stocks, their form and composition varying according to the particular source. Sword-shaped bars are phosphoritic, whereas the spit-shaped bars are low in phosphorus. Their distinctive forms would have enabled smiths to differentiate between the iron sources in selecting material for manufacturing a particular implement.[64] This functional role, of course, need not preclude their social or ritual use as well, while the known distribution need only reflect the limits of hoarding conditioned by different cultural attitudes to the storage of wealth outside the South-East, rather than the full extent of their exchange or use.[65] The control and technology of coin production, too, became increasingly sophisticated from the second century B.C. onwards.[66]

Bronze production rose markedly towards the end of the period and also became increasingly specialised. Northover notes a clear distinction between lost-wax casting, which is concentrated on open settlements such as Gussage All Saints and Beckford, and sheet metalworking which is particularly associated with hillforts.[67] A further tier of sites such as Hengistbury Head and Glastonbury shows a complex range of activities, including the actual production of copper-alloys.[68] Hengistbury Head and Meare are the only known sites involved in glass-working, the latter apparently the centre of glass bead production in England,[69] while at Hengistbury the grain assemblage implies that until the later first century B.C. it was a consumer site whose inhabitants were divorced from primary agricultural production.[70] The location of these primary producing sites in environmentally restricted areas can be paralleled in other areas, e.g. iron production in East Yorkshire, leading Sharples to suggest that for social reasons these activities were deliberately sited in marginal areas to exclude them from the tribal heartlands.[71] Alternatively, the settlement of increasingly specialised and often agriculturally unpromising environments during the later Iron Age perhaps led these communities to develop products for exchange to offset these other disadvantages,[72] although this argument cannot be taken far, as the population of many core areas also opted for change.

Many attribute the economic changes of the later Iron Age to social pressures arising from the supposed reduction in overseas contacts from the fourth century B.C.. Bradley, for example, argues that the leading groups may deliberately have stimulated specialised production to promote their own position, in effect using their patronage to increase the dependency of the remainder of the population by undermining their self-sufficiency.[73] For others, however, population pressure remains the preferred explanation. Although absolute figures remain controversial, the marked increase in site numbers compared to the earlier Iron Age and densities of between one to three sites per square kilometre now being reported for widely separated areas leave little doubt that by the Conquest Britain was much more densely populated than anyone

62. R.M. Ehrenreich, 'Blacksmithing technology in Iron Age Wessex', *OJA* v (1986), 165–183.
63. D.F. Allen, 'Iron currency bars in Britain', *PPS* xxxiii (1967), 307–335.
64. op. cit. (note 62).
65. Trow, op. cit. (note 1).
66. C.C. Haselgrove, 'Coinage and complexity: archaeological analysis of socio-political change in Britain and non-mediterranean Europe during the late Iron Age', in D.B. Gibson and M.N. Geselowitz (eds.), *Tribe and polity in late prehistoric Europe* (New York, 1988), 69– 96.
67. P. Northover, 'Iron Age bronze metallurgy in central southern England', in Cunliffe and Miles, op. cit. (note 11), 126–45.
68. Cunliffe, op. cit. (note 17).
69. J. Henderson, 'The raw materials of early glass production', *OJA* iv (1985), 267–91; idem, 'The Iron Age of Loughey and Meare: some inferences from glass analysis', *Antiq. Journ.* lxvii (1987), 29–42; and idem, 'The Glass' and 'Glassworking', in Cunliffe, op. cit. (note 17), 160–3 and 180–5.
70. S. Nye and M.K. Jones, 'The carbonised plant remains', in Cunliffe, op. cit. (note 17), 323–8.
71. Sharples, op. cit. (note 13). For East Yorkshire, see Millett and McGrail, op. cit. (note 41).
72. Bradley, op. cit. (note 7).
73. op. cit. (note 7).

had previously thought possible.[74] It is equally possible, however, that this demographic growth was a direct result of the agricultural changes of the period, rather than their cause. Gent has shown that the food-storage capacity of hillforts is much greater than the resident communities would have required, while the experimental yields obtained by Reynolds at Butser imply that food production was not limited either by the crops or the technology.[75] If there was a limiting factor, it was probably the resources which could be invested.[76] Even so, by the first centuries B.C. and A.D., the agricultural economy of at least Lowland Britain was almost certainly capable of generating a substantial food surplus, allowing communities to sustain population growth and an increasing measure of economic specialisation, while still leaving a disposable surplus to support elite status-building activities such as prestige exchange and acts of conspicuous consumption.

SETTLEMENT PATTERN AND HIERARCHY

The biggest problem in later Iron Age settlement studies is still our knowledge of open sites. Several recently investigated sites were only recognised incidentally to earlier or later enclosure phases, e.g. Gussage All Saints, Thorpe Thewles and Winnall Down, or were found through excavation of other threatened sites and landscapes, e.g. Little Waltham, Mucking or Wetwang Slack.[77] Those sites – just like such upland counterparts as the hut cluster settlements at Kilphedir, Sutherland or Roxby, Cleveland[78] – are probably exceptional only in being known. Their importance in the later Iron Age landscape can only therefore be guessed, leaving our perceptions still massively biased towards the more visible cropmark enclosures and the well-preserved – but not necessarily typical – earthwork sites in marginal upland valleys such as Teesdale.[79] The continuing preoccupation with areas such as Wessex merely compounds this problem. Only recently, for example, has the first fully excavated rural farmstead from so important an area as Kent been published, at Farningham Hill.[80]

Over much of southern England and the Welsh Marches, the pre-first-century B.C. settlement pattern was dominated by 'developed hillforts' such as Danebury or Maiden Castle, fairly regularly spaced across the landscape as if each controlled a discrete territory.[81] Arguably, these sites housed the elite, functioning as administrative and economic central places for dependent rural settlements,[82] though other interpretations are possible. Developments in eastern England and other lowland areas where hillforts are rare, follow superficially different lines, with a new class of extended open settlements, or 'villages', such as Dragonby and Mucking, emerging from the third century B.C. onwards. Some of these sites, however, are within the hillfort zone, as at Beckford, Worcestershire, and no absolute division can be made.

These changes need not necessarily reflect a smooth, continuous process of settlement

74. e.g. B.W. Cunliffe, 'Settlement and population in the British Iron Age: some facts, figures and fantasies', in B.W. Cunliffe and T. Rowley (eds.), *Lowland Iron Age Communities in Europe* BAR Int 48 (1978), 3–24; Knight, op. cit. (note 39); Williamson, op. cit. (note 38); cf. Fowler, op. cit. (note 47).
75. H. Gent, 'Centralised storage in later prehistoric Britain', *PPS* xlviii (1983), 243–267; and P.J. Reynolds, 'New approaches to familiar problems', in Jones and Dimbleby, op. cit. (note 6), 19–49.
76. Jones, op. cit. (note 6).
77. G.J. Wainwright, *Gussage All Saints: an Iron Age settlement in Dorset* DOE Arch. Rep. 10 (London, 1979); Heslop, op. cit. (note 29); Fasham, op. cit. (note 32); P. Drury, *Excavations at Little Waltham 1970–71* CBA Res Rep 26 (London, 1978); Dent, op. cit. (note 44).
78. H. Fairhurst and D.B. Taylor, 'A hut circle settlement at Kilphedir, Sutherland', *PSAS* ciii (1970–1), 65–99; and R. Inman, D.R. Brown, R.E. Goddard and D.A. Spratt, 'Roxby Iron Age settlement and the Iron Age in north-east Yorkshire', *PPS* li (1985), 181–213.
79. D. Coggins, *Upper Teesdale: the archaeology of a north Pennine Valley* BAR 150 (1986).
80. B.J. Philp, *Excavations in the Derwent Valley Kent* (Dover, 1984).
81. Cunliffe, op. cit. (note 12).
82. Alternatives to the models set out by Cunliffe, op. cit. (note 16) are discussed in C.C. Haselgrove, 'Central places in British Iron Age studies: a review and some problems', in E. Grant, *Central places: archaeology and history* (Sheffield, 1986), 3–12 and in Stopford, op. cit. (note 33).

nucleation linked to population growth.[83] Many hillforts, Collis suggests, reflect the aggregation of settlements into larger units in response to a particular crisis or some other rapid change in conditions.[84] The division of many villages and some later defended sites like Dyke Hills, Dorchester, Hod Hill or Salmonsbury, into numerous separate compounds resembling single unit settlements[85] is certainly compatible with such a model. A different manifestation of the process may be the clusters of individual settlements or 'neighbourhood groups', frequently found along the terraces of rivers like the Nene, the Ouse and the Thames.[86] Hingley suggests that these were corporate communities holding their land in common, unlike contemporary isolated farmsteads in areas such as the Oxfordshire uplands which continued to cultivate their land independently.[87]

Whichever model is preferred – gradual growth or sudden reorganisation – we still need to ask why such changes, like the agricultural developments of the period, were so widespread? Whatever the answer, the 'developed hillforts', nucleated villages and 'neighbourhood groups' all in their different ways imply a mosaic of relatively small corporate groups covering much of England. Whether they were integrated by elite control or by more egalitarian forms of social organisation, these entities, in turn, constituted the sub-units from which all wider late Iron Age cultural or political configurations were formed. During the third and second centuries B.C., many communities also began to differentiate themselves more markedly at both local and regional levels, as is reflected in the highly decorated fineware assemblages that appeared at this time throughout most of eastern and southern England,[88] a development which can hardly be coincidental.

The first century B.C. onwards brought relatively little change to the settlement pattern in many areas and a marked restructuring in others. In Lincolnshire, activity at Dragonby reached its maximum and throughout eastern England there was further settlement nucleation, both north and south of the Thames, where the recently constructed Wealden hillforts were rapidly abandoned.[89] There was also relative stability throughout Atlantic Britain, with the raths and rounds of Wales and the South-West and the larger multiple enclosure forts and cliff castles all continuing in use. However, certain features, such as the sheer density of sites in some areas, over two per square kilometre around Llawhaden, Dyfed,[90] and the one new settlement type in Cornwall – the enclosed courtyard house clusters with their associated souterrains, e.g. Carn Euny[91] – may imply processes of settlement aggregation similar to those already discussed for the South and East. In Scotland, too, the enigmatic brochs were apparently the only new type of dwelling site. The use of hillforts and homesteads such as crannogs and the fortified dun enclosures all continue much as before.[92]

In the Upper Thames Valley, however, the landscape appears more nucleated and tightly organised than before.[93] In Wessex too, the 'developed hillforts' such as Danebury and Maiden

83. Champion, op. cit. (note 10).
84. J. Collis, 'A theoretical study of hillforts', in G. Guilbert (ed.), *Hillfort studies* (Leicester, 1981), 66–76.
85. Bradley, op. cit. (note 7).
86. Jones, op. cit. (note 42).
87. R. Hingley, 'Towards social analysis in archaeology: Celtic society in the Iron Age of the Thames Valley', in Cunliffe and Miles, op. cit. (note 11), 72–88.
88. Cunliffe, op. cit. (note 11); Millett, op. cit. (note 1).
89. S. Elsdon and J. May, *The Iron Age pottery from Dragonby: a draft report* (Nottingham, 1987) and F.H. Thompson, 'Three Surrey hillforts: excavations at Anstiebury, Holmbury, and Hascombe, 1972–77', *Antiq. Journ.* lix (1979), 245–318.
90. Darvill, op. cit. (note 8).
91. P.M.L. Christie, 'The excavation of an Iron Age souterrain and settlement at Carn Euny, Sancreed, Cornwall', *PPS* xliv (1978), 309–434.
92. E. Mackie, 'The Brochs of Scotland', in P.J. Fowler (ed.), *Recent work in rural archaeology* (Bradford on Avon 1975), 72–92; D.W. Harding, 'The function and classification of brochs and duns', in Burgess and Miket, op. cit. (note 9), 206–20.
93. R. Hingley and D. Miles, 'Aspects of Iron Age settlement in the Upper Thames Valley', in Cunliffe and Miles, op. cit. (note 11), 52– 71.

Castle were either abandoned or declined in favour of non-defended sites. A new class of cohesive rural settlement also made its appearance, comprising an extended complex of ditched compounds.[94] Similar processes occurred further afield. In parts of north-east England, traditional enclosed farmsteads gave way to extended enclosure complexes such as Thorpe Thewles and Catcote, and something approaching 'neighbourhood groups' began to form in some of the more circumscribed parts of the landscape.[95]

Back in the south, the shift away from traditional community centres may account for the wealth of farms such as Owslebury after 50 B.C.[96] Coin lists imply that some rural settlements were of higher social status than the rest.[97] As we have seen, the elite may already have been rurally based even when the hillforts were still occupied. The restructuring of the southern settlement pattern did not occur everywhere at the same time and different regions were not equally affected. On the Sussex coastal plain, for example, marked changes only occur late in the first century B.C. and were possibly followed by further developments in the earlier first century A.D.[98]

There remains the problem of the so-called oppida which developed late in the Iron Age and whether these represent a significant break with the pre-existing settlement pattern. Unfortunately, the diversity of the sites which have been classed as oppida does not make discussion any easier. The 'enclosed oppida',[99] in fact, mix late hillforts (e.g. Bigbury, Oldbury) and large valley-slope or bottom fortifications (such as Dyke Hills, Dorchester; Salmonsbury; Stonea Camp; and Orams Arbour, Winchester). We currently know very little about those latter sites, except that they are generally later and larger than the 'developed hillforts', and their lowland situation implies a greater emphasis on accessibility and communications. Many important new unenclosed settlements, e.g. Baldock, Cleaval Point on Poole Harbour and perhaps Leicester share this tendency.[100] However, proximity to better agricultural land may also have been an important locational consideration, just as access to particular resources presumably influenced the siting of earlier nucleated settlements such as Dragonby.

The remaining oppida include the well-known south-eastern dyke complexes at Colchester, Chichester, St Albans and Silchester, their supposed counterparts in outlying regions at Bagendon and Stanwick, and important extended settlement complexes at Braughing, Canterbury and perhaps Sandy.[101] Again, they constitute a chronologically and morphologically diverse grouping. Braughing, Silchester, and probably Canterbury were all important nucleated settlements by the late first century B.C.,[102] whereas activity at Bagendon and Stanwick was most intensive after the invasion.[103] Neither of the latter sites is apparently nucleated to the same degree as some south-eastern sites.

Archaeological perception of these 'territorial oppida' is heavily coloured by the civitas capitals frequently established on or near the same site. Further distortion has arisen from the frequent

94.   Cunliffe, op. cit. (note 12).
95.   Haselgrove, op. cit. (note 34).
96.   J. Collis, 'Excavations at Owlesbury, Hants. A second interim report', *Antiq. Journ.* l (1970), 246–261.
97.   C.C. Haselgrove, *Iron Age coinage in south-east England: the archaeological context* BAR 174 (1987).
98.   O. Bedwin and R. Holgate, 'Excavations at Copse Farm, Oving, West Sussex', *PPS* li (1985), 215–246; Haselgrove, op. cit. (note 97).
99.   e.g. Cunliffe, op. cit. (note 12); Rodwell, op. cit. (note 2).
100. I.M. Stead and V. Rigby, *Baldock: the excavation of a Roman and pre-Roman settlement, 1968–72* Britannia Monograph 7 (London, 1986); P. Woodward, *Romano-British industries in Purbeck* Dorset Natur Hist. Arch. Soc. Monograph 6 (Dorchester, 1987) and P. Jarvis, 'The early pits of the Jewry Wall site, Leicester', *Trans. Leics. Arch. Hist. Soc.* lx (1986), 7–15.
101. C. Partridge, *Skeleton Green: a late Iron Age and Romano-British site* Britannia Monograph 2 (1981); Haselgrove, op. cit. (note 97).
102. M. Fulford, 'Calleva Atrebatum: an interim report on the excavation of the oppidum, 1980–6', *PPS* liii (1987), 271–8; P. Arthur, 'Roman amphorae from Canterbury', *Britannia* xvii (1986), 239–58; Partridge, op. cit. (note 101); Haselgrove, op. cit. (note 97).
103. Trow, op. cit. (note 1); C.C. Haselgrove and P. Turnbull, *Stanwick, excavations and fieldwork: Interim Report 1981–3* Univ. Dur. Dept. Arch. Occ. Paper 4 (Durham, 1984).

failure to differentiate the processes which were at work. In one sense, these larger settlements simply continue the process of nucleation which began in the third century B.C.,[104] but we must avoid automatically equating this development with urbanisation. If anything, our meagre knowledge of the internal organisation of Colchester or St Albans suggests a spatially extensive version of existing settlement types, albeit with more pronounced functional zoning. The sites comprise elite and lower status residential compounds separated by their fields, with other discrete areas of the overall territorial enclosure reserved for burial, ritual and industrial activities.[105] The same model seems applicable to the recently elucidated relationship between The Ditches hillfort, North Cerney, and Bagendon.[106] Against this, many sites do show signs of the total occupied area having expanded over time, as well as changes in layout and surprisingly frequent shifts in the focus of settlement activity.[107] At Silchester, for instance, major changes took place at the heart of the settlement complex during the later first century B.C., involving the imposition of an orthogonal street plan;[108] a similar development may have occurred at Canterbury in the earlier first century A.D.. At Braughing, on the other hand, the focus of occupation shifted several times during the life of the settlement.[109]

Most of the 'territorial oppida' apparently had zones where there were frequent transactions using coinage, to judge from the intensive coin losses in these areas.[110] However, we must be cautious of automatically assuming from this and the other features that the oppida formed the apex of a settlement hierarchy on which other lesser sites and rural farmsteads were economically or even politically and socially dependent. The economic interpretation, in particular, enshrines a view of Iron Age societies which is generally accepted as anachronistic. Economic transactions were probably mainly a function of social relations between individuals, involving exchanges between equals and along kinship networks and the discharge of obligations between those of lower status and the elite, the latter extending their patronage and protection in return for the services and tribute of their subordinates. Elite dealings, especially, probably played the determining role in the circulation of most commodities and produce, and the scope of those transactions mediated by low value coinage need not have been large.[111] The fundamental question, therefore, is how the relationships between individuals and groups translate into particular Iron Age settlement patterns; we must be wary of assuming that these social and political hierarchies necessarily coincided with settlement hierarchies hypothesised from criteria of our own imposition.

The idea of a late Iron Age settlement hierarchy dominated by the territorial oppida has, in fact, little empirical substance. As in Continental Europe, many traits we might expect to be restricted to the highest ranking sites, such as coin production, luxury goods manufacture and prestige imports, are all attested on other settlements. The pattern of rural elite residence suggested for central southern England is echoed there and elsewhere in the dispersed distribution of gold coinage.[112] In the South-East, the richest late Iron Age burials appear to be primarily associated with lesser settlements, such as Baldock or Welwyn, and rural sites.[113] The principal exception, the Lexden tumulus at Colchester, is also unusual in other respects.[114] A further problem arises from using their large extent and linear dykes to define the 'territorial oppida' in the first place, since these attributes appear to be exclusive neither to the period nor to

104. Bradley, op. cit. (note 7).
105. Haselgrove, op. cit. (note 2); Nash, op. cit. (note 2); Champion, op. cit. (note 10).
106. Trow, op. cit. (note 1).
107. Haselgrove, op. cit. (note 97).
108. Fulford, op. cit. (note 102).
109. Haselgrove, op. cit. (note 97).
110. Haselgrove, op. cit. (note 97).
111. Haselgrove, op. cit. (note 97).
112. J. Collis, 'Functional and theoretical interpretations of British coinage', World Arch. iii (1971), 71–84.
113. Rodwell, op. cit. (note 2).
114. J. Foster, The Lexden tumulus: a reappraisal of an Iron Age burial from Colchester, Essex BAR 156 (1986).

the most extensive settlements. On the one hand, the process of constructing large-scale enclosures seems to be linked with the earlier revival of the insular habit of boundary building. On the other hand, several other probable late Iron Age dyke complexes exist, differing from the 'territorial oppida' only in lacking a recognisable core settlement. These include Arundel; Gussage Down, Dorset; Minchinhampton Common; the north Oxfordshire Grim's Ditch and perhaps Ilchester.[115]

These developments may well express less new defensive requirements than a desire for increased isolation and prestige by the social elite.[116] The linear dykes may simply have formalised the boundaries of what had become private estates – the ramparts at Stanwick largely follow pre-existing land divisions[117] – or delimited the land associated with a particular elite centre. A range of focal functions for the place will have automatically followed from the permanent, or – like the Saxon *villa regalis* – occasional residence of 'central persons' there. Continued over a long period of time, this can only have promoted the growth and importance of the settlement, as the centre from which these functions were exercised. In most cases, the record is silent, but a few sites – Colchester, St Albans, Silchester and perhaps Canterbury – can be identified from the inscribed coinage as the seats of particular rulers.[118] The coinage also suggests that during the late Iron Age, individual political authority was being exercised on a greater scale and more continuously than before, both in the widening coin distributions and in the frequency with which individual rulers stress their descent, suggesting that real or fictional inheritance was an important consideration in their authority.[119] Such developments, if true, would make sense of the relatively sudden prominence of the territorial oppida, as selected elite settlements became focal centres for the larger political groupings being fashioned by their rulers.

Unfortunately, we still know far too little of how the labour needed to construct these linear earthworks was mobilized, or of the timespan over which the sites were occupied. In any case, the same processes are unlikely to have operated to an equal extent everywhere. Millett suggests that some 'territorial oppida' may have originated as neutral meeting-places for several smaller social units rather than as elite centres.[120] As these units gradually coalesced into larger groupings, such locations acquired additional integrative functions and eventually came to symbolise the tribal identity. Only at this stage of institutional development did the elite establish permanent residence at these tribal centres, at which point, the pathways merge. On the evidence available, this model perhaps has relevance for rather more Gaulish sites than British.[121]

CONTINENTAL INFLUENCE DURING THE LATER IRON AGE

The basic Continental influences on late Iron Age Britain have received extensive discussion. The more important first-century B.C. innovations with obvious Continental connections include fine wheel-made pottery, a flat-grave cremation rite which is closely paralleled in northern France, a coinage directly based on Gallo-Belgic models, and new imports from the Roman world.[122] Initially, the main imports were Italian wine amphorae and prestige metalwork, but after the Caesarian conquest and especially the Augustan reorganisation of Gaul, the range diversified to include Spanish amphora-borne products, brooches and finewares.[123] The earliest pottery imports, from *c.*25 B.C., were a group of micaceous platters, jars and flagons originating in central Gaul, Samian pottery and north French Gallo-Belgic wares taking over in the final decade

---

115. e.g. Bradley, op. cit. (note 7); Trow, op. cit. (note 1).
116. M. Bowden and D. McOmish, 'The required barrier', *Scot. Arch. Rev.* iv (1987), 76–84.
117. Haselgrove and Turnbull, op. cit. (note 103).
118. Haselgrove, op. cit. (note 97).
119. Haselgrove, op. cit. (note 1).
120. op. cit. (note 1).
121. cf. Collis, op. cit. (note 50).
122. Haselgrove, op. cit (note 1); Rodwell, op. cit. (note 2).
123. For amphorae, see A.P. Fitzpatrick, 'The distribution of Dressel 1 amphorae in north-west Europe', *OJA* iv. 3 (1985), 305–340; and P. Sealey, *Amphoras from the 1970 excavations at Colchester, Sheepen* BAR 142 (1985).

of the century.[124] Outside the South-East, these imports are largely restricted to the principal settlements.[125] Further indications of the high level of material Romanisation amongst the south-eastern elites, apart from their burial rite, include the adoption of Gaulish – and thus essentially Roman – dietary preferences and the highly Romanizing inscribed coinages.[126] The custom of building formal temples, e.g. at Hayling Island, may also be Roman, although the claims of Frilford and Woodeaton to similar pre-Conquest developments have recently been minimised.[127]

Discussion of these changes is still bedevilled by the vexed question of the Belgae, an immigrant group to the maritime part of Britain, of unknown size and date, to whom Caesar alludes.[128] This Belgic immigration, however, continues to elude archaeological identification, notwithstanding recent attempts to relocate it from Kent to the Solent area.[129] For many other recent commentators, Caesar's reference to raiding followed by settlement is perfectly consonant with military activity in northern Gaul to obtain goods and slaves for the southern markets which developed following the Roman foundation of Gallia Transalpina between 121–118 B.C..[130] This raiding perhaps paved the way for more permanent political alliances and domination, involving some colonisation, and ultimately leading to Britain perhaps providing northern Gaul with military aid against Caesar.[131] Beyond that, however, we should heed Bradley's advice that 'if we cannot recognise the Belgae in the archaeological record, we should be reluctant to make them responsible for too many changes in British society.'[132]

Three other aspects of Continental influence on British later Iron Age developments do warrant a brief review. The first is the argument that Britain was largely isolated from the Continent until c.100 B.C., and that its subsequent reintegration came about, as has already been implied, because Gaulish economic interests were expanded northwards to meet the ever growing demands of Roman trade.[133] The cross-Channel trade network focused on Hengistbury Head is widely held to be the most tangible expression of these changes. Whatever their consequences, we need to ensure, first and foremost, that these developments do not obscure the important changes that insular societies were already experiencing at the time this contact commenced.

In fact, the idea that reviving Mediterranean economic interest in temperate Europe postdates the foundation of the southern Gaulish province needs reconsideration. Italian wine amphorae were reaching the southern German site of Manching throughout the second century B.C..[134] This implies that Mediterranean trade with temperate Europe was already on the increase shortly after Rome's victory in the second Punic war and her acquisition of overseas possessions in Spain, although we do not know how the contacts with Manching were mediated. The Gaulish evidence needs re-examining first, and Britain, in any case, need not have been affected, but if this interpretation is correct, the orthodox view may require revision. The alternative argument that Mediterranean interest in particular northern lands only revived once sufficient productive power had been generated there to make trade with them worthwhile[135] cannot be taken very far, since this could easily already have been the case in Britain by the second century B.C..

124.   Trow, op. cit. (note 1).
125.   Haselgrove, op. cit. (note 2).
126.   Foster, op. cit. (note 114); King, op. cit. (note 34); Haselgrove, op. cit. (note 97).
127.   R. Downey, A. King and G. Soffe, 'The Hayling Island temple and religious connections across the channel', in W. Rodwell (ed.), *Temples, churches and religion: recent research in Roman Britain* BAR 77 (1980), 289–304 and D.W. Harding, *Excavations in Oxfordshire 1964–66* Univ. Edin. Dept. Arch. Occ. Paper 15 (Edinburgh, 1987).
128.   *De Bello Gallico* V, 12.
129.   Cunliffe, op. cit. (note 2).
130.   e.g. Bradley, op. cit. (note 7); Haselgrove, op. cit. (note 1); Nash, op. cit. (note 2).
131.   *De Bello Gallico* IV, 20.
132.   Bradley, op. cit. (note 7), 145.
133.   e.g. Bradley, op. cit. (note 7); Cunliffe, op. cit. (note 17).
134.   E.L. Will, 'The Roman amphoras from Manching: a reappraisal', *Bayerische Vorgeschichtsblätter* lii (1987), 21–36.
135.   C. Gosden, 'Gifts and kin in early Iron Age Europe', *Man* xx (1985), 475–93.

Marked material culture discontinuities at boundaries often conceal an intensive pattern of interaction across them.[136] Such evidence as we have for cross-channel contacts prior to 100 B.C. is therefore all the more damaging to the argument of insular isolation. Continental contact with the South-West quite possibly continued throughout, with a Mediterranean interest in Cornish tin an important factor,[137] though its influence on insular material culture was limited. In the South-East, too, occasional early Belgic gold coin-finds could imply contacts going back to the later third century B.C., and during the later second century Gallo-Belgic A and B coins were imported in quantity.[138] Whether these finds reflect elite alliances or mercenary payments or yet other mechanisms, they give some substance to the extensive cross-channel contacts presented in Caesar's[139] text. The development of potin coinage, ultimately based on a Massaliote model also shows emphatically that Britain was not completely closed to Continentally-based innovations during the later second century B.C..[140]

Why then did Britain become so much more open to emulating Continental material culture during the first century B.C.? An increasingly likely answer is that social and cultural change, rather than opportunity, was the root cause. In this respect, the early trade through Hengistbury Head, which brought few changes outside the site's immediate hinterland,[141] may be more important for understanding why cross-channel contacts had so little impact earlier, than as a phenomenon in its own right. Sharples suggests that the Iron Age communities of Dorset and Hampshire deliberately excluded the specialist manufacturing industries at Hengistbury and the extensive contacts these required from their territories (hence their marginal location) until a deepening of the social hierarchy rendered the area more open to external stimuli during the later first century B.C..[142]

The second aspect of the current orthodoxy which needs reassessment is that after 50 B.C., the axis of cross-channel trade shifted decisively from the South-West and central southern England to the South-East. This is supposedly a result of the Roman conquest of Gaul and of the treaties forged by Caesar,[143] particularly reflected in the differing distributions of the earlier Dressel 1A and later Dressel 1B Italian wine amphora forms.[144] This view, however, neglects marked changes in the South-East during the earlier first century B.C., notably the import of Gallo-Belgic C and D coinages and the striking of Insular gold coinages based on these Continental prototypes. Together, these changes ruptured the pre-existing patterns of circulation and established axes which many other late Iron Age, continentally-inspired innovations seem to follow.[145] *Pace* Thompson, the late Iron Age grog-tempered pottery tradition quite possibly had pre-Caesarian beginnings[146] and other Continental La Tène III innovations started to exert their influence on insular material culture at about the same time. The amphora evidence also needs reassessment. The earliest Dressel 1B types were reaching Manching well before the mid-first century B.C., as well as north French sites such as Villeneuve St Germain.[147] There is therefore no

136. I.R. Hodder, *Symbols in action* (Cambridge, 1982).
137. C.F.C. Hawkes, 'Ictis disentangled and the British tin trade', *OJA* iii (1984), 211–33.
138. Haselgrove, op. cit. (note 97); D. Nash, *Coinage in the Celtic world* (London, 1987).
139. Haselgrove, op. cit. (note 1); cf. *De Bello Gallico* II, 4, 14; IV 20, 21; V, 12.
140. Haselgrove, op. cit. (note 97). Van Arsdell's recent analysis of the striations on potin coins has, however, convincingly refuted the suggestion that papyrus – with its intimations of pre-Caesarian Mediterranean contacts, e.g. op. cit. (note 15) – was employed to press out the moulds for some of these coins, see R. Van Arsdell, 'An industrial engineer (but no papyrus) in Celtic Britain', *OJA* V(2) (1986), 205–221.
141. Cunliffe, op. cit. (note 17).
142. Sharples, op. cit. (note 13).
143. Haselgrove, op. cit. (note 1).
144. e.g. Fitzpatrick, op. cit. (note 123), fig.4.
145. Haselgrove, op. cit. (note 97).
146. The ceramic sequence at several sites e.g. Baldock, Stead and Rigby, op. cit. (note 100), and Silchester, Fulford, op. cit. (note 102) suggests a date earlier than the second half of the first century B.C. inception proposed by Thompson, op. cit. (note 57), probably in the first half of the century.
147. Will, op. cit. (note 134). Villeneuve, M-F Devos, *Essai d'analyse spatiale à partir de l'étude des amphores d'un site de la Tène tardive: Villeneuve St Germain (Aisne, France)* (Memoire du DEA, Université de Paris X, 1986).

reason why some could not also have reached south-east England before 50 B.C.. Indeed the recently published example from the Baldock burial, if not even earlier, could well be attached to this group.[148] Conversely, the chronological specificity of the fabric used to attribute several central southern English finds to the Dressel 1A variant is now in doubt.[149] In any case, cross-channel trade to the latter region undoubtedly continued after the conquest of Gaul, albeit on a diminished scale.[150] Chronological factors alone, therefore, cannot explain why in one area these contacts had manifestly more impact on subsequent developments than in the other.

The final aspect of current orthodoxy concerns the potential role of direct trade with the Roman world after 50 B.C. in promoting political centralisation in the South-East, compared to the areas further west and north. In recent years, a 'core-periphery' model has been widely canvassed as a helpful framework for explaining these developments,[151] as well as why Roman Britain, in turn, evolved as it did. Briefly, the model suggests that new prestige goods brought into Britain through direct trade with the Roman world played a critical part in a process of wealth-accumulation by the competing elites of the south-eastern core area. Initially, this brought about frequent shifts in political power between different centres as trade fluctuated, but in the long-term, the establishment of virtual monopolies over external trade by geographically well-placed groups, notably in eastern England, was a key factor in their imposing political power on other regions.[152] This process culminated in the political hegemony exercised by the eastern ruler, Cunobelinus, whose domains, the coin-distributions suggest, eventually extended over most of the South-East. To obtain the commodities which they needed in exchange for Roman goods – chief among them the minerals, slaves and agricultural exports listed by Strabo[153] – the elites had to look largely beyond the South-East. They did this by a combination of military force and developing further exchange networks. A limited quantity of Roman imported goods was therefore passed on to the resource-rich periphery through dendritic trade networks radiating out from the South-East, making this periphery, in effect, economically dependent on the core area. In both areas, these demands would therefore stimulate increased production for export. Outside this inner periphery, however, in Atlantic Britain, these developments probably had little or no impact.[154]

Although this model is undeniably useful, various criticisms can also be levelled. Firstly, the quantity of Roman imports has probably been over-estimated.[155] While this will have enhanced their prestige value in the core area, the overall economic impact of Roman trade will have been significantly lower. Secondly, evidence of direct Roman involvement in the trade is lacking. Indeed, the idea of strongly exploitative Roman trade networks on which the core-periphery model ultimately depends is probably anachronistic. Instead, Millett suggests that goods entered and left Britain through a network of alliances and exchanges between Romanised Gauls and their British kin or clients, in effect an intensification of the earlier first-century B.C. social and political links between Belgic Gaul and south-east England.[156] This view allows for the reasonably complex developments in the core, while requiring only minimal impact on the periphery. Thirdly, far fewer imports penetrate into the periphery than the model predicts, although there are enough to show that these regions were in contact, however indirectly, with the Continent.[157] Equally, the main developments at Bagendon, Stanwick and perhaps Redcliffe

148. Stead and Rigby, op. cit. (note 100). The Dressel 1A form proper is known in south-east England at Braughing and at Stanstead Essex, where at least three vessels are represented (A.P. Fitzpatrick, pers. comm.).
149. A.P. Fitzpatrick, pers. comm.
150. Cunliffe, op. cit. (note 17).
151. e.g. Haselgrove, op. cit. (note 2); Bradley, op. cit. (note 7); Nash, op. cit. (note 2); Darvill, op. cit. (note 8); and most recently, B.W. Cunliffe, *Greeks, Romans and Barbarians: spheres of interaction* (London, 1988).
152. Haselgrove, op. cit. (note 2).
153. *Geography* IV, 5, 3.
154. Haselgrove, op. cit. (note 2); Darvill, op. cit. (note 8).
155. Millett, op. cit. (note 1); Trow, op. cit. (note 1).
156. Millett, op. cit. (note 1); cf. Haselgrove, op. cit. (note 97).
157. Trow, op. cit. (note 1).

on the Humber crossing, are Claudio-Neronian, suggesting that their raison d'être lies in post-Conquest developments. Finally, the core-periphery model perhaps lays insufficient emphasis on the threat of a Roman invasion, from Caesar onwards, and on Roman diplomatic manoeuvering and subsidies, as factors in late Iron Age political developments. In particular, Augustus concluded new treaties with various British rulers (most probably in the penultimate decade B.C.), effectively making them Roman client kings. These alliances are reflected in the rulers' Romanizing coinages[158] and must surely have had an influential centralising role.

CONCLUSIONS: LATER IRON AGE SOCIETIES c.50 BC – AD 70

Insular later Iron Age societies were still essentially agrarian, although they inhabited a highly developed landscape with a well-adapted settlement pattern and communication network, and some areas at least were supporting an increasing degree of specialisation. Warrior activities undoubtedly also played a part in all these communities, but their relative importance at different times is difficult to read directly from archaeological patterns such as the earlier prevalence of developed hillforts.[159] The dichotomy which Nash draws between primarily warrior societies and other agrarian communities is therefore highly suspect.[160] Since later Iron Age population was probably rising, this may have put pressure on land in more circumscribed regions and thereby increased tension,[161] but in most areas the agricultural economy was probably perfectly capable of generating a substantial surplus.[162]

By the second century B.C., both settlement evidence and material culture suggest that the basic social and political matrix of Britain was made up of relatively small-scale corporate groups, each headed by an elite, but retaining a strong emphasis on the communal control of resources within the collective territory. These basic units were also loosely linked together in wider, culturally differentiated configurations by ties of clientage and shared ancestry.[163] These larger entities correspond reasonably well with those known in the later first century A.D.,[164] although the boundaries between them must still have been fairly fluid. Some regional groupings evidently laid greater stress on their shared identities than others, e.g. in Dorset,[165] but everywhere their capacity for common action was surely weak and political authority transient, being restricted to periods of common danger or such matters as mediation in disputes, and lacking lasting coercive powers.[166] This appears to be what happened in the South-East at the time of Caesar's invasions, Cassivellaunus becoming war leader only by virtue of the emergency.[167] History, as a result, has perhaps given him greater prominence than he deserves. His power was probably short-lived, and was certainly insufficient to prevent four Kentish leaders from breaking away to make their separate peace with Caesar.[168]

The settlement evidence from Atlantic Britain suggests that similar conditions of political decentralisation and minimal social hierarchy persisted there right down to the Conquest. Indeed, the crisis precipitated by the Claudian invasion and further Roman advances was probably in itself the single most important unifying factor throughout this zone. Differences in the social structure are underlined in other ways, such as these regions' failure to adopt coinage. By contrast, in the South-East and adjacent areas, the combination of Roman diplomacy, trade – however mediated – and the threat of invasion from 50 B.C. onwards, seems to have promoted

158.   Haselgrove, op. cit. (note 97).
159.   Bowden and McOmish, op. cit. (note 116).
160.   In Nash, op. cit. (note 2).
161.   Dent, op. cit. (note 44).
162.   Reynolds, op. cit. (note 75).
163.   Haselgrove, op. cit. (notes 1, 34).
164.   Millett, op. cit. (note 1).
165.   Sharples, op. cit. (note 13).
166.   Haselgrove, op. cit. (note 34).
167.   *De Bello Gallico*, V, 11.
168.   ibid., V, 22.

moves towards greater political centralisation and more absolute forms of social ranking between the elites and their dependents. There are many historical parallels for similar developments when other expansive states came into direct contact with more egalitarian societies.[169] After A.D. 43, these changes were partly echoed in northern England, where the formation of a Brigantian confederation, apparently in treaty with Rome, finds physical expression in the complex site of Stanwick.[170]

A steepening of the social hierarchy in south-east England can be inferred in several ways: the embellishment of the principal settlements; increased emphasis on forms of material culture by which individual rank could be further defined; relatively restricted access to prestigious Continental imports; and the adoption of a minority, Romanising burial rite.[171] Although, almost by definition, those burial rites which we can detect earlier in the Iron Age are also minority practices,[172] this new rite differs in its emphasis on overt wealth consumption. The quantity of prestige metalwork deposited during the period, e.g. as offerings in watery places,[173] or at temples like Hayling Island, implies that other forms of conspicuous consumption increased too. Altogether, throughout the South-East, there appears to be greater emphasis on individual expression of rank and less on adherence to a particular identity group, which was largely subsumed by the wholesale embrace of Romanised Belgic culture. By the Conquest, several hitherto distinctive regional coinage traditions had been almost completely subsumed into a single series emanating from the Eastern region, only the issues of the Southern kingdom retaining a partial independence.[174] However, in peripheral areas like Dorset, elite status expression laid greater emphasis on the common cultural framework afforded by membership of a wider regional grouping[175], although some new practices, such as warrior burials and rich female graves containing mirrors,[176] clearly had a significance which went far beyond any particular regional group.

Both zones, therefore, saw the development of a numerous elite, whose position was founded on absolute distinctions of rank and wealth. This was surely a common factor in their subsequent successful Romanisation,[177] just as the different foundations of the social hierarchy in each zone (which in the South-East possibly included a more developed concept of private ownership) may go far to explaining the more rapid rate of overt Romanisation in the core, both before and after the Conquest. Similarly, the cultural dominance of the South-East and the stresses which its predatory relations on its neighbours must have engendered throughout the peripheral zone does appear to provide a satisfactory explanation of the markedly greater emphasis which these peoples placed on their common tribal identities.[178]

The two zones also diverge in their apparent degree of pre-Conquest political centralisation, the clearest evidence of which comes from the different regional coinages. In eastern England, under Cunobelinus, the control exercised over minting, the standardisation of issues, the range of denominations, and the propaganda use of coin-types all speak for a high measure of political authority. Most of the peripheral coinages, however, hint at subdivisions within the overall tribal region, each of which may have had their own separate rulers. Nowhere does the conservative repertoire of these peripheral series convey the same message of centralised political authority as the standardised sets and symbolism of Cunobelinus' coinage, especially his later issues.

169.   M.H. Fried, 'On the concept of the tribe', in *Essays on the problem of the tribe* American Ethnological Society (New York, 1968), 3–22.
170.   Haselgrove, op. cit. (note 34); see also N. Higham, 'Brigantia revisited', *Northern History* xxiii (1987), 1–19.
171.   Haselgrove, op. cit. (note 2).
172.   G.A. Wait, *Ritual and religion in Iron Age Britain* BAR 149 (1985).
173.   A.P. Fitzpatrick, 'The deposition of late Iron Age metalwork in watery contexts in Southern England', in Cunliffe and Miles, op. cit. (note 11), 178–90.
174.   Haselgrove, op. cit. (note 97).
175.   Sharples, op. cit. (note 13).
176.   e.g. Cunliffe, op. cit. (note 12).
177.   Millett, op. cit. (note 1).
178.   Haselgrove, op. cit. (note 2).

Although the inscribed coinages provide evidence for legitimation by descent, as well as implying that several south-eastern rulers must have been recognised as client kings by Augustus and Tiberius, these political developments still need not amount to the formation of hereditary kingdom states. Firstly, the time scale is too short, not more than three generations. Secondly, the coinage and the number of known client kings, ending up as supplicants to the emperor[179] imply that political power was frequently unstable. Thirdly, the circulation history of the coinage indicates clearly the cellular structure even of Cunobelinus' domains, several of whose territories were evidently piecemeal additions during his reign.[180] On balance, Cunobelinus' hegemony therefore probably had more the characteristics of a paramount chiefdom. His kingdom was, in effect, an aggregate of smaller territorial groups, like those of Caesar's time, each controlled by local client elites or, in some cases, by Cunobelinus' own relations. These sub-units will have been bound together by a complex network of alliances and personal ties between the paramount ruler, his client elites and their dependants, backed up by military force.[181] Once this complex structure collapsed after the invasion, many dependent elites must have been quick to throw in their lot with Rome, perceiving in her the key to their future position. For them and their territories this amounted to little more than the exchange of one paramount for another – the emperor.

179. e.g. *Res Gestae Divi Augusti* 6, 32.
180. Haselgrove, op. cit. (note 97).
181. Haselgrove, op. cit. (note 1). When Britain was in due course formally incorporated as a province, the administrative arrangements for the South-East evidently fell back partly on the looser tribal groupings which had existed prior to Cunobelinus' paramountcy, of whom only the Trinovantes are recorded by Caesar (*De Bello Gallico* V, 20) rather than adopting the political arrangements in force at the time of the invasion. All the south-eastern *civitates* were, thus, to a greater or lesser extent artificial creations. This contrasts markedly with the adjacent peripheral regions where there were already meaningful divisions which could be adopted intact, reflected in the cultural distinctiveness and strongly emphasised tribal identities of the four major groupings: the Corieltauvi, the Dobunni, the Durotriges, and the Iceni.

CONQUEST AND AFTERMATH

By Valerie A. Maxfield

In the mid–1950s when Sir Ian Richmond produced his classic *Roman Britain* (first published in 1955) there was very little archaeological evidence which could be brought to bear upon the problem of the conquest of Britain. The broad outline of the story could be told from the fragmentary accounts of Cassius Dio and Tacitus; some detail on the major movements of the individual legions could be added to this from the evidence of epigraphy but there was little archaeological flesh which could be added to the bare historical bones. Now, some thirty years later, there is a welter of archaeological data, a mass of military sites which must be related in some way to the imposition of Roman rule on Britain. And herein lies the dilemma of the archaeologist whose material must be brought into contact with, and explained in the context of, an historical narrative. Conquest is a dynamic affair: armies may change winter-base from one season to the next: their summer encampments may change from day to day. The fortunes of war fluctuate in a way which is far too swift to be detected adequately in archaeological evidence which is, by its very nature, static and unsubtle. Even with the *relatively* good archaeological dating which we have for the Claudio-Neronian period it is rarely, if ever, that a single military establishment can be dated to the span of a single governorship and thus correlated with a narrative which presents the trend of conquest in terms of what was accomplished by the individual governors appointed to the province. What can be seen are general trends of conquest rather than the nuances which lie behind those trends. The elusiveness of even a major campaigning army until such time as that army starts to construct substantial winter-bases, may be appreciated from the fact that despite several decades of intense archaeological activity there is still not one jot of direct archaeological evidence for the presence of Julius Caesar's armies in Britain in 55 and 54 B.C..[1]

One area in which there has been a considerable increase of knowledge over the last three decades or so is that of pre-Flavian legionary bases. This is due in large part to city-centre redevelopment and the growth of urban rescue archaeology. While epigraphic evidence has long pointed to Colchester, Lincoln and Wroxeter as early bases associated respectively with Legions XX, IX and XIV, it was not until the 1970s that traces of the fortresses themselves came to light and with them complications as well as clarification.[2] In most cases we are dealing with multi-phase, multi-site military complexes (long familiar from military sites in the Rhineland) whose individual histories as established by archaeological investigation do not always fit happily with one another, nor with the neat scenario which has often in the past been adduced from the scant written record.[3]

---

1. The identification of the hillfort of Bigberry in Kent as the native fortification stormed by Caesar's army in 54 B.C. (*de Bello Gallico* 5.9) is an attractive one but by no means as certain as is implied by F.H. Thompson, 'Excavations at Bigberry, near Canterbury, 1978–80', *Antiq. Journ.* lxiii (1983), 237. The identification was proposed by T. Rice Holmes, *Ancient Britain and the Invasions of Julius Caesar* (Oxford), 678–85.
2. *RIB* 200 (Colchester); *RIB* 254–257 (Lincoln); *RIB* 292–294 (Wroxeter).
3. G. Webster (ed.), *Fortress into City. The Consolidation of Roman Britain, First Century AD* (London, 1988), contains the latest statements by the excavators of all these sites.

At Colchester a legionary base of Claudian date has been shown to underlie the western half of the later *colonia*, with suggestions of an annexe to its east, and traces of an earlier establishment, of indeterminate nature, underlying it. Just to the west of the fortress site in the Sheepen area, Fitzpatrick and Todd have separately drawn attention to distinct areas of military activity of an early date, while about three and a half kilometres to the south-west in the Gosbecks area (still within the pre-Roman Camulodunum complex) aerial reconnaissance has revealed a small fort of some 1.6 ha internal area.[4] The chronological relationship between the various components of this complex is uncertain, though there is no reason to believe, as is often stated, that the fort must pre- or post-date the fortress. The two could well have co-existed.[5] Tombstones of a centurion of Legion XX and a *duplicarius* in an ala Thracum attest the presence of both legionaries and auxiliaries, possibly contemporaneously, perhaps housed together, perhaps separately. The separation of legionary and auxiliary troops, characteristic of the later army of occupation, need in no way apply to an army on campaign.

At both Lincoln and Wroxeter, legionary bases have been found to underlie the later Roman cities, but in neither case have they produced the anticipated Claudian material. Hence neither may be the establishments at which were based the soldiers of Legions IX and XIV respectively whose tombstones first hinted at a legionary presence at these two sites. These incognominate stones should date no later than *c*.54 while Jones proposes a date no earlier than 60–70 for the Lincoln site, Webster a 'Neronian' date for Wroxeter.[6] There is a distinct possibility that in both cases earlier military establishments existed on sites separate from the Neronian fortresses, in the case of Lincoln, in the area to the south of the Brayford Pool, at Wroxeter perhaps at the undated 8-hectare site of Eaton Constantine.

Unencumbered by modern urban development, the complexity of the Roman military situation in the Wroxeter area is readily apparent. Though it was not until 1975 that the legionary fortress itself came to light during excavation in the later *civitas*, aerial reconnaissance in the vicinity has revealed the presence of some 15 Roman camps, indicative of the strategic importance of the area which sits at the gateway to central Wales via the valley of the river Severn.

A base for the fourth of the British invasion legions, II Augusta, has now been identified at Exeter. The legion has long been known from the evidence of Suetonius to have operated in the south in the early years of the conquest, and Exeter has been postulated from time to time as a likely location for a base. The site had, however, produced no military inscriptions, no military finds and no traces of military buildings. In the early 1960s the first hint of a military presence came to light, in 1971 the first indications of a legionary-sized establishment, in the form of a large bathhouse and parts of a couple of barrack buildings. Again, as at Lincoln and Wroxeter, the foundation date would appear to be Neronian rather than Claudian, and various contexts

4.   A. Fitzpatrick, 'Camulodunum and the early occupation of south-east England. Some reconsiderations', in C. Unz (ed.), *Studien zu den Militärgrenzen Roms III* (Stuttgart, 1986), 35–41; M. Todd, 'Oppida and the Roman Army: a review of recent evidence', *Oxford Journ. Arch.* 4.2 (1985), 187–99, esp. 192–5; D.R. Wilson, 'A first-century fort near Gosbecks', *Britannia* viii (1977), 185–7.

5.   Compare, for example, the situation at Mainz in the Tiberian period: a 2-legion fortress at Mainz plus forts at Mainz-Weisenau (to the south-east) and Mainz-Kastel to the east, across the Rhine.

6.   L.R. Dean, *A Study of the Cognomina of Soldiers in the Roman Legions* (Princeton, 1916), 108–110. M.J. Jones and G. Webster in G. Webster (ed.), op. cit. (note 3). For a summary of the samian pottery evidence for Lincoln cf. B.R. Hartley in A.C. & A.S. Anderson (eds.), *Roman Pottery Research in Britain and North-West Europe* (Oxford, 1981), Part. i, 239–48. The belief that these inscriptions date rather earlier than the earliest identified structural evidence at either of these sites has led to doubt being expressed about their dating. This is certainly more secure than the fluctuating evidence of archaeology, being based on Empire-wide epigraphic criteria. For example, an analysis of the tombstones of soldiers serving in Legions VII and XI in Dalmatia has shown that while incognominate soldiers feature commonly among those whose memorials record the legions without the titles *Claudia pia fidelis* which they won in 42 in connection with the suppression of the revolt of Camillus Scribonianus, they are singularly rare on stones commemorating soldiers after 42. Thus the use of *cognomina* has become the general rule by this date.

between 55 and 65 have been proposed.[7] While epigraphic proof of the identity of the garrison is still lacking, a decorated antefix of a design produced by II Augusta at its later base at Caerleon is convincing enough evidence of an association with that unit.[8]

The identification and dating of what may reasonably be seen as the four primary bases of the four British legions, leads on to two further problem areas which have received considerable attention. Firstly there is the question as to the dispositions of II, IX and XIV before the units settled at their individual full-legion sized bases at Exeter, Lincoln and Wroxeter.[9] Secondly, there is the problem of the later movements of the legions between existing and new bases as the progress of the conquest advanced west and north.

To look at this second problem first; it is apparent that the interrelationship of legionary movements and the later histories of individual legionary bases in the pre-Flavian period is a complex one. It may be convenient firstly to remind ourselves what little firm information is provided by written sources. In the winter of 49/50 Colchester was turned over to a veteran colony; its creation is linked with the need to establish a legionary base in touch with the tribe of the Silures who were in a state of unrest. From this it may be inferred that the legion which had been stationed at Colchester was now moved west.[10] Legions XIV and XX both took part in the suppression of the rebellion of Boudica, for both won honorific titles on this occasion, but neither is specifically located. Legion II (again unlocated) failed to send the requested rein-forcements and its camp prefect committed suicide (why was he and not one of his superiors the legate or laticlave tribune deemed to be responsible?). Legion IX suffered a serious defeat at the hands of the rebels and returned to its camp (unlocated). In A.D. 66 or 67 Legion XIV was moved out of Britain in connection with Nero's projected eastern war. It returned briefly during the civil war year of 69 but within a matter of months was moved away again.[11]

A serving soldier of Legion XX died in the Gloucester area some time in the middle years of the first century.[12] A soldier of this same legion is also attested as having died at Wroxeter. However, the soldier in question is a *beneficiarius legati pr(opraetore)*, an aide to the governor, an appointment which involves absence from the parent legion. Hence no firm inference regarding the location of the legion should be drawn from the place of the soldier's demise.[13] Numerous inscriptions of Legion XX point to its subsequent sojourn at Chester, where it was to remain based until it finally left Britain.[14] Legion II Augusta was the first (and only) legion attested at Caerleon. Such is the sum total of available facts, but on the basis of them alone it has been possible in the past to construct a neat and simple scenario. In A.D. 49/50 Legion XX moved west to Gloucester where it was well positioned on the edge of the then conquered territory, to deal

7. Todd has pointed to the possibility of an earlier foundation date on the basis of the samian: 'Dating the Roman Empire: the contribution of archaeology', in B. Orme (ed.), *Problems and Case Studies in Archaeological Dating* (Exeter, 1982), 35–56, esp. 54–55. The present writer favours the earlier rather than the later end of the proposed date range, *pace* the arguments recently advanced by N. Holbrook in an appendix to N. Holbrook and A. Fox, 'Excavations in the legionary fortress at Bartholomew Street East, Exeter, 1959', *Proc. Devon Arch. Soc.* 45 for 1987 (1989), 23–57, esp. 51–5.

8. P. Bidwell and G. Boon, 'An antefix of the Second Augustan Legion from Exeter', *Britannia* vii (1976), 278–80. Ptolemy's confusion in placing II Augusta *incorrectly* at Isca Dumnoniorum (Exeter) rather than at Isca Silurum (Caerleon) where it was based at the time he wrote, may be due to his using a first-century source for southern England, a source which *correctly* located the legion at Exeter in the pre-Flavian period.

9. The debate over whether Exeter was large enough to accommodate a full legion revolved in part around the assumption that the site was only 15.4 hectares in size. Recent excavation has shown it to cover some 16.6 hectares (measured over the ramparts), and Henderson has now even suggested that two auxiliary units were accommodated in addition to a full legion: 'Exeter' in Webster (ed.), op. cit. (note 3). This speculation is based on a very hypothetical reconstruction of barrack accommodation.

10. Tacitus, *Annals* 12.32.

11. Tacitus, *Histories* 2.66: 4.68.

12. *RIB* 122.

13. *RIB* 293. The legion lacks the titles *Valeria victrix*, which it won in connection with the suppression of the Boudican rebellion.

14. *RIB* 489–516.

with the Silurian problem beyond. In 68 when Legion XIV left Britain, Legion XX took its place at Wroxeter, while Legion II moved into Gloucester. Here the three legions remained until the resurgence of military activity in the Flavian period, with wars in Wales and in northern Britain, led to further troop movements, including the addition of Legion II Adiutrix to the British legionary establishment, bringing it back up to four. II Augusta moved from Gloucester to the newly established fortress of Caerleon: II Adiutrix moved into Lincoln and IX shunted north to York. Wroxeter remained the base of XX until its projected move north to Inchtuthil in the mid–80s. Apart from the question of the location of XIV during its brief sojourn in Britain in 69 all was straightforward. While the trends underlying this pattern remain true, the detail as seen through the archaeological evidence is considerably more complicated.

At the nub of the problem is the Gloucester complex. Here there are now known to be two distinct areas of military activity, one below the later *colonia* site in the modern city centre, the other to the north-west in the Kingsholm area. Coin evidence provides a firm *terminus post quem* of 67 for the primary phase of the city-centre fortress. The material from the Kingsholm area is of an earlier complexion, terminating in the mid-60s.[15] There are two distinct structural phases represented, the earlier one extending over an area of some 8 ha (20 acres), the later possibly as much as 22 ha (56 acres), a size adequate to accommodate a force numerically well in excess of a single legion or its equivalent. The two tombstones of serving soldiers known from Gloucester (a legionary of Legion XX and a cavalryman of cohors VI Thracum) very probably relate to the Kingsholm rather than the city-centre occupation.[16] An unfinished cheekpiece from an auxiliary cavalry helmet was retrieved from the site, though its relevance to the garrison is uncertain since it was in the process of manufacture, not in use. Thus it could be evidence of a legionary *fabrica* rather than an auxiliary cavalry presence.[17] There is thus a reasonable case for believing that part or all of Legion XX was based at some time in the Claudio-Neronian period at Gloucester-Kingsholm. The recent discovery of a centurial stone of Legion XX VV, hence after A.D. 60, is of doubtful relevance to the garrison of Kingsholm. The inscription presumably came from a stone building, the only such likely to have existed in the Kingsholm complex being a bathhouse. The stone was reused in the Cathedral and hence may be thought more likely to derive from a city-centre building. Hurst suggests that it relates to the second (stone) structural phase in the city fortress. Equally it may relate not to any military building but to a building in the *colonia*, which was certainly settled by veterans of Legion XX and may well have been built by serving soldiers of that legion.[18] This same legion has also been associated with a base at Usk in south Wales, a 19.4-hectare site founded some time during the 50s and occupied into the 60s. On the basis of excavations conducted here in the late 1960s and early 1970s, Manning interpreted the site as a fortress of Legion XX, the unit being identified through a small bronze roundel depicting a running boar, symbol of this legion.[19] The area excavated by Manning was dominated by granary buildings, very suggestive of a campaign supply base. More recent work by the Glamorgan and Gwent Archaeological Trust in the north-western corner of the site (probably the *retentura*) has produced, in addition to yet another granary, the first evidence for residential accommodation – barrack-like buildings, some of which were converted in a secondary (but still pre-Flavian) stage of occupation into what have tentatively been identified as stables.[20]

To return to Gloucester; the city-centre site was founded in the late 60s, its first phase of

15.   H.R. Hurst, *Kingsholm* (Gloucester, 1985).
16.   *RIB* 121, 122. Hurst has recently suggested that the legionary could as well relate to the later phase (Hurst in Webster (ed.), op. cit. (note 3)). The internal dating evidence, the omission of *VV* from the legion's titles and the writing out of *stipendiorum* and *annorum* in full, make this unlikely.
17.   The published evidence attributes it variously to Periods 1 and 2 – Hurst, op. cit. (note 3), 27, 117.
18.   *Britannia* xvii (1986), 429; Hurst in Webster (ed.), op. cit. (note 3), 70.
19.   W. Manning, *Report on the Excavations at Usk 1965–1976. The Fortress Excavations 1968–1971* (Cardiff, 1981), 39.
20.   On the granaries; D.R. Evans and V.M. Metcalf, 'Excavations at 10 Old Market Street, Usk', *Britannia* xx (1989), 23–68 on the barracks and stables interim statements (subject to reinterpretation on further analysis) by A. Marvell (pers. comm.) and *Archaeology in Wales* 27 (1987), 49–52.

occupation coming to an end no earlier than the late 70s.[21] The site was rebuilt in stone in the late 80s, a rebuild which was initially interpreted as relating to the establishment of a *colonia* at Gloucester, but which has recently been reinterpreted by its excavator as a final military phase, with the army remaining in occupation into the 90s.[22] What unit(s) occupied this new fortress? One possibility is that part or all of II Augusta was responsible for its original construction and initial garrison. This would be consistent with the evidence from Exeter, where there appears to have been a reduction in intensity of use at about this same time. The conclusion of Phase I at Gloucester would then coincide with the transfer of the legion to Caerleon where construction commenced in the mid-70s, though was not completed until some considerable time later.

Of the moves of Legion XX between the later 60s and the 80s there is no firm evidence. The common assumption that it replaced Legion XIV at Wroxeter and remained there until it started on its (abortive) move into Inchtuthil in the mid-80s is incapable of proof but makes good sense in terms of the overall strategy of legionary movements. Legion IX, once established at Lincoln, appears to have remained there until the Flavian advance northwards when it moved into a forward base at York, being replaced at Lincoln by II Adiutrix. Despite several attempts to prove pre-Flavian military occupation at York, there is still no good evidence for it, and certainly no reason to postulate a legionary presence.[23]

The evidence on these various legionary sites is steadily increasing: as it does the interpretations placed on it are evolving and, at times, radically changing. The views presented by the individual excavators are often not only at variance with one another but mutually inconsistent.[24] This is due not only to the often ambiguous nature of the evidence itself, but to the problems inherent in using something as static and imprecise as archaeological evidence to interpret a dynamic process. What has become very clear is that these early campaign bases should not be regarded in the same light as the later substantive legionary fortresses, the long-term 'permanent' homes of the provincial legionary garrison, disposed one legion per fortress. These Claudio-Neronian sites are the *castra hiberna*, the winter-bases, of a mobile army, brought together to campaign in the summer, distributed into winter-quarters in whatever troop combinations were deemed prudent. The divorce of legions and *auxilia* so characteristic of the later frontier armies is simply not appropriate here. Both legionary and auxiliary troops are attested at Colchester, Wroxeter and Gloucester (as well as numerous pre-Flavian sites on Rhine and Danube) and although contemporaneity of occupation can in no place be proved, it is a very likely option.[25]

The archaeological evidence which has accrued in such quantities over the last decade can help in our understanding of the broad sweep of military affairs, but will never be able adequately to reflect the subtleties of the situation. Only further epigraphic evidence is capable of providing the necessary precision of interpretation, and all too often, as we have seen, it too is capable of more than one interpretation. Attempts to identify the nature of troops in occupation on the basis of building plans and scraps of equipment are also fraught with difficulty. The notion that the *lorica segmentata* is distinctively and exclusively the equipment of the legionary has been thrown into doubt, while the accommodation provided for legionaries in some early military bases cannot be shown always to be so different from that occupied by auxiliaries.[26]

In other respects, too, the work of the last few decades has brought about a radical reappraisal of some of our fundamental assumptions about the army in the field. For example, a completely

21. Coins of 64 and 66 in primary construction trenches date its foundation.
22. The reinterpretation of the original report appears in H. Hurst, 'Gloucester' in Webster (ed.), op. cit. (note 3), 51ff. This reinterpretation raises grave problems (outside the scope of this paper) in relation to the deployment of Legion XX in the Flavian period.
23. B.R. Hartley, 'The Brigantes and the Roman Army', in K. Branigan (ed.), *Rome and Brigantes* (Sheffield, 1980), 2–7, esp. 2–4.
24. See notably in Webster (ed.), op. cit. (note 3).
25. The presence of the odd piece of horse-trapping or 'possible stable' building, often used as evidence for the presence of an auxiliary cavalry unit should, however, be viewed with caution. A legion included 120 cavalry: its officers were mounted and its bulky equipment transported by baggage-animals.
26. V.A. Maxfield, 'Pre-Flavian forts and their garrisons', *Britannia* xvii (1986), 59–72.

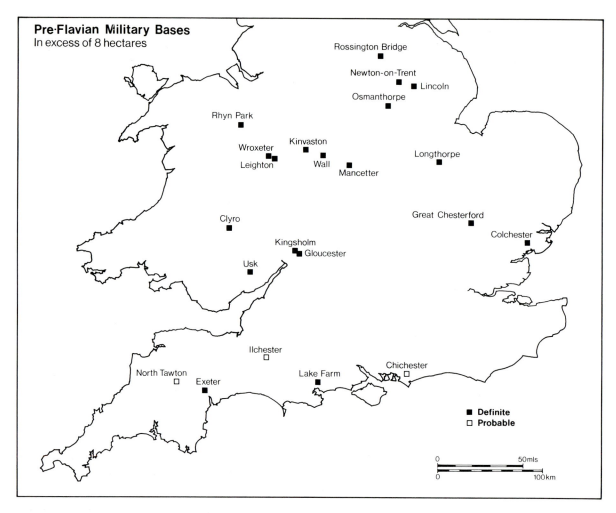

FIG. 1   Pre-Flavian military bases in excess of 8 hectares (*c.* 20 acres).

new category of military site has been defined, the so-called 'vexillation fortress'. This term embraces a category of site which is too small to have accommodated a full legion, too large for an auxiliary site (FIG. 1). Examples tend to cluster in the 10–12 hectare range.[27] This group of sites was first defined by Frere and St Joseph in their report on excavations at Longthorpe, which remains the most fully excavated example of the category.[28] It is sites of this general character which on present evidence would appear to fill in the gap between the arrival of the legions in A.D. 43 and the construction of the first full-sized legionary fortresses in *c.*60, for, as has already been observed, with the exception only of Colchester, there is no evidence for any sites capable of accommodating a force equivalent in size to a complete legion, until well into the reign of Nero when Lincoln, Wroxeter, Kingsholm Phase 2, Gloucester and Exeter were constructed. Frere has suggested that Legion IX is associated not only with Longthorpe but also Newton on Trent, Rossington Bridge and Malton, to which should be added the putative early base at Lincoln itself. In the area of Legion XIV he points to Leicester (though the existence of a large early base here is,

---

27.   Being roughly half the size of later legionary fortresses, these sites were at first often referred to as 'half-legionary fortresses', an unfortunate term since it begs the question of their garrison. The vaguer term 'vexillation' is more satisfactory, as a detachment may consist of legionaries, auxiliaries or a combination of the two. However, in view of our present state of ignorance of the interior arrangements of the majority of these sites, the interpretation of their function must remain open. Some could have served, for example, as supply-bases, as has been suggested of the Flavian site of Corbridge Red House: W.S. Hanson, C.M. Daniels, J.N. Dore and J.P. Gillam, 'The Agricolan supply base at Red House, Corbridge', *Arch. Ael.*[5] vii (1979), 1–97.

28.   S.S. Frere and J.K. St. Joseph, 'The Roman Fortress at Longthorpe', *Britannia* v (1974), 1–129.

on present evidence, highly speculative), Wall, Kinvaston and Leighton (otherwise known as Eaton Constantine or Eye Farm). To these may be added Towcester and Mancetter. In the south of England, where Legion II Augusta is known to have operated, lie Chichester where traces of military activity appear to extend over an area in excess of 16 hectares and Lake Farm, a site of at least 13 hectares.

The fragmentation of the legions in the early stages of the conquest, which is implied by this interpretation, is surprising and in many ways unexpected. Strength lies in numbers and prudent commanders do not weaken their armies at a time when, distributed to their winter-quarters to rest and recoup for the season ahead, they are perhaps less ready to deal with trouble. Caesar's armies hardly ever went into winter-quarters in strength below that of a full legion (and usually in considerably stronger groups).[29] Likewise, the Augustan armies on the Rhine were often accommodated in two-legion bases, but despite the intensity of recent fieldwork including aerial reconnaissance, such large bases are still totally lacking in Britain. Lack of evidence or evidence of a lack? The disposition of troops in winter-quarters could be determined by a number of inter-related factors: the strength and location of the enemy; the desire to protect an ally; the need for security in the 'off-season'; the availability of local food supplies and the accessibility of the site for shipping them in from outside. It is perhaps no coincidence that the largest known of the early bases was sited in the *oppidum* associated with the heart of the anti-Roman coalition – Colchester. The apparent lack of large troop concentrations elsewhere, even within the very early years of the conquest, implies that no major threat was envisaged: the army evidently felt secure.

Another interesting characteristic of early military dispositions in Britain which has emerged only in the last few years, is the reuse of native hillforts. The case of Hod Hill is well known, but for many years it stood alone – an isolated example, a sole exception to the rule that Roman forts lie in accessible sites chosen for ease of access not strength of defence. There are now several such sites, predominantly in the south and west, where the army exploited the natural advantages of hill-top sites, though the chronological (and hence the military) relationship of the Roman and native use of the sites is not always clear. At Hod Hill Richmond believed that Roman defeated and ejected native immediately prior to constructing the fort, and while there is no conclusive archaeological evidence of actual attack, nor is there a demonstrable chronological gap between native and Roman occupation.[30] At Hembury, on the other hand, Todd has demonstrated that the army constructed its encampment on a disused site. The position is unclear at Brandon Camp.[31] Nor (as far as the evidence takes us) is the nature and extent of these encampments the same in all cases. Only at Hod Hill does the army appear to have constructed its own circuit of defences, though at Hembury they may have rebuilt one of the hill-fort gates.[32] Frere sees

29.　The one occasion when a legion was divided between winter-quarters, it suffered an attack. Servius Galba, wintering with Legion XX in the Alpine area, stationed two cohorts in the territory of the Nantuates, the remaining eight at Octodurus (Martigny) in the territory of the Veragri. The Gauls, we are told, 'despised the small numbers of a legion from which, never at full establishment, two cohorts had been withdrawn, and a considerable number of soldiers sent off to seek supplies.' (Caesar, *de Bello Gallico* 3.1–2).

30.　The catapult-bolts deemed by Richmond to be evidence of a Roman attack on the native fortification, could equally well derive from the Roman fort period, when the area not enclosed within the Roman defences could have been used as a practice-ground: Richmond himself suggested that the area may have been used for cavalry exercises. *Hod Hill* Vol. II (London, 1968), 91; cf. R.W. Davies, 'The Training grounds of the Roman cavalry,' *Arch. Journ.* cxxv (1969), 73–100.

31.　Richmond, op. cit. (note 30): M. Todd, 'Excavations at Hembury, Devon 1980–83; a summary report', *Antiq. Journ.* lxiv (1984), 251–68: S.S. Frere, 'Brandon Camp, Herefordshire', *Britannia* xviii (1987), 49–92: on the one hand, a ring-ditch which underlay one of the Roman structures at Brandon had silted up and developed a turf-line prior to the construction of the military building above it, yet the pottery from the site included types which were current at the very end of the Iron Age and into the early years of the Roman period.

32.　M. Todd, 'Hembury (Devon): Roman troops in a hillfort', *Antiquity* lviii (1984), 172–3, fig. 3. The cross-dykes which straddle Hembury hillfort (defining a roughly rectangular area of some 2.5 ha at the northern end of the site) may conceivably relate to the period of Roman use. They were dated to the late Iron Age by D.M. Liddell (*Proc. Devon Arch. Expl. Soc.* I.2 (1930), 40–63; II.3 (1935), 135–175 esp. 164). More recent excavation 'has added little of substance to her account. They do appear to date from the Late Iron Age or later.'; M. Todd, op. cit. (note 31) esp. 262–3.

Brandon, which was provided with a large granary building, as a supply-base. The accommodation at Hod Hill is more that of a conventional fort. The reason for the choice of these hill-top sites must remain a matter for speculation: clearly the hills offered some protection; they also provided a wide outlook. By occupying these hillforts the army denied them to the enemy.[33]

The problem of trying to use the evidence of archaeology to write history has already been touched on. One particular area in which this has been tried relates to the question of the extent of Claudius's original ambitions in Britain. When Claudius told Aulus Plautius to conquer 'the rest' did he mean the whole of the rest of Britain or, as is commonly argued, merely the rest of the lowland zone? Either theory is tenable on the grounds of the historical evidence which is totally ambiguous on the point. One piece of archaeological evidence which is often adduced in favour of the latter hypothesis is the existence of the so-called 'Fosse Frontier'. It was R.G. Collingwood who, in a paper published in 1924, first propounded the idea of the Fosse Frontier, suggesting that the Fosse Way, the road which strikes diagonally across Britain from the area of Exeter in the south-west to Lincoln in the north-east, was intended to be the line of the first frontier of Britain, a frontier established by the second governor of the province, Ostorius Scapula.[34] The starting-point for his premise was the assumption that the road suffered from an 'obvious lack of utility as an ordinary traffic line' (he pointed to the fact that neither later roads nor railways followed its general course); hence, he suggested '(it) was intended as a *limes* in the sense of a transverse fortified road acting as a frontier – a purely temporary frontier – for a conquered district.' Elsewhere he wrote '(Ostorius Scapula) drew a frontier line across Britain, disarmed all the tribes on his own side of it and fortified and patrolled it to keep out raids from beyond. This frontier line was the road known as the Fosse Way. It was meant to hold down the entire country up to the Trent and Severn.'[35] This idea of a Fosse frontier has been taken up and embellished by subsequent commentators, who have, in so doing, departed in two particularly significant respects from Collingwood's original hypothesis. Firstly they have transferred its authorship from Ostorius Scapula (governor from 47–52) to Aulus Plautius (governor from 43–47) and secondly they have argued that it was designed, not as a temporary expedient, but as the boundary of the Claudian province, marking the limit of the area which Claudius intended to conquer.[36] The logic of the line has been variously explained as the boundary between highland and lowland, between semi-nomadic peoples and sedentary tribes capable of romanization, between areas of predominantly pastoral and predominantly arable economy – all distinctions which are, to a greater or lesser degree, over-simplistic and inaccurate. The case for the Fosse Frontier has been advocated most vigorously by Graham Webster, who in a number of important and influential books and articles, has brought archaeological evidence to bear on the problem, attempting to identify many of the *castella* which Collingwood assumed (but could not demonstrate) to lie along the frontier road.[37] Webster pointed out that to have any meaning as a frontier line, the Fosse must predate the advance westwards into Wales, the Scapulan thrust forward to Trent and Severn and the transfer of Legion XX into a position (wherever that position was) to deal with the Silures in the winter of 49/50. In practice, few of the military sites which can now be shown or suggested to lie along the line of the Fosse Way can be closely dated. Of those that can, only Cirencester, perhaps Bath, and the putative early site at Lincoln appear to be as early as Plautian. Exeter, assumed to be the south-western terminus, is certainly later (even

33. A similar range of hill-top military sites has emerged in the upper Rhineland and Raetia, dating between the 20s and 40s A.D.. There are Trajanic examples in Dacia, and Antonine examples in the area beyond the middle Danube. All appear to relate to periods of active campaigning in the areas in question.
34. 'The Fosse', *JRS* xiv (1924), 252–56.
35. R.G. Collingwood, *The Archaeology of Roman Britain* (Oxford, 1930), 66.
36. See, for example, S.S. Frere, *Britannia* (London, 1967), 76: 'As the basis of a *limes* it marks the intended limits of the first Claudian province, and it follows that imperial policy at first envisaged occupation only of the lowland zone.'
37. G. Webster, 'The Roman military advance under Ostorius Scapula', *Arch. Journ.* cxv (1958), 49–98; 'The military situations in Britain between AD 43 and 71', *Britannia* i (1970), 179–97; (with D. Dudley) *The Roman Conquest of Britain AD 43–57* (London, 1965); *The Roman Invasion of Britain* (London, 1980).

on the very earliest estimate of its foundation date). So, too, are Ilchester and Margidunum.[38] But what of the practicality of the Fosse Way as a frontier line? It is just about the longest line which could possibly be chosen within Britain. The concentration of known (though not necessarily contemporary) sites along its line averages out at no more than one site in forty kilometres, and even though there are probably more sites to be identified we are still a very long way from the fort-spacing characteristic of other known frontier lines, the eleven-kilometre spacing on Hadrian's Wall for example, or the three on the Antonine Wall. There is, in fact, no closer spacing of forts along the Fosse Way than along the other major roads of the province. It is worth, then, examining Collingwood's fundamental premise that the Fosse lacked utility as a road line. The fact that this is true of the nineteenth and twentieth centuries does not make it true of the Roman period. The road clearly was important in the late Saxon and early Norman periods when it featured as one of the four great highways which came under the King's Peace.[39] As far as the Roman period was concerned it linked two legionary fortresses: it formed part of the road network which covered the whole country, facilitating movement by military and civilian. It is a *limes* in this early sense of the word, rather than in the later sense of a fortified frontier.[40] The static frontier has no place in the dynamic campaigning situation of the mid-first century, when the boundaries of the *provincia* will have existed in a notional rather than a physical sense, enforced by the armies which in the winter will have been distributed around the province, and in summer will have been engaged in campaigning beyond to extend it.

Looking at this distribution of troops around the province, it is apparent that military sites were built in the territory of Rome's allies, as well as in areas directly conquered. It is often assumed, without justification, that the territory of the 'client' rulers, will have entertained no soldiers. Hence, for example, forts identified in the territory of the Iceni, have automatically been dated (without excavation) as post-Boudican. Written evidence from elsewhere shows how the Roman army might base itself in an allied kingdom to protect and secure the throne of a friendly ruler.[41] As regards Rome's allies within Britain, recent work has touched on two. While archaeology has brought to light a supply-base (Fishbourne) and a major military establishment (Chichester) within the territory attributable to the kingdom of Cogidubnus, the re-reading of the well-known Chichester inscription has changed somewhat our perception of his status – not 'King and imperial legate' but 'Great King', no longer a member of the Roman senate, but nonetheless recognized as an eminent ruler.[42] Further north, in the territory of Cartimandua, Queen of the Brigantes, there has been a reconsideration of the site of Stanwick. As a result of the eloquent report produced on the excavations carried out here in the early 50s by Wheeler, the site has become woven into the historical narrative of the conquest of the north as the location of Venutius's last stand.[43] In many a history book 'the battle of Stanwick' features with the status of a historical fact. The notion that a man such as Venutius, whom Tacitus describes as skilled in military matters, should try to defend the Stanwick enclosure is, of itself, highly questionable.[44] Recent excavations on the site have confirmed the doubts expressed by Dobson on the

38. On the question of the Fosse Way in general and on its intended south-western terminus in particular cf. V.A. Maxfield, 'Devon and the End of the Fosse Frontier', *Proc. Devon Arch. Soc.* 44 (1986), 1–8. The discovery of increasing numbers of military sites in the south-west peninsula, well beyond Exeter and the Fosse Way, have changed perceptions of the conquest of this area.
39. *Leges Edwardi Confessoris* 12. Published in F. Liebermann, *Die Gesetze der Angelsachsen* (Vol. I, 1903), 637–9.
40. de Ruggiero, *Dizionario Epigrafico* (Rome, 1950), sv. *Limes.*
41. One contemporary example, is the garrison based at Gorneae to protect the king of the turbulent kingdom of Armenia. Tacitus, *Annals* 12.45. On the various factors lying behind fort siting cf. V.A. Maxfield, 'The Army and the Land in the Roman South-West', in R.A. Higham (ed.), *Security and Defence in South-West England before 1800* (Exeter, 1986), 1–25.
42. J. Bogaers, 'King Cogidubnus: Another reading of RIB 91', *Britannia* x (1979), 243–54.
43. R.E.M. Wheeler, *The Stanwick Fortifications, North Riding of Yorkshire* Soc. of Antiqs. Research Report xvii (London, 1954).
44. Doubts about the nature of the site were first expressed by B. Dobson, 'Roman Durham', *Trans. Architect. & Arch. Soc. Durham & Northumberland* 2 (1970), 40.

three-phase development of the site proposed by Wheeler (who tied each phase in neatly with an historically documented episode in the history of the Brigantes), substituting instead the hypothesis that the distinction between the three enclosures is one of function rather than chronology. It is also now apparent that substantial quantities of imported fine pottery of Claudio-Neronian date were reaching the site.[45] Its occupant would appear to have been economically if not politically pro-Roman, and it has been suggested that far from being the enclave of an anti-Roman faction, Stanwick was the *oppidum* of the pro-Roman Cartimandua.[46] (below, p. 31)

The last thirty years of archaeological activity have thus combined to bring about a fairly radical reappraisal of the nature of the conquest and, in particular, of the question of military deployment. The discovery of large numbers of new sites has brought about a qualitative as well as quantitative increase in information. New categories of site have been identified and apparent gaps in our knowledge filled in. The 1956 edition of the Ordnance Survey Map of Roman Britain, for example, shows not a single military base in the West Country, west of a line from Gloucester to Hod Hill (and even these two appear as 'probable' not 'certain'). We now know of some fourteen definite and five probable sites, thus firmly ruling out of court the notion that the Roman army never penetrated Devon and Cornwall. The next thirty years may well see an equally radical rethink, discarding many of our present hypotheses and will, it is to be hoped, bring to light new evidence on matters about which we remain, at present, very much in the dark. Comparatively few *castra aestiva* of Claudio-Neronian date have yet been identified: none at all of Caesarian date. The identification and particularly the excavation of more 'vexillation fortresses' is desirable if we are properly to understand the nature and role of these early bases. Categorisation by size alone, which is what we are doing at present, may well be very misleading, for these bases could have served a wide variety of functions which can be identified only with increased knowledge of their internal plans. Excavation needs, however, to be fairly extensive if it is to elucidate non-standard layouts. Early Roman timber buildings are too irregular for their plan to be recovered satisfactorily by small-scale trenching and extrapolation. Our knowledge of military cemeteries is lamentably poor, as is our understanding of the nature and function of the military annexe and of extra-mural activity in general, though excavation is now starting to produce important evidence for industrial activity (metal-working and pottery production, for example) in the vicinity of military bases. Colchester and Longthorpe have both been the subject of recent monographs on this subject.[47] The whole question of army supply, both of food-stuffs and of durables, is a matter of considerable importance. Some individual artefact types, particularly ceramics and various categories of specifically military equipment, are receiving attention, and there is scope for a more comprehensive look at the whole question of the mechanics of supply of an army on campaign, as of the later settled army of occupation.[48]

Even the question of the composition of the army itself is still open to debate. We do not, for example, have any idea of the number of auxiliary units which accompanied the four legions to Britain in 43, an unfortunate state of affairs which is due in large part to Britain's meagre epigraphic record: few soldiers' tombstones, no building inscriptions and no military diplomas of pre-Flavian date. The oft-quoted statement that there were about 20,000 legionaries and a

45.   On the recent excavations see P. Turnbull, *Durham Arch. Journ.* 1 (1984): *Yorks Arch. Journ.* liv (1982), 174.
46.   W.S. Hanson and D.B. Campbell, 'The Brigantes: from Clientage to Conquest', *Britannia* xvii (1986), 73–90.
47.   R. Niblett, *Sheepen: an early Roman Industrial site at Camulodunum* (London, 1985). G.B. Dannell and J.P. Wild, *Longthorpe II. The military works depot: an episode in landscape history* (London, 1987).
48.   On pottery see, for example, papers in J. Dore and K. Greene (eds.), *Roman Pottery Studies in Britain and Beyond* (Oxford, 1977). On military equipment see, M.C. Bishop (ed.), *The Production and Distribution of Roman Military Equipment* (Oxford, 1985). A paper by D.J. Breeze on supply on the northern frontier, contains many points of general application: 'Demand and supply on the northern frontier' in R. Miket and C. Burgess (eds.), *Between and Beyond the walls. Essays on the Prehistory and History of North Britain in honour of George Jobey* (Edinburgh, 1984), 264–286.

comparable number of auxiliaries, is (where the *auxilia* are concerned) an hypothesis and not a matter of fact.[49]

Last, but by no means least, an area of very considerable, not to say fundamental, continuing concern, is that of the overall impact of the army on settlement and economy. The investigation of patterns of settlement on the eve of the Conquest, the demonstration that many hillforts had gone out of use well before the invasion of 43, and the increasing evidence for continuity in the rural landscape, is gradually moulding our perception of the relationship between the military and the native population, our understanding of 'Conquest and Aftermath' as perceived from grass-roots level.

49.   In his summary of military dispositions in A.D. 23 (*Annals* 4.5), Tacitus indicates that the number of auxiliary troops was but slightly inferior to the number of legionaries. The comment is of a general nature and cannot necessarily be taken to apply to the army within any one province. On the one hand, Paul Holder has recently published a survey of the *auxilia* in Britain which suggests that the bulk of the troops attested in the province came over in 70 and not in 43, while, on the other, Graham Webster has published a Plautian fort distribution map which implies contemporary occupation of sites sufficient to accommodate an auxiliary garrison well in excess of that which it is reasonable to expect. P. Holder, *The Roman Army in Britain* (London, 1982); G. Webster, *The Roman Invasion of Britain* (London, 1980), 112, Map II.

THE FLAVIAN AND TRAJANIC NORTHERN FRONTIER*

By Charles Daniels

'But when Britain . . . was restored by Vespasian, generals became great, armies excellent, and the enemy's hopes diminished' (Tacitus *Agricola* 17.1). The first Flavian appointment saw Petillius Cerialis (A.D. 71–73/4) return to Britain as governor, clearly with the task of terminating the unfinished war with Venutius. Polarization of the Brigantes into pro- and anti-Roman factions had occurred under Cartimandua and Venutius on the breakdown of their marriage, when Vettius Bolanus had been able to do no more than rescue the queen during the civil war following Nero's death.

As Tacitus tells it this was the second and final of the pair's matrimonial upsets, the earlier having occurred in the governorship of Didius Gallus (A.D. 52–7). Most accept this statement, although the question of duplication of a single event has been raised, if not satisfactorily answered, and the single event attributed to A.D. 69.

Cerialis moved Legion IX Hispana forward to York and by permanent conquest or campaigning dealt with the Brigantes. Wheeler's interpretation of the date and sequence at Stanwick has been seriously questioned, especially his view that it was the scene of Venutius' last stand. Fresh excavation and reconsideration of the old evidence have thrown doubt on there ever having been a Roman attack, or destruction, of the fortress. In fact the nature and quantity of Roman material which it has produced has even allowed the suggestion that far from being an anti-Roman stronghold, it could have been Cartimandua's capital.[1] (above, p. 28)

Cerialis' campaigning has been identified in the three Stainmore marching camps of Rey Cross, Crackenthorpe and Plumpton Head, approximately a day's march apart. Most accept Carlisle as the next halting place, although whether anything in the way of a more permanent base was placed there at this time is uncertain. In view of the fact that the site is hardly less than 100 miles by foot from York it is still perhaps a little rash to see anything beyond a temporary halt there. Milton, in Dumfriesshire, was long ago dismissed as a contemporary fort, but the possibility of the military strike-force having camped at Dalswinton before returning south is not totally out of the question.

The case for a Cerialan fort at Corbridge, once considered a possibility, has been greatly reduced with the discovery and excavation of a 'vexillation fortress' at Beaufort Red House, just

---

* Some repeated references are: S.S. Frere, *Britannia*, 3rd edn. (1987). P. Salway, *Roman Britain* (1981).
  W.S. Hanson and D.B. Campbell, 'The Brigantes: from Clientage to Conquest,' *Britannia* xvii (1986), 73–90.
  W.S. Hanson, *Agricola and the Conquest of the North* (1987).

1. D. Braund, 'Observations on Cartimandua,' *Britannia* xv (1984), 1–6, especially for older references, and Hanson and Campbell (1986) for references to recent works by Mitchell, Dobson, Hartley, Fitts, Turnbull and Haselgrove; Sir Mortimer Wheeler, *The Stanwick Fortifications* (1954); Frere (1987) and Salway (1981) take the traditional view.

west of Corbridge, in 1974. An Agricolan date was proved.[2] The second Flavian governor, Julius Frontinus (A.D. 73/4–77/8), completed the conquest of Wales. His successor was another legate with previous experience of Britain: Gn. Julius Agricola.

Because his son-in-law Tacitus wrote a life of him, Agricola is better known than any other governor of Britain. But Tacitus' life was by its very nature heavily eulogistic (he wrote to praise Agricola, not to bury him) and for that reason it has produced differences of opinion over its reliability.[3] Tacitus' use of sweeping descriptions coupled with his almost total lack of the names of peoples and places has meant that aerial photography, excavation and fieldwork have come into their own in attempting to provide the locations of the events described. While excavation and fieldwork has been carried out by many people, the photographic exploration was for long predominantly the work of one man, Professor Kenneth St Joseph, although others are now flying, and discovering, on a regular basis.

Problems principally arise because of the short time-scale for the first Flavian period in Scotland. Agricola arrived in Britain in 77 or 78, won his victory at Mons Graupius in 83 or 84, and in 86 or 87 everything north of Dalswinton and Newstead was abandoned on the withdrawal of Legion II Adiutrix, and auxiliary troops, from the province. To date sites to a single year within this decade is impossible on the evidence available, although it is often tried.[4]

Agricola's first season saw the suppression of a revolt in Wales and his second an advance to the north, though probably not far beyond the area already traversed by Cerialis. In his second winter he is credited with fostering the education and Romanization of the civilian part of the province. Precisely how much should be attributed to him, as opposed to any other Flavian governor, is not clear, although fragments of a stone building inscription from Verulamium bear his name.[5]

In his third season Roman arms were carried to the Tay, which would fit with Titus' fifteenth imperial salutation taken in 79. Seasons four and five were spent in the creation of a further line on the Forth-Clyde isthmus (*inventus in ipsa Britannia terminus*, Tacitus *Agricola* 23.1) and the consolidation of the territory to the south. Macdonald's belief that the Agricolan line of forts underlay many of the later Antonine Wall forts is now mostly disproved, but differences of opinion exist as to whether any, or all, of the area previously overrun as far as the Tay was included within the frontier. Likewise the details of the campaign in southwest Scotland in the fifth season are still differently interpreted.[6]

Agricola's last two seasons culminated in his defeat of the Caledonian tribes at Mons Graupius. The evidence for the campaigns leading to this is entirely that of marching camps, of which St Joseph has identified several groups of probable or possible relevance. The so-called 'Stracathro' type with its unusual but characteristic gate form is generally accepted as Agricolan, although it is frequently added that it would have been better to have named it after Dalginross, where Roy drew not only the ditches but also the standing banks of a gate of this type, since totally destroyed. Likewise, a group of camps of about 30 acres is generally taken to be Agricolan, as are three large camps of some 115 acres each at Dunning, Abernethy and Carpow. This leaves

2. B. Hartley, 'Some problems of the Roman Military Occupation of the North of England,' *Northern History* i (1966); Hanson and Campbell (1986); Hanson (1987); W.S. Hanson, C.M. Daniels, J.N. Dore and J.P. Gillam, 'The Agricolan Supply Base at Red House, Corbridge,' *Arch. Ael*[5] vii (1979), 1–97.

3. Sir Ian Richmond and R.M. Ogilvie, *Cornelii Taciti de Vita Agricolae* (1967) and A.R. Burn, *Agricola and Roman Britain* (1953) for older views, against which see Hanson (1987), critically reviewed by C.M. Daniels, *Arch. Ael*[5] xvi (1988), 259–61.

4. Revised dates for governorship: A.R. Birley, 'The Date of Mons Graupius', *Liverpool Class. Monthly* 1.2 (1976), 11–14.

5. Salway (1981), 142; S.S. Frere, *Verulamium Excavations* II (1983), 55–72; M. Fulford, 'Excavations at . . . Silchester,' *Antiq. Journ.* lxv (1985), 39–60; Hanson (1987), Chapter 4.

6. Sir George Macdonald, *The Roman Wall in Scotland*, 2nd edn. (1934); D.J. Breeze, *The Northern Frontiers of Roman Britain* (1982), 45–46; Hanson (1987), 107–113; C.M. Daniels, *Scottish Arch. Forum* ii (1970), 92; G.S. Maxwell, 'New Frontiers: The Roman Fort at Doune,' *Britannia* xv (1984), 217–23; S.S. Frere, 'The Flavian Frontier in Scotland,' *Scottish Arch. Forum* xii (1981), 89–97; N. Reed, 'The Fifth Year of Agricola's Campaigns,' *Britannia* ii (1971), 143–148; Hanson (1987), Chapter 6.

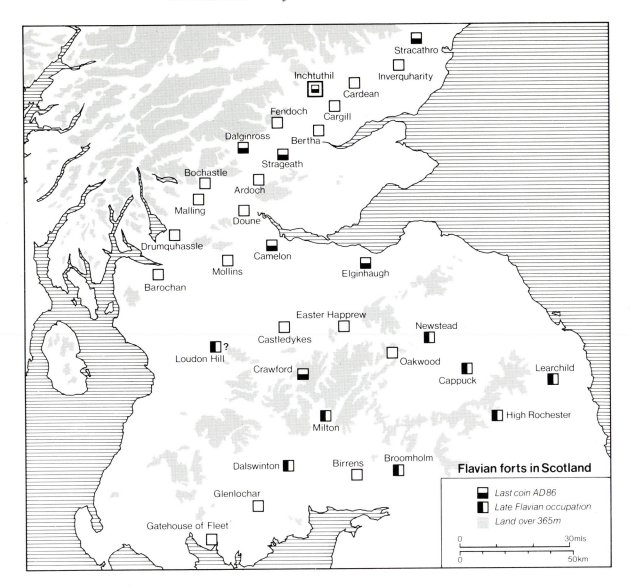

FIG. 1 Flavian forts in Scotland. (A. Hobley)

several other groups, including one at 63 acres and one at *c.*110 acres, to be connected with later campaigning, principally Severan. However, in 1978 St Joseph published a 144-acre camp at Durno just to the north of the local landmark of Bennachie (Aberdeenshire), which he argued to have been the battlefield of Mons Graupius. In addition, he claimed that this carried the whole 110 acre series over to an Agricolan date. By no means all scholars agree with this abrupt *volte-face*, the more so because by any reasonable calculation the army encamped at Durno must have been from 2½ to 4 times the size of the force Agricola had with him at Graupius, if Tacitus is to be given any credibility.[7]

The battlefield itself has long been chased about the counties of Scotland and identified at Duncrub in Strathearn, Raedykes and Durno in Aberdeenshire and Knock Hill in Banff. Perhaps, it has even been suggested, it lay in Nairn, Inverness, or even beyond. While no site carries complete conviction Duncrub has least of all.[8]

7. J.K. St Joseph, 'The Roman Camp at Durno, Aberdeenshire, and the Site of Mons Graupius,' *Britannia* ix (1978), 271–287, and 'Air Reconnaissance in Roman Britain 1973–6,' *JRS* lxvii (1977), 131– 145 for full references; Salway (1981), 146; Frere (1987), 94–6; J.C. Mann, 'Two 'topoi' in the *Agricola,'* *Britannia* xvi (1985), 21–4; Hanson (1987), Chapter 6.
8. L. Keppie, 'Mons Graupius: The Search for a Battlefield,' *Scottish Arch. Forum* xii (1981), 79–88; A.A.R. Henderson, 'From 83 to 1983: On the Trail of Mons Graupius,' *The Deeside Field* xviii (1984), 23–29.

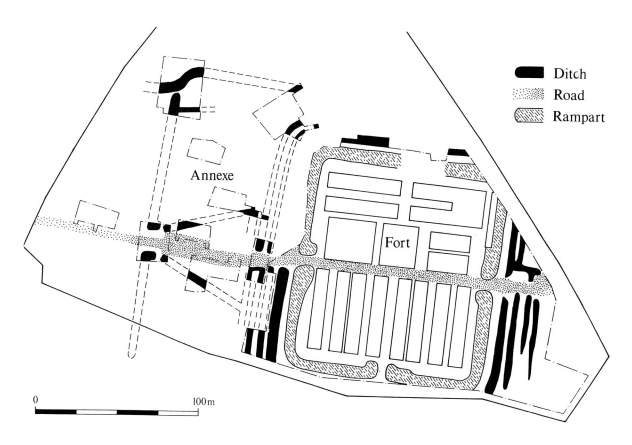

FIG. 2   Elginhaugh: fort and annexe. (W.S. Hanson)

Continued discovery and excavation have gone far to our building up a picture of the post-Agricolan frontier which faced the Highland Line from Loch Lomond up through Strathmore. Where once less than 10 possible fort sites were known, and far fewer excavated, today twice that number are recorded and mostly tested. The understanding of this system has recently received a most important boost with the publication of the legionary fortress of Inchtuthil, the scene of Sir Ian Richmond's excavations 1952– 65. Unfortunately he himself died in the autumn of 1965. Of perhaps equal importance is a study of the currency of Domitian, with particular regard to the withdrawal from Flavian Scotland, which shows most convincingly that *everything* north of the Newstead-Dalswinton line was abandoned at a single stroke late in 86 or early in 87, thus placing the Gask watchtower system as part of Agricola's dispositions.[9] (Fig. 1)

Domitian's final line (Flavian II) seems to have been to hold the forts of Glenlochar, Dalswinton, Milton, Oakwood and Newstead as the basis for controlling lowland Scotland. Behind these Broomholm, High Rochester, Learchild and others provided a back-up garrison – but one in total considerably smaller in size than the Agricolan (Flavian I) occupation had required. But it was apparently not under Domitian but Trajan that the full extent of Tacitus' statement *perdomita Britannia et statim omissa* (Tacitus, *Histories* 1.2) occurred, with the creation of yet another frontier, this time based on the line of the Stanegate. The term Stanegate really only correctly applies to the road running between Corbridge and Carlisle, but under the name 'Western Stanegate' the system has been traced from Carlisle via Burgh by Sands to Kirkbride in the west. Nothing similar is as yet known between Corbridge and the east coast, although aerial photographs show a multiperiod (apparently timber) fort at Washing Wells, Wickham, just south

9.   S.S. Frere, 'The Flavian Frontier in Scotland,' *Scottish Arch. Forum* xii (1981), 89–97; L.F. Pitts and J.K. St Joseph, *Inchtuthil, the Roman Legionary Fortress* (1985), reviewed by G.D.B. Jones, *Britannia* xix (1988), 527–530; the coinage review is by A. Hobley, *Britannia* xx (1989), 69–74.

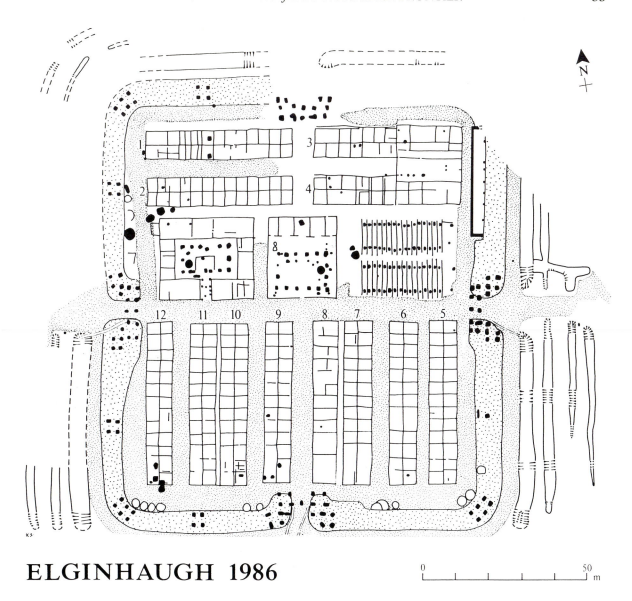

ELGINHAUGH 1986

0 [scale] 50 m

FIG. 3 Elginhaugh: plan of fort. (W.S. Hanson)

of the Tyne. In the absence of any evidence, for or against, this site is usually placed on maps as an 'Eastern Stanegate' fort.

That the Trajanic frontier used the Stanegate road as its principal lateral connection is generally accepted, and has been for some time. Forts are known at Corbridge, Chesterholm, Nether Denton, Brampton Old Church, Carlisle, Burgh by Sands and Kirkbride, with the further possibility of one at Carvoran, but the only evidence to date from Newbrough is fourth-century pottery. Other sites may await detection further east. Fortlets have been excavated at Haltwhistle Burn and Throp, and another is suggested at Castle Hill Boothby. Whether yet more existed is by no means certain, and the likelihood of a regular system with forts and fortlets alternating is far from proved. The fort, fortlet and tower model once seemingly presented by the Taunus sector of the Upper German frontier is now known not to have possessed forts until late in the reign of Hadrian, and, therefore, not to provide a parallel for the Trajanic Stanegate.[10]

10. E. Birley, *Research on Hadrian's Wall* (1961), Chapter 5; B.R. Hartley, 'Some Problems of the Roman Military Occupation of the North of England,' *Northern History* i (1966), 7–20; G.D.B. Jones, 'The Solway Frontier: Interim Report 1976–81', *Britannia* xiii (1982), 283–285; C.M. Daniels (ed.), *Collingwood Bruce, The Roman Wall* (1978), *vide* Stanegate; H. Schönberger, 'The Roman Frontier in Germany', *JRS* lix (1969), 164–167,

THE NORTHERN FRONTIERS*

By David J. Breeze

HADRIAN'S WALL

1961 was a landmark in the study of Hadrian's Wall for in this year Eric Birley published his *Research on Hadrian's Wall*. Here were collected and distilled the descriptions and interpretations of antiquarians and archaeologists from the 16th century onwards. Thus this work forms the starting point for any subsequent treatment of Hadrian's Wall. Whilst *Research on Hadrian's Wall* will never require to be repeated, the acquisition of new data and the re-examination of existing material has continued and thus our view of Hadrian's Wall has been modified.

Several general books have brought this new work to wider audiences. The 'official' guide-book, *The Handbook to the Roman Wall*, has passed through two new editions. The twelfth by the late Sir Ian Richmond was published in 1966 and the thirteenth, considerably expanded by Charles Daniels, in 1978. These have been supplemented by a wide range of general and detailed guide-books to the Wall.[1] *Hadrian's Wall* by David J. Breeze and Brian Dobson offers a different treatment, a history of the Wall.[2] More specialised treatments have also appeared in David Divine's *The North-West Frontier of Rome* and Hunter Davies' *Walk along the Wall*.[3] An attempt to place Hadrian's Wall in its wider setting on the northern frontier was made by David J. Breeze in *The Northern Frontiers of Roman Britain*, while Hadrian's Wall has also been considered in the many general books on Roman Britain which have been published since 1961. Mention must be made of the useful compilation of the primary literary sources for the northern frontier by John Mann.[4] Further books and articles will be considered below.

---

*   I am pleased to acknowledge the help I have received from Dr B. Dobson, Dr L.J.F. Keppie and Dr Valerie Maxfield in preparing this paper.

1. For example, R. Birley, *Guide to the Central Sector of Hadrian's Wall* (1972); David J. Breeze, *Hadrian's Wall, A souvenir guide to the Roman Wall* (1987); J. Crow, *Hadrian's Wall* (1985); R.W. Davies, *Hadrian's Wall, A practical guide to the visible remains* (1972); T.H. Rowland, *A Short Guide to the Roman Wall* (1973); L. Turnbull, *Hadrian's Wall*, History Trails in 4 books (1974).
2. David J. Breeze and Brian Dobson, *Hadrian's Wall* (1st ed., London, 1976; 2nd ed., 1978; 3rd ed., 1987).
3. Other books on Hadrian's Wall include, D.J. Breeze and B. Dobson, *The Army of Hadrian's Wall* (1972); R. Embleton and Frank Graham, *Hadrian's Wall in the days of the Romans* (1984); Frank Graham, *The Roman Wall* (1979); J. Forde-Johnston, *Hadrian's Wall* (London, 1977); Barri Jones, *Hadrian's Wall from the air* (1st impression, 1976; 2nd impression 1978); F. Gerald Simpson, *Watermills and Military Works on Hadrian's Wall*, edited by Grace Simpson (Kendal, 1976). Most excavation reports and many discussion papers on Hadrian's Wall have appeared in the two appropriate county journals, *Arch. Aeliana* and *Trans. Cumberland Westmorland Antiq. Arch. Soc.*; others have been published in *Britannia*.
4. J.C. Mann (ed.), *The Northern Frontier in Britain from Hadrian to Honorius: Literary and Epigraphic Sources*. Cf. J.C. Mann and R.G. Penman (eds.), *Literary Sources for Roman Britain* LACTOR II (1987).

The Wall or Curtain

Several miles of the curtain have been uncovered since 1945. Much of this is unpublished, but English Heritage is in process of preparing a detailed survey of those stretches in State care. Among the discoveries were three shaped stones at Cawfields which Dorothy Charlesworth interpreted as part of the parapet.[5] Recent work by Jim Crow for the National Trust between Housesteads and Peel Crag has revealed evidence for extensive repair of the wall, probably, he suggests, under Septimius Severus. The original narrow wall appears to have been so badly built as to require extensive replacement less than 100 years after its construction.[6] The hard white mortar used by the rebuilders appears to have been so liberally spread over the face of the stones as to suggest that the whole wall was plastered.[7] Further stretches of original clay core have been uncovered, re-opening the question of the significance of the differential use of clay and mortar without answering it.[8]

Milecastles

Analysis of milecastle plans by R. Hunneyset revealed the use of different setting-out lines by the legionary builders, thus providing an additional indicator of the builder, though the use of an external or an internal setting-out line can only be recognised today in narrow wall milecastles.[9] The discovery of a milecastle in the 'wrong' position on Westgate Road, Newcastle, will force a re-consideration of 'the accepted positions and numbering of milecastles generally on the eastern stretch of the Wall'.[10] The excavation of MC 35 made a valuable addition to the small number of completely excavated milecastles, presenting a detailed history of the Roman structure and the succeeding medieval settlement. The lack of a north gate was remarkable, though it was not clear that the milecastle was built without one.[11] The accommodation initially was a small building, similar in size to a fort barrack-room, but this was replaced on several occasions by up to two larger buildings during an occupation which continued well into the fourth century, emphasising the different histories of milecastles and turrets.

Turrets

Turrets have been the subject of detailed consideration by Dorothy Charlesworth.[12] The small finds from turrets were considered by Lindsay Allason-Jones, who has made a valuable contribution to the question of the source of the troops stationed at these structures.[13] She noted both the quantity and quality of the material. Turrets on both the stone and turf walls have been excavated, many in advance of consolidation. Of particular importance were the group examined in 1958 and 1959, for the report, by Charmian Woodfield, set new standards for the publication of these structures.[14] One turret, 45a, was known to be earlier than the wall but was re-dated to the early Hadrianic period on the basis of a sherd of Hadrianic pottery in the foundations. Many of the turrets excavated were found to have gone out of use before the end of the second century,

5.   D. Charlesworth, *Arch. Ael.*[4] xlvi (1968), 73–4.
6.   *Current Arch.* xcvi (April 1985), 16–9; *Britannia* xiv (1983), 290–1; xv (1984), 280; xvi (1985), 271. Further work on the curtain in the crags sector is described in D. Haigh and Revd. M. Savage, *Arch. Ael.*[5] xii (1984), 33–147.
7.   Cf. *Britannia* xix (1988), 433 for excavation by P. Bidwell revealing 'the imprint of seven courses . . . on a slab of fallen plaster'. Traces of plaster adhering to the faces of stones in consolidated stretches of the wall can be seen, for example, at Heddon-on-the-Wall and at Blackcarts.
8.   J. Bennett, *Arch. Ael.*[5] xi (1983), 43–5. Cf. *Britannia* xix (1988), 433 for clay core at Denton Burn.
9.   R. Hunneysett, *Arch. Ael.*[5] viii (1980), 95–107.
10. Barbara Harbottle, R. Fraser and F.C. Burton, *Britannia* xix (1988), 153–62.
11. Haigh and Savage, op. cit. (note 6), 33–147. Work at MC 39 is reported in *Britannia* xvii (1986), 378–81; xviii (1987), 316; xix (1988), 434.
12. D. Charlesworth in M.R. Apted, R. Gilyard-Beer and A.D. Saunders (eds.), *Ancient Monuments and their Interpretation* (London, 1977), 13–26.
13. L. Allason-Jones in J.C. Coulston (ed.), *Military Equipment and the Identity of Roman Soldiers* BAR Int. Ser. 394 (1988), 197–233.
14. C.C. Woodfield, *Arch. Ael.*[4] xliii (1965), 87–200.

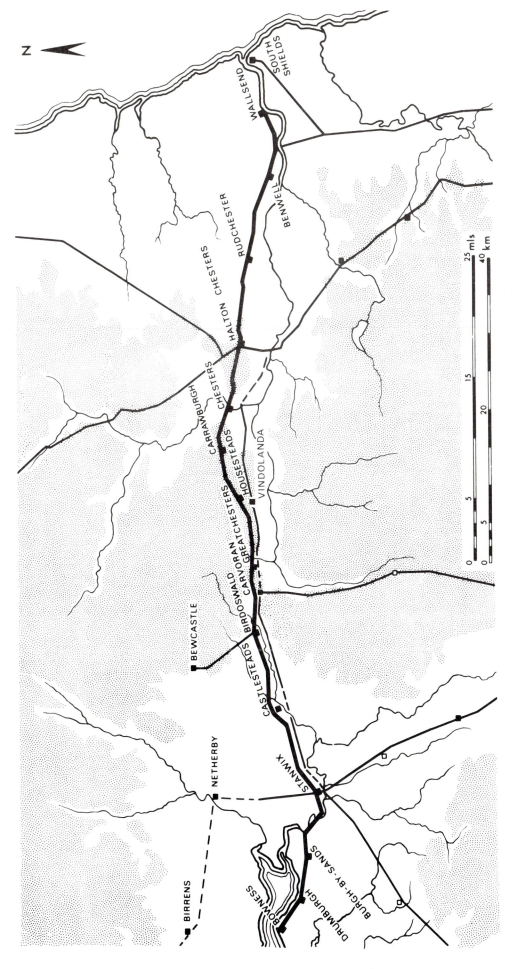

FIG. 1 Hadrian's Wall at the end of Hadrian's reign. (T. Borthwick & D.J. Breeze)

a conclusion supported by Allason-Jones.[15] One, 51b, was re-occupied in the late fourth century when a hut was built within it. Two, 18b and 26a, furnished evidence for metal-working. These excavations have led to renewed discussion of the purpose of the stone platforms found in both stone and turf wall turrets. Charlesworth suggested they were to provide the bases for ladders rather than stairs, though she interpreted some as the bases of benches.[16] In 1986 Jim Crow discovered a new turret between T39a and T39b, a hitherto unexpected addition to the Wall.[17]

Bridges
Both Chesters Bridge and Willowford Bridge have been examined.[18] At Chesters part of the original abutment was discovered below the tower, which was linked with the construction of a road leading up to the second phase bridge, which was dated to the early third century. Excavations at Willowford similarly revealed evidence for an original abutment. Following flood damage, probably in the early Antonine period, the bridge was rebuilt, being extended westwards.

Gateways
A search for the Portgate, where Dere Street passed through the Wall, resulted in the discovery of traces of a projecting gateway.[19]

The Vallum
While several sections have been cut across the Vallum, the single greatest contribution to the study of this earthwork has been Brenda Heywood's 'The Vallum – its problems restated', a distillation of her 1954 PhD thesis, the conclusions of which were cited in *Research on Hadrian's Wall*.[20]

The Cumbrian Coast
R.L. Bellhouse's energies have been primarily directed at extending knowledge of the location of the milefortlets and towers, combined with excavation of selected examples.[21] He has been able to demonstrate that the fort at Maryport was used as the starting-point for laying out the system in that area,[22] and has traced the system a little further to T26b (Risehow),[23] but evidence for structures further south remains sparse, though the possibility of milefortlets as far south as Ravenglass has been mooted.[24] Significant discoveries have come to light as a result of G.D.B. Jones' flying and subsequent excavations.[25] The discoveries are complex, but can be summarised as follows: for the first 1.5 km beyond Bowness a pair of ditches has been located; 1 km on, this is reduced to a single ditch; a further 3 km on at Tower 4b there is both a single ditch and a palisade (the palisade of two phases) while a road has also been discovered; both phases of palisade and road were also located at Silloth; at Tower 4b a further, third, phase was identified in a stone tower which overlay the ditch, fronting the palisade. Professor Jones has suggested that the palisade is one of those referred to in the *Historia Augusta, Life of Hadrian*.[26] The discovery of these ditches led to the realisation that the milefortlets, which were placed between the ditches,

15. op. cit. (note 13), 219–220.
16. op. cit. (note 12), 18.
17. *Current Arch.* cviii (February 1988), 14–7; *Britannia* xix (1988), 434.
18. P. Bidwell and N. Holbrook, *Hadrian's Wall Bridges* (1989), forthcoming.
19. D. Charlesworth, *Arch. Ael.*[4] xlv (1967), 208.
20. B. Heywood in M.G. Jarrett and B. Dobson (eds.), *Britain and Rome* (Kendal, 1966), 85–94.
21. Reports of R.L. Bellhouse's work on the Cumbrian Coast have appeared regularly in *Trans. Cumberland Westmorland Antiq. Arch. Soc.* since 1954; note in particular lxix (1969), 65–101; lxx (1970), 34–47. For the near-complete excavation of a milefortlet see T.W. Potter, *Britannia* viii (1977), 149–83.
22. R.L. Bellhouse, loc. cit. (note 21).
23. R.L. Bellhouse, *Trans. Cumberland Westmorland Antiq. Arch. Soc.* lxxxi (1981), 12–3; lxxxiv (1984), 41–59.
24. T.W. Potter, *Romans in North-west England* (Kendal, 1979), 14–9.
25. N.J. Higham and G.D.B. Jones, *Arch. Journ.* cxxxii (1975), 20–23; G.D.B. Jones, *Britannia* vii (1976), 236–43; xiii (1982), 283–97. Cf. R.L. Bellhouse, *Britannia* xii (1981), 135– 42.
26. Jones, op. cit. (note 25), 294–5.

ought to have both front and rear entrances to allow movement across the frontier line. Excavation by R.L. Bellhouse at MF20 confirmed that this milefortlet did have two gates.[27] Bellhouse's excavations on the coast have demonstrated that very few of the towers were re-commissioned in Period 1B, though some milefortlets are known to have been re-occupied only to be abandoned before the end of the second century.[28] A handful of sites have yielded fourth-century pottery.[29]

Forts

Excavations have taken place in eleven out of the sixteen Wall forts, four of the contemporary forts on the isthmus and three of the four Cumbrian Coast stations, since 1961. Only the more significant results can be listed here. The fort at Newcastle has been located, though it appears to have been constructed no earlier than the late second or third century.[30] The size of the fort at Stanwix has been re-defined, making it slightly larger than before.[31] The stone north defences were dated to the Antonine period: an absence of third- and fourth-century pottery was noted. Excavation at Bowness resulted in a redefined fort, rather smaller than before, while here the excavator remarked on the lack of fourth-century wares.[32] Wallsend has been almost completely excavated (FIG. 2).[33] The Hadrianic plan, while conforming generally to the 'norm', departed from it in some interesting details, particularly in planning and in the division of the men's quarters in each of the seven barrack-blocks examined into nine double rooms. In the late third or early fourth century chalet-style barrack-blocks replaced the earlier buildings in the southern part of the fort, while the *praetentura* was occupied by several 'casually-built hutments'. Work earlier at Housesteads, where English Heritage has been conducting a long-running programme of excavation and consolidation, led to an important study of late fort buildings, and, in particular, late barrack-blocks, the so-called chalets[34] (Fig. 3). More recently, a new type of barrack-block, dated to the mid-third century, has been recognised at Chesterholm-*Vindolanda* and at South Shields.[35] A major programme of excavation at South Shields, sponsored by Tyne and Wear County Council, began in 1977, and has led to the suggestion that the Hadrianic fort was of timber and the first stone fort Antonine.[36] Under Severus, when the fort was turned into a supply-base, it was extended southwards, to its final size; at the same time the headquarters-building was demolished and replaced by two granaries; a new headquarters-building was erected in the southern extension. The old headquarters-building was replaced about 220 but facing the other way. Later in the third century a courtyard building and a barrack-block (see above) were erected in the south-east corner of the fort.

27. R.L. Bellhouse, *Trans. Cumberland Westmorland Antiq. Arch. Soc.* lxxxi (1981), 7–13.

28. T.W. Potter, *Britannia* viii (1976), 182–3; note R.L. Bellhouse, *Trans. Cumberland Westmorland Antiq. Arch. Soc.* lxxxi (1981), 11 for the suggestion of brief occupations of the milefortlets at the beginning of Periods I and II only.

29. T.W. Potter, loc. cit. (note 28), 183.

30. C. Daniels and Barbara Harbottle, *Arch. Ael.*[5] viii (1980), 65, with the comment that the stone fort was not the earliest Roman activity on the site.

31. J.A. Dacre, *Trans. Cumberland Westmorland Antiq. Arch. Soc.* lxxxv (1985), 53–69.

32. The most recent excavations at Bowness were undertaken by Paul Austen, to whom I am grateful for advance information. See also, T.W. Potter, *Romans in North-west England* (Kendal, 1979), 321–49; R.L. Bellhouse, *Trans. Cumberland Westmorland Antiq. Arch. Soc.* lxxxviii (1988), 33–53.

33. C. Daniels in W.S. Hanson and L.J.F. Keppie (eds.), *Roman Frontier Studies 1979* BAR Int. Ser. 71 (1980), 173–93. Regular statements on the progress of the excavations have appeared in 'Roman Britain in 19—' in *Britannia* from vii (1976), to xvi (1985).

34. J.J. Wilkes in M.G. Jarrett and B. Dobson (eds.), *Britain and Rome* (1966), 114–38. Cf. now C. Daniels loc. cit. (note 33); D.A. Welsby, *The Roman Military Defence of the British Provinces in its Later Phases* BAR Brit. Ser. 101 (1982).

35. P. Bidwell, *The Roman Fort at Vindolanda* (London, 1985), 79–84; *Britannia* xix (1988), 431–2.

36. R. Miket, *The Roman Fort at South Shields, Excavation of the Defences 1977–1981* (1983). For subsequent reports see, *Britannia* xv (1984), 277; xvi (1985), 268; xvii (1986), 374–6; xviii (1987), 314–5; xix (1988), 431–3, with the latest plan in *Britannia* xix (1988), 432. See also, J.N. Dore and J.P. Gillam, *The Roman Fort at South Shields, Excavations 1875–1975* (Newcastle, 1979).

WALLSEND   SEGEDUNUM

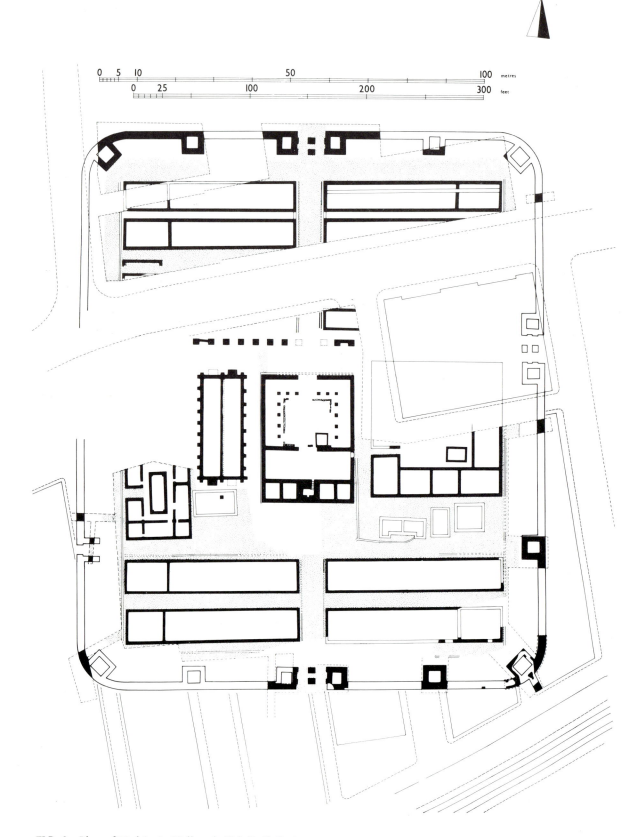

FIG. 2   Plan of Hadrianic Wallsend. (E.J.G. Bailey)

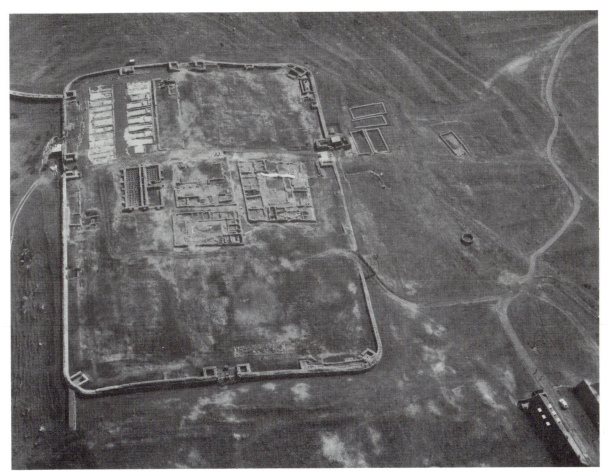

FIG. 3 Housesteads from the air, looking east. The programme of re-excavation and consolidation has clearly revealed the commanding officer's house and the hospital (to the right and behind the headquarters). The fourth-century chalet-style barracks are evident in the north-east corner. (Cambridge University Collection)

Large-scale excavations have allowed the different histories of the Wall forts to become better defined. For example, the relatively few buildings within fourth-century Wallsend contrast sharply with Housesteads, where even the rampart backing was utilised.[37] At Halton Chesters and Rudchester Wall Period III (conventionally dated to c.300 to 367) was absent from the areas excavated, and at both sites the final barrack-blocks were of timber with the uprights resting on stone pads.[38] Current excavations at Birdoswald are yielding evidence of late- to post-Roman occupation.[39]

While the many seasons of excavation at the six superimposed forts at Corbridge have now been published,[40] excavation at the west end of the Stanegate has revealed that a military presence continued at Carlisle into the third century.[41] The chance find of part of an altar at Chesters demonstrated that the original garrison was the *ala Augusta ob virtutem appellata*, thus confirming Eric Birley's earlier suggestion that the fort was built for a cavalry unit.[42] His argument that all

37. Daniels, op. cit. (note 33), 176 and 191.
38. J.P. Gillam, *Durham Univ. Gazette* new ser. ix no. 2; J.P. Gillam, R.M. Harrison and T.G. Newman, *Arch. Ael.*[5] i (1973), 81–5.
39. *Britannia* xix (1988), 436–7; *Current Arch.* cxii (December 1988), 158.
40. J.P. Gillam, *Arch. Ael.*[5] v (1977), 47–74; L. Allason-Jones and M.C. Bishop, *Excavations at Roman Corbridge; the Hoard* (London, 1988); M.C. Bishop and J.N. Dore, *Corbridge: Excavations of the Roman fort and town, 1947–80* (London, 1989).
41. *Current Arch.* ci (August 1986), 172–7.
42. P.S. Austen and D.J. Breeze, *Arch. Ael.*[5] vii (1979), 115–26; E. Birley, *Research on Hadrian's Wall* (Kendal, 1961), 270.

projecting forts were built for cavalry units, however, has been challenged by the proposition that the original idea was for all forts to lie astride the Wall where possible.[43] An inscription of 213 found at Newcastle revealed that the regiment based there at that time was *cohors I Cugernorum*, and not *cohors I Cornoviorum*, listed there in the *Notitia Dignatatum*; rare additional evidence for change of units between the early third century and the *Notitia*.[44]

Reconsideration of the *Notitia Dignitatum*, and other sources for the names of the Wall forts, has led to the suggestion that the name of Birdoswald was *Banna* not *Camboglanna*, which was Castlesteads, whilst the name of Stanwix was *Uxellodunum*.[45]

Outposts

At Birrens Professor Anne S. Robertson identified a pre-Hadrianic enclosure and examined the Hadrianic and Antonine forts.[46] The Antonine I fort she suggested was destroyed by enemy action prior to the rebuilding attested by an inscription dated to 158, this final fort continuing until its destruction in the invasion of about 180. More limited work at Bewcastle by Paul Austen located a stone barrack-block built in the late second century and rebuilt about a century later.[47] No trace was found of the fourth phase previously identified at Bewcastle which suggests that the fort may have been reduced in size in the early fourth century.

A reconsideration of the dating evidence from the outpost forts led John Casey and Mark Savage to propose abandonment of all these sites by Constantine I in 312, rather than in 342/3 and the 360s as previously argued by Richmond.[48]

The Hinterland

A recent paper in *Britannia* has collated the evidence for the occupation of the forts in northern England and offered a series of eleven distribution maps illustrating the changing pattern from about 75 to the *Notitia Dignitatum*, with analysis, so that further detailed discussion is not required here[49] (Fig. 4). Mention must be made, however, of the important regional studies by Dr N. Higham and Professor G.D.B. Jones in Cumbria and Dr B. Dobson in County Durham.[50]

Finds

An encouraging trend has been the publication of existing collections of finds. These have taken the form of catalogues of material from sites ranging in size from turrets to forts, as well as publication of different types of finds.[51] The *Vindolanda* writing-tablets, although pre-Hadrianic in date, cast an interesting and unique light upon life on the northern frontier.[52]

43. D.J. Breeze and B. Dobson, *Britannia* iii (1974), 193.
44. Daniels and Harbottle, op. cit. (note 30), 65– 73.
45. M. Hassall in R. Goodburn and P. Bartholomew (eds.), *Aspects of the Notitia Dignitatum* BAR Int. Ser. 15 (1976), 112–3; A.L.F. Rivet and C. Smith, *The Place Names of Roman Britain* (London, 1979), 221; D.J. Breeze and B. Dobson, *Hadrian's Wall* (London, 1987), 272–4.
46. Anne S. Robertson, *Birrens (Blatobulgium)* (Glasgow, 1975). For a comment on the cause of the destruction in 158 cf. D.J. Breeze, *Britannia* viii (1979), 459.
47. P.S. Austen in B. Dobson (ed.), *The Tenth Pilgrimage of Hadrian's Wall* (1979), 20.
48. P.J. Casey and M. Savage, *Arch. Ael*[5] viii (1980), 75–87; Cf. P.J. Casey in J. Bird *et al.* (eds.), *Collectanea Londiniensia* (London, 1978), 181–93. I.A. Richmond, *The Romans in Redesdale* (Newcastle, 1940), 112–6.
49. D.J. Breeze and B. Dobson, *Britannia* xvi (1985), 1– 19. Cf. P.R. Wilson, R.F.J. Jones and D.M. Evans (eds.), *Settlement and Society in the Roman North* (Bradford, 1984). R.F.J. Jones in A. King and M. Henig (eds.), *The Roman West in the Third Century* BAR Int. Ser. 109 (1981), 393–414.
50. For the work of N. Higham and G.D.B. Jones see now *The Carvetii* (Gloucester, 1985), and the papers cited therein. For Cumbria see D.C.A. Shotter, *Trans. Cumberland Westmorland Antiq. Arch. Soc.* lxxx (1980), 1–15; D.J. Breeze, *Trans. Cumberland Westmorland Antiq. Arch. Soc.* lxxxviii (1988), 9–22; and more generally D. Shotter, *Roman North-West England* (1984). B. Dobson, *Trans. Architect. Arch. Soc. Durham Northumberland*, new ser. ii (1970), 31–43. On northern England now B. Hartley and L. Fitts, *The Brigantes* (Gloucester, 1988).
51. For example, Lindsay Allason-Jones and Roger Miket, *The Catalogue of small finds from South Shields Roman Fort* (Newcastle, 1984); Lindsay Allason-Jones and Bruce McKay, *Coventina's Well* (1988); W.H. Manning, *Catalogue of Romano-British Ironwork in the Museum of Antiquities, Newcastle upon Tyne* (1976); C.S.I.R. I, I; I, 6.
52. A.K. Bowman and J.D. Thomas, *Vindolanda: The Latin Writing-Tablets* (London, 1983); *Britannia* xviii (1987), 125– 42.

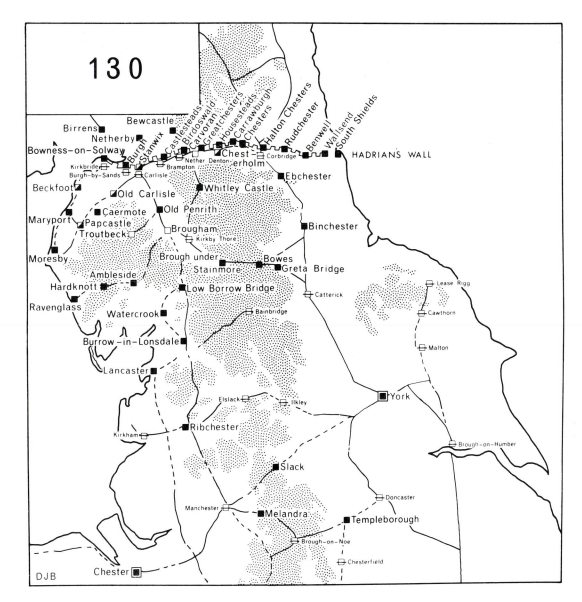

FIG. 4   Military dispositions in northern Britain about A.D. 130. Black square = occupied. Half-filled square = possible occupation. Open square = uncertainty. Open square with horizontal stroke = abandonment within previous 20 years. (D.J. Breeze)

The Building of Hadrian's Wall

Research on Hadrian's Wall took account of C.E. Stevens' Horsley lecture on the building of Hadrian's Wall. In 1966 this was republished.[53] A reply to this appeared two years later, essentially offering a simplified version of Stevens' scheme.[54] The discovery of a Legion VI building stone reused in T33b, a structure seemingly abandoned before the end of Wall Period IB, has led to the suggestion that the normal allocation of structures to Legions VI and XX should be reversed.[55] The discovery of some centurial stones on the north face of the wall suggests that our views on the location of these records must be revised.[56]

53.   C.E. Stevens, *The Building of Hadrian's Wall* (Kendal, 1966).
54.   J. Hooley and D.J. Breeze, *Arch. Ael.*[4] xliv (1968), 97–114.
55.   V.A. Maxfield and R. Miket, *Arch. Ael.*[4] l (1972), 158. D.J. Breeze and B. Dobson, *Hadrian's Wall* (London, 1987), 68–9.
56.   *Britannia* ii (1971), 291, no.11; iii (1972), 354, no. 12; v (1974), 462, no. 7.

A different approach to the building of Hadrian's Wall appeared in a paper by Peter Hill, who considered the stone-masonry of the curtain and several different structures, pointing out that the Wall was not as well constructed as archaeologists tend to imply by their descriptions and calling for a more rigorous description of stone structures.[57]

The Function of Hadrian's Wall

Eric Birley noted that Hadrian's Wall did not 'serve as a military fortification' and 'that the stationing of units . . . in forts on its line was merely coincidental, to give them a convenient springboard . . .'.[58] This offered implicit rejection of Richmond's well-known diagram illustrating the use of Hadrian's Wall as first planned and after the addition of forts to the linear barrier,[59] though this diagram continues to be repeated. The Richmond system was explicitly rejected by Brian Dobson in the seventh Horsley lecture on 'The function of Hadrian's Wall'.[60] Among the other aspects of the Wall covered in this lecture were the existence of a parapet along the top of the wall and the nature of turrets. The possibility of a sloping top to the wall was considered, as was the existence of turrets like those on Trajan's Column rather than the normal flat-topped structure. The towers on the Wall (both turrets and at milecastles) have been considered by David Woolliscroft, who has suggested that in the original plan for the Wall these towers were carefully positioned to link back to the Stanegate where the army units lay.[61]

THE ANTONINE WALL

Sir George Macdonald's *Roman Wall in Scotland*, published in 1934, was the magisterial statement on the Antonine Wall. Since that date there have been two reviews of work in the journals of this society, the first by Kenneth Steer and the second by Lawrence Keppie.[62] Anne Robertson's guide, *The Antonine Wall*, is the most complete introduction to the Wall for visitors.[63] The first detailed treatment of the frontier since Macdonald is *Rome's North-West Frontier* by W.S. Hanson and G.S. Maxwell.[64]

The Advance into Scotland

Maxwell and Hanson have proposed an Antonine date for some camps in southern Scotland, the first indication of routes taken by the invading army.[65] The rediscovery of part of the Ingliston milestone enabled it to be dated to either 139 or 140–144, depending upon the consular date which lies at the damaged part of the stone.[66]

The Rampart and Ditch

Lawrence Keppie has collected the evidence for the differences in the stone base of the Wall, its turf superstructure and the ditch.[67] He related these to the evidence provided by the distance slabs

57. P.R. Hill, *Arch. Ael.*[5] ix (1981), 1–22.
58. E. Birley, *Research on Hadrian's Wall* (Kendal, 1961), 270.
59. I.A. Richmond (ed.), *Handbook to the Roman Wall* (Newcastle, 1966), 26.
60. B. Dobson, *Arch. Ael.*[5] xiv (1986), 1–30. For a challenge to the preferred reconstruction of turrets see Lindsay Allason-Jones in J.C. Coulston (ed.), *Military Equipment and the Identity of Roman Soldiers* BAR Int. Ser. 394 (1988), 218–9.
61. D. Woolliscroft, *Archaeology Today* xx (March 1987), 37–44; xx (April 1987), 10–15.
62. K.A. Steer, *JRS* l (1960), 84–93; L.J.F. Keppie, *Britannia* xiii (1982), 91–111. For a review of inscriptions found in Scotland since the cut-off date of *RIB* I (1954), see L.J.F. Keppie, *PSAS* cxiii (1983), 391–404; on sculpture *CSIR* I, 4. On coins A.S. Robertson, *PSAS* cxiii (1983), 405–48. Excavation reports and discussion papers on the Antonine Wall are usually published in either *PSAS* or *Glasgow Arch. Journ.*
63. Anne S. Robertson, *The Antonine Wall* (1st edition 1960; 6th edition 1979). Cf. L.J.F. Keppie, *Scotland's Roman Remains* (Edinburgh, 1986).
64. W.S. Hanson and G.S. Maxwell, *Rome's North West Frontier, the Antonine Wall* (Edinburgh, 1st ed. 1983; pbk. 1986).
65. ibid. 64–8.
66. G.S. Maxwell, *PSAS* cxiii (1983), 379–85.
67. L.J.F. Keppie, *PSAS* cv (1972–4), 151–65.

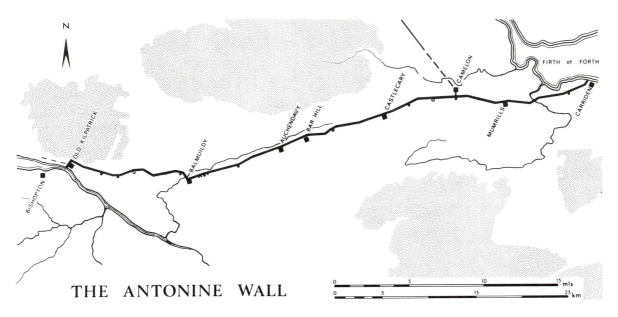

THE ANTONINE WALL

FIG. 5   The Antonine Wall as originally planned. Located fortlets and small enclosures are marked. Both Auchendavy and Bar Hill forts are included as there is doubt about which is primary. (T. Borthwick)

and the temporary camps, though without being able to draw any firm correlations. Keppie's tables did, however, demonstrate that the 'normal' width of the ditch, 40 feet, is only found in less than half of the Wall, while the base may have been intended to be fifteen Roman feet wide. Differences in the width of the base 'seem sufficiently distinct to reflect different work-squads'. Evidence for junctions between different work-squads has been found during excavations at Garnhall and Kemper Avenue, Falkirk and also possibly at Bantaskin.[68] The discovery of three culverts through the base at Bantaskin offers the hint that these might have been regularly provided. Repairs to the turf superstructure have also been recorded.[69]

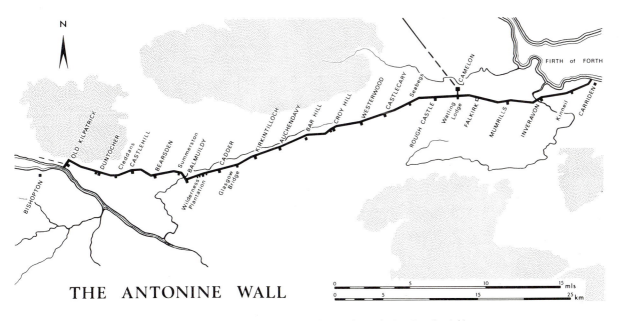

THE ANTONINE WALL

FIG. 6   The Antonine Wall as completed, with located fortlets indicated. (T. Borthwick)

68.   L.J.F. Keppie, *PSAS* cvii (1975–6), 69; L.J.F. Keppie and D.J. Breeze, *PSAS* cxi (1981), 245.
69.   Keppie and Breeze, op. cit. (note 68), 245.

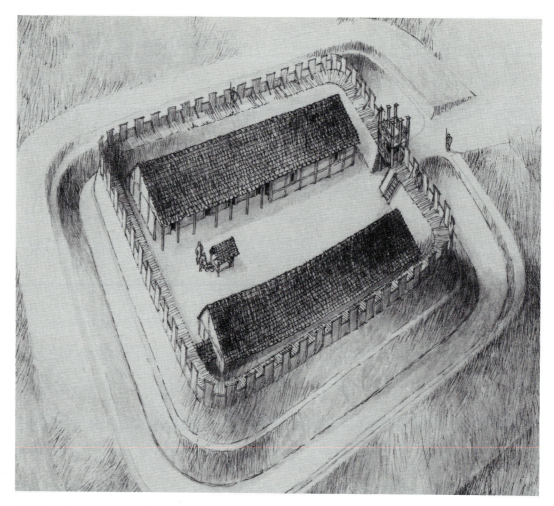

FIG. 7   Reconstruction of the fortlet at Barburgh Mill. (M.J. Moore)

Fortlets

The existence of a fortlet guarding the point where the road north passed through the Antonine Wall at Watling Lodge has been known since the end of the last century.[70] In the years following 1945 three new fortlets were discovered; that at Duntocher preceded the construction of both an adjacent fort and the Antonine Wall rampart.[71] Since 1975 five new fortlets have been located, and their significance is discussed below.[72]

'Small Enclosures'

RCAHMS' Lanarkshire Inventory drew attention to the existence of three small enclosures in the Wilderness Plantation section of the Wall.[73] These were spaced about one-sixth and one-third of a mile west of the Wilderness Plantation fortlet and about one-sixth of a mile to the east. Subsequent excavation of one of these structures provided a plan (an area about 6m square within a turf rampart) but no evidence for its function.[74]

70.   The size of the fortlet was redefined during recent excavations: D.J. Breeze, *PSAS* cv (1972–4), 166–75.
71.   Anne S. Robertson, *An Antonine Fort, Golden Hill, Duntocher* (1957).
72.   Bill Hanson and Lawrence Keppie, *Current Arch.* lxii (June 1978), 91–4; L.J.F. Keppie and J.J. Walker, *Britannia* xii (1981), 143–62; 320.
73.   RCAHMS, *Lanarkshire* (1978), 113 and 159.
74.   W.S. Hanson and G.S. Maxwell, *Britannia* xiv (1983), 227–43.

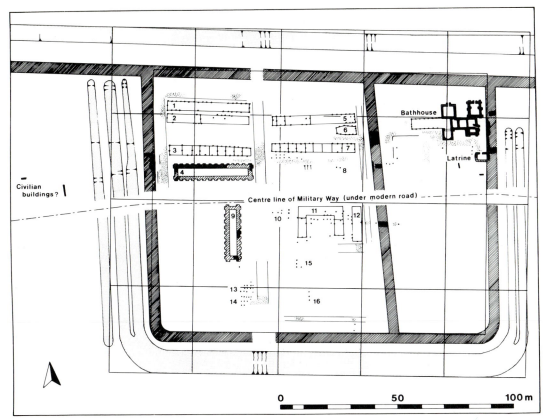

FIG. 8   Plan of fort at Bearsden on the Antonine Wall with superimposed grid measuring 5 × 4 actus. Numbered
Key: 3 and 7 barracks; 4 and 9 granaries; 10 site of headquarters; 11 workshop?; 12 storehouse; 16 open space;
the rest unknown. (D.B Gallagher)

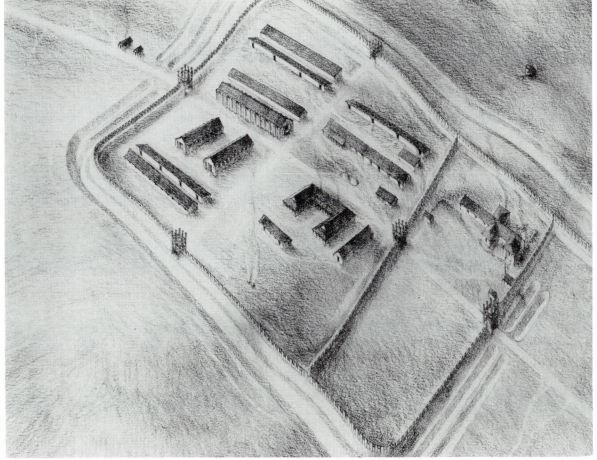

FIG. 9   Reconstruction of fort at Bearsden. (M.J. Moore)

Forts

Work here has been limited to five sites. At both Croy Hill (Fig. 10) and Bar Hill the earlier enclosure was found to be early Antonine, not Agricolan.[75] At all sites the internal buildings were investigated, but the most extensive excavations were at Bearsden where much of the fort was examined[76] (Figs. 8 and 9). The fort was found to have had an unusual layout, with no headquarters-buildings; evidence was also found to suggest that the fort and annexe were planned within a framework based upon the *actus*. The original plan for a large fort was amended during building operations with the enclosure divided into fort and annexe, while only one structural phase, Antonine I, was found. Analysis of sewage from the latrine in the outer annexe ditch led to the suggestion that the soldiers' diet was mainly vegetarian.[77] The discovery of a hypocausted building, possibly a bath-house, at Falkirk has provided a valuable hint of the probable location of the fort.[78] An inscription found at Old Kilpatrick recorded *cohors I Baetasiorum* dedicating under the command of a centurion of *Legion I Italica*.[79]

Military Way

A single section across the road at Rough Castle provided rare evidence for the form of construction.[80] The cobbles forming the base of the road were laid upon two layers of turves.

The Flanks

In 1970 Frank Newall discovered a second fortlet on the south side of the Clyde estuary, perched on the hills high above the coast.[81] Subsequent excavation revealed two phases of stone buildings of Antonine date. The exact location, size and the history of the fort at Cramond had been determined by A. and V. Rae in the 1950s.[82] This work has been continued by N.M. Holmes, who has found an area devoted to industrial activity outside the fort.[83]

The Outpost Forts

Excavation or re-assessment has taken place at all four outpost forts. Extensive excavations by Professors S.S. Frere and J.J. Wilkes at Strageath have furnished plans of the Antonine I and II forts,[84] while at Camelon the annexe was investigated by Valerie Maxfield revealing extensive evidence of industrial activity.[85] As a result of a re-assessment of the earthworks at Ardoch D.J. Breeze suggested that, rather than the defences of the Antonine fort being extended by the digging of new ditches, this fort was placed within the abandoned earthworks of the first-century fort.[86]

75. W.S. Hanson in D.J. Breeze (ed.), *Roman Scotland: Some Recent Excavations* (Edinburgh, 1979), 19–20; L.J.F. Keppie, *Glasgow Arch. Journ.* xii (1985), 51–8.

76. D.J. Breeze in D.J. Breeze (ed.), *Studies in Scottish Antiquity* (Edinburgh, 1984), 32–68. For Rough Castle see: I. MacIvor, M.C. Thomas and D.J. Breeze, *PSAS* cx (1978–80), 230–85.

77. B.A. Knights, Camilla A. Dickson, J.H. Dickson and D.J. Breeze, *Journ. Arch. Science* x (1983) 139–52. Cf. Camilla and James Dickson, *Plants Today* (July–August 1988), 121–6. Cf. R.W. Davies, *Britannia* ii (1973), 122–42 = R.W. Davies, *Service in the Roman Army*, edited by Valerie A. Maxfield and D.J. Breeze (Edinburgh, 1989), 187–206, for a discussion of the place of meat in the Roman military diet.

78. L.J.F. Keppie and J. Frances Murray, *PSAS* cxi (1981), 248–62.

79. *Britannia* i (1970), 310–1, no. 20; R.L.N. Barber, *Glasgow Arch. Journ.* ii (1971), 117–9 offered various possibilities for the date; E. Birley, *Latomus* xlii (1983), 73–83 = *The Roman Army Papers 1929–1986* (Amsterdam, 1988), 221–31, argued for a Severan date.

80. L.J.F. Keppie, *PSAS* cvii (1975–6), 63–4.

81. F. Newall, *Glasgow Arch. Journ.* iv (1976), 111–23.

82. A. and V. Rae, *Britannia* v (1974), 163–224.

83. N.M. McQ. Holmes in D.J. Breeze (ed.), *Roman Scotland: Some Recent Excavations* (Edinburgh, 1979), 11–4.

84. S.S. Frere and J.J. Wilkes, *Strageath: Excavations within the Roman Fort, 1973–86* (London, 1989).

85. Valerie A. Maxfield in D.J. Breeze (ed.), *Roman Scotland: Some Recent Excavations* (Edinburgh, 1979), 28–32; *Scot. Arch. Forum* xii (1981), 69–78.

86. D.J. Breeze in Anne O'Connor and D.V. Clarke (eds.), *From the Stone Age to the 'Forty-five'* (Edinburgh, 1983), 224–36. For the work at Bertha see: Helen C. Adamson and D.B. Gallagher, *PSAS* cxvi (1986), 195–204.

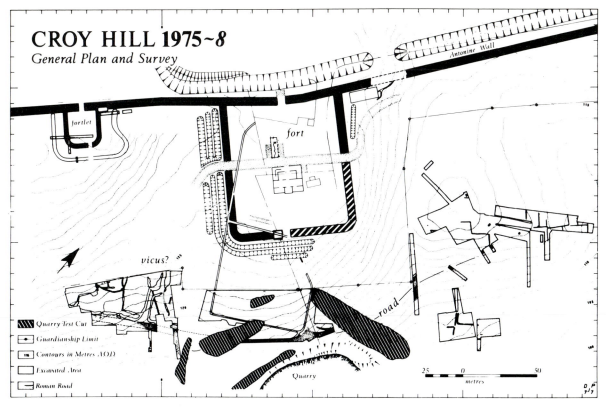

FIG. 10   Plan of fortlet, fort and *vicus* at Croy Hill on the Antonine Wall. Enclosure beneath the fort shown to be early
Antonine by Dr W.S. Hanson. (D. Powlesland)

The Hinterland
Several syntheses have considered the occupation of southern Scotland,[87] but excavation has been
concentrated within the south-western sector. At Crawford the small fort was examined by
Gordon Maxwell with the demonstration that it could not have held a complete unit in either of
the Antonine periods and, most importantly, that there was only a brief interval between the two
periods.[88] At Barburgh Mill a fortlet, probably occupied by a century, was completely excavated
and dated to the Antonine I period.[89] Further fortlets have been discovered through aerial
reconnaissance.[90]

The Building of the Wall
In 1975 J.P. Gillam put forward a new hypothesis for the building of the Antonine Wall.[91]
Noting the different relationships of the forts to the Wall (preceding, contemporary or later) and
also the fortlets (contemporary or later), he suggested that the Antonine Wall was planned
broadly on the same lines as the abandoned Hadrian's Wall with forts every eight miles and
fortlets, similar in size to the milecastles on Hadrian's Wall, at mile-intervals in between; during
building operations the number of forts was increased by replacing every other fortlet by a fort
(Figs. 5 and 6). In the following years, stimulated by this proposal, five new fortlets were found
and the hypothesis considerably strengthened,[92] though the situation may have been more

87.   For example, G.S. Maxwell, *PSAS* civ (1971–2), 147– 200; *Studien zu den Militärgrenzen Roms* (1977), 23–30;
       D.J. Breeze in W.S. Hanson and L.J.F. Keppie (eds.), *Roman Frontier Studies 1979* BAR Int. Ser. 71 (1980),
       45–60.
88.   G.S. Maxwell, *PSAS* civ (1971–2), 178.
89.   D.J. Breeze, *Britannia* v (1974), 130–62.
90.   G.S. Maxwell and D.R. Wilson, *Britannia* xix (1988), 22–6.
91.   J.P. Gillam, *Scot. Arch. Forum* vii (1976), 51–6.
92.   For bibliographical details of the sites see note 72.

complicated than Gillam allowed.[93] Further consideration has also been given to the details of the construction of the barrier through analysis of the distance slabs.[94] The discovery of a new distance slab at Hutcheson Hill enabled Steer and Cormack to demonstrate that each legionary length must have been marked not only at each end but both north and south of the Wall.[95] The discovery of more temporary camps along the Wall line has enabled Maxwell to suggest the division of the Wall builders into separate gangs.[95a]

The Reason for the Construction of the Antonine Wall

It has generally been considered that the Antonine Wall was built in the face of hostility from the northern tribes,[96] either directly, or indirectly, in that Hadrian's Wall may have been built too far from the main enemy in the north, the Caledones.[97] More recently other reasons have been advanced for the move north in the early 140s: Antoninus Pius was offering a sop to his generals, Trajan's marshals, kept inactive by Hadrian's policies;[98] it was in order to provide the new emperor with a triumph and consolidate his position on the throne;[99] the Romans desired to take into the empire the good farmland of the eastern Tyne-Forth province.[100] In the face of the lack of a clear statement by the Romans for the move north, the reason will remain a matter for speculation.

HISTORY

The Late Second Century

Excavation from the 1890s on demonstrated that there were two main periods of occupation at the Antonine Wall forts, followed by a shadowy third of uncertain significance. Haverfield argued in 1899 for the abandonment of the Antonine Wall in the 160s.[101] Macdonald, making greater use of the numismatic evidence, proposed occupation continuing into the early 180s, linking its abandonment to the invasion of the northern tribes at that time;[102] the break between the two periods was placed in the mid–150s. Epigraphically the break is attested by the rebuilding inscription of 158 from Hadrian's Wall and inscriptions of the same date at Birrens and Brough-on-Noe: these were linked by Haverfield to the attack on the Genounian district by the Brigantes described by Pausanias, the coin issue of 154/155 supposedly showing Britannia subdued, and the arrival of reinforcements for the three British legions at the mouth of the Tyne: all three have been challenged, as has the whole concept of a 'Brigantian revolt'.[103] The Antonine

93.   D.J. Breeze in W.S. Hanson and L.J.F. Keppie (eds.), *Roman Frontier Studies 1979* BAR Int. Ser. 71 (1980), 52.
94.   G.S. Maxwell in D. Pippidi (ed.), *Actes du IXe Congres international d'études sur les frontiers romaines* (Bucuresti and Köln, 1974), 327–32; *Britannia* xvi (1985), 25–8.
95.   K.A. Steer and E.A. Cormack, *PSAS* ci (1968–9), 122– 6; *Britannia* i (1970), 309, no. 19. For a general treatment of the distance slabs see L.J.F. Keppie, *Roman Distance Slabs from the Antonine Wall* (Glasgow, 1979).
95a. Maxwell, op. cit. (note 94), 329. Cf. W.S. Hanson and G.S. Maxwell, *Rome's North West Frontier, The Antonine Wall* (Edinburgh, 1986), 117–121.
96.   For example, K.A. Steer, *Arch. Ael.*⁴ xlii (1964), 19–21.
97.   J.P. Gillam in I.A. Richmond (ed.), *Roman and Native in North Britain* (Glasgow, 1958), 66-7.
98.   A.R. Birley, *Trans. Architect. Arch. Soc. Durham Northumberland new ser.* iii (1974), 13–25.
99.   D.J. Breeze, *Scot. Arch. Forum* vii (1976), 67–80.
100. W.S. Hanson and G.S. Maxwell, *Rome's North West Frontier, The Antonine Wall* (Edinburgh, 1986), 68–9.
101. F. Haverfield in *The Antonine Wall Report* (Glasgow, 1899), 157–9.
102. G. Macdonald, *The Roman Wall in Scotland* (Oxford, 1934), 478–82.
103. F. Haverfield, *Arch. Ael.*² xxv (1904), 142–4. J.G.F. Hind, *Britannia* viii (1977), 229–34 (on the location of the Brigantes). J.C. Mann (ed.), *The Northern Frontier in Britain from Hadrian to Honorius: Literary and Epigraphic Sources* (n.d.), no. 62 (commenting on the coin). J.J. Wilkes, *Zeitschrift für Papyrologie und Epigraphik* lix (1985), 291–5 suggests that the vexillations were contributed from Britain for the armies of the Germanies under Julius Verus, not that reinforcements came from Germany for the British legions; S.S. Frere, *Britannia* xvii (1986), 329 prefers the orthodox interpretation; M. Speidel, *Britannia* xviii (1987), 235–6 argues that 'these were drafts of the British legions sent to the German armies years earlier and that in 155 under Julius Verus they returned to Britain'. Cf. D.J. Breeze and B. Dobson, *Hadrian's Wall* (London, 1987), 112–5 for general comment.

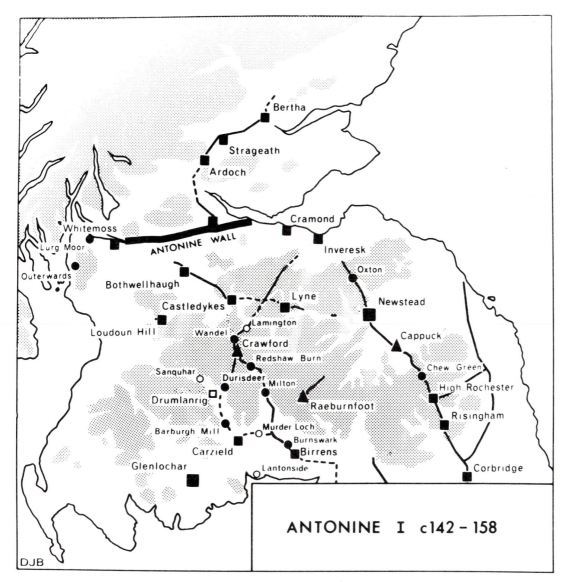

FIG. 11   Military dispositions in Scotland during the first Antonine period (*c.* A.D. 142–58). Large square = fort over 8
acres; smaller square = smaller fort; triangle = small fort, probably serving as base for unit with outposted
troops; circle = fortlet. (D.J. Breeze)

Wall chronology clashed with that adopted by archaeologists on Hadrian's Wall, who dated their
structural periods – and thus the Antonine Wall – differently. Four main periods were identified
on Hadrian's Wall: I 122–197; II 197–296; III 296–367; IV 368–410.[104] The first was divided into
two phases: IA 122–142 and IB 158–197. Antonine Wall I was dated 142–158 and II 184–197. As a
result of these different chronologies different dates were offered for different types of pottery
from the same deposit.[105] The break-through came in 1972 when Brian Hartley published his
detailed study of the samian ware from the two Walls.[106] This argued that the two Walls could
not have been held at the same time, and that the Antonine Wall was abandoned in the mid- 60s
(Fig. 11). This archaeology-inspired date was linked to the literary and epigraphic evidence for
Calpurnius Agricola in north Britain (161–6).[107] Hartley still retained the date of 197 for the end

104.   Cf. E. Birley, *Research on Hadrian's Wall* (Kendal, 1961), 247–65. Cf. A.R. Birley, *Hadrian's Wall* (London,
        1963), 19.
105.   This was brought out most clearly in K.A. Steer, *PSAS* xciv (1960–1), 98–9.
106.   B.R. Hartley, *Britannia* iii (1972), 15–42.
107.   Cf. J.P. Gillam, *Trans. Architect. Arch. Soc. Durham Northumberland* x pt. 4 (1953), 359–75.

of HW IB. Three years later John Gillam accepted the earlier date for the abandonment of the Antonine Wall, but linked it to HW IB ending and II beginning in 180.[108] Not all evidence will support this date, but there the argument rests in the meantime.[109] It is not easy to see how new evidence might come to light: a new inscription or a dendrochronological date seems the most likely.

The Severan Campaigns
Professor J.K. St. Joseph has defined and redefined the series of camps which he suggests should be related to these campaigns (see FIG. 12).[110] The discovery of the legionary base at Carpow on the south bank of the Tay estuary by Robin Birley added flesh to the bald statements of the contemporary historians.[111] Sculpture and tile stamps attest the involvement of Legions II and VI in the building of the fortress, but do not necessarily reflect the garrison.[112] The excavations, firstly by Birley and subsequently by Professor Wilkes, have revealed that the principal buildings were of stone and the barrack-blocks of timber.[113]

   The era of peace which seems to have lasted through the third century is usually considered to have been the result of the 'Caracallan settlement'.[114] This settlement, however, is a modern invention. We know of no actions of Caracalla beyond his abandonment of his father's conquests and forts. The nature of the disposition of Roman forces in the north seems to have been very similar after as well as before the Severan 'interlude', so far as we can tell, the main arrangements having been initiated in the 160s following the abandonment of the Antonine Wall.[115] These included the strengthening of the screen of outpost forts beyond Hadrian's Wall. It seems to have been during Wall Period IB (*c*.163–180) that some consideration was given to the occupation of the minor structures on the Wall and at least one turret appears to have been abandoned. Many more were given up before the end of the century. Other changes included the narrowing of milecastle gateways and the abandonment of the Vallum (these two actions may be connected). The pattern for Hadrian's Wall established in the last decades of the second century seems to have continued to the end of the fourth century if not into the early fifth.

The Third and Fourth Centuries
Inscriptions take the late-second–early-third-century regiments stationed in northern Britain through to the 240s; the *Notitia Dignitatum* presents a very different picture of the north with many of the hinterland forts being the bases for new, fourth-century, style *numeri* and *vexillationes*. John Mann has drawn the conclusion from this that in between, probably in the late third century, many units left their forts never to return.[116] This may be presumed to have been a tangible result of the peaceful conditions obtaining on the northern frontier in the third century. The rise in power of the Picts in the fourth century brought the new units to Britain to support the troops on the Wall.

108.   J.P. Gillam in A. Detsicas (ed.), *Current Research in Romano-British Coarse Pottery* (London, 1973), 55–62; J.P. Gillam, *Arch. Ael.*⁵ ii (1974), 1–15. D.C.A. Shotter, *PSAS* cvii (1975–6), 81–91, argues that the coin evidence would support abandonment of the Antonine Wall in the 160s.

109.   For reference to the problems of the date of *c*. 165 for the abandonment of the Antonine Wall see D.J. Breeze, *Scot. Arch. Forum* vii (1976), 67–80. Cf. A.R. Birley, *Arch. Ael.*⁴ 1 (1972), 175–89, on the significance of 197; D.A. Welsby, *Arch. Ael.*⁵ viii (1980), 89–94 on the interpretation of the building inscriptions.

110.   J.K. St Joseph, *JRS* lxiii (1973), 230–3; lxvii (1977), 141–5. Cf. G.S. Maxwell, *Scot. Arch. Forum* xii (1981), 40.

111.   R.E. Birley, *PSAS* xcvi (1962–3), 184–207.

112.   J.D. Leach and J.J. Wilkes in J. Fitz (ed.), *Limes, Akten des XI Internationalen Limeskongresses* (Budapest, 1977), 47–62; R.P. Wright, *PSAS* xcvii (1963–4), 202–5; *Britannia* v (1974), 289–92.

113.   Leach and Wilkes, loc. cit. (note 112); in D.J. Breeze (ed.) *Roman Scotland: Some Recent Excavations* (Edinburgh, 1979), 46; *Britannia* xi (1980), 351.

114.   K.A. Steer in I.A. Richmond (ed.), *Roman and Native in North Britain* (Glasgow, 1958), 91–111. For the use of subsidies as a means of control of the tribes beyond the frontier following 211 cf. now M. Todd, *PSAS* cxv (1985), 229–32.

115.   D.J. Breeze and B. Dobson, *Hadrian's Wall* (London, 1987), 143–4.

116.   J.C. Mann, *Glasgow Arch. Journ.* iii (1974), 34–42.

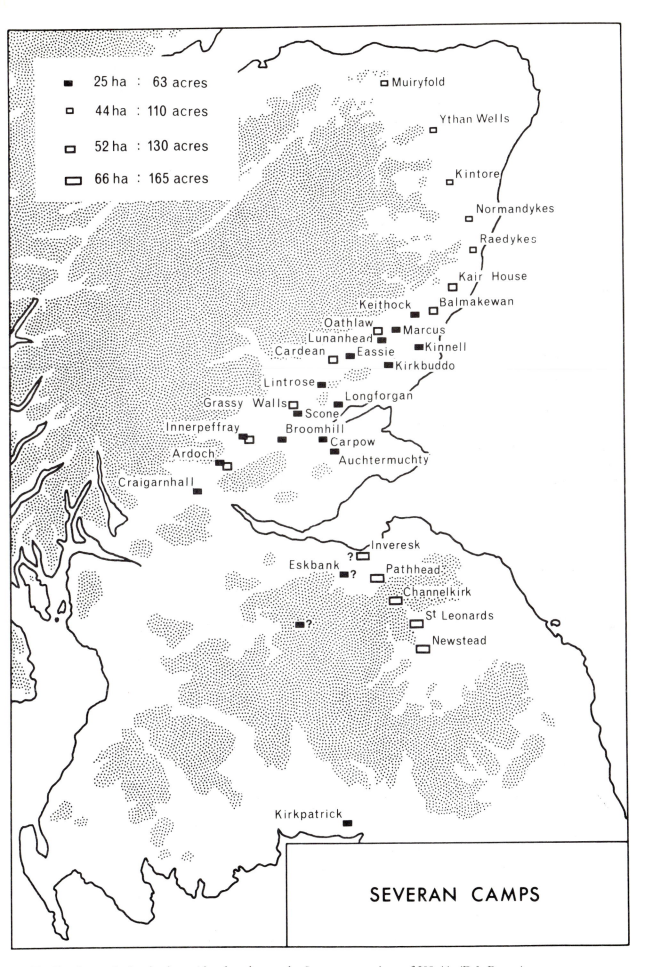

Legend:

- ■ 25 ha : 63 acres
- ▫ 44 ha : 110 acres
- ▭ 52 ha : 130 acres
- ▭ 66 ha : 165 acres

Muiryfold
Ythan Wells
Kintore
Normandykes
Raedykes
Kair House
Balmakewan
Keithock
Oathlaw   Marcus
Lunanhead   Kinnell
Cardean   Eassie
Kirkbuddo
Lintrose
Longforgan
Grassy Walls
Scone
Innerpeffray   Broomhill
Carpow
Ardoch   Auchtermuchty
Craigarnhall

Inveresk
Eskbank   ?
?   Pathhead
Channelkirk
?   St Leonards
Newstead

Kirkpatrick

SEVERAN CAMPS

FIG. 12 Camps in Scotland considered to date to the Severan campaigns of 208–11. (D.J. Breeze)

FIG. 13   Fort and *vicus* at Chesterholm-Vindolanda from the air, looking east. *Vicus* to either side of the road running
west from the fort. Fort bath-house to north (left) of the road. Bottom right are reconstructions of Hadrian's
Wall, a turret, section of the Turf Wall and a Turf Wall milecastle gate. (Cambridge University Collection)

Richmond, in his consideration of the outpost forts in the 1930s, linked their abandonment to
the establishment of friendly buffer states in the Scottish Lowlands.[117] As noted above, the
abandonment of these forts has now been brought forward from the 340s and 360s to 312.[118]
Furthermore, John Mann has suggested that the use of Roman names by the earliest rulers of
these northern kingdoms, seen by Richmond as evidence of their Roman establishment, may
reflect adoption of Christianity rather than the exercise of imperial power.[119] John Casey has
emphasised the role of Magnus Maximus in the defence of the north in the late fourth century,
suggesting that the Yorkshire coast signal-stations date to the 380s rather than the late 360s.[120]

CIVILIAN SETTLEMENTS

There have been two general surveys of this subject, by Peter Salway and Sebastian Sommer.[121]
The most important work in the field has been at *Vindolanda*[122] (Fig. 13). Here Robin Birley has

117.   I.A. Richmond, *The Romans in Redesdale* (Newcastle, 1940), 112– 6.
118.   See note 48.
119.   Mann, op. cit. (note 116). Note that R.S.O. Tomlin, *Britannia* v (1974), 303–9, argued that 'the "barbarian
        conspiracy" should . . . be redated to June 367' with London recovered by the autumn and the second
        campaigning season falling in 368.
120.   P.J. Casey in P.J. Casey (ed.), *The end of Roman Britain* BAR Brit. Ser. 71 (1979), 66–79.
121.   P. Salway, *The Frontier People of Roman Britain* (Cambridge, 1965); C.S. Sommer, *The Military Vici in Roman
        Britain* BAR Brit. Ser. 129 (1984).
122.   R.E. Birley, *Vindolanda, a Roman frontier fort on Hadrian's Wall* (London, 1977); *Vindolanda I, 1976 Excavations*
        (Bardon Mill, 1977), 8, 25–6; *Civilians on the Roman Frontier* (Edinburgh, 1973). Sommer, op. cit. (note 121).

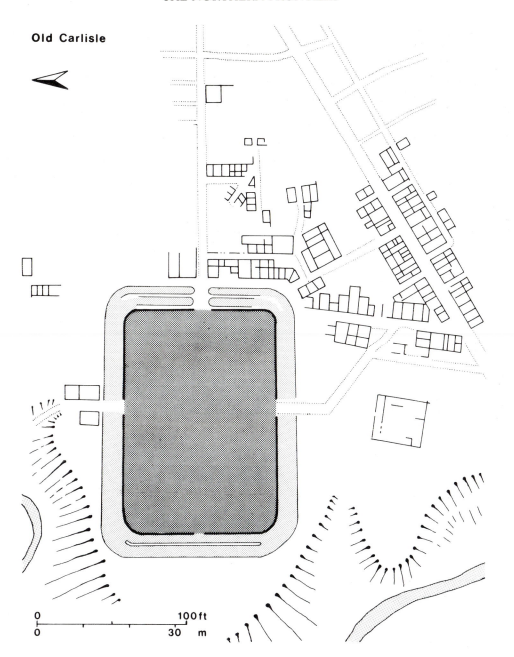

Old Carlisle

FIG. 14   Fort and *vicus* at Old Carlisle, drawn from air photographs. (D.B. Gallagher after G.D.B. Jones)

excavated large areas of the civil settlement, and subsequently laid it open for public inspection. The two main phases of the *vicus* are now dated to the second half of the second century and the third century, ending in or very soon after 270. Excavations in Carlisle are providing the first modern information on the urban settlement, as well as the military complex.[123] On the Antonine Wall the search for civil settlements has been less successful, though some evidence has come from Croy Hill, while both timber and stone buildings have been examined at Inveresk on the eastern flank of the Wall.[124] Beyond the immediate locality of forts the survey and excavation programme of George Jobey has considerably extended our knowledge of Iron Age and native settlements.[125] Jobey has considered the inter-action between Roman and native, military and

123.   D. Charlesworth, *Arch. Journ.* cxxxv (1978), 115–37 for a general survey; M.R. McCarthy, T.G. Padley and M. Henig, *Britannia* xiii (1982), 79–89 for a report on more recent work.
124.   W.S. Hanson in D.J. Breeze (ed.), *Roman Scotland: Some Recent Excavations* (1979), 19–20; G. Thomas in Breeze, op. cit., 8–10.
125.   See the papers published by G. Jobey in *Arch. Ael.*[4] xxxv (1957) to *Arch. Ael.*[5] xvi (1988).

civilian, and this field of research has received much attention from others. Of particular note is the work of N. Higham and G.D.B. Jones in Cumbria.[126] In several studies Professor Jones has attempted to relate the differences in the settlements revealed by aerial photography north and south of the Solway to the existence of Hadrian's Wall.[127] Several other publications have examined the nature of the impact of the Roman army on the indigenous inhabitants of north Britain.[128]

ENVIRONMENT

Richmond made use of botanical evidence in the 1930s, not only in helping to date but also as an aid to understanding the landscape within which the Romans operated. Over the last 20 years considerably more resources have been channelled into environmental studies. As a result we can see more clearly that most of the uplands must have been cleared of trees by the time that the Romans arrived in north Britain.[129] Elsewhere there was more tree-cover than today, but many areas had been cleared for farming. The date of the ard-marks found below many Roman military sites on the northern frontier is uncertain, and the possibility of ploughing by the Romans before construction has been suggested, though a Neolithic/Bronze Age date still seems preferable.[130]

RELIGION AND CEMETERIES

The most fruitful source of new discoveries of religious inscriptions, sculptures and artefacts has been the civil settlements at *Vindolanda*.[131] At Yardhope in Northumberland a shrine to Cocidius has been recognised.[132] The neglected field of cemeteries has received more attention than usual, with work at Brough under Stainmore, Brougham and at High Rochester, where Beryl Charlton and John Day surveyed a barrow cemetery and excavated some examples.[133]

CONCLUSIONS

One of the main attractions in the study of Roman Britain lies in the relationship between the literary and archaeological sources. This relationship is nowhere closer than on the northern frontier where literary, epigraphic and documentary sources are the most plentiful within the island and can be supplemented by analogy with the rest of the empire. Yet the historical events cannot be said to form a continuous narrative, more a series of isolated statements. Archaeology

---

126.   See note 50.
127.   G.D.B. Jones and J. Walker in J.C. Chapman and H.C. Mytum (eds.), *Settlement in North Britain 1000BC – AD 1000* BAR Brit. Ser. 118 (1983), 185–204.
128.   For example, J. Turner, *Journ. Arch. Science* vi (1979), 285–90; M. Jones in M. Jones and G. Dimbleby (eds.), *The Environment of Man: the Iron Age to the Anglo-Saxon Period* BAR Brit. Ser. 87 (1981), 95–127; Helen Porter in A. King and M. Henig (eds.), *The Roman West in the Third Century* BAR Int. Ser. 109 (1981), 353– 62; D. Wilson in J.C. Chapman and H.C. Mytum (eds.), *Settlement in North Britain 1000 BC – AD 1000* BAR Brit. Ser. 118 (1983), 29–53; K. Branigan (ed.), *Rome and the Brigantes* (Sheffield, 1980); P. Clack and Susanne Haselgrove (eds.), *Rural Settlement in the Roman North* (Durham, nd); J.C. Barrett, A.P. Fitzpatrick and L. Macinnes (eds.), *Barbarians and Romans in North-west Europe from the later Republic to late Antiquity* BAR Int. Ser. 471 (1988). Cf. W.H. Manning in J.G. Evans, Susan Limbrey and H. Cleere (eds.), *The effect of man on the landscape: The Highland Zone* (London, 1975), 112–6. On the supply of the army cf. D.J. Breeze in R. Miket and C. Burgess (eds.), *Between and Beyond the Walls* (Edinburgh, 1984), 264–86; K.F. Hartley, *Glasgow Arch. Journ.* iv (1976), 81–9; D.J. Breeze, *PSAS* cxvi (1986), 185–9.
129.   W.S. Hanson and L. Macinnes, *Scot. Arch. Forum* xii (1981), 98–113; N. Higham, *The Northern Counties to AD 1000* (London, 1986), 182–5. Cf. n. 127.
130.   J. Bennett, *Arch. Ael.*⁵ xi (1983), 54–8.
131.   R.E. Birley, *Vindolanda, A Roman frontier post on Hadrian's Wall* (London, 1977), 73–5.
132.   D.B. Charlton and M.M. Mitcheson, *Britannia* xiv (1983), 143–53.
133.   M.J. Jones *et. al, Trans. Cumberland Westmorland Antiq. Arch. Soc.* lxxvii (1977), 17–47. Brougham: *JRS* lvii (1967), 177; lviii (1968), 179. High Rochester: D.B. Charlton and M.M. Mitcheson, *Arch. Ael.*⁵ xii (1984), 1–31.

FIG. 15   Reconstructed Wall and turret at Chesterholm–Vindolanda. (D.J. Breeze)

FIG. 16   Reconstructed west gate of the fort at South Shields.

can illuminate these statements, but must be treated circumspectly if used to amplify the documentary evidence.[134] Yet archaeology offers the only hope of increasing knowledge, be it through the steady accumulation of structural and artefactual information, the discovery of more inscriptions or writing-tablets, the excavation of types of monuments hitherto little examined such as cemeteries, or the improvement in archaeological and scientific techniques.

The methods of undertaking archaeological research have changed significantly over this century. The era of privately inspired and funded research lasted well into the era of scientific excavation. The local societies often provided a framework for this work – and some finance – but primarily a vehicle for publication, as they still do. The first university appointment of a Roman archaeologist in north Britain was in 1931: Eric Birley. His career spanned the whole period of university primacy in research on Hadrian's Wall. Following 1945 the role of the state increased through the funding of rescue archaeology and some research at sites in care. In the 1980s local authorities have become more involved in excavation, mainly through their appreciation of the potential of both Walls for tourism. At the same time private research has returned, in particular through the activities of the Vindolanda Trust. Today there is a flexible approach to work on the northern frontiers with English Heritage, Historic Scotland and the Royal Commissions on behalf of central government, several local authorities, the National Trust, universities and museums all contributing and collaborating in both large-scale operations and selective investigations, in planning and discussion and in publication. This offers the best chance that northern studies can continue in the same vital manner as in the past.

134. R. Reece, *Scot. Arch. Rev.* iii (1984), 113–5.

BEYOND THE NORTHERN FRONTIER: ROMAN AND NATIVE IN SCOTLAND*

By Lawrence Keppie

This paper differs from the others contained in this volume in that it deals with that part of the island of Britain which never, or only briefly, formed part of the Roman province of *Britannia*. When Claudius quitted the island after his brief visit in A.D. 43, he is said, according to Dio, to have instructed Plautius to conquer 'the remaining areas';[1] Roman propaganda soon claimed that Britain had been completely conquered by Claudius, as far as the Orkneys.[2] In reality, successive governors endeavoured to extend the limits of the province or secure its borders according to political circumstances or military capacity. The advances achieved under Julius Agricola brought Roman forces to the edge of the Scottish Highlands and culminated in a much heralded victory at the still unidentified site of *Mons Graupius*. It was precisely at this moment that the best opportunity lay of carrying through the conquest of the island to its logical end. Whether Agricola's unnamed successor attempted to better his achievements is not known, but with the withdrawal of troops to continental postings in the later 80s, the opportunity of complete conquest, if it had ever really existed, slipped away. Most if not all the territory north of the Tyne-Solway line had been given up by *c.* A.D. 105.[3]

Agricola himself had advocated a halt at the Forth-Clyde line,[4] and his reports to the emperor, or those of his successor, must surely have emphasised the difficulty of penetrating the northern mountains as soon as their geographical extent became obvious. The Antonine re-advance to the Forth-Clyde isthmus, an advance linked as much to political expediency as to military necessity, lasted only a generation. The early third-century campaigns of Severus had a limited impact; it is by no means certain how much of the northern part of the island Severus intended Roman forces to garrison on a permanent basis.[6] With the departure to Rome of Caracalla in 211, the period of direct Roman intervention in Scotland north of the Cheviots was effectively ended. It had lasted for no more than 40–50 years in total, in comparison with nearly four centuries of direct Roman control on the South. Thereafter, though we may presume attempts on the part of the Romans to influence political events in the North, we lack secure evidence for any physical involvement

---

*   I am grateful to Mr G.S. Maxwell, Dr D.J. Breeze and Dr E.W. MacKie for reading an early draft of this paper. Their many comments have much improved the final version.

1. Dio, lx.21.5.
2. Silus. Italicus., *Punica* iii.597ff.; Valerius Flaccus, *Argonautica* i.8; and (later) Eutropius vii.13.2; Oros. vii.6.10; see G.S. Maxwell, *Scot. Arch. Forum* vii (1976), 31–49. The Elder Pliny, writing in the later 70s A.D., could claim conquest 'nearly 30 years ago' of land almost as far as the Caledonian Forest (*NH* iv.102).
3. See *ILS* 1338 for a *censitor Brittonum Anavion[ens(ium)]* whom some have seen operating in Annandale. A date of *c.* 110 has been suggested, which would imply occupation of at least a small part of SW Scotland, after the main Trajanic withdrawal, *c.* 105; see A.R. Birley, *The Fasti of Roman Britain* (Oxford, 1981), 302.
4. Tacitus, *Agricola*, 23.
5. A.R. Birley, *Trans. Archit. and Arch. Soc. Northumberland Durham* iii (1974), 13–25; D.J. Breeze in W.S. Hanson and L.J.F. Keppie (eds.), *Roman Frontier Studies 1979* BAR Int. ser. 71 (Oxford, 1980), 47.
6. D.J. Breeze, *The Northern Frontiers of Roman Britain* (London, 1981), 135.

within the modern boundaries of Scotland. The distribution of outpost forts north of Hadrian's Wall in the third and early fourth centuries may indicate a desire to protect areas of north-east Northumberland to the Tweed, but no further. The view that a group of *loca* (places) mentioned in the Ravenna Cosmography represented 'tribal meeting-places' of the third and fourth centuries under Roman suzerainty as far as the Forth-Clyde isthmus and even beyond, is no longer widely accepted.[7]

Though Tacitus claimed, in the prologue to his *Histories*, that Britain had been thoroughly conquered (*perdomita*) in his day,[8] the floodtide of the Roman advance had reached only to the edge of the Highland massif. Roman authors were well aware in succeeding centuries that the island consisted of a Roman part (the province called *Britannia*) and a non-Roman part to which the name *Caledonia* might be applied. Caledonia was seen by authors of the Neronian period onwards as a wild, trackless, densely forested zone, where military glory might be sought.[9] The noun *Caledonia* appears first in Tacitus, by which he meant Britain north of the Forth-Clyde line.[10] Ptolemy's *Caledones* lay further north, seemingly in a band of territory across the Grampians, or along the Great Glen, with the Caledonian Forest beyond them.[11] Tacitus provides some useful, if vague, details on the physical geography of the North. The Caledonians were 'large-limbed and red-haired';[12] but he tells us little of the political organisation or about settlement and economy. For undiscerning authors, the name *Caledonia* could be applied to that part of the island not currently held by Rome, whatever its extent.

We are fortunate that Ptolemy's world map, compiled about A.D. 140, included a fairly detailed tribal map of Scotland, and many place-names along the coastline, and inland. The details, which have been closely studied, seem likely to have their origin in information-gathering by Agricola's forces, the extent of whose penetration they closely mirror.[13] The Novantae are shown as occupying the South-West, the Selgovae the southern uplands, between the major north-south communication routes, and the Votadini are given the Lothian plain and a spread of territory southwards across the Cheviots to the Tyne. The Damnonii (some prefer the spelling Dumnonii)[14] are assigned territory in the Clyde valley and Stirlingshire, with the Venicones perhaps in Fife, or in Strathmore, and the Vacomagi beyond them. To the north and north-west political control was evidently more fragmented, as the geography itself might lead us to expect. Many of these tribal names do not recur in other, independent sources, and we must beware of over-reliance on Ptolemy. Some of the tribal territories and the assignment to them of place-names do not always correspond well with unchanging geographical realities.[15]

The time has long passed since accounts of Roman invasions and occupations of North Britain were seen in isolation, as though Scotland was entirely uninhabited when they arrived, or remained so throughout their sojourns. For Scotland, the Roman period and the Iron Age were contemporary; or rather the Roman penetrations represented a short-lived intrusion into an Iron Age society. A collection of essays, *Roman and Native in North Britain* (edited by Sir Ian Richmond, Edinburgh, 1958) placed this subject firmly before the eyes of archaeologists and historians alike. It has remained a topic for detailed investigation ever since.[16]

7. I.A. Richmond and O.G.S. Crawford, *Archaeologia* xciii (1949), 1ff.; K.A. Steer in I.A. Richmond (ed.), *Roman and Native in North Britain* (Edinburgh, 1958), 139. *Contra*, A.L.F. Rivet and C. Smith, *The Place-names of Roman Britain* (London, 1979), 212.
8. Tacitus, *Histories* i.2; cf. *Agricola* 10.1.
9. Lucan, *Pharsalia* vi.68; Pliny, *NH* iv.102; Statius, *Silvae* v.2.142 (*Caledonios campos!*); Martial, *Epig.* x.44; Silus Italicus, *Punica* iii.597–600. See J.G.F. Hind, *PSAS* cxiii (1983), 373–78 for a citation of the literary evidence.
10. Tacitus, *Agricola* 10.3, 25.3, 27.1, 31.4.
11. Ptolemy ii.3.8.
12. Tacitus, *Agricola* 25.3.
13. Rivet and Smith, op. cit. (note 7), 123ff.
14. ibid., 324–44.
15. J.C. Mann and D.J. Breeze, *PSAS* cxvii (1987), forthcoming.
16. See esp. Maxwell, loc. cit. (note 2); idem in Hanson and Keppie (eds.), op. cit. (note 5), 1–14; idem in J. Chapman and H. Mytum (eds.), *Settlement in North Britain, 1000 B.C.–1000 A.D.* BAR Brit. Ser. 118 (Oxford, 1983), 233–62; D.W. Harding (ed.), *Later Prehistoric Settlement in South-East Scotland* (Edinburgh, 1982); P. Clack in D. Miles (ed.), *The Romano-British Countryside* BAR Int. ser. 103 (Oxford, 1982), 377–402; R. Miket and C. Burgess (eds.), *Between and Beyond the Walls* (Edinburgh, 1984); D.J. Breeze, *PSAS* cxv (1985), 223–28.

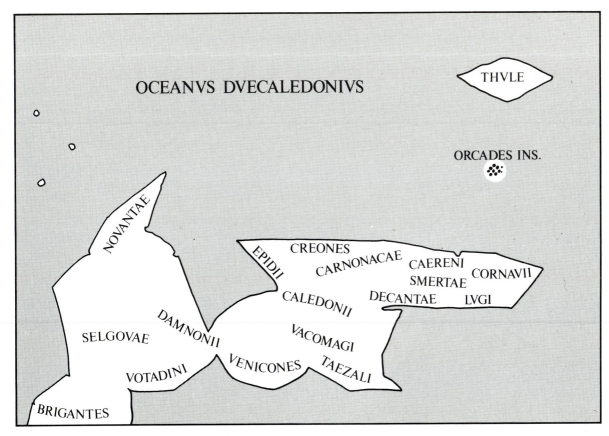

OCEANVS DVECALEDONIVS

THVLE

ORCADES INS.

NOVANTAE

CREONES
EPIDII
CARNONACAE CAERENI
CORNAVII
SMERTAE
CALEDONII DECANTAE LVGI

DAMNONII
SELGOVAE VACOMAGI
VOTADINI VENICONES TAEZALI

BRIGANTES

FIG. 1 The tribes of northern Britain, according to Ptolemy.

If we are to assess the impact of Rome on the northern half of the island, it is helpful to pose a series of questions: (1) what was the settlement landscape which met the eyes of the advancing troops of Agricola in the later 70s A.D. ?; (2) to what extent would the pattern have been visibly different by the time that the army withdrew at the end of the Flavian, or indeed the Antonine occupations?; (3) how much of any Roman influence would have remained to greet the expeditionary force marching north under Severus in A.D. 209? While we are in a position to provide a generalised answer to the first question, the second and third are more problematical.

How much we are dependent on Ptolemy's record becomes apparent when we try to build up a picture of the political geography of Scotland without the help of the specific information he provides, on the basis of archaeological information alone. We are dealing with a time period of half a millennium, into which the hiccup of the Roman occupations has to be inserted. Recent surveys and settlement studies have done much to illuminate our appreciation of the communities of Iron Age Scotland, but our knowledge remains inevitably uneven. Pride of place must go to the work over many decades of the investigators of the Royal Commission on the Ancient and Historical Monuments of Scotland, whose inventories of the counties of Roxburghshire (1956), Selkirkshire (1957) and Peeblesshire (1967) established the broad outlines of the settlement sequence among the Votadini and the Selgovae. The publication of Stirlingshire (1963) and Lanarkshire (1977) extended the coverage into the lands of the Damnonii, and more recently the territory of the Epidii and other tribes of the western coastline can be studied with the aid of inventories of Argyll (1971 onwards). Equally a deep debt is owed to the endeavours of Professor George Jobey and his pupils which have embraced much of the 'Tyne-Forth' province.[17] Professor Jobey has been active too in the South-West, where his efforts have more

17. G. Jobey, *A Field-Guide to Prehistoric Northumberland, Part 2* (Newcastle, 1974); idem, *Arch. Ael.*[5] ii (1974), 17–26; idem in P. Clack and S. Haselgrove (eds.), *Rural Settlement in the Roman North* (Durham, 1982), 7–20; L. Macinnes in Harding (ed.), op. cit. (note 16), 176–98.

recently been supplemented by aerial reconnaissance by Professor G.D.B. Jones and Dr N.J. Higham.[18] Mr Frank Newall has spent a lifetime plotting sites in Ayrshire and Renfrewshire by orthodox field survey.[19] But north of the Forth-Clyde line systematic survey in recent years has been of limited extent, except that the initiatives of Mr Ian Shepherd and Dr Ian Ralston in Grampian must be warmly commended.[20] Aerial reconnaissance over the last decade by the Royal Commission under the supervision of Mr G.S. Maxwell, taking up the mantle formerly assumed by Professor St. Joseph, has added immeasurably to our awareness of the intensity of settlement and the distribution of known (and novel) house and settlement types.[21] Attention has always been directed to those structures peculiar to the Scottish scene: the brochs of the north and west,[22] the duns of Argyllshire and the western coastline,[23] the souterrains of Fife, Angus and the Mearns,[24] and the loch-side or loch-island crannogs which are widely distributed.[25] There are no neat dividing lines between house- or settlement-types, and on archaeological evidence alone we can proceed only a short way towards defining tribal boundaries to match those indicated by Ptolemy.

This was an essentially country-based society, led by a warrior aristocracy, whose dress and equipment can be reconstructed from artefactual evidence. We have almost no information about tribal organisation, leadership, about internal alliances or changing attitudes to Rome. Any assertions have to be concocted by analogy with Celtic society in southern Britain or continental Europe. Careful study of clan society in the Highlands in the centuries down to Culloden (1746) could offer useful analogies.

The native economy can be reconstructed from a variety of sources. Cultivation of land for crops was well established, as was cattle-rearing, and pasturing of sheep on higher ground. Excavations have yielded ploughshares, quernstones, sickle blades, sheep-shears, spindle whorls, and carbonised grain, especially barley. Animal bones have been found. Pollen diagrams reveal considerable clearance of woodland.[26] Plough marks have been detected on the ground below Roman forts.[27] Field-systems and stock-enclosures have been plotted near several native sites; doubtless many more will be detected.[28]

At the battle of *Mons Graupius* Tacitus makes Agricola assert that his opponents were the Britons who had escaped from earlier battles and fled northwards.[29] Earlier he had claimed that Agricola's garrison posts on the Forth-Clyde isthmus had the effect of sweeping back recalcitrant Britons 'as though into another island.'[30] The tribal names Damnonii and Cornavii in central and north-west Scotland recall similar tribal-names in England; moreover, artefactual evidence of

18. J.Condry and M. Ansell, *Trans. Dumfries. & Galloway Nat. Hist. & Antiq. Soc.* liii (1977–78), 105–13; G. Jobey, *PSAS* cv (1972–74), 119–40; N.J. Higham and G.D.B. Jones, *The Carvetii* (Gloucester, 1985); G.D.B. Jones and J. Walker in Chapman and Mytum (eds.) op. cit. (note 16), 185–204; N.J. Higham in Clack and Haselgrove (eds.), op. cit. (note 7), 105–22.
19. *PSAS* xcv (1961–62), 159–70; idem, *Glasgow Arch. Journ.* iv (1976), 111–23.
20. I. Ralston, K. Sabine and W. Watt in Chapman and Mytum (eds.), op. cit. (note 16), 149–73.
21. *Aerial Archaeology* ii (1978), 37–44; idem, *Scot. Arch. Rev.* ii.1 (1983), 45–52.
22. E.W. MacKie in P.J. Fowler (ed.), *Recent Work in Rural Archaeology* (Bradford on Avon, 1975), 72–90; N. Fojut, *Glasgow Arch. Journ.* ix (1982), 38–59; idem, *PSAS* cxi (1981), 220–28.
23. R.W. Feachem, *The North Britons* (London, 1965), 122ff.
24. F.T. Wainwright, *The Souterrains of Southern Pictland* (London, 1963); T. Watkins, *PSAS* cx (1980), 165–208.
25. R. Munro, *Ancient Scottish Lake Dwellings* (Edinburgh, 1882); I. Morrison, *Landscape with Lake Dwellings; the Crannogs of Scotland* (Edinburgh, 1985); cf. T.N. Dixon, *PSAS* cxii (1982), 17–38 for recent underwater survey in Loch Tay.
26. J. Turner, *Journ. Arch. Science* vi (1979), 285–90; W.E. Boyd, *Glasgow Arch. Journ.* xi (1984), 75–81; idem, *Britannia* xvi (1985), 37–48; W.S Hanson and L. Macinnes, *Scot. Arch. Forum* xii (1981), 98–113; J.H. Dickson, *Scot. Arch. Forum* ix (1977), 62–65.
27. G.S. Maxwell in Chapman and Mytum, op. cit. (note 16), 243.
28. T. Gates in Clack and Haselgrove (eds.), op. cit. (note 17), 21–42; S.P. Halliday in Harding (ed.), op. cit. (note 16), 74–91.
29. *Agricola* 34.1.
30. *Agricola* 23; cf. SHA, *Vit. Ant. Pii.* v.5.

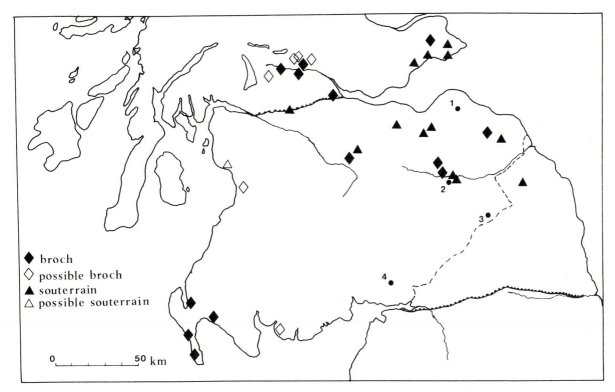

FIG. 2   Brochs and souterrains south of the River Tay (1 = Traprain Law; 2 = Eildon Hill North; 3 = Woden Law; 4 = Burnswark).

contacts between the south and the Atlantic seaboard of Scotland has been adduced, but not with total scholarly agreement.[31]

On the other hand, it has been averred that we can detect, by the presence of distinctive house- or settlement-types in areas outwith their main concentrations, the movements of tribesmen southwards or eastwards into new territory, and indeed that these movements can be tied in with the arrival, presence, or withdrawal of Roman forces. Particularly noticeable is the growing number of brochs attested on Tayside, in the Forth Valley, and in the Border counties. Many have on excavation yielded Roman material, or have been dated by the C14 method to the first or second centuries A.D.. It has been variously supposed that their occupants moved southwards either to help friendly tribes to fend off the Roman invaders;[32] or that they were invited southwards by the Romans either to occupy empty territory or to fill a vacuum in the immediate aftermath of Roman withdrawal.[33] What does seem clear is that the occupants had access to a wide range of sophisticated Roman artefacts, in pottery, metal, glass and stone (below, p. 68). Often the brochs have been shown to overlie round timber houses or the defences of a hillfort.[34] Traditionally the builders have been seen as immigrants, but a well argued case has been made for seeing here, in some instances at least, the adoption by increasingly prosperous landowners of these impressive defensive towers as symbols of their status.[35]

A number of souterrains have been found in central and southern Scotland in contexts which clearly suggest that they postdate a Roman withdrawal from Scotland.[36] At Shirva on the

31.   E.W. MacKie, *Glasgow Arch. Journ.* ii (1971), 39–71.
32.   J.R.C. Hamilton, *Excavations at Clickhimin, Shetland* (London, 1968), 108; cf. R.W. Feachem, *The North Britons* (London, 1965), 124–26.
33.   E.W. MacKie, *Glasgow Arch. Journ.* ix (1982), 60–72.
34.   S. Piggott, *PSAS* lxxxv (1950–51), 92ff. (Torwoodlee); RCAHMS, *Berwickshire* (Edinburgh, 1915), 60ff. (Edinshall); D.B. Taylor, *PSAS* cxii (1982), 244 (Hurly Hawkin); MacKie, loc. cit. (note 33) (Leckie); L. Main, *Forth Naturalist & Historian* iii (1978), 99–111 (Buchlyvie).
35.   L. Macinnes, *PSAS* cxiv (1984), 235–49.
36.   H. Welfare in Miket and Burgess (eds.), op. cit., (note 16), 305–23.

Antonine Wall, east of Kirkintilloch, a souterrain was constructed in the conveniently available hollow of the Antonine ditch, which we must assume was now disused. For building material nearby forts and cemetery-plots were robbed of upstanding stonework.[37] At Newstead at least two souterrains were built some 400 m SW of the fort, one utilising building stones from some structure there.[38] At Crichton, on the line of Dere Street in Midlothian, dressed stonework was taken from an as yet unlocated Roman fort or fortlet to construct a souterrain. One large block bears the foreparts of a pegasus, the emblem of Legion II Augusta.[39] The chronological implications are clear. Some duns, typical of the western coastal districts, have been observed in the Forth Valley with an outlier on the Upper Tweed. A few of these sites have yielded Roman material thus indicating a general date for occupation and use.[40] But whether these duns are evidence of the movement of population into new areas before the Romans arrived, while they were present, or in the wake of a withdrawal can only be guessed at. Note that population movement, if it did occur, might have been prompted by pressures from other tribal groups in the North and West rather than in response to Roman campaigning.

We remain largely ignorant as to the extent to which Roman advances were in fact resisted by the native population, but there are no good grounds for supposing that the presence was in fact generally welcomed, except perhaps in south-east Scotland (below, p. 70). In describing Agricola's advance to the Tay, Tacitus is able to note that the army was buffeted by bad weather; but the tribes dared not attack it.[41] North of the Tay, Agricola found resistance hardening, and tough fighting followed.[42] In the speech attributed to Calgacus before the battle of Mons Graupius, Tacitus implies that the Romans adopted a scorched earth policy in newly won territory; but no hint is given that Agricola's troops acted in this way.[43] No written source survives to tell us whether the forces of Lollius Urbicus needed to fight their way northwards to the Forth-Clyde line and beyond; the distance slabs show conventional scenes of combat, and Roman victory.[44] Cassius Dio's and Herodian's accounts of Severus' campaigns imply hard fighting throughout with no indication of success on the battlefield.[45] Obtaining confirmation of this by archaeological means is a hard task. The excavator of Leckie broch has argued that the site was besieged and stormed by Roman troops.[46] At Buchlyvie, part of the broch wall was dismantled or fell; but whose hands were at work remains a mystery.[47] It is often assumed that the presence atop Eildon Hill North of a timber-framed signal-tower serving the Roman fort at Newstead implies abandonment of the hill by its substantial community,[48] but in the absence of extensive excavation it is rash to draw conclusions; a few of the hut platforms have recently been examined.[49] One result of the Roman advance must have been to put an end to the traditional inter-tribal warfare of which Tacitus speaks.[50] But it is no longer possible to argue that the Romans brought about the abandonment of hillforts in the areas overrun. In many cases their defences had long since been overlaid by domestic habitation, a sign perhaps of increasing prosperity or more settled conditions.[51]

---

37. L. Keppie and J.J. Walker, *Britannia* xvi (1985), 29–35; L.J.F. Keppie and B.J. Arnold, *CSIR, Great Britain*, vol. i.4, *Scotland* (London, 1984), nos. 108–114.

38. RCAHMS, *Roxburghshire* (Edinburgh, 1956), no. 611.

39. Welfare, loc. cit. (note 36), pl.48; Keppie and Arnold, op. cit. (note 37), no. 58.

40. R.W. Feachem, *PSAS* xc (1956–57), 24–51. Attention may be drawn to the splendid (unpublished) dissertation, N. Aitcheson, *The Brochs and Duns of the Forth Valley* (Glasgow, 1982).

41. *Agricola* 22.1.

42. *Agricola* 25ff.

43. *Agricola* 30.5.

44. L. Keppie, *Roman Distance Slabs from the Antonine Wall* (Glasgow, 1979).

45. Dio lxxvi. 15–17; Herodian iii. 14–15.

46. MacKie, loc. cit. (note 33).

47. Main, loc. cit. (note 34).

48. RCAHMS, *Roxburghshire* (Edinburgh, 1956), no. 597.

49. *Discovery and Excavation in Scotland* 1986, 1f.

50. *Agricola* 12. On the location of the Genunian territory, attacked by the 'Brigantes' during Pius' reign, see J.G.F. Hind, *Britannia* viii (1977), 229–34; Rivet and Smith, op. cit. (note 7), 47.

51. RCAHMS, *Roxburghshire* (Edinburgh, 1956), 15ff.

Earlier generations of scholars discerned on Burnswark Hill, that table-top summit near Ecclefechan in Dumfriesshire, visible on clear days from Hadrian's Wall, evidence for a Roman siege of the hilltop, in the form of siege-camps bracketing the summit to north and south. Here, if anywhere, was dramatic evidence of collision between the incoming Romans and the local population, a Scottish Masada. However, excavations in the 1960s showed conclusively that the hillfort defences were long disused by the time that Roman projectiles landed in their midst.[52] It was then argued that Burnswark deserved a place among those practice-works which had been receiving close scrutiny.[53] Yet a case could still be made for a brief siege of the hilltop, say during the Antonine period, or even in Severan times, when recalcitrant elements had retreated to the old hillfort as a natural stronghold.[54] On the other hand, the long known siege-works at Woden Law hillfort, beside Dere Street, have more recently been seen as of native origin, perhaps defensive against attack from the south.[55] The recent publication of excavations conducted at these works in 1949 has done nothing to convince the present writer that the hillfort was the subject of hostile military action, or even of a mock attack, by Roman forces.[56]

The arrival of Roman forces in a locality, whether in a temporary capacity or intending a longer-term stay, must have created an impact on the local community. The troops needed a substantial area to lay out their encampments or to establish permanent garrison-posts, and the raw materials to construct them.[57] There is no indication that they were prepared to respect pre-existing settlements where strategic considerations necessitated the use of the best available ground. Existing habitation sites (or their remains) were swept away.[58] At Carronbridge and Dun (Montrose) aerial reconnaissance has shown Roman camps sited amid evidence for pre- and post-Roman native settlement.[59] The Antonine Wall rampart itself overlay the outer defences of the Iron Age hillfort at Castlehill. Roman roads have been seen to cut through native habitations.

The positioning of a substantial number of troops permanently in a locality must have resulted in an considerable impact on the native economy, until the tribesmen adapted to serve it.[60] Initially, we can suppose that the troops were supplied from the south, by road or by sea. But local sources of foodstuffs, clothing and other materials must have been tapped in due course. Pottery manufacture in the vicinity of forts got underway.[61] Doubtless young men were conscripted, by treaty obligation upon the tribal chiefs, to serve in the Roman army, outside Britain itself;[62] but it remains hard to pinpoint them among cohorts of *Brittones* attested at continental postings.[63]

It is common to base discussions of 'Romans and Natives' in Scotland on a study of trade and consumer-goods which found their way into the hands of the native communities. Contacts between the Roman world and the tribes beyond its frontiers have been closely studied,

52. G. Jobey, *Trans. Dumfries & Galloway Nat. Hist. & Antiq. Soc.* liii (1978), 57–104.
53. R.W. Davies, *Historia* xxi (1972), 99–113.
54. S.S. Frere and J.K. St. Joseph, *Roman Britain from the Air* (Cambridge, 1983), 32–35.
55. S.P. Halliday in Harding (ed.), op. cit. (note 16), 75–91.
56. I.A. Richmond and J.K. St. Joseph, *PSAS* cxii (1982), 277–84.
57. W.S. Hanson, *Britannia* ix (1978), 293–305; K. Greene, *The Archaeology of the Roman Economy* (London, 1986), 124ff.
58. RCAHMS, *The Archaeological Sites and Monuments of Ewesdale and Lower Eskdale* (Edinburgh, 1981), 14 (Broomholm); L.J.F. Keppie, *Glasgow Arch. Journ.* viii (1981), 49 (Bothwellhaugh); A.S. Robertson in D. Haupt and H.G. Horn (eds.) *Studien zu den Militärgrenzen Roms* II (Köln/Bonn, 1977), 72 (Cardean); I.A. Richmond, *PSAS* lxxxv (1950–51), 142 (Cappuck); G.S. Maxwell, *Britannia* xiv (1983), 176; W.S. Hanson and P.A. Yeoman, *Elginhaugh: A Roman Fort and its Environs* (Edinburgh, 1988), (Elginhaugh).
59. J. Clarke and A.B. Webster, *Trans. Dumfries. & Galloway Nat. Hist. & Antiq. Soc.* xxxii (1955), 9–34, pl. 1; W.S. Hanson, *Agricola and the Conquest of the North* (London, 1986), pl.23.
60. See esp. D.J. Breeze in Miket and Burgess (eds.), op. cit. (note 16), 264–86; also R.W. Davies, *Britannia* ii (1971), 122–42; B.A. Knights, C.A. Dickson, J.H. Dickson and D.J. Breeze, *Journ. Arch. Science* x (1985), 139–52.
61. D.J. Breeze, *PSAS* cxvi (1986), 185–89.
62. Tacitus, *Agricola* 13.1, 31.1; B. Dobson and J.C. Mann, *Britannia* iv (1973), 191–200.
63. J.P. Gillam in Miket and Burgess (eds.), op. cit. (note 16), 287–94.

especially in recent years.[64] A special session was devoted to this topic at the XIVth International Limeskongess at Carnuntum in 1986. For Scotland, impressive surveys by James Curle long ago laid the groundwork, and fresh tables were prepared by Professor Anne Robertson in a memorable article published in 1970.[65] A new collection of data, from which computer indexes have been generated, now forms part of the *Roman Scotland Archive* held at the Hunterian Museum. Such lists also include material deriving from what appear to be isolated contexts, but in the writer's view a good proportion will in due course be shown to derive from Roman or native sites which have not yet been identified.[66]

If our study is restricted to objects deriving from known native sites, we can form some impression of the types of material which came into native hands. As was already noted by Professor Robertson, the range is wide, and of notable quality: glassware for the table, bronze mirrors, samian ware, jewellery, paterae and other bronze vessels. In fact the standard of living seems higher in some native sites than in Roman forts themselves! Missing from native sites is the abundance of coarse wares, of continental or local manufacture, which would normally form the bulk of ceramic finds from any Roman fort in the North, and which we might have supposed would reach native sites most easily, at reasonable cost.[67] From this it might be concluded that native customers were discerning buyers. More probably, the more exotic and most valuable material came into their hands as gifts. Coins too reached native purses, including gold and silver issues of high quality.[68] To some extent this may indicate the beginnings of a money-based economy. Coins of course may also have reached Scotland as subsidies paid to individual chieftains to consolidate their allegiance or, later, to buy off their threats of attack.[69] We must suppose other perishable materials, textiles, leatherwork, and foodstuffs.[70] A note of caution is not out of place here: some have doubted Scottish sites yielding Roman material need be strictly contemporary with the centuries of Roman occupation, and have suggested that high quality objects were 'hoarded' over long periods. Similarly, some have supposed that certain items might have been kept as ritual objects; but such theories are difficult to substantiate.[71]

In the case of jewellery, there is often a fine line between items of Roman provincial and of local native manufacture. Glass bangles, seemingly manufactured along Hadrian's Wall and in Scotland, have a distribution roughly equivalent to the furthest areas garrisoned by Roman troops. Though Celtic in ultimate origin, such objects may have reached Scotland in the wake of the Roman advance.[72] Roman ironwork has turned up in several hoards, in loch deposits. The depositors have long been assumed to be native,[73] but a recent study has suggested that most of

64.   R.E.M. Wheeler, *Rome Beyond the Imperial Frontiers* (London, 1954); R. Bartel, *World Arch.* xii (1980–81), 11–26; R. Brandt and J. Slofstra (eds.), *Roman and Native in the Low Countries, Spheres of Interaction* BAR Int. ser. 184 (Oxford, 1983); L. Hedeager in K. Kristiansen and C. Paludan-Muller (eds.), *New Directions in Scandinavian Archaeology* (Copenhagen, 1978), 191–216; for material from Ireland, see J.D. Bateson, *Proc. Roy. Irish Acad.* lxxiii (1973), 21–97.

65.   *JRS* iii (1913), 99–115; ibid. xii (1932), 73–77; idem, *PSAS* lxvi (1931–32), 277–397; A.S. Robertson, *Britannia* i (1970), 198–226; cf. D.V. Clarke, *Scot. Arch. Forum* iii (1971), 22–54.

66.   To be the subject of a forthcoming paper in *Glasgow Arch. Journ.*

67.   Roman coarse wares are present on native sites in Cumbria; see Higham, loc. cit (note 18). The absence of Roman pottery of the third and fourth centuries in Scotland is used by J.C. Mann to indicate a lack of direct contact at that time, see *Glasgow Arch. Journ.* iii (1974), 34–42.

68.   A.S. Robertson, *PSAS* cxiii (1983), 405–48; P.J. Casey in Miket and Burgess (eds.), op. cit. (note 16), 295–304 reassesses the fourth-century coin finds.

69.   A.S. Robertson in R.A.G. Carson and C.M. Kraay (eds.), *Scripta Nummaria Romana: Essays presented to Humphrey Sutherland* (London, 1978), 186–216; M. Todd, *PSAS* cxv (1985), 229–32.

70.   Notice the model bale of hides, in terracotta, found in a broch in Skye, *PSAS* lxvi (1931–32), 289, fig.; Mann, loc. cit. (note 67). A finely decorated Roman shoe is reported from a crannog site in Dumfriesshire, see J.G. Scott, *Glasgow Arch. Journ.* iv (1976), 38, fig. 3.

71.   R.B.K. Stevenson, *PPS* xxi (1955), 282–94; L. Alcock in P.J. Casey (ed.), *The End of Roman Britain* BAR Brit. ser. 71 (Oxford, 1979), 134–42; notice the remarks by P. Hill, J. Close-Brooks and N. Aitcheson on the Traprain assemblage in *Scottish Arch. Rev.* iv.2 (1987), 85–97.

72.   R.B.K. Stevenson in A.L.F. Rivet (ed.), *The Iron Age in North Britain* (Edinburgh, 1966), 25 ff; idem, *Glasgow Arch. Journ.* iv (1976), 45–54.

73.   S. Piggott, *PSAS* lxxxvii (1952–53), 1–50.

the material was of Roman origin, and that those responsible were Celtic auxiliaries from nearby forts.[74]

Conversely, we should expect native material to have reached the forts, and attention has been drawn to pottery, wooden wheels, jet bangles, bronze terrets and other items.[75] Here too there is a hazy dividing-line between Roman-provincial and locally produced items. It is difficult to discern direct Roman influence on the range of items produced by native communities essentially for their own use; but a recent study has proposed that 'Donside' terrets, normally regard as Pictish or Proto-Pictish and produced in North-east Scotland in the early centuries A.D., drew inspiration from equipment in use by Roman cavalry which had penetrated into *Caledonia* in the second or third centuries.[76]

Whether Roman material reached native communities by direct purchase from merchants, or by exchange with other communities, or by gift-exchange, or at shops in the *vici* of forts, or by looting of the forts themselves after abandonment can never be determined in specific instances. (We must not assume that all such goods arrived only after the first appearance of Roman troops in Scotland: Gaul and, later, southern Britain were penetrated by Roman merchants before direct conquest). A case has been made for seeing high quality goods as reaching only the most sophisticated of the native settlements, so illuminating the purchasing-power or social status of the elite;[77] but it is hard to know whether this is a result of the accident of excavation which has concentrated on the most imposing sites. Distribution maps prepared by Professor Robertson show the spread of Roman material from the first and second centuries A.D..[78] Most items derive from sites within, or within close reach of, territory encompassed by Roman garrisons. More surprisingly perhaps, a similar map of third- and fourth-century material, when the country was not occupied at all, shows a remarkably similar distribution.

It must be clear that the forts themselves and the associated *vici* provided the most likely and sympathetic environment for social and economic intercourse between Roman and native.[79] We remain largely ignorant in any detail as to who lived in the *vici* and set up shop there, but there is a growing body of evidence from Hadrian's Wall to bring into play, and modern parallels make it possible to posit a mix of friendly natives, merchants and pedlars, itinerants, con-men, and soldiers' families, and craftsmen seeking a living, all enduring the harsh climate and the uncertainties of the far northern outposts. For example, excavation and aerial reconnaissance at Inveresk have suggested a substantial community in well-built stone structures, with a field-system beyond.[80] Two inscriptions attest to the presence there, probably in the Antonine period, of a *procurator*, evidence of the imperial government's financial involvement in economic activities.[81] At Cramond, excavation and isolated finds suggest a similar level of development, and the possible continuation of the settlement long after the garrison withdrew.[82] An inscription on an altar from Carriden, at the east end of the Antonine Wall, indicates the formal presence of *vicani*.[83] The altar itself came from an area east of the fort where aerial photographs indicate field-boundary or drainage ditches which are presumably contemporary with the fort and which suggest either stock-management enclosures or cultivated plots.[84] At Castledykes aerial photography and limited excavation have provided evidence of field-systems north and south of the

74. W. Manning, *Britannia* iii (1972), 224 ff; idem, *Scot. Arch. Forum*, xi (1979), 52–61.
75. L. Allason-Jones, 'Introductory Remarks on Native and Roman Trade in North Britain' (forthcoming paper).
76. L. and J. Laing, *PSAS* cxvi (1986), 211–21.
77. L. Macinnes, *PSAS* cxiv (1984), 242ff.
78. loc. cit. (note 65).
79. P. Salway, *The Frontier People of Roman Britain* (Cambridge, 1965); C.S. Sommer, *The Military Vici in Roman Britain* BAR Brit. ser. 129 (Oxford, 1984); P.J. Casey in Clack and Haselgrove (eds.), op. cit. (note 17), 123–32.
80. I.A. Richmond (ed. by W.S. Hanson), *PSAS* cx (1980), 286–305; *Britannia* ix (1978), 416 with figs; G. Thomas, *PSAS* cxvii (1987), forthcoming.
81. *RIB* 2131; G.S. Maxwell, *PSAS* cxiii (1983), 385ff; Birley, op. cit. (note 3), 294.
82. A. and V. Rae, *Britannia* v (1974), 163–224; see annual reports of work in *Britannia* vii (1976) onwards.
83. I.A. Richmond and K.A. Steer, *PSAS* xc (1956–57), 1–6; *AE* 1962, 249; L.J.F. Keppie, *PSAS* cxiii (1983), 400, no. 10.
84. Sommer, op. cit. (note 79), pl. 11.

fort;[85] from the latter zone, between the fort and the River Clyde, have come numerous coins and small bronzes, of personal adornment and military horse-furniture, hinting at the nature of the garrison, but also indicating a substantial civil population living outside the fort itself, perhaps well beyond the chronological limits of direct military occupation.[86] But on the Antonine Wall evidence for civilian presence remains patchy.[87] Some evidence of a field-system was detected recently from the air south of Rough Castle fort; other such systems are suspected.[88]

In any assessment of the extent of penetration of Roman goods into the native economy, a major difficulty lies in identifying sites which were strictly contemporary with the Roman occupation, if Roman material is itself absent. Only a small number of native sites have been dated by scientific means. Certainly excavation reports of Iron Age sites published in recent years have frequently reported Roman artefacts.[89] Many habitation sites had a lengthy lifespan, into which Roman material made a short-lived intrusion and impression, with the occupants continuing in a traditional life-style.[90] Undoubtedly we must beware of assuming that the presence of Roman material, of however high a quality, presupposes a friendly attitude towards the occupying power. The widespread penetration of western, especially American products into the Middle East or Africa need not indicate courteous relationships at government level.

Precisely how the Romans proceeded to impose an administrative structure on southern Scotland during their occupations eludes us. In the early decades of conquest in southern Britain, alliances were formed with adjacent groups, and the opposition effectively divided. We can assume that alliances with northern tribes too remained an important aspect of Roman policy.[91] Where client status was not granted, or feasible, we can look for a semi-military administration. Presumably taxation was imposed. But we have no clues from Scotland itself to match those being provided by recent finds of writing-tablets from Vindolanda.[92]

The absence of Roman roads and military installations from Berwickshire and the Lothians, north of the Tweed, has long been noticed. Despite repeated and intensive aerial sorties in recent years, which have brought to light a wealth of native settlements, the Roman map remains as devoid of sites as ever.[93] The natural conclusion has been to suppose that the tribe here, whom we must identify (from Ptolemy) as a part of the Votadini, had established, and indeed through much of the Roman occupation were able to maintain, a close alliance with the Roman authorities. In effect they may well have constituted a client kingdom.[94] Here if anywhere north of the Cheviots the positive impact of Roman presence might be looked for. There are grounds for supposing that the population expanded.[95] Rectilinear enclosures similar to those noted in Northumberland have been detected from the air on the Lothian plain.[96] The suggestion has been made that we can begin to discern a Votadinian culture. The archaeological record suggests variations in settlement north and south of the Tweed, which might be taken as reflecting some

85. Information from Mr G.S. Maxwell; also *Discovery & Excavation in Scotland 1987*, 45.
86. Small finds to be published by L. Keppie and J.D. Bateson in due course.
87. Richmond and Steer, loc. cit. (note 83); W. Hanson and G. Maxwell, *Rome's North West Frontier* (Edinburgh, 1983), 186–91.
88. Information from Dr D.J. Breeze and Mr G.S. Maxwell.
89. In addition to those already cited, see E.M. Wilson, *PSAS* cx (1978–80), 114–21 (West Mains of Ethie); T. Watkins, ibid., 122–64 (Dalladies); J. Close-Brooks, ibid. cxvi (1986), 117–84 (Clatchard Craig).
90. Note the percipient comments of T. Watkins, *PSAS* cx (1978–80), 199ff.
91. In general, D. Braund, *Rome and the Friendly King* (London, 1984); for the Brigantes, see W.S. Hanson and D.B. Campbell, *Britannia* xvii (1986), 73–89.
92. A.K. Bowman and J.D. Thomas, *Vindolanda: The Latin Writing-Tablets* (London, 1983), 105ff. for a *centurio regionarius* based at Carlisle under Trajan; eidem, *Britannia* xviii (1987), 125–42. Cf. also *RIB* 583.
93. A line of temporary camps has been identified south of the Tweed, between Newstead and Berwick.
94. A.H.A. Hogg in W.F. Grimes (ed.), *Aspects of Archaeology in Britain and Beyond* (London, 1951), 200–213. A century-long gap in the coin series from the site, beginning in the mid 150s, suggests a hiatus in direct contact after the Antonine withdrawal from Scotland; see M.F. Sekulla, *PSAS* cxii (1982), 285–94.
95. G. Jobey, *Arch.Ael.*[5] ii (1974), 17–26.
96. G.S. Maxwell, *Scot. Arch. Forum* ii (1970), 86–90.

differences in treatment by the Romans. Whether that portion of the tribe living north of the Tweed was at some time hived off to become a separate entity, following upon adjustments in the formal frontier of the Roman province, is for future researchers to examine. The hillfort at Traprain Law continued to house a community throughout much of the Roman period.[97] Indeed, it seems to have acted as a centre of commercial production and distribution of goods to both Roman and native customers. The very substantial collection of Roman finds from the site has included door-keys and locks, toilet articles and fine glassware, as well as pottery, brooches, dress-fasteners and agricultural tools.[98] Rectangular stone buildings have been noted. Some of the population knew, or were learning, Latin.[99] It seems reasonable to suppose that successive refurbishments of the fortifications on the hilltop might be linked to the ebb and flow of Roman control, or – it may be – pressure from the North. In the later fourth century a section of the tribe, then occupying a zone on the south bank of the River Forth, was transferred to North Wales.[100] We may easily interpret this movement as a reward for loyalty, to a group now dangerously exposed. The late-fourth-century 'Traprain Treasure' has been interpreted as loot from southern Britain or the Continent, but might equally have originated as a gift from the Roman authorities to a northern ally.[101] Whether similar alliances were entered into, briefly or over a longer timespan, with other tribes is not known.[102]

It is hard for us to reconstruct internal political change in Scotland during the four centuries of the Roman province of *Britannia*. Ptolemy provides a map which effectively outlines political control in the later first century A.D.. We know nothing about those tribal groups encountered during the Antonine re-advance; but we should beware of assuming that the position was unchanged from the Flavian period. Dio knew of two tribes whom he names as Maeatae and Caledonians; he notes that 'the names of the others have been merged in these two'.[103] Of these the Maeatae lay 'closer' to the Roman province, and we could think of them as constituting an alliance or coalition of tribes in central and southern Scotland. Perhaps, as in the Flavian advance, Roman onslaughts encouraged tribal unity. The Picts (*Picti*) are first mentioned by a Roman author in the year 297;[104] but popular (modern) imagination supposes the Romans and Picts locked in conflict during earlier centuries as well. The origin of the Picts is not a subject requiring elaboration here.[105] Suffice it to say that by the later third century A.D., and perhaps some time before, Rome's enemies in the North had acquired, if not a new coherence, at least a new name. The Picts were to remain the bogeymen of the Roman authorities down to the end of the Western Empire. 'Picts vanquished, enemy destroyed' reads the hopeful message on the side of an early-fourth-century bronze gaming-piece dispenser, in the form of a tower, found recently at a villa between Aachen and Bonn.[106] Ammianus could speak of the Picts in the 360s as divided into two groups, the Dicaledones and the Verturiones; it would seem that the Caledonians had become subsumed in the new groupings.[107] In past generations discussion on the Picts has centred on their artistic output and the impact of Christianity. More recently attention has shifted

97. G. Jobey in D.W. Harding (ed.), *Hillforts* (London, 1976), 191–204. There is as yet no evidence that occupation ever spilled over into the plain below.
98. A.O. Curle, *PSAS* l (1915–16), 90–144; E. Burley, *PSAS* lxxxix (1955–56), 118–226.
99. J. Curle, *PSAS* lxvi (1931–32), 359, fig. 42 (2 items); *RIB* 2131.
100. A.H.A. Hogg, *Antiquity* xxii (1948), 201–5.
101. Alcock, loc. cit. (note 71); G. and A. Ritchie, *Scotland: Archaeology and Early History* (London, 1981), 142ff.
102. J.G. Scott, *Glasgow Arch. Journ.* iv (1976), 29ff., argues for differing relationships in the later first century A.D., based on presence or absence of Roman small finds in SW Scotland; but it is difficult to consider his scheme for inclusion or exclusion of tribes in the Roman province as militarily feasible.
103. lxxvi.12.1.
104. *Pan.Lat.* iv.11.4; cf. ibid. vii.7.2.
105. F.T. Wainwright, *The Problem of the Picts* (Edinburgh, 1955; repr. Perth, 1980).
106. PICTOS VICTOS HOSTIS DELETA LVDITE SECVRI. H.G. Horn, *Ausgrabungen im Rheinland 83/84*, 171–73 offers a somewhat different translation. But cf. C. Hülsen, *Röm. Mitt.* xix (1904), 142ff. for parallels, including another reference to Britain.
107. Amm. Marc. xxvii.8.5; cf. xxvi.4.5.

towards identifying their settlements.[108] Some hillforts which had gone out of use were reoccupied in the third or fourth centuries; other forts were on fresh sites.[109] Many duns continued in occupation in the third and fourth centuries, and even if most brochs were now ruinous, communities continued to huddle around them, or utilised their stonework as convenient building material. Crannogs too remained in use into the Middle Ages and beyond.[110]

Much has been made of evidence suggesting hurried Roman withdrawal and hasty firing of garrison-posts, which presupposes hostile pressure, but the archaeological evidence alone rarely provides unequivocal evidence as to whose hands were at work, Roman or native.[111] Though care was taken to conceal some re-usable items, much evidently remained to be 'liberated' by the local people.[112] The decision to leave the northern part of the island in alien hands left a base for raiding parties by land and sea, which carried off loot from the province in the South.[113] Initially the tribes in the North, swept by Roman forces 'as though into another island', must have seemed no more than an irritant, but as the generations passed, they came to constitute a serious threat, which had on occasion to be bought off. Several emperors had to undertake, or threaten to undertake, punitive expeditions.

By the early second century it was probably clear to most Roman observers that the island of Britain would be permanently partitioned between that part which was deemed Roman and the tribes living beyond. Severus' expedition was to teach the Romans, if they had not realised it already, that attempts to adjust the territorial balance further in Rome's favour would come to grief against the triple rocks of fierce resistance, the climate and the mountainous terrain. In truth, the Scottish Highlands were no more impenetrable than the mountains of northern Spain or eastern Turkey. But the Romans had begun the conquest of Britain rather later in their quest for world domination and their initial successes in the island only served to draw them further from their Empire's Mediterranean focus. Appian implies in the proemium to his Roman History that the part of Britain not then (? *c.* A.D. 150) within the province of *Britannia* was simply not worth conquering, in the absence of any recognisable economic advantage.[114]

It is a reasonable conclusion that the Roman impact on non-Roman Britain was slight and short-lived. There is no evidence at all for settlement or colonisation in southern Scotland, in that bodies of Roman citizens or Romanised provincials from southern Britain decamped to Scotland with some degree of official encouragement or coercion. Agricola is praised by Tacitus for fostering a Roman lifestyle, language and dress in southern Britain.[115] There, the military *vici* might grow into small towns, maintaining an existence after the garrisons moved away. Many tribal centres were shifted to lower ground, and the beginnings of urban life encouraged. This is not documented for those parts of Scotland which fell within the Empire. No towns grew up, though the *vici* outside such forts as Inveresk and Cramond could have formed the bases of independent communities in due course. No villa-type structures have been identified, even on

108. J.G.P. Friell and W.G. Watson, *Pictish Studies: Settlement, Burial and Art in Dark Age Northern Britain* BAR Brit. ser. 125 (Oxford, 1984); I. Ralston and J. Inglis, *Foul Hordes: The Picts in the North East and their Background* (Aberdeen, 1984); I.A.G. Shepherd in Chapman and Mytum (eds.), loc. cit. (note 16), 327–56.

109. J.C. Greig, *Scot. Arch. Forum* iii (1971), 15–21 (Cullykhan); A. Small and B. Cottam, *Craig Phadrig* (Dundee, 1972) (Craig Phadrig); A. Small, *Scot. Arch. Forum* i (1969), 61–68; K.J. Edwards and I. Ralston *PSAS* cix (1977–78), 202–210 (Burghead). Cf. L. Alcock in Hanson and Keppie (eds.), op. cit. (note 5), 61–69.

110. L.R. Laing, *Settlement Types in Post-Roman Scotland* BAR 13 (Oxford, 1975); Alcock, loc. cit. (note 71).

111. K.A. Steer, *Arch. Ael.*⁴ xlii (1964), 1–39; Hanson, op. cit. (note 59), 143ff.; L.F. Pitts and J.K. St. Joseph, *Inchtuthil, the Roman Legionary Fortress* (London, 1985), 109ff.

112. Concealment of the distance slabs accounts for the high survival rate; Keppie, op. cit. (note 44), 7f.; for re-used material, above, p. 66. Stonework now known to be from the bathhouse at Elginhaugh was utilised in a long cist at Parkburn, Lasswade; see A.S. Henshall, *PSAS* xcviii (1964–66), 204ff. Diamond-broached building stones were re-used in the defences of the Dark Age fort on Ruberslaw, Roxburghshire.

113. Keppie and Arnold, op. cit. (note 37), nos. 45 and 57; and above, p. 71 for the Traprain Treasure.

114. Appian, *Proem.* 5–7; cf. Pliny, *NH* xvi.4 (on the Chauci).

115. Tacitus, *Agricola* 21.1.

the good soils of the Lothians; no tribal rulers constructed lavish buildings in the Roman manner. It should not be supposed that rural settlement (say) 30 miles north or south of Hadrian's Wall would have been radically different.[116] To what extent the presence or proximity of the Romans to communities in central and southern Scotland had some effect on the annual cycle or crop-growing and animal husbandry is as yet difficult to gauge. Better woodworking and agricultural tools would have become available, and certainly reached some native sites. An increased sophistication in woodworking in the construction of crannog platforms at the time of the Roman presence, and a decline in standards in later generations, has been ascribed to the availability of a wide range of quality iron tools.[117] We cannot even be sure that the adoption of stone round-houses or rectangular buildings by the northern tribes was directly suggested by Roman models. We may doubt whether Latin would be heard much beyond the immediate vicinity of the forts. Essentially, the periods of occupation were, even cumulatively, too short for the normal process towards a Romanised lifestyle to make much headway.

116.   A distinction in sophistication is alleged by Jones and Walker, loc. cit. (note 18), between homesteads north and south of the Solway; but lack of excavation and dating deters interpretation.

117.   J.G. Scott, *Glasgow Arch. Journ.* iv (1976), 29–44.

THE EARLY CITIES

By Malcolm Todd

The earliest phases of Romano-British cities were first clearly illumined by Sheppard Frere's excavations at Verulamium from 1955 to 1961.[1] Before that, glimpses of the early development of urban centres had been gained at Camulodunum, London, Silchester, Wroxeter and Exeter,[2] but it was Frere's work that provided coherence and, above all, sequence for the first time. The great expansion of urban excavation in the 1960s and 1970s produced a welter of information on all phases of Romano-British cities, much of it still undigested or even unpublished. The decreasing pace and scale of excavation from the later 1970s has allowed an interval for assessment and appraisal which in some respects is timely. This chapter is an attempt at establishing an outline of what is now known of the first half-century of the better recorded cities in Britannia.

The results of work at Verulamium have been published in full and require only brief summation. A planned layout of streets emerged in the years immediately following A.D. 43 and timber buildings of advanced and thoroughly Roman technique went up at a similarly early date. A unified complex of shops and workshops in Insula XIV, erected about A.D. 50, displays such a degree of order in its plan, as well as an impressive mastery of large-scale construction in timber, as to raise the possibility of immigrant craftsmen, supported by external capital. Even after the destruction of 60/1, admittedly with a delay of about fifteen years, the same site still housed craftsmen in a continuous range of shops and this use of the frontage extended well into the second century. By the seventies, public buildings were going up. The forum was dedicated in 79 or in 81, having presumably been begun earlier in the seventies.[3] Its plan points to Gaul for its inspiration and it may reasonably be seen as the work of an architect trained in Gaul. A *macellum* and a temple of Romano-Celtic type were added in the following decade or so. By about 100, or a little before, Verulamium was a thriving city of some 15 hectares. This steady growth, interrupted by the events of 60/1, could not have been achieved without the active co-operation of leading members of the Catuvellauni. The early development of villas in the vicinity of the city is eloquent testimony to the interest shown in the urban centre of the *civitas* by at least some of its *principes*.[4] It was this interest, or conversely the lack of it, that largely determined the pace of urban development in the first century. Official encouragement may have provided a favourable climate for such growth: the finance, or most of it, had to be found locally.

1. S.S. Frere, *Verulamium excavations I* (London, 1972); II (London, 1983); III (Oxford, 1985).
2. M.R. Hull, *Roman Colchester* (Oxford, 1958); R.E.M. Wheeler, *Roman London* (RCHM London, 1928); D. Atkinson, *Report on excavations at Wroxeter, 1923–7* (Oxford, 1942); A. Fox, *Roman Exeter* (Manchester, 1952); G.C. Boon, *Calleva. The Roman town of Silchester* (Newton Abbot, 1974).
3. S.S. Frere, *Verulamium excavations II* (London, 1983), 69–72; W. Eck, 'Senatoren von Vespasian bis Hadrian', *Vestigia* xiii (1970), 48–9 points to A.D. 81 as a possibility.
4. Lockleys: *Antiq. Journ.* xviii (1938), 339–76; Park Street: *Arch. Journ* cii (1945), 21–110; Gorhambury: D.S. Neal in M. Todd (ed.), *Studies in the Romano-British villa* (Leicester, 1978), 33–58: Gadebridge Park: D.S. Neal, *The excavation of the Roman villa in Gadebridge Park, Hemel Hempstead, 1963–8* (London, 1974).

The Verulamium evidence, so cogently presented in the published record, has dominated views on the early development of cities for nearly thirty years. Its main features, the growth of the place in the Neronian and early Flavian period, the building of public structures between 70 and 90, the contribution of commerce to the local economy, have been fitted into a model to which other cities have been assumed to conform. Romano-British specialists have often tended to extrapolate from one site to others of its category. The inadequacies and dangers of such an approach are revealed by an examination of those cities that have produced coherent evidence for their early growth.

THE MILITARY COLONIAE

The graphic account by Tacitus of the destruction of the *colonia Victricensis* at Camulodunum in 60 provides us with an invaluable brief catalogue of the major buildings which had been erected there in the decade following the foundation of the city in 49.[5] As well as the notorious *Templum divi Claudii*, there existed a basilica (presumably a forum-basilica) and a theatre. As is well known, no defences surrounded the city, the legionary rampart and ditches having been levelled, in part at least, to assist the provision of new urban amenities. Archaeological investigation has considerably enlarged our knowledge of the transition from legionary fortress to *colonia* at Camulodunum, providing thereby invaluable insights into Roman practice in urban foundation in an emergent province.[6] The *colonia* took over the site of the fortress, several of the streets in the *retentura* being retained. To the east, however, a new grid of streets was laid out over the fortress-annexe, on a slightly divergent alignment. This was to be the site of several large public and official structures, which could not easily be accommodated within the old fortress area, as a considerable number of the military structures were retained in use. The *praetorium* and *principia* were probably demolished, but this still did not release sufficient space for the public buildings envisaged for the premier colony. There may have been a brief hiatus between the evacuation of the fortress and the laying-out of the *colonia*, but this cannot have been more than a year or two.

It has steadily become apparent that a number of buildings were retained from the legionary fortress, sometimes remodelled. These include residential accommodation at Lion Walk and Culver Street in the southern half of the city.[7] This reuse, or rebuilding, of military blocks is understandable enough and is encountered also at Gloucester later (below, p. 78). Even for legionary veterans, Roman government was not prepared to go to any expense. The public and official structures of the *colonia* before the Boudiccan sack are as yet recorded in little more than outline. The massive podium of a major classical temple beneath the Norman keep of Colchester castle is safely assumed to be the only remnant of the *Templum divi Claudii*, built and dedicated after the emperor's death in 54.[8] It stood in a large temenos, 177 m by 107 m in its ultimate form, occupying most of a large insula. Within this temenos the altar which presumably preceded the temple-building in Claudius' own lifetime, is to be sought. South of the temple lay two large buildings, mainly of timber, which were adorned with elaborate stucco work: these were almost certainly public structures, though their purpose is not known. Both were begun, but probably not completed, before 60. The early forum at Camulodunum has not yet been certainly located, but the site of a stone theatre is now known, in the area of Maidenburgh Street, immediately west of the great temple, where a massive curving wall was first noted in 1891.[9] The date of this building is uncertain, but it seems unlikely to be the structure mentioned by Tacitus as already existing in 60. That building, however, may have lain on the same site.

5.   Tacitus, *Annales* xiv, 32.
6.   P. Crummy, 'Colchester: the Roman fortress and the development of the colonia,' *Britannia* viii (1977), 65–105; idem, 'Colchester (Camulodunum/Colonia Victricensis)', in G. Webster, *Fortress into City* (London, 1988), 24–47.
7.   P. Crummy, *Excavations at Lion Walk, Balkerne Lane, Middleborough, Colchester, Essex* (London, 1984).
8.   P.J. Drury, 'The temple of Claudius at Colchester reconsidered,' *Britannia* xv (1984), 7–50.
9.   P. Crummy, 'The Roman theatre at Colchester,' *Britannia* xiii (1982), 299–302.

Domestic and commercial buildings in the pre-Boudiccan *colonia* were constructed to high standards. Some of the Claudian and Neronian buildings on North Hill were developed in plan and carefully constructed, with mortared pebble sill-walls and walling of clay blocks above.[10] Tiled roofs and painted walls are in evidence, and at least one building in Insula 10 was equipped with a piped water-supply. The western and central parts of the city were already heavily built up before 60 and the level of prosperity evinced by the find-record was high: large stocks of imported pottery, glass and lamps were present in the shops destroyed in the rebellion.[11]

The early community at Camulodunum was not confined to the urban centre. Activities outside the early *colonia*, but clearly related to it, have been illumined by work on the lower part of Sheepen Hill, 0.75 km to the north-west.[12] During the life of the legionary fortress, craft-working was carried on at Sheepen and this was continued, or resumed, in the fifties. Metalworking was a particular concern of the craftsmen at work here, much military scrap being at their disposal, though pottery-making and perhaps leather-making were also practised. The known buildings are rectilinear in plan, with verandahs fronting on to a street. The prevailing picture is that of a highly Romanised craftsmen's quarter which supplied the early *colonia* with a variety of goods. That some, perhaps most, of these artisans were immigrants is highly probable. This suburb was destroyed in 60–1 and occupation was not later resumed.

Restoration of the *colonia* after 61 may not have been immediate, but once begun it was energetically pursued. From the late sixties, the devastated area on North Hill was extensively rebuilt, masonry footings and timber-framed superstructures now being common. There were changes to the street-pattern, the streets in the eastern part of the city being added to. A water supply was laid on in a series of timber pipes held in iron collars. Sewers, too, were provided, at least on the principal streets, masonry structures nearly a metre high and a metre wide at the base, with inspection shafts at the junctions and with drains leading from houses and other buildings. It is reasonable to expect the building of defensive works after 61. A substantial ditch noted at Balkerne Lane may belong to this time, but its life was short, being filled in again before A.D. 85. The Flavian period saw a continuation of the programme of building and rebuilding. Restoration of the public buildings in the eastern part of the city may not have occurred until the final decade of the first century. Elsewhere in the *colonia* there are signs of major works of construction about A.D. 100 and into the following century. A stone defensive wall, freestanding, was erected early in the second century, a rampart being added to its rear about 150. But already before 100, probably in the seventies or eighties, an imposing gate had been constructed, the Balkerne Gate, astride the road leading to London.[13] This was an exceptionally elaborate structure for Roman Britain and belongs more to the tradition of impressive urban gates of the late first century B.C. and first century A.D. still to be seen in Italy, at Aosta, Turin and Spello. The Balkerne Gate incorporated in its structure an earlier ornamental arch, triumphal or commemorative in character. This is undated, but it is likely to belong to the foundation of the colony or to its rebuilding in the sixties.

Other nuclei of settlement continued to exist in the vicinity and there must have been considerable interaction between them and the urban centre. These included the site at Gosbecks, 5 km to the west, where a religious complex extended over 12 hectares (30 acres), comprising a temple in its own temenos, a theatre and a walled space or fairground.[14] The temple originated in the Iron Age, the Roman building probably dating from the late first or early second century. The theatre in its first, timber form was contemporary with that temple and was not replaced in stone until the middle of the second century. Settlement continued also at Sheepen and here too temples were going up by the early second century, if not earlier. Although not in the strictest sense urban, the communities responsible for these buildings were clearly connected with Camulodunum and did not represent any purely rural society.

10.   B.R.K. Dunnett, 'Excavations on North Hill, Colchester, 1965,' *Arch. Journ.* cxxxiii (1967), 27–61.
11.   M.R. Hull, *Roman Colchester* (Oxford, 1958), 153–6.
12.   R. Niblett, *Sheepen: an early Roman industrial site at Camuloaunum* CBA Research Report 57 (London, 1985).
13.   P. Crummy, *Excavations at Lion Walk, Balkerne Lane, Middleborough, Colchester, Essex* (1984), 14–16.
14.   B.R.K. Dunnett, 'The excavation of the Roman theatre at Gosbecks,' *Britannia* ii (1971), 27–47.

Both the other military *coloniae* have produced important information on their early state in the past twenty years. The physical transition from legionary fortress to *colonia* has been illumined with useful clarity of detail at Gloucester in particular.[15] The legionary defences were retained in the early city, may indeed have received strengthening in the form of a new revetment at the front. More compelling and interesting is the retention of at least several accommodation blocks in the fortress for use in the *colonia*, with appropriate rebuilding where this was necessary. We may suspect that this was a solution that had been applied in earlier *coloniae* in the western provinces, though nowhere revealed in so vivid a way. The most impressive information from Gloucester comes from the Berkeley Street area on the west side of the city, and from a site close to the eastern defences. On both sites, blocks in the second-period fortress were renewed and converted into residences for the original colonists and their families. These renovated structures remained in use for the first half-century or so of the *colonia*. This may seem like an unduly economical approach to the creation of a new city. But the buildings of the second fortress were little more than twenty years old and piecemeal reconstruction could transform them into dwellings of above-average comfort for a frontier province. There may, of course, have been more elaborate buildings in other areas of Glevum, not yet examined or already destroyed. Not all the military structures were retained. Some are known to have been demolished and their sites left empty. The Gloucester evidence thus throws light not only on the earliest phase of this *colonia*, but also on the attitudes of Roman officials to colonial foundations in general about A.D. 100. It was not that of 'no expense spared'. The evidence from the British *coloniae* reveals the truth that the best thing to do with veterans was to get them out of the way as quickly and as cheaply as possible.

The public buildings of Glevum have not been extensively revealed. Part of the forum has been excavated and it is clear that this overlay the *principia* of the fortress and shared the same alignment as the fortress streets.[16] Most of the military street-plan indeed seems to have been preserved in the *colonia*. The date of the forum is not firmly fixed, but probably followed shortly after the foundation, about A.D. 100. Another large complex lay to the north of the forum, a colonnaded precinct, perhaps of a major Classical temple[17] (of the Imperial cult?). This too is not securely dated but is unlikely to have been built later than the middle of the second century at the latest.

The imposing site of Lincoln, controlling the gap cut through the Lincolnshire limestone ridge by the Witham, was bound to appeal to the eye of a Roman commander seeking a strategically important site that was also tactically strong. To the legionary fortress founded about 60 or a little later, and possibly an earlier but still elusive auxiliary fort, we must now add Iron Age settlement to the factors contributing to the growth of a community here in the early Roman period.[18] The evidence for pre-Roman settlement by the side of the Brayford Pool has accumulated steadily over recent years, particularly on the valley floor. Few structures can be convincingly associated with the Iron Age finds and the material itself cannot be dated with any precision. But the cumulative information now available does point to a native settlement, or settlements, in existence here shortly before and about the time of the Roman conquest.

The legionary fortress occupied the commanding height now crowned by the cathedral and castle.[19] Abandoned as a military base in the seventies, probably by 78 at the latest, the site retained its defensive enceinte thereafter. The foundation date of the *colonia* is uncertain. It must date between 78 and 96, most probably between 86 and 96, after the withdrawal from Scotland and before the death of Domitian. The legionary defences provided the frame for the early city and the street-pattern of the fortress was formative for the urban plan. Excavation of a part of the

15.   H. Hurst, 'Excavations at Gloucester: first interim report,' *Antiq. Journ.* lii (1972), 24–69; idem in G. Webster, *Fortress into City* (1988), 48–73.
16.   H. Hurst, *The Roman forum and post-Roman sequence at Gloucester* (forthcoming).
17.   H. Hurst, in G. Webster, *Fortress into City* (1988), 65.
18.   M.J. Darling and M.J. Jones, 'Early settlement at Lincoln,' *Britannia* xix (1988), 1–58.
19.   M.J. Jones, in Webster, *Fortress into City* (1988), 145–66.

forum complex reveals that it overlay the *principia*, though the forum-basilica did not succeed the legionary basilica on the same site.[20] Instead, it lay on the opposite side of the courtyard, backing on to the main north-south street. The identification of the forum allows two long-known features of Roman Lincoln to be placed in their proper architectural context. The colonnade on the western side of Bailgate, the main north-south street, uncovered between 1878 and 1897 and still partly visible in cellars, is now revealed with fair certainty as part of the frontage of the forum, while the Mint Wall, a length of obviously Roman masonry still standing up to 7.25 m above the present ground surface, should belong to the north range of the forum. The date of construction is not fixed with any precision. The first phase of the forum may be represented by a well paved area, dating from about A.D. 100, the fully developed complex dating from later in the second century. It is sometimes suggested that the Lincoln forum was of the double precinct type, as at Verulamium. This now seems to be excluded by what is known of the plan. The date of the street-system and of the impressive sewers lies within the first half of the second century. Thus far, the internal buildings of the fortress seem to have been demolished and the colonial buildings begun anew. But too little examination of the accommodation blocks has been carried out for certainty on the point. The legionary defences remained standing, though they received refurbishment in the form of a stone wall at the front early in the second century.[21] That work of refurbishment may not have been completed until about 120. Aside from the forum, the only major structure known for certain in the early city is the baths in the north-eastern quarter. This building went up about or shortly after 100 and was most probably the public *thermae*.[22]

It is possible that the early city extended outside the confines of the old fortress, though no building plans of the first and early second century have yet been recovered. The topography of Lincoln is not conducive to rectilinear planning, except on the flat hill-top, and the structures on the steep slope leading down to the Witham may have been added to the plan in stages as terraces were constructed. It is this area that is likely to have seen the development of commercial quarters, particularly close to the river frontage. Lincoln was very well placed to exploit trade and commercial connexions with the rest of eastern England and may indeed have been an inland port of some consequence. When opportunity to examine the river frontages presents itself, the commercial importance of the *colonia*, in its locality and further afield, should become clearer.

LONDINIUM: A COMMERCIAL AND ADMINISTRATIVE CENTRE

The origins and early history of Londinium are difficult, probably impossible, to parallel in the western provinces. There was no major Iron Age nucleus, unless a striking concentration of Iron Age coins to the west of modern London is a relic of an oppidum; no legionary base was sited here and no other military installation has yet been located where it might have been predicted, at the Thames crossing, despite several false alarms; no colonial foundation was established here; no native *civitas* was to be administered from a *chef-lieu* at London. For the first twenty-five years of Roman Britain, Londinium seemingly enjoyed only a modest ranking in the official structure of the province. But within the following twenty years it contained the residence of the governor as well as the *officium* of the procurator and was graced by public buildings which can bear comparison with any in the West. The anomalous beginnings of Londinium – as they appear to us – are a useful reminder that we should not seek underlying principles that will explain all aspects of the early growth of cities. Londinium, of course, owed its rapid early development to the commercial advantages offered by direct maritime connections with the Continent via the Thames estuary, and information on the exploitation of its waterfront has been the most important single result of recent work in the city.[23]

20. M.J. Jones and B. Gilmour, 'Lincoln, principia and forum: a preliminary report,' *Britannia* xi (1980), 61–72.
21. M.J. Jones, *The defences of the upper Roman enclosure. The Archaeology of Lincoln* 7.1 (1980).
22. The excavation of this building is unpublished.
23. G. Milne, *The port of Roman London* (London, 1985), 25–9.

Already by A.D. 60, London was thronged with *negotiatores*,[24] so that the early provision of quays and storebuildings was to be predicted. The beginnings of this process have been discerned in the building of revetments and the insertion of rows of piles along a stretch of waterfront to the east and west of London Bridge, all this about the middle of the first century. This development was not notably orderly, but it was soon followed by a much more purposeful layout. From the seventies onward, the waterfront west of London Bridge was transformed by the construction of a massive artificial terrace, up to 15 metres in advance of the old foreshore, framed by braced timbers laid on one another. This represents a considerable engineering task, which could only have been undertaken by specialists working within a well-planned programme. Buildings were constructed on this terrace, including a large and complex masonry structure, a store-building and a series of what may have been timber warehouses. Upstream of London Bridge, masonry structures were built in this same early Flavian phase as far as the mouth of the Walbrook, more than 200 m. away to the west, an astonishingly large enterprise at so early a date. Before the end of the first century, a terrace-quay was added east of the Bridge and two open-fronted buildings, each of five bays, built on it. These buildings were plainly store-buildings or transit-sheds.

This immense programme of riverside building could only have been undertaken by some official agency or an agency which enjoyed considerable official support, probably the latter. A *conventus civium Romanorum* with strong commercial interests in the developing province and in cross-Channel trade probably based itself in London, may indeed have been active there before A.D. 60. The connections of such men among provincial administrators could have been both wide and influential,[25] and the rapid growth of Londinium from the sixties onward may have owed much to them.

The sixties and seventies saw the emergence of a fully urban Londinium as well as the flowering of a commercial centre. The building around a piazza north of Lombard Street and Fenchurch Street, variously dubbed the 'proto-forum' and 'pre-forum' is fairly certainly the earliest forum and basilica of the city, erected in the seventies (or in the early eighties at the latest) to a plan and proportions that recall Gallic fora rather than those of Roman Britain.[26] The *praetorium* of the provincial governor, overlooking the Thames east of the mouth of the Walbrook, went up in the eighties or nineties, its positioning recalling that of the *praetorium* at Cologne.[27] At least two bath-suites, at Huggin Hill and Cheapside, belong to the closing years of the first century, that at Huggin Hill near the Thames representing substantial and public *thermae*.[28] The fort on the north-east side of the city was built about or shortly after A.D. 100[29] and that is the likely date of the construction of the recently located amphitheatre at Guildhall, close by the fort-defences. Its position suggests that this was originally a military *ludus*, though it may well have served a variety of purposes after its construction. No remains of a theatre have yet been identified, but such a building will surely have existed by the early second century. No defensive circuit, even of the simplest kind, is known to have been provided for the early city. Temples appropriate to the capital of a province have so far proved elusive. A Capitolium may be predicted, while a temple of the Imperial cult is more firmly indicated by a dedication to the *numen* of the Emperor by the province of Britannia,[30] though the site of the building is unknown. Another inscription, of the later first or early second century, attests the presence in London of a slave of the provincial *Concilium*,[31] so that institution was probably based here too by A.D. 100 if not earlier.

24.   Tacitus, *Annales* xiv, 33.
25.   We may surmise that the attitude of Alpinus Classicianus towards the repressive measures of Suetonius Paullinus after the revolt of 60/1 owed something to this kind of connection.
26.   P. Marsden, *The Roman forum site in London* (London, 1987).
27.   P. Marsden, 'The excavation of a Roman palace site in London, 1961–72', *Trans. London and Middx. Arch. Soc.* xxvi (1975), 1–102; xxix (1978), 99–103.
28.   P. Marsden, 'Two Roman public baths in London,' *Trans. London and Middx. Arch. Soc.* xxvii (1976), 1–70.
29.   Not fully published. W.F. Grimes, *The excavation of Roman and medieval London* (London, 1968), 15–46.
30.   *RIB* 5.
31.   *RIB* 21.

Of equal interest is the demonstration that the early layout of Londinium was not as haphazard as was once thought. Although the two low hills separated by the Walbrook valley did not provide the most convenient of sites for a large planned town, the lineaments of a planned settlement have begun to emerge. These are particularly clear to the west of the Walbrook, in the form of a rectilinear street-pattern, but can be traced also on the eastern side of the valley between the forum site and the river.[32] This area had seen much development before A.D. 60, notably of rectangular buildings with dried brick walls on stone footings, divided into shops and workshops, some of them perhaps fronting on to a gravelled space on the top of the eastern hill, the later forum site. Across the river in Southwark occupation also began before 60. The most active development of residential and commercial properties came in the Flavian period. This is now well attested in all those areas of London where extensive excavation has taken place. Some of the Flavian buildings, although conforming to the well known type of strip-building, are rather more elaborate than those known at Verulamium, for example. Some more ambitious dwellings existed before the end of the first century. At Watling Court, for instance, one substantial house possessed at least three mosaics and was built to a plan more reminiscent of the Mediterranean provinces than Britain. The possibility that this was the property of an immigrant *negotiator* is strong. More typical are the shops-cum-dwellings at Newgate Street (GPO Site), which contained one principal chamber, reached by a passageway and with an adjoining service-room and more private quarters to the rear.[33] Infilling of the areas sloping down to the Thames on both sides of the Walbrook continued apace during the Flavian period, until, by 100, most or all of the ground was occupied. There can have been little in the way of space for gardens or yards, so that large houses set within their own policies can scarcely have stood on these slopes. They may, of course, have lain further out to east and west. The unusually rapid growth of residential and lesser commercial quarters at London, and the overall character of the development, are clearly products of the commercial and administrative functions of the place.

The status of early Londinium continues to provoke a great deal of discussion without producing any conclusive result. The city which grew so rapidly from the Boudiccan sack can scarcely have had the status merely of a *vicus*, whatever its rank before A.D. 60. As the provincial capital and as a thriving commercial community with strong cross-Channel connections, Londinium may be safely presumed to have enjoyed appropriate urban status. We know that in the early Empire it was not a *colonia*, nor was it the principal centre of a *civitas peregrina*. No precise analogy can be quoted, but it is probable that Londinium attained the rank of a *municipium* in the later first century, presumably with *ius Latii*, possibly in the reign of Vespasian, when so many provincial communities achieved municipal rank, in Spain in particular.

THE NATIVE COMMUNITIES

Silchester has claimed a high degree of interest from students of this subject, the possible links with Commius and his descendants, and later with the realm of Cogidubnus, offering much scope for speculation. The extensive excavations of the later nineteenth century provided at least the framework of a Romano-British city at Calleva, without revealing much of its early history.[34] More recently, the field-work and excavation of George Boon and Michael Fulford have added a wealth of detailed evidence.[35] Fulford's work since 1977 has indeed provided us with some of the most important information about the development of an Iron Age oppidum in

32. D. Perring in J. Maloney and B. Hobley (eds.), *Roman urban topography in Britain and the western empire* CBA Research Report 59 (London, 1985), 94–8.
33. idem, 96–8.
34. Summarized in G.C. Boon, *Calleva. The Roman town of Silchester* (1974), 36–48.
35. G.C. Boon, 'Belgic and Roman Silchester,' *Archaeologia* cii (1969), 1–81; M.G. Fulford, 'Excavations on the sites of the amphitheatre and forum-basilica at Silchester, Hampshire; an interim report,' *Antiq. Journ.* lxv (1985), 39–81; idem, *Silchester: excavations on the defences, 1974–80* Britannia Monograph 5 (1984).

southern Britain yet obtained.[36] The bearing of this evidence on our understanding of early Roman urbanism in Britain is of major significance.

About the middle of the first century B.C., a major impetus was given to development of the site. The material associated with this phase indicates long-distance trade-contacts and other pointers to external influence, so that the temptation to link this phase with the appearance in the region of Commius and his entourage is strong and reasonable. Development of the site thereafter was steady and it now seems likely that the defensive line known as the Inner Earthwork dates from the period 50– 20 B.C. and not to the period about the time of the Claudian conquest. The later Iron Age introduces a major step towards an orderly plan. A settlement laid out in a series of rectilinear blocks defined by a grid of streets was established by about 20 B.C., the whole covering some 32 hectares (60 acres). This period of Calleva is that to which the inscribed coinages of Tincommius and Eppillus belong, with their clear references to Roman influence or even recognition. An increasing impact of table- and other wares from the western provinces was felt at the same time. Connections with other southern British oppida were now developing, such intercourse being certainly not confined to trade. Significant progress in urbanisation had thus been made by the community at Silchester in the second half of the first century B.C.. Further developments included the development of craft-working, certainly in metal, possibly too in glass and/or in enamel.

The early Roman town began its growth about or shortly after A.D. 50. Whether or not the origins of the Roman street-pattern are so early has not yet been determined, but that possibility remains open following the recent work. The earliest Roman buildings may also belong to the fifties, for even major structures in timber may be difficult to detect below the massive stone footings of later buildings. The identification of a large timber building at Silchester below the stone basilica[37] illustrates the point admirably and serves as a salutary reminder of what may lie undetected below stone public buildings in other cities. The territory of the Atrebates is a strong candidate for inclusion among those *civitates* which were handed over to Cogidubnus at a date which is unlikely to have been much later than the mid- or late forties. The impetus towards the provision of urban amenities at Silchester is thus likely to have been as strong or stronger than at other southern *civitates*. Certainly, some unusually forceful agent must have been behind the building of a timber amphitheatre in the fifties or sixties (or at latest by the early seventies) and a sizeable bath-house in the same period.[38] The presence of bricks stamped with the legend NER CL CAE AVG GER, perhaps products of a manufactory at Little London 3 km south-west of the city, has often been taken to indicate some form of imperial concern with Calleva at this date, though precisely what that concern was is unknown. It is going too far to see these brick-stamps as revealing that Calleva had been transferred or confiscated to the imperial patrimonium. More plausibly, they represent a venture which involved agents of the procurator of the province, alive to the chance of profit in an enlarging building market.

The street-plan of Calleva had begun to develop by the sixties at the latest, possibly even in the previous decade. There is no evidence that the emerging city was affected by the revolt of A.D. 60–1 and progress from Nero's reign into the early Flavian period was steady. The timber basilica beneath the stone forum-basilica was constructed in the eighties, certainly after 78. That this building formed part of a forum complex does not seem to be in doubt. The presence of such an ambitious timber building in an early city is a reminder of what we have lost or not yet seen in the frontier provinces, and its relatively late date in a city which got off to a vigorous early start is matter for remark. The rapid early growth of Calleva is best attributed to local political factors and not to any wider significance in the formative years of the province. Indeed, in the strategic sense Calleva was not of outstanding importance. If held by a friendly king, this region could be regarded as safe; certainly not in need of intensive military supervision. The same was true of

36.   M.G. Fulford, 'Calleva Atrebatum: an interim report on the excavation of the oppidum, 1980–86,' *PPS* liii (1987), 271–8.
37.   Fulford, *Antiq. Journ.* lxv (1985), 39–81.
38.   M.G. Fulford, *The Silchester Amphitheatre* Britannia Monograph 10 (1989).

Chichester and its territory, and it is striking that similar evidence for the early development of urban structures has steadily accumulated here too.

The site of Chichester itself has not produced any clear indication of a major Iron Age nucleus. Iron Age coins and pottery of Tiberio-Claudian date are known from the site but none of this material certainly comes from a pre-Conquest deposit and no Iron Age structures have been noted. The impressive system of dykes to the north, however, should relate to a late Iron Age centre of authority (and probably not the presumed oppidum at Selsey) in the Chichester region.[39] Claudian activity at Chichester itself is well represented, though it is not clear whether this was military, civilian or both. That a military unit was stationed here seems beyond reasonable doubt, given the array of military equipment from several sites. The timber buildings of this phase are not readily identifiable as military structures by their plan, though their structural details and orderly planning are certainly reminiscent of military work.[40] They may belong to the annexe of a fort or to a civilian *vicus* which had been able to draw on the expertise of military builders. After about A.D. 50 these buildings were demolished, giving way to much more varied occupation. Substantial timber structures existed and a variety of crafts were being pursued: pottery-making, bronze-working and enamelling among them. That these activities are those of an early urban community, plausible in any case, receives support from the fact that ambitious structures are reliably attested for the fifties and sixties. A dedication to Nero, perhaps of a statue, dated to A.D. 57–8, was found in 1740 in a central position in the town,[41] and the famous dedication of a temple of Neptune and Minerva, most Roman of all early inscriptions from a Romano-British city, set up by a *collegium* of smiths at the behest of Tiberius Claudius Cogidubnus,[42] could date from the late fifties, or later in Nero's reign, or (at the outside) to the early Flavian period. Two further inscribed monuments may also date from the second half of the first century. One is the base of a statue or other sculpted monument, dedicated to Jupiter Optimus Maximus, *in honorem domus divinae*.[43] This could perhaps be the base of a Jupiter column, so widely attested in northern Gaul and the Rhineland. The other, now in poor condition, is an altar dedicated by one Lucullus, son of Amminius or Adminus, to a Genius.[44] This came from a central position in the city, the junction of North Street and West Street, and may originally have lain within the forum. It would be unwise to place too much emphasis upon the occurrence of a single name, but the regal associations of Amminius/Adminius do have some resonance, especially within this area of southern Britain. This group of monuments, of the period from Nero's reign to the Flavian period in all probability, comprises the most graphic epigraphic testimony we so far possess for the embellishment of an early city in Britain.

Two peregrine *civitates* had centres which grew at the former sites of legionary fortresses: Wroxeter and Exeter. The Wroxeter evidence must await Dr Graham Webster's full publication of many years of excavation. The story appears to be a complex one and dates are sparse in the most recent interim statement.[45] The legionary base can have had no significant function after the late seventies or 80 at latest. Webster has argued that it was retained until about 90, but if this was the case no obvious reason presents itself. The fortress left its mark on the emergent city. The *via praetoria* survived the demolition of the fortress, while a block of several insulae based on the fortress layout formed a central element in the city. The early city may have been relatively small, possibly even confined to the area of the fortress. Its buildings were largely of timber and only fragmentary plans have so far been recovered. An occasional sign of the reuse of military buildings has been noted, but this was evidently no more than sporadic. The city of the late first and early second centuries was unpretentious in its layout and, so far as we can judge, in its

39.   R. Bradley in B. Cunliffe, *Excavations at Fishbourne, 1961–9* (London, 1971), 17–36.
40.   B. Cunliffe in A. Down, *Chichester excavations 3* (Chichester, 1978), 177–83.
41.   *RIB* 92.
42.   *RIB* 91.
43.   *RIB* 89.
44.   *RIB* 90.
45.   G. Webster, *Fortress into City* (London, 1988), 120–44.

architecture. The only known building of any scale is the unfinished bath-house below the later forum. This has been interpreted in almost every conceivable way.[46] Until its date is more firmly fixed, it is difficult to place in the history of Viroconium. It sits uneasily in the early city as it is known at present. More plausibly, it belongs to the latter days of the legionary occupation.

The unremarkable buildings of the period c. 90 to 120 were swept away in a major scheme of rebuilding in the first half of Hadrian's reign. The city was enlarged to west and north, a forum was constructed over the remains of the first-century *thermae*, a fine new suite of baths went up across the street from the forum and a *macellum* was included in the same insula. The forum was completed by A.D. 128/9, as the splendid dedicatory slab indicates[47] and the *thermae* were probably contemporary with it or not much later. The Hadrianic city was more than twice the size of its predecessor and adorned with public structures that could stand comparison with any in the province. It is reasonable to link the Hadrianic replanning of Wroxeter with the recognition of the Cornovii as a *civitas peregrina*. This could have occurred earlier, but if so then local energies and enthusiasm were slow to react to the normal demands of urban foundation. More probably, official recognition came early in Hadrian's reign and was quickly followed by a building programme of appropriate scale.

Exeter may reasonably be compared with Wroxeter, being a legionary fortress site with no sizeable pre-Roman native community evidently in the near-vicinity.[48] The possibility of some pre-Roman occupation in the Exeter area must be allowed for, but at present this appears to be scattered and not necessarily immediately prior to the Roman conquest. The fortress was finally abandoned in the seventies, probably between 71 and 74, though the fortress defences were retained unmodified thereafter for some time, perhaps for twenty or thirty years. The legionary baths were reduced in size in the early to mid-seventies, but in their modified form could have continued in use for some little time after that date. The site of the baths and the ground to the south-west was adopted for the forum and basilica, again recalling the sequence at Wroxeter. The date of the construction of the forum is far from well established. The samian pottery from primary deposits includes material of the late seventies or even early eighties, providing a *terminus post quem* not before 80/85. But the fact that earlier activities on the site, including the deposition of rubbish from elsewhere, will have left behind residual pottery in some quantity is a matter to be taken seriously. Also hinting at a later date for the construction of the stone forum is a samian fragment which might be as late as the nineties or about 100.[49] The matter is complicated by what appears to be a substantial timber structure antedating the stone forum, of which only a small area has so far been examined, on the site of the *palaestra* and south-west *caldarium* of the baths.[50] With the example of Silchester now before us, it is worth allowing for the possibility of a timber forum, perhaps dating to the later Flavian period. The building of the stone forum and basilica might then have followed as late as 100 or even somewhat later. The street-plan of the early city was in essence that of the fortress, with a few modifications. Additions to the grid outside the bounds of the fortress probably were not made until later in the second century. To that rather limited extent, early Isca was a planned city, but excavation has not yet revealed much in the way of planning within individual insulae in the early decades. Several sites have yielded evidence for late Flavian occupation but building-plans of that period are few and necessarily incomplete. It is notable that some areas of the city remained free of buildings from the beginning until the end of the Roman period.

Early Roman Canterbury seems to have owed little to its Iron Age predecessor in terms of layout. The present indications are that the development of an ordered plan did not precede the late first century and even then the street-grid was laid out piece-meal.[51] Elements were still

46.   S.S. Frere, *Britannia* (3rd. ed., London, 1987), 104 note 20.
47.   *RIB* 288.
48.   P.T. Bidwell, *The legionary bath-house and basilica and forum at Exeter* (Exeter, 1979), esp. 67–90; C. Henderson in Webster, *Fortress into City* (1988), 91–119.
49.   Bidwell, op. cit. (note 48) 86–8.
50.   Bidwell, op. cit. (note 48) 73.
51.   P. Bennett, 'The topography of Roman Canterbury; a brief reassessment,' *Arch. Cantiana* c (1984), 47–56.

being added early in the second century. The known public buildings, likewise, show no signs of early foundation. The theatre in its first form, a modest gravel bank revetted by a stone wall, was not built until after 80 and may be as late as 100. The more classical structure which replaced it was not built until the early third century.[52] Both structures were oddly aligned in relation to the street-grid, though it is not easy to discern which was primary, the streets or the early theatre. Other structures belong to the early second century, including a bath-building (near St. Margaret's church) and a temple-precinct west of the theatre. The forum almost certainly lay in the area of High Street, about the junction with Guildhall Street, but its plan cannot be reconstructed with certainty and its date has not been fixed.[53] On present evidence, then, Roman Canterbury seems to have been taking shape about and after A.D. 100 rather than in the Flavian period. And there are suggestions of piecemeal growth in its plan and the absence of a master design.

For so important a city, surprisingly little is known of the early phases of Venta Belgarum.[54] A major Iron Age settlement existed here and the earthwork known as Oram's Arbour may have partly enclosed it on one side at least. An early Roman fort is to be expected at the Itchen crossing, though its site has not been certainly fixed. Early civilian development is patchily known, but it is clear that a sizeable settlement existed by about A.D. 60. Before that date, terracing of the western slope of the Itchen valley had been carried out and on the platform thus created timber buildings had been erected. These, or some of them, were destroyed in a conflagration about 60, quite possibly in disturbances connected with the great revolt. By this time the town may have covered 25 to 30 hectares. Earthwork defences seem to have existed by the early Flavian period, but were swept away by the later extension of the city. Evidence for an early street-grid or a planned layout is sparse. The main development of streets came in the late first century, perhaps in the nineties, partly on the valley floor, partly on the lower slope of the western hill. The incompletely known forum was probably constructed about or shortly after 100 on a site where timber buildings had earlier stood.[55] Other public buildings have not yet been identified, though a major structure (a theatre or amphitheatre?) may lie beneath the medieval castle on rising ground.

Claudian material is recorded from several sites and some of the main roads are probably Claudian or early Neronian in date, e.g. those leading towards Cirencester and Silchester. But the main development was evidently from the later fifties. The early Roman deposits are usually deeply buried below medieval and later Roman accumulation, lying on the lowest terrace of the valley and thus only seen in limited areas so far. Little is known of the early development of the town plan. It is notable that the forum was sited in the eastern part of the town, replacing earlier timber structures. The western area seems to have developed more slowly, towards the end of the first century. No plans of first-century buildings have yet been recovered, but there is at least one indication of early commercial activity. A first-century ditch west of the area later defended, in Crowder Terrace, has yielded debris from the manufacture of bone objects. Beyond the urban nucleus, rural settlements of the later Iron Age continued to flourish, for example at Winnal, Milland and Highcliffe. In all of these, a high level of prosperity is evidenced by the contents of first-century graves.

The *chef-lieu* of the Corieltauvi at Leicester was another instance of an Iron Age settlement, the site of which was taken over, in part at least, by the Roman army.[56] The Iron Age material so far known seems to belong to the first century A.D., so that the settlement need not have been long established before the Conquest. A military post here is indicated by military equipment and Claudian material in some quantity, but the record of contemporary buildings is patchy and incoherent. Early civilian structures pose similar problems of chronology and plan. Timber

52.   S.S. Frere, 'The Roman theatre at Canterbury,' *Britannia* i (1970), 83–112.
53.   Bennett, op. cit. (note 51), 50–1.
54.   The excavations on the Roman city are largely unpublished.
55.   *Antiq. Journ.* xliv (1974), 189, 214.
56.   P. Clay and J.E. Mellor, *Excavations in Bath Lane, Leicester* (Leicester, 1985), 29–32.

buildings at Jewry Wall, Bath Lane and Butt Close Lane may all be Neronian in date and that may also be true of structures at Elbow Lane, earlier seen as military.[57] The Jewry Wall buildings are of particular interest, though obtained in limited excavation. They were haphazardly laid out and are more reminiscent of civilian than military structures, whether in a fort-*vicus* or more purely native settlement is impossible to decide. Not until the end of the first century was there any evident attempt at orderly planning, and this may have accompanied the first grid of streets at this time.[58] There appears to have been a phase of demolition of timber structures at several sites in the early eighties, followed by occupation that was far from ambitious or carefully planned. Not until the close of the century or the beginning of the second, are there clear signs of a controlling hand behind the planning of Ratae. At Jewry Wall, timber buildings of about 100 were on the same alignment as the later public baths and structures at Butt Close Lane were on a similar alignment to that of the street-grid. Both at Bath Lane and Butt Close Lane, a phase either of vacancy or very slight activity seems to have occurred after 100, and lasted for some thirty or forty years. It was in the second quarter of the second century that the major advances in the development of the city came, with the building of the forum, the public baths and a number of private residences. After a slow start, and rather undistinguished growth in the first century, perhaps mainly commercial in character, the city matured rapidly between 120 and 150.

Cirencester is a classic case, so far as can be seen, of a town which emerged from the *vicus* of a Roman fort.[59] No Iron Age community existed on the site, the main pre-Roman centre being at Bagendon 5 kilometres to the north, with other settlements possibly still occupied at Trewsbury and Ranbury Ring, both within 6 kilometres of Corinium. Occupation continued at Bagendon until at least the reign of Nero, so that the shift of population towards Cirencester may have been gradual, over two or three decades. Military occupation at Corinium itself probably did not end before the early seventies, by which time a sizeable *vicus* existed.[60] The lay-out of the early city followed in the final two decades of the first century, accompanied by the first public buildings, the forum and basilica. Elsewhere, there is clear indication of an increase in activity in the later Flavian period, but few buildings have been excavated of this phase. The basilica was an extremely ambitious structure, 100 metres long, and may have absorbed much of the finance available for the city in the late first century.[61] The planning of the new city owed little, if anything, to the earlier *vicus*. A fresh start seems to have been made at Corinium about or after A.D. 80.

Although Bath was not a city, but essentially a religious complex and healing centre, the remarkable buildings erected here in the first century can be appropriately discussed within an urban framework. Late Iron Age occupation or use of the site is revealed by the quantity of Iron Age coins thrown into the sacred spring, but no nucleus of pre-Roman settlement has yet been identified.[62] A Claudian fort may have existed at the Avon crossing north of the later town, surrounded by the superb theatre of hills which gives the site of Bath its peculiar attraction. Claudio-Neronian occupation of an unspecified kind is also attested near to the hot springs, so that the early history and layout of the place may not have been simple. As yet, however, there is no indication of planning in early Roman Bath. Nothing prepares us for the building of the fine classical temple in its precinct and the great bath-complex which seem to belong to one programme of construction dating to the sixties or early seventies. Direct dating evidence is indeed sparse, but the architectural detail is best accommodated in that period.[63] The fact that visitors from Gaul were already at Bath in the late first century,[64] leaving epigraphic memorials

57. Clay and Mellor, op. cit. (note 56). The site at Butt Close Lane is unpublished.
58. K.M. Kenyon, *Excavations at the Jewry Wall site, Leicester* Res. Rep. Soc. Antiq. 15 (Oxford, 1948), 10–14.
59. A. Macwhirr in G. Webster, *Fortress into City* (1988), 74–90.
60. J. Wacher and A. Macwhirr (eds.), *Early Roman occupation at Cirencester* (Cirencester, 1982).
61. Macwhirr, op. cit. (note 59), 82, fig. 4.7.
62. B. Cunliffe and P. Davenport, *The temple of Sulis Minerva at Bath I* (Oxford, 1985). B. Cunliffe (ed.), *The finds from the sacred spring II* (Oxford, 1988). B. Cunliffe, *Roman Bath*. Res. Rep. Soc. Antiq. (Oxford, 1968).
63. T.F.C. Blagg, 'The date of the temple of Sulis Minerva at Bath,' *Britannia* x (1979), 101–7.
64. *RIB* 140.

behind them, is sound evidence for the existence of a substantial structure by 100 at the latest and probably some time earlier.

Not the least interesting of the questions surrounding early Aquae Sulis is: Who was responsible for this remarkable architectural complex? Bath was not the administrative centre of a *civitas*, although it was mentioned by Ptolemy as a *polis* of the Belgae, along with Venta (Winchester). Whatever its legal status in the first century (and that was surely humble), it is difficult to believe that decurions of the Belgae alone were both wealthy and ambitious enough to aspire to the architectural heights which Aquae Sulis displayed in the first century. Whoever was responsible for the development of Bath had connections with craftsmen familiar with recent trends in architecture and sculpture in the great cities of the West, including Rome itself. It is difficult to resist the conclusion that imported capital as well as imported expertise lay behind the development of Bath. But why such an investment should have been made is still far from certain.

DISCUSSION

It is becoming clearer that the tendency of the past thirty years to assign the main advances in urbanization to the Flavian period obscures much of the truth. The well known congruence of Tacitus' *Agricola* 21 and the forum dedication at Verulamium, welcome though such evidence always is, has been used too freely to provide a chronological and political context for the development of cities in southern Britain. We do not know what later Flavian and Trajanic governors did to stimulate urban life, but in the period of consolidation which followed the abandonment of the northern conquests it would not be surprising if considerable attention was paid to this aspect of the province, not least because of the net effect it would have had in reducing the burden of general administration. Certainly, the archaeological evidence now indicates that the period from about 90 to 120 saw important growth in a wide range of cities, from a major commercial and administrative centre like London to largely native communities like Leicester, Exeter and Wroxeter. For the province as a whole, this period may well prove to have been more formative than the seventies or the early reign of Hadrian.

The influences at work in the early cities of Britannia were no doubt various and we are only just beginning to appreciate what they were. The British *curiales* are mute, as yet, but they cannot have been inactive. The ties that bound craftsmen to their masters may help to explain the evidence for a multiplicity of crafts and minor industries in the early cities. Increasingly, too, the contribution of outsiders is harder to deny. Students of Roman Britain have by tradition been reluctant to admit immigrants to the province, partly because the epigraphic record rarely shows them, partly because to leave Gaul or the Germanies for Britain seemed to many modern observers a poor exchange. But people did move into frontier provinces and no doubt some came to Britain, especially from Gaul. Southern Britain was much closer to Gaul, in all senses, than to the north of the island. Reflections of contacts with northern Gaul are now more clearly evident in the early cities, in architecture, planning, sculpture and constructional details. The progress of urbanization in Britain can be seen to be broadly similar to that of northern Gaul, with due allowance for an earlier start across the Channel. Amiens and Carhaix and Tongres would have been entirely familiar to a Briton from Silchester or Winchester.

The relatively early date of planned layouts in Britain is much less surprising than it seemed two decades ago. The beginnings of urban development in northern Gaul can now be traced back to the later reign of Augustus and the early years of his successor. Practical experience and expertise in the physical planning of cities were thus close at hand from the very beginnings of Roman Britain. The Gaulish contribution has not been sufficiently emphasized by British scholars. Too much weight, by contrast, has been placed on the role of the army in the planning and construction of the early cities in Britain. Firm evidence for military involvement is hard to come by, if it exists at all, whereas the Gaulish connexion is evident in the architecture of public buildings and in monumental sculpture. The forum-basilicas of both Silchester and Caerwent were embellished with Corinthian capitals which were broadly based on models from north-eastern Gaul, while another large building at Canterbury (a temple?) was adorned with similar capitals. That skilled masons came from Gaul is as certain as it can be and is supported by at least one inscription from Bath.[65] Even quantities of fine stone for architectural detail may have been imported from Gaul, as is suggested by non-British limestone fragments found at Canterbury.[66]

There has been – and probably still is – a general tendency to assume that large public structures were built in a relatively short time and completed, unaltered, to the original plan. The assumption is at least unwarranted and requires superhuman feats of organized endeavour from the early urban communities of Roman Britain. No matter how much encouragement and material aid they received from Imperial representatives, it seems incredible that the larger fora, temples and baths were normally completed within a decade or so. The great forum at London, for example, seems likely to have occupied a work-force of between one and two hundred men for between ten and twenty years, probably more. In cities which had less obvious access to large sums of money, the span of years needed to construct the principal buildings may have been much longer. These were the largest buildings to be constructed in western Europe before the great cathedrals of the twelfth and thirteenth centuries. The main elements of those medieval structures were rarely completed in less than half a century, even when the driving forces were the wealth and ambition of a prince-bishop.[67]

Nor is it wise to imagine that the plan as originally conceived was realised in full. There will have been frequent modification above the level of the foundations during construction, and such changes will almost always be lost to us. These are matters to be borne in mind when we are assessing the date of a forum or baths, as defined by the dating evidence found in its primary levels. Construction deposits containing material of about A.D. 90 may indicate a building not completed until the 120s or 130s. Conversely, a dated dedication-slab, such as those at Verulamium and Wroxeter, presumably marks the completion of work that may have begun years, perhaps a decade, earlier.

Too little allowance has also been made in the past for more than one structural phase in public buildings. The appearance of a timber basilica at Silchester and an early stone forum at London, along with hints of alteration, rebuilding and even replanning elsewhere, must direct closer attention to structures that appear unitary, but which may be the culminating phase of a long process of building. Much the same kind of development is being recorded elsewhere in the western provinces, for example at Glanum and Conimbriga.[68]

Street-grids may also have taken a longer time to develop than is commonly assumed. Individual streets are usually difficult to date and it is too easily deduced that all the elements in a street-grid are contemporary when they share a common alignment. Reconstruction on the drawing-board can obscure differences of date when there are no obvious discrepancies of alignment. In some cases, including Canterbury, Cirencester, Leicester and Winchester, there are clear suggestions of addition to an original core layout. This is also seen in certain Gaulish cities, Bavay and Tongres among them, while both Amiens and Trier were considerably enlarged during the first century A.D.[69]

It is regrettable that we know so much less about private dwellings and related structures than about the larger public buildings. The gap in our knowledge not merely embraces the kinds of houses erected in the early cities and the traditions of living which they represented, but, equally important, the relationships between residences and commercial quarters. In those cities of the western provinces for which the appropriate evidence is available, mainly in Italy and Gaul, it is plain that the owners of houses were usually prepared to put their properties to commercial use. This has long been known at Pompeii, where very few of the larger houses show no evidence at all of commercial, or even industrial, activity on the part of proprietors. In the north African cities, there are abundant indications of direct participation in money-making enterprises: the higher up the social scale, the more heavily involved owners appear to have been. At Timgad, for

65. *RIB* 149.
66. Import of fine stone from much further afield is attested in the first century, e.g. at London and Camulodunum.
67. One of the most expeditious of such buildings, the nave of Durham cathedral, took forty years to complete.
68. Glanum: *Gallia* xliv (1986), 453–4; Conimbriga: J. Alarção and R. Etienne, *Conimbriga I* (1977).
69. E.M. Wightman, *Gallia Belgica* (London, 1985), 75–80.

example, it was the splendid house of a third-century equestrian officer and magistrate which contained the largest number of shops.[70] There are glimpses of the same relationship between commerce and the urban properties of *curiales* in the cities of Gaul, for example at Vaison and St. Bertrand-le-Comminges. There is no reason to think that the tribal magnates of Britain will have been slow to seize the opportunities offered by an expanding economy. Capital, in the form of loans, will have been freely available, and investment in urban property, both residential and commercial, was well established and profitable. In an emergent province like Britain the risks could be considerable, as residents of Camulodunum, Londinium and Verulamium found in A.D. 60, but the potential for money-making was not inconsiderable.

Given the relative scarcity of private structures so far excavated in the early cities, it is rash to draw too firm conclusions about the prevailing character of houses and their purlieus.[71] But in summarizing what is known at present, one or two features may be commented on, if only to provide a framework to be modified by later research. First, the simplicity of most of the early houses appears to be established fact. Buildings of complex plan, when they appear at London and Camulodunum, are conspicuous. The dwellings recorded in two of the early colonies, Camulodunum and Gloucester, are notably simple in their planning, as well as economic in their siting. Secondly, the frequent appearance of buildings devoted to craft-working and small-scale industry needs emphasis, without in any way rebutting the idea that city economy in the Roman provinces was based first and foremost upon agriculture. The appearance of craftsmen in cities from the very beginning, in some instances clearly operating in organized groups, as at Verulamium, Chichester and Camulodunum, is one of the most distinctive features of early Romano-British cities as we now know them. The place of these craftsmen in the social order is not yet to be fixed with complete certainty. Some were probably immigrants from adjacent provinces, attracted by the opening up of new markets in Britain. It is likely that such men will have been attracted to the more prominent cities such as London and Camulodunum, though some evidently found their way to Bath. Others, probably the majority, were of local origin and worked under the patronage of a British master, on terms that had changed little, if at all, since the Roman conquest. Those members of the emerging curial order who were quick to appreciate the entrepreneurial advantages provided by the new cities could have located within them their dependent craftsmen to exploit the commercial opportunities of the new communities. The fact that commercial quarters were sited in prominent places in the cities, as at Verulamium and London, and that a commercial group might provide a building such as the temple of Neptune and Minerva at Chichester, underlines the link between artisans and leaders of the communities in the early years.

The early physical development of cities is often linked, and with reason, to their constitutional status. Unfortunately, although these two aspects of urban affairs are interrelated, the evidence from the British cities for their constitutional basis and the chronology of its endowment is slight indeed. If we accept that Verulamium was a *municipium* (but probably not until the Flavian period?) and that the Cornovii were a self-governing *civitas peregrina* by the early reign of Hadrian, those are the limits of our certain knowledge outside the ranks of the *coloniae*. It is frequently argued that the *civitates* of southern Britain became self-governing units in the seventies and eighties A.D., as most of the army was then transferred to the North and West. This is to assume too much and the longer span of urban planning outlined above suggests a more prolonged period in which administrative responsibilities were taken up by the various native communities. The clear and direct evidence which inscriptions alone can provide is scarce. It is useful to note that the two relevant inscriptions, from Verulamium and Wroxeter, are fifty years apart. The cities of Roman Britain, or most of them, took shape over that half-century, not solely under the direction of the Flavian governors.

---

70. E. Boeswillwald, R. Cagnat and A. Ballu, *Timgad, une cité africaine sous l'empire romain* (Paris, 1905), 325–6.
71. The comments of C.V. Walthew on this matter in 'The town house and the villa house in Roman Britain,' *Britannia* vi (1975), 189–205, receive little support from the results of recent work.

CITIES FROM THE SECOND TO FOURTH CENTURIES*

By John Wacher

The last two or three decades have seen great strides made in the knowledge and understanding of Romano-British urban structures and institutions. Major excavations in centres like London, Colchester, Lincoln, Canterbury, Silchester and Exeter have not only produced more detailed plans of streets and buildings, but also illuminated historical, economic and social development; ideas have abounded, interpretations flourish, so that it is sometimes difficult to assess the real advances. Yet even now there are still some uncomfortable gaps. Despite the huge amounts of money sunk into excavations at York, it remains probably the least well-known of our major Roman cities; Winchester must run it a close second. In contrast, excavations in many other urban centres have revealed a wealth of information, which, in some cases, is still being analysed and is awaiting publication. Much of the earlier work on individual sites was carried out, as it had been before the Second World War, by *ad hoc* excavation committees, such as those at Canterbury, Exeter and London where the large open bombed areas made excavation possible for the first time in the hearts of these Romano-British cities. The middle 50s and 60s saw the maximum flourishing of these committees to cope then with the rising tide of modern development; Verulamium, Cirencester, Colchester, Lincoln, Chichester, Winchester were among those to follow the trend. But many of these committees were inadequately financed, until a radical change occurred in government funding during the early 70s which led to the establishment first of the trusts and then of the large urban units, often with the co- operation of local government. Now the wheel has turned full circle and many of these units are not only seriously underfunded and understaffed, but sometimes in danger of imminent collapse due to new policies implemented by English Heritage. Urban archaeology is undoubtedly expensive, but it should be remembered that the returns often far outweigh the cost. Help may be at hand. It is now becoming increasingly common for property developers, with the notable exception of some government departments, to pay all or part of the cost for archaeological investigation of their building sites. All this work has gone hand-in-hand with several important syntheses, often bred, and later published, from a variety of conferences, which have included such diverse subjects as topography[1] and fortifications.[2] More recently, a summary of the state of knowledge has been published in an all-embracing volume on urban archaeology.[3]

*   The writer would like to thank the following for providing the illustrations: Peter Marsden for FIGS. 1, 9 and 10; Michael Fulford for FIGS. 2, 4 and 6; Philip Crummy for FIGS. 5, 16–18; Michael Jones for FIGS. 3, 7 and 12; Alan McWhirr for FIGS. 8 and 15; Richard Brewer for FIG. 14; Paul Bennett for FIG. 11.

1. F. Grew and B. Hobley (eds.), *Roman Urban Topography in Britain and the Western Empire* CBA Res. Rep. No.59 (1985).
2. J. Maloney and B. Hobley (eds.), *Roman Urban Defences in the West* CBA Res. Rep. No.51 (1983).
3. J. Schofield and R. Leech (eds.), *Urban Archaeology in Britain* CBA Res. Rep. No.61 (1987). For the main Roman section see pp. 27–45, with further sections under individual topics.

GENERAL CHRONOLOGY

The second century A.D. could be called the peak of urban development in Roman Britain, although there are some puzzling gaps to be found at London and Verulamium, where major fires seem to have caused recessions. By 100, most of the cities of the province had been founded and some had already been furnished with street-grids and a few with imposing public buildings; a small minority had been given fortifications.[4] It used to be thought that much of this urban building was the work of Agricola, as indicated by the famous passage in his biography by Tacitus.[5] But it is becoming clearer, after the results of more and more excavations, that the dates previously given to many of the grander public buildings were much too early (above, p. 88). It is one of the defects of archaeology that, short of an accurately-dated inscription, the dates provided by artefactual relationships can only give an approximate indication of the actual dates of construction. Consequently every new excavation carried out is liable to make that date later than was ascribed before; this is particularly true of urban fortifications.

A recent instance where this type of re-assessment has come about has followed Fulford's discovery of a timber-framed forum and basilica at Silchester.[6] Similar structures may yet be found in other cities, and there are strong suspicions of ones at Lincoln[7] and Exeter.[8] The effect of this discovery, though, has been to advance the date of the masonry forum at Silchester well into the second century, probably c.125–50.[9] It now, therefore, joins the growing company of second-century fora, such as those at Leicester,[10] Caistor-by-Norwich,[11] Wroxeter[12] and possibly Caerwent[13] and Exeter.[14] To this list can probably be added London,[15] unless the so-called 'proto-forum' is accepted as the first attempt to provide this type of public building for a newly-promoted *municipium*. A second-century date of construction is, of course, much more in keeping with what was happening in Gaul and Germany, where many of the great Gallic fora in their fully developed forms also belong to the second century.

Among other public structures mainly attributable to the second century are urban bath-houses, such as Leicester,[16] Wroxeter,[17] and Caistor-by-Norwich,[18] and, indeed, it may be significant that Tacitus does not mention them in the passage cited above. Bath-houses also imply aqueducts and sewers. The majority of masonry theatres and amphitheatres, such as those at Verulamium,[19] the as-yet-to-be-located Brough-on-Humber,[20] Cirencester[21] and probably the recently-confirmed theatre at Colchester,[22] likewise belong to the same century or later, although they were sometimes preceded by first-century timber structures. In most cases nearly all of these massive public buildings were inserted into existing street systems, which occasionally had to be adapted to fit. Temples, as might be expected, show a more variable

4.   The most recent view on this complex subject of early fortifications is Frere's paper in *Britannia* xv (1984), 63–74.
5.   *Agricola*, 21, 1.
6.   *Antiq. Journ.* lxv (1958), 47–9.
7.   *Britannia* xi (1980), 66.
8.   P.T. Bidwell, *The Legionary Bath-House and Basilica and Forum at Exeter* (Exeter, 1979), 73.
9.   op. cit. (note 6), 52.
10. *Britannia* iv (1973), 40.
11. *Britannia* ii (1971), 8–9.
12. *RIB* 288.
13. *Britannia* xviii (1987), 309, with reference to a corinthian capital and comments upon it by M.G. Fulford in *Antiq. Journ.* lxv (1985), 58.
14. op. cit. (note 8), but see also Fulford, op. cit. (note 13).
15. *Britannia* viii (1977), 37; but see also P. Marsden in J. Bird, H. Chapman and J. Clark (eds.), *Collectanea Londiniensia* (London, 1978), 89–103.
16. J.S. Wacher, *Towns of Roman Britain* (London, 1975), 342.
17. G. Webster, *The Cornovii* (London, 1975), 60.
18. *Britannia* ii (1971), 22.
19. *Archaeologia* lxxxiv (1934), 213. But see also S.S. Frere, *Verulamium Excavations, Vol.II* (London, 1983), 74.
20. *RIB* 707.
21. *Antiq. Journ.* xliii (1963), 25; xliv (1964), 18.
22. *Britannia* xiii (1982), 302.

chronology, especially when they occupy sites of obviously ancient sanctity. Last of the major public works to be considered here are fortifications, and the most recent view, as cited above,[23] would see the first systematic attempt, in earthwork, to defend Romano-British cities and towns as coming in the aftermath of a northern rebellion in 180–4. Thereafter, it is now generally agreed that masonry walls were added to these fortifications, where they existed, over an extended period beginning in the third century, although in a minority of cases such as Caerwent[24] and some minor towns,[25] a fourth-century date is more appropriate. For the latter, it may be argued that the 'extended period' of the third century had simply not been extended far enough by archaeologists. The later addition of external towers to these walls is still the subject of controversy. Once thought to have been added by Count Theodosius c.A.D.367, when he was reorganising city and town defences in Britain for the purpose of mounting *ballistae*,[26] it is now becoming clearer that: (1) this date is being put too late; (2) they were not intended as *ballistaria*. Moreover, compared with continental examples, their provision was haphazard and fitful even in a single city, while some sites have none at all; no adequate explanation has yet been made to account for these differences. A date nearer the middle of the fourth century is now perhaps more acceptable;[27] while Baatz's suggestion[28] that the towers provided vertical concentrations of missile-throwing defenders has an element of simplicity about it which is most convincing.

The second century also saw the development of more complex urban domestic housing. Walthew has drawn a comparison in the genesis of urban and rural housing,[29] and has shown ostensibly that the rate was much faster in the countryside, at least in south-east Britain, with the emergence of the rural corridor-house during the first century. This compares with an early-to-mid-second-century date for similar buildings in towns. Superficially this may well be so, but Walthew fails to look deeply enough into the respective origins. It may be that the villas he cites as showing a high degree of romanisation in the first century were special cases, no more representative of the indigenous Romano-British farmer than perhaps the shops and work-shops of his urban neighbours. There is more than a suspicion that a great many urban houses began life as commercial premises, some even remaining linked to such activities even after their enlargement.[30] (above, p. 88–9) But, however we view the origins of urban housing, Walthew is probably correct to argue that it was around the middle of the second century before houses of quality and distinctive plan began to appear in cities. It was certainly the age when luxuries such as elaborate mosaics and wall-paintings made their first appearance generally. Yet many of these houses were still constructed with wattle and daub on timber frames or of mud-brick, even in areas where there was abundant building stone. This may well explain a point recently raised by Reece in his attempt to show that cities ceased to function in the third century.[31] His argument partly depends on what he calls the preponderance of second-century layers over those, in particular, of the late fourth century. But these enhanced deposits can be explained in two ways. They either came from the digging of deep foundation trenches when timber structures were rebuilt in stone, or they were the result of the destruction and levelling of wattle-and-daub or cob walls. In contrast, when a masonry structure is rebuilt, the same foundations can often be re-employed, while any stone derived from the destruction can normally be reused. So once a city has been converted to masonry not only does the frequency of reconstruction decline, but also there is less waste material when it happens.

23. See note 4.
24. J. Casey, 'Imperial Campaigns and fourth-century defences in Britain', in J. Maloney and B. Hobley (eds.), *Roman Urban Defences in the West* (London, 1983), 122.
25. Such as Catterick and Thorpe.
26. *Arch. Journ.* cxii (1955), 20–42.
27. op. cit. (note 24).
28. For doubt on the use of towers as *ballistarii* see G. Webster, 'Late Roman civil defences in Britain', in J. Maloney and B. Hobley (eds.), *Roman Urban Defences in the West* (London, 1983), 118–120. For Baatz's views see 'Towns Walls and defensive weapons', in ibid. 136–140.
29. *Britannia* vi (1975), 189–205.
30. See p. 111–3 below for examples cited from Colchester.
31. *World Archaeology* 12, no.1, 77–92.

Urban decline in the third century, widespread throughout the Empire, is now generally believed to have largely passed Britain by.[32] Explanations are offered to allow for the observed fact that little or no new building took place during this century. One, already given above, points to the need to replace masonry buildings only infrequently.[33] Another would have it that the cost in money, skilled men and materials of the construction of massive urban fortifications meant that there was little to spare for private enterprise;[34] despite these views, however, quite a number of new buildings overall in British cities date to the third century. Yet it would be surprising if changes did not occur in the very early third century, as the result of the probable punitive measures employed by Severus against the supporters of Clodius Albinus; Spain was badly hit and there is no reason to believe that Britain did not suffer likewise. Certainly a palatial courtyard house in the centre of Leicester was in a derelict state by the turn of the second century and being used for industrial purposes.[35] Shortly after, it was completely demolished and its place taken by a large public market-hall. The transfer of private property to public ownership can only mean that the owner had died without successor, had vacated the property or had been absent for a long time. In the circumstances surrounding the accession of Severus, confiscation seems its most likely fate. Summed up, the evidence for the third century in Romano-British cities and towns would point more to an uneven stagnation than to genuine decline.

A return to more stable government towards the end of the third century seems to have restored confidence among the population. New building schemes were begun in cities, such as the large block of shops in Insula XIV at Verulamium,[36] constructed on a site which had long been vacant. Refurbishment and sometimes alterations were also carried out on public buildings, such as the Verulamium theatre,[37] while radical changes were introduced into the forum and basilica at Cirencester.[38] But the revival was uneven. London presents some puzzling and contradictory features.[39] Wroxeter lost its forum and basilica[40] to a fire in the late third century, while the baths opposite had reached a stage of dereliction thought to have been beyond repair shortly afterwards.[41] It has been argued that the cities of Roman Britain had shrunk and completely changed their character by the early fourth century.[42] This may well have been true in Gaul, where the circuits of the late-third-century defences often included only a fraction of the total town area, sometimes but not always containing the principal public buildings.[43] The contrast with Britain could not be more marked. Here the circuits may be marginally earlier than their Gaulish counterparts, but only seldom do they deviate from the lines of fortifications laid out in the late second century. Certainly there were changes, although these still remain puzzling and little understood. It has been long argued, for instance, that, by the middle of the fourth century, the period of recovery was over and that large areas of each city were falling into decay and disuse, with only some individual, large, stone buildings continuing to flourish.[44] The mistake, though, that we may be making is to equate apparent disuse, or dereliction, with the loss of a city's vitality and function. For several decades after the Second World War, numerous blitzed towns in Britain possessed large derelict areas – even the City of London; some still do, caused by delayed redevelopment. But these towns continued to function properly; there was no

32. S.S. Frere, *Britannia: a history of Roman Britain* (London, 1987), 172, 244.
33. A.L.F. Rivet, *Town and Country in Roman Britain* (London, 1964), 93.
34. op. cit. (note 24), 123.
35. op. cit. (note 16), 348.
36. S.S. Frere, *Verulamium Excavations, Vol. I* (London, 1972), 98–112.
37. *Archaeologia* lxxxiv (1934), 232–39.
38. *Antiq. Journ.* xliv (1964), 9–14.
39. P. Marsden, *Roman London* (London, 1980), chap. IX.
40. D. Atkinson, *Report on the Excavations at Wroxeter, 1923–1927* (Oxford, 1942), 105.
41. P. Barker, 'Aspects of the topography of Wroxeter', in F. Grew and B. Hobley (eds.), *Roman Urban Topography in Britain and the Western Empire* (London, 1985), 114.
42. op. cit. (note 31).
43. S. Johnson, 'Late Roman urban defences in Europe', in Maloney and Hobley, op. cit. (note 24).
44. e.g. R.G. Collingwood, *Roman Britain and the English Settlements* (Oxford, 1936), 206–7.

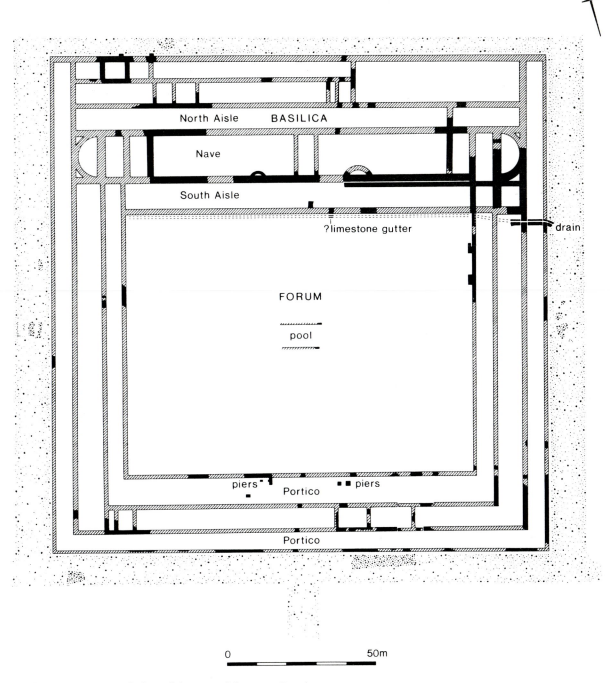

FIG. 1 Reconstructed plan of the second forum at London.

noticeable depopulation, nor lack of vitality. We should, perhaps, not be too ready to degrade the idea of continuing urban life in fourth-century Britain into a mismatch of villages and villas. Change there may have been; it was occurring throughout the Roman Empire. But cities and towns still had an important part to play in the provinces and most continued to do so well into the fifth century.

SOME RECENT DISCOVERIES

As indicated at the very beginning of this paper, the last decades or so have seen some remarkable discoveries in Romano-British cities which have considerably enhanced our knowledge. Space does not permit the examination of more than a selection here.

Some of the most interesting discoveries have been made in a city that Sheppard Frere had early made peculiarly his own: Canterbury. His chasing of the plan of the large, early third-century theatre through small excavations and modern cellars was a remarkable feat.[45] Excavations by the Canterbury Archaeological Trust have now amplified and added detail to it. But most important of all has been the discovery of what has long been suspected, that across the street on its north-western side lay a large colonnaded and porticoed courtyard which is known to contain at least one Romano-Celtic temple.[46] This temple was not placed centrally within the precinct and others may well have existed, not unlike perhaps the temple enclosure at Silchester;[47] it is tempting to suggest a major temple in the centre, or perhaps some sort of totem, since it has not yet been established if the site was of pre-Roman sanctity. The precinct itself is a slightly irregular trapezoid, while the street separating it from the theatre does not line up with the street grid. A triumphal arch may have straddled this street close to the western corner of the theatre. Dating apparently to the early second century, the precinct could have been laid out after the construction of the first theatre, which was built c.80–90; it must be admitted, though, that the dates are so close that both structures could be contemporary. The precinct's portico on the north-east side, where it faces the likely forum across a main street, seems to have been of monumental proportions, and it may have been intended to unite both buildings as an architectural whole. Quantities of imported marbles imply buildings with considerable pretensions. Unfortunately, it is still not known how far to the south-west the forum extended, otherwise it would be tempting to interpret the temple precinct as a *capitolium* in the later Gallic manner, with the four main architectural elements of forum, basilica, *capitolium* and first theatre being part of a piece of deliberate planning. As at Verulamium, it is possible to detect here the germination of italianate seeds, which ultimately reached their full flowering in Gaul, Germany and some other provinces later in the second century.[48] The most surprising aspect of all, though, is that later British fora, such as Leicester and Wroxeter,[49] eschew such models and adopt a much less elaborate form, it usually being claimed that, because they resembled military *principia*, they were built with the help of military architects. If so, it would be a surprising regression with two models of proto-tripartite fora already existing in Britain from which to copy and it possibly indicates a poverty, perhaps not so much in cash, but in ideas, of some Romano-British cities.

While on the subject of fora it is worth mentioning some five other excavations in the last two decades which have been concerned with them and which have greatly improved our understanding of these structures: London, Silchester, Lincoln, Exeter and Leicester.

Of these the chief problem in London is concerned with the building of first-century date which preceded the Hadrianic forum and is consequently beyond the scope of this contribution (above p. 80). The Hadrianic forum[50] though has a number of unusual features, such as a double row of shops or offices behind the basilica and what appears to be a pool in the centre of the piazza (Fig. 1). The two fora and basilicae at Silchester[51] and Lincoln[52] are of especial interest, for the former has produced evidence for a first-century timber basilica, while evidence from the latter indicates a similar possibility. The effect of these discoveries has been to project the dates of their masonry successors into the second century, which at Silchester may be as late as c.150. The basilica there now also exhibits a different plan, since the westerly of the two internal aisles has been shown by Fulford to have been an invention of the earlier excavators. The existence of only

45. *Britannia* i (1970), 1–33.
46. *Arch. Cant.* xcii (1976), 238; xciv (1978), 275; xcv (1979), 270; xcvi (1980), 406; xcvii (1981), 279; xc (1984), 47–56.
47. op. cit. (note 16), 267.
48. S.S. Frere, *Verulamium Excavations, Vol. II* (1983), 68.
49. op. cit. (note 16), fig.5 (p.42).
50. *Britannia* viii (1977), 1–64; R. Merrifield, *The Roman City of London* (London, 1965), 136; P. Marsden, *The Roman Forum Site in London* (London, 1987).
51. *Antiq. Journ.* lxv (1985), 47–60.
52. *Britannia* xi (1980), 66.

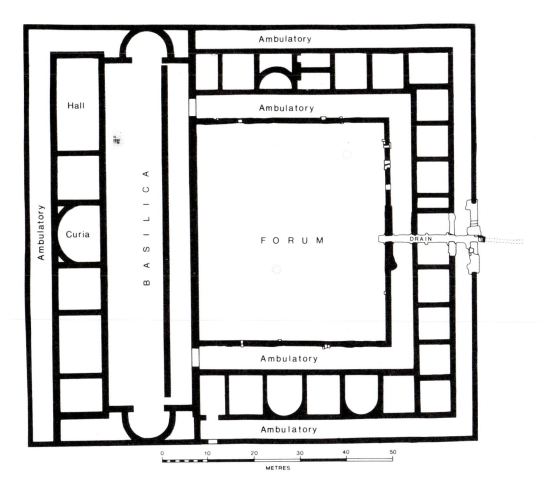

FIG. 2 The second forum at Silchester.

a single aisle is becoming a more-commonly recognised feature in Romano-British basilicae, being matched at Exeter,[53] certainly at Caistor-by-Norwich[54] and possibly at Caerwent.[55] The last two are probably contemporary with Silchester. Recent excavations by Richard Brewer in the basilica at Caerwent have identified the *curia*, with foundations for a stepped dais and slots in the floor to support wooden seating.[56]

The masonry forum at Lincoln,[57] as at Gloucester,[58] was built on the site of the legionary principia, and may, as indicated above, have been preceded by a wooden version (Fig. 3). This reuse of the site of a legionary building resulted, in both cities, in the forum interrupting the line of one of the principal streets, a feature which can only be matched elsewhere in Britain at London[59] and at Exeter where the forum occupied the site of the legionary baths.[60] In this respect, though, Lincoln and Exeter are different from the other two, for the basilicae run parallel with the intersecting streets and not across their lines. It is not impossible, therefore, that both fora, dating at Lincoln probably to the Trajanic or Hadrianic periods, and possibly slightly earlier at Exeter, were of tripartite form, with the main streets between east and west gates running through the piazzas; admittedly this would leave only little space for a temple of any size, unless it

53. op. cit. (note 8), 69. But the aisle was only constructed in a later phase.
54. *Britannia* ii (1971), 14–20.
55. op. cit. (note 16), 46.
56. Pers. comm.
57. See note 52, 71–2.
58. *Antiq. Journ.* lii (1972), 52–8.
59. op. cit. (note 16), 88–9.
60. op. cit. (note 8), fig.22.

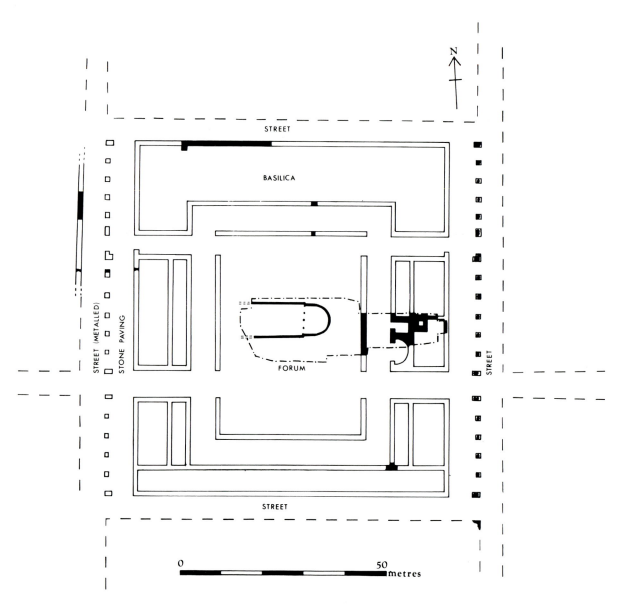

FIG. 3   Reconstructed plan of the forum at Lincoln.

was embedded in the southern range of the forum. At Lincoln the point of entry of the street on the east side is marked by the double inosculating columns of the Bailgate colonnade.[61]

Another recently excavated urban public building is the Silchester amphitheatre[62] (Fig. 4). A first-century timber phase of almost circular form was replaced by a near oval shape, also of timber in the second century, before being rebuilt in masonry in the third century. The seating banks were composed of material dug from the arena, the floor of which was sunk nearly 2m below the natural ground surface. In all three phases recesses had been built into the arena wall at the ends of the short axis, probably to act as shrines to Nemesis. In the early phases the outer revetment of the *cavea* was made of turf, which, unusually, was retained in the masonry reconstruction. One extremely interesting discovery in the arena was what was identified as an early medieval timber-framed hall, with suggestions of an enclosing palisade situated on the crest of the seating bank, coupled with fortification of the south entrance; these apparently date to the middle of the twelfth century. It is tempting, though, to ascribe an earlier date to them since the

61.   *Archaeologia* lvi (1899), 371.
62.   *Antiq. Journ.* lxv (1985), 60–78.

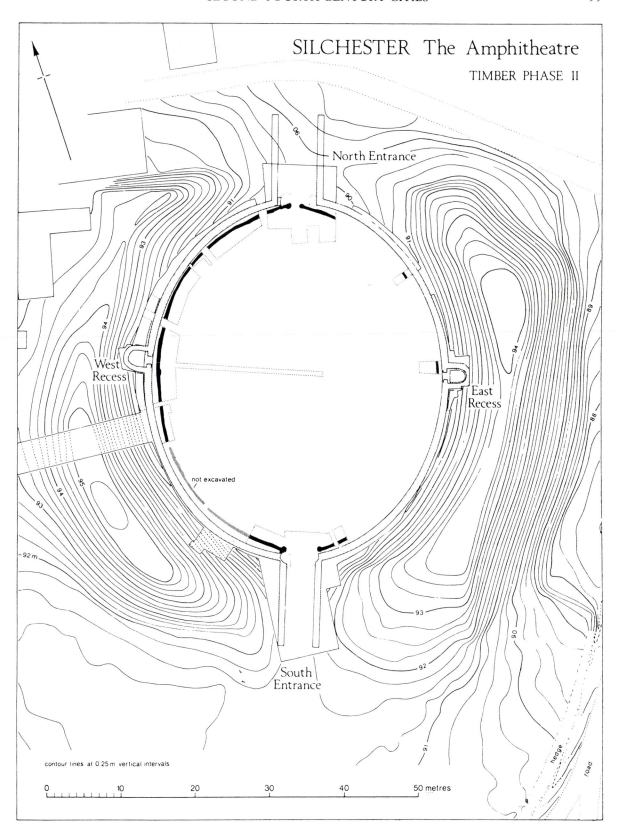

FIG. 4   The timber amphitheatre at Silchester.

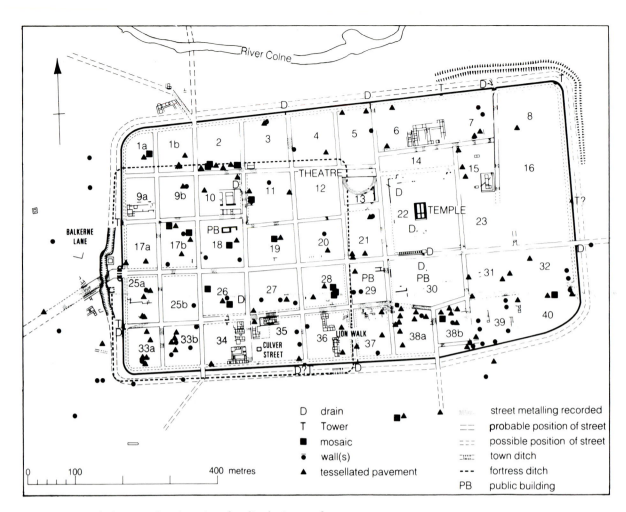

FIG. 5   Camulodunum, showing site of earlier legionary fortress.

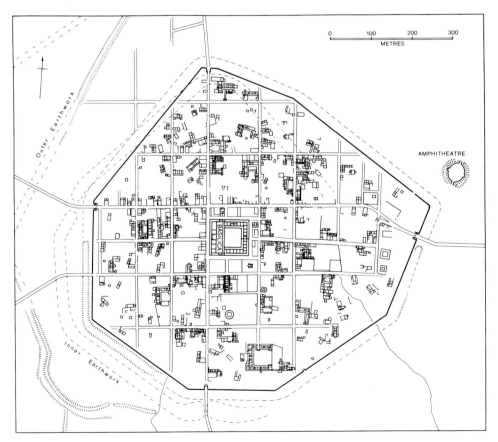

FIG. 6   Silchester in the later Roman period.

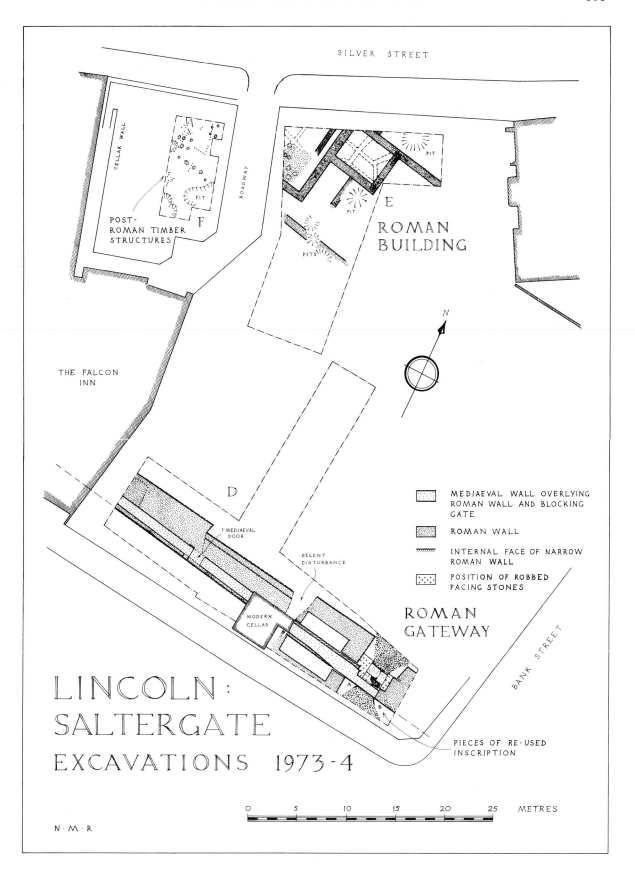

FIG. 7   Excavations at Saltergate, Lincoln: the defences and south gate of the lower town.

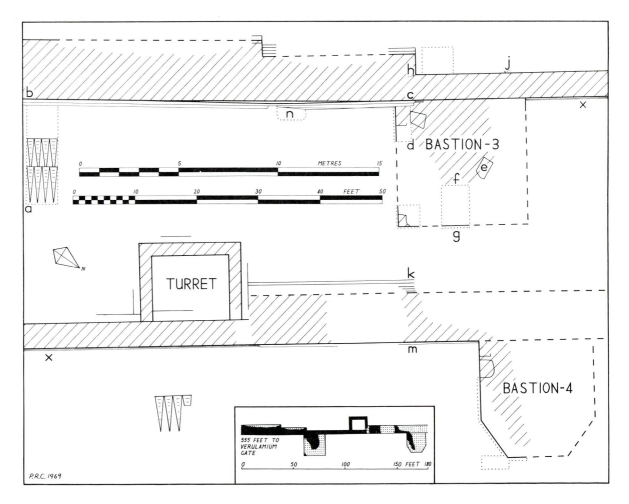

FIG. 8   A stretch of the north-east defences of Cirencester.

hall is reminiscent of a very similar building constructed in the arena of the amphitheatre at
Cirencester, where the north-east entrance passage was also fortified in timber. These structures
were associated with the only sherds of grass-tempered pottery to be found in the Cirencester
region and probably date to the fifth or sixth century.[63]

As in the past, urban fortifications still attract a good deal of attention, and it is becoming
increasingly apparent that individual circuits have a much more complex history of development
than was once thought. This is certainly true of the three *coloniae*, Colchester (Fig. 5), Lincoln and
Gloucester[64] and of Verulamium[65] and Silchester[66] (Fig. 6) where there are circuits on different
alignments, while Cirencester has produced a whole sequence of development stages on the same
alignment.[67] In view of these complexities, it is probably no longer adequate to cut comparatively narrow sections across the line in a number of different places; where possible whole
lengths should be investigated, because only by so doing can local variations from the norm be
detected. This has been done most effectively at Lincoln on the defences of both the upper and
lower enclosures[68] (Fig. 7). For instance, it is now apparent that some cities, such as Cirencester
(Fig. 8), Gloucester and both enclosures at Lincoln, were fortified by narrow-gauge walls when

63. *Antiq. Journ.* xliii (1963), 26; xliv (1964), 18. See also J.S. Wacher, 'Late Roman developments', in A. McWhirr
     (ed.), *Archaeology and History of Cirencester* (Oxford, 1976), 16.
64. M. Jones, '*Coloniae* in Britain', in Maloney and Hobley, op. cit. (note 2), 90–5.
65. S.S. Frere, *Verulamium Excavations, Vol.II* (London, 1983), 33–54.
66. M. Fulford, *Silchester Defences, 1974–80* (London, 1984).
67. e.g. *Britannia* i (1970), 227–39.
68. *Antiq. Journ.* lv (1975), 227–66; lix (1979), 50–91; M.J. Jones, *The Defences of the Upper Roman Enclosure* (London,
     1980).

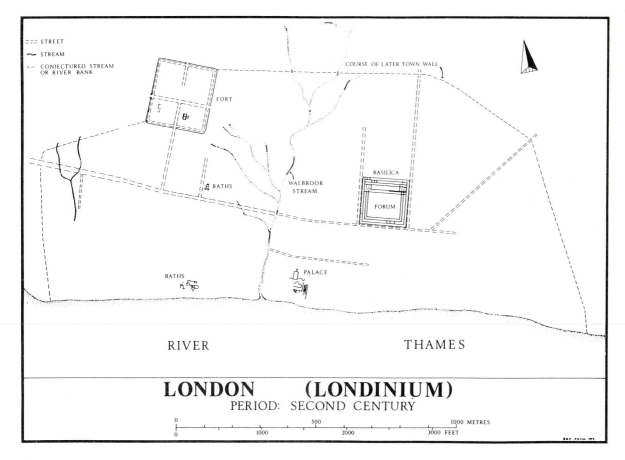

FIG. 9 London in the second century A.D.

the first masonry circuits were constructed. Subsequently, lengths were often strengthened by complete rebuilding to a wider gauge, or an additional thickening was added by cutting down into the rampart against the inside face. It is often not clear, however, when these thickenings were carried out, or even, when some lengths remained untreated, whether all the widened sections were contemporary with one another. Additional complications arise when there are internal or external towers, which are not always contemporary with the various phases of curtain wall. Furthermore, local repairs may add to the complexities, and may not always be distinguishable from the original work when seen only in short lengths at a time. It is, therefore, becoming hazardous to ascribe the *terminus post quem* for the initial construction of a walled circuit to the sum of the dates obtained from individual sections across it, no matter how numerous they are. Indeed, what is becoming increasingly apparent is that, once started, programmes of urban fortification required an almost continuous commitment on the part of the community to keep them effective and in good order.

Another public work of an exceptional nature has been revealed by the uncovering of the successive river frontages, with their quays, on the north bank of the Thames at London, the latest of which seems to date to the third century[69] (Fig. 9). A considerable length, possibly up to 800m long, ran between London Bridge and the Tower of London and consisted of a massive framework of oak beams built in a box-like pattern. In its earliest stages, the first-century quay was backed with a row of warehouses, or granaries[70] (Fig. 10).

Progress has also been made on less prominent public works. The street grid at Canterbury has been shown to be much more irregular than Frere's original projections and is probably of later

69. *Trans. London and Middx. Arch. Soc.* xxv (1974), 117– 28.
70. *Britannia* xiv (1983), 207–26.

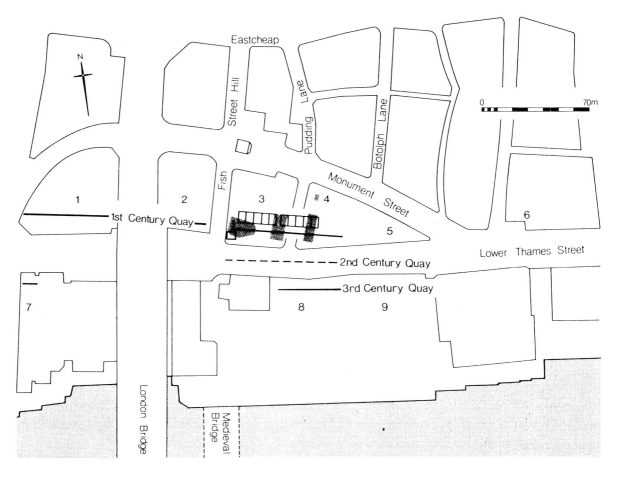

FIG. 10   Storebuildings and quays on the Thames frontage at London.

date, with the main lay-out belonging to the early second century[71] (Fig. 11). At Lincoln, more is now known of the street plan of the lower enclosure[72] (Fig. 12), while Exeter has produced evidence for a fairly regular grid.[73] The problems surrounding the water supply of Lincoln have received attention[74] and the pipe-line originally excavated by Thompson has been traced for some distance along the Nettleham Road towards the city walls; the reservoir built against the north wall has also been more extensively examined, and there is now very little doubt as to its function.[76] More remarkable though at Lincoln has been the discovery of a well of considerable dimensions situated in the east range of the forum,[77] which must have provided an alternative source of water to the rather puny amount supplied by the aqueduct.

The crucial importance of urban cemeteries is also being increasingly appreciated. Several have been excavated on a sufficient scale for evidence to be accumulated, not only on burial rites and the palaeopathology of the skeletal material, but also on various socio-economic problems. The large cemetery at Poundbury, just west of Dorchester[78] (Fig. 13), has revealed some interesting masonry mausolea, with internal mural decorations; they seem to be connected with a definite hierarchy of burials, possibly associated with family groups. Poundbury has also produced some

71. *Arch. Cant.* c (1984), 50–2.
72. M. Jones, 'New streets for old: the topography of Roman Lincoln', in Grew and Hobley, op. cit. (note 1), 86–93.
73. P.T. Bidwell, *Roman Exeter: Fortress and Town* (Exeter, 1980), 47.
74. op. cit. (note 16), 126–31.
75. *Arch. Journ.* cxi (1955), 106–28.
76. *Britannia* ii (1971), 257; vii (1976), 325; viii (1977), 390; ix (1978), 434; x (1979), 294.
77. *Britannia* xi (1980), 67.
78. Interim notes and plans in *Proc. Dorset Nat. Hist. and Arch. Soc.* lxxxviii onwards; *Current Archaeology* 20 (May 1970), 259– 60; *Britannia* ii (1971), 280–1.

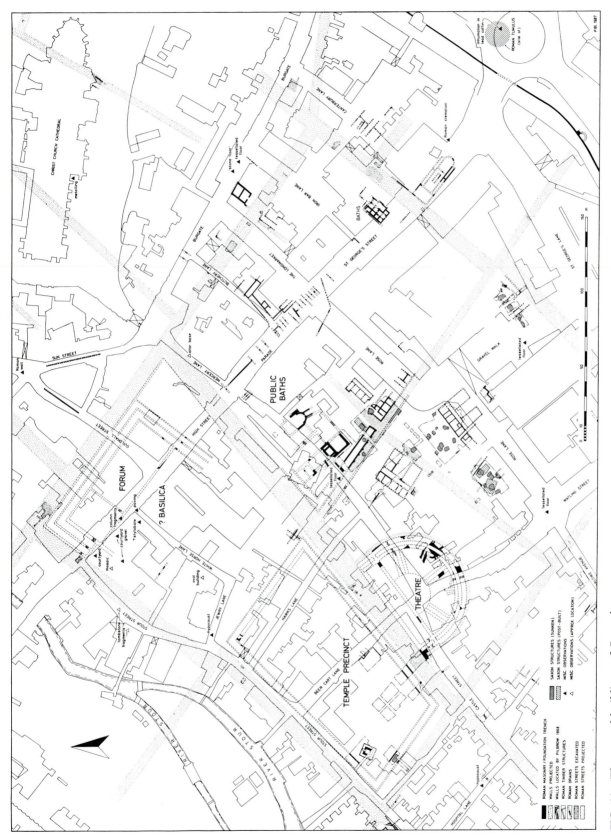

FIG. 11   The central buildings of Canterbury.

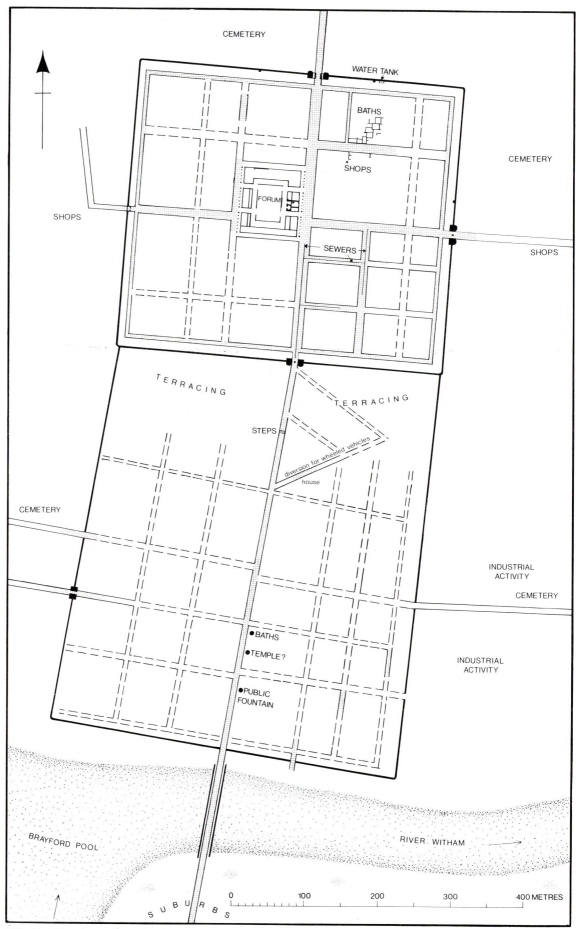

FIG. 12 Lincoln at the peak of its development.

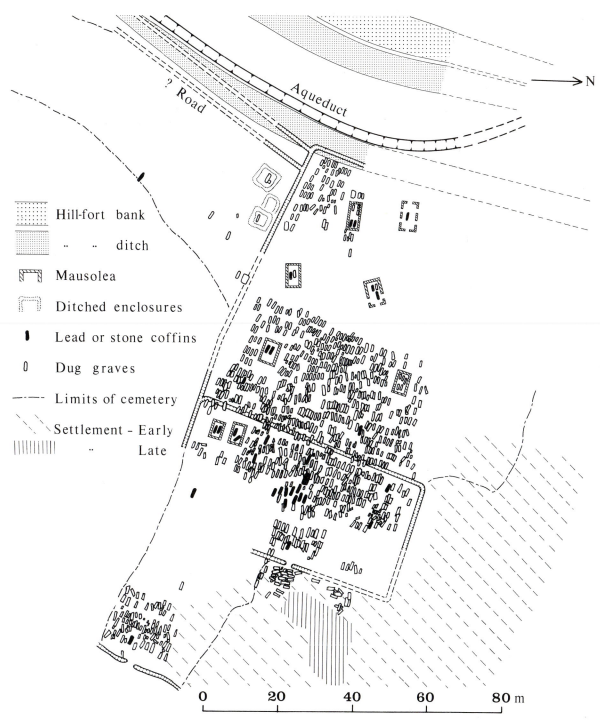

FIG. 13   The late Roman cemetery at Poundbury Camp, Dorchester, Dorset.

gypsum burials, a form of interment more widely recognised at York. The suggestion has been made that, in Britain, to which province the custom was introduced, these burials may be associated with Christianity.[79] The skeletal material from another large cemetery to the west of Cirencester,[80] threw some light, although not conclusive, on the damage that high lead concentrations might have on the human body. Most samples analysed were abnormally high in

79.   H.G. Ramm, 'The end of Roman York', in R.M. Butler (ed.), *Soldier and Civilian in Roman Yorkshire* (Leicester, 1971), 179–200; C.J.S. Green, 'The significance of plaster burials for the recognition of Christian cemeteries', in R. Reece (ed.), *Burial in the Roman World* (London, 1977), 46–52.
80.   A. McWhirr, L. Viner and C. Wells, *Romano-British Cemeteries at Cirencester* (Cirencester, 1982).

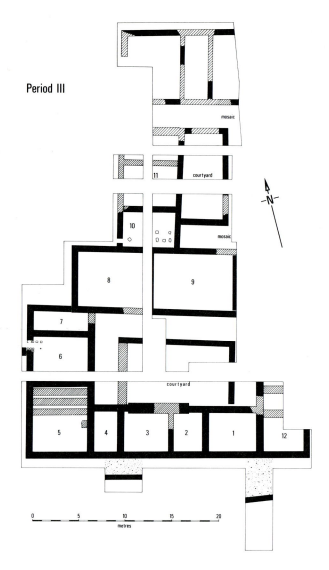

FIG. 14   Town-house at Caerwent.

lead content and it was concluded that, in some children, it may have been sufficient to cause death. What was not revealed, though, was how the lead reached the diet, since even if drinking-water had been universally carried in lead pipes, the hard water of the Cirencester region would have rendered them nearly harmless. This cemetery also produced evidence for the existence of gout among the local population; no other cases are known from Roman Britain. It may be no more than coincidence, but even today colonies of *Colchicum officinale* are found in the Cotswold region.[81] The alkaloid Colchicine and its associated compounds derived from the corms are still used as a specific remedy for gout.[82]

The recent excavation of numerous urban domestic houses and commercial premises has increased our knowledge immeasurably of these buildings. Caerwent has produced another courtyard house, on the very edge of the town in Insula I[83] (Fig. 14). The earliest structure was dated to the mid to late second century, but it was replaced by a more substantial house in the early third century, containing at least one mosaic. The courtyard house replaced it in turn probably in the late third century; it too possessed a mosaic and one room at least was heated by a hypocaust. This adds to the sum of courtyard houses at Caerwent, and, for a town of its size, its

81.   Information from Professor Clive Stace, Dept. of Botany, University of Leicester.
82.   Information from Professor Sir Robert Kilpatrick, Dept. of Medicine, University of Leicester.
83.   *Britannia* xiii (1982), 334; xiv (1983), 283; xv (1984), 270; xvi (1985), 259.

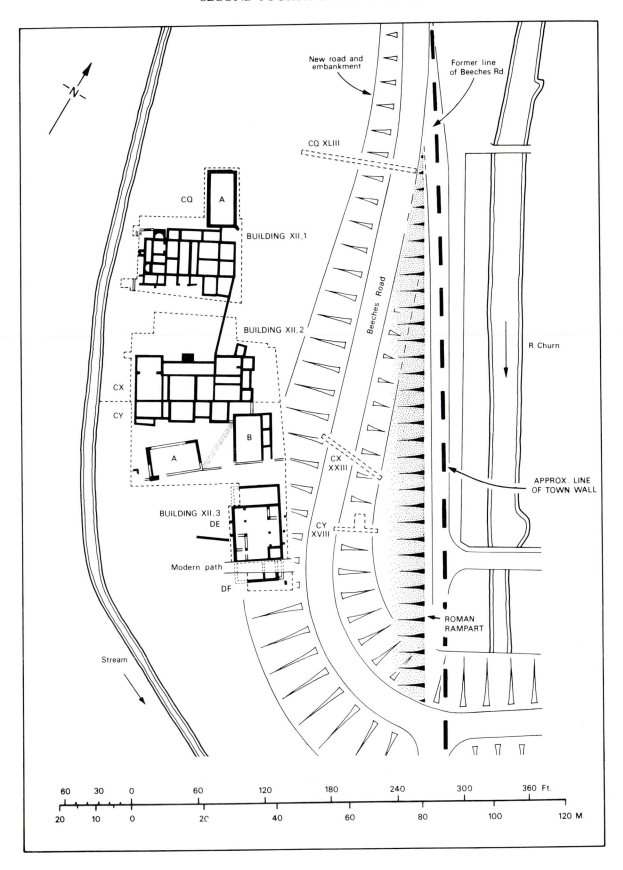

FIG. 15 Farmhouses and outbuildings of the fourth century close to the eastern defences of Cirencester.

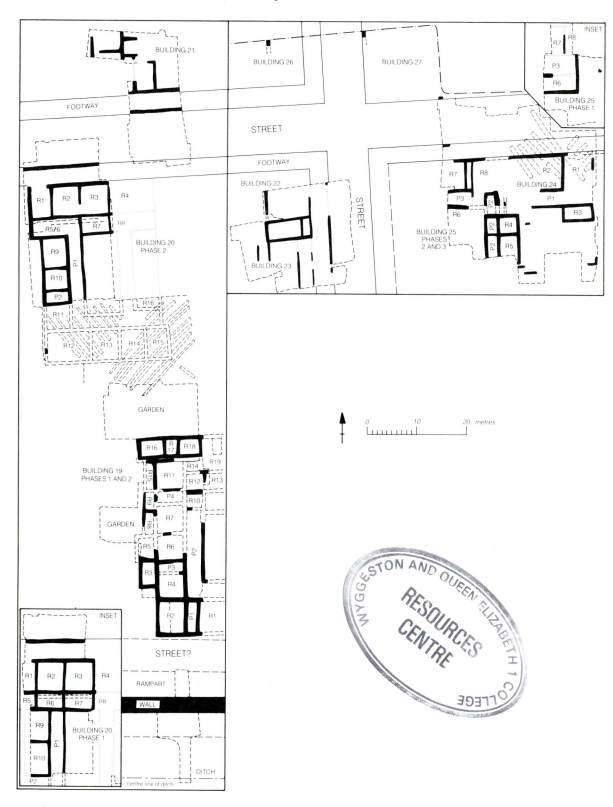

FIG. 16   Town-houses at Lion Walk, Colchester, second to fifth century.

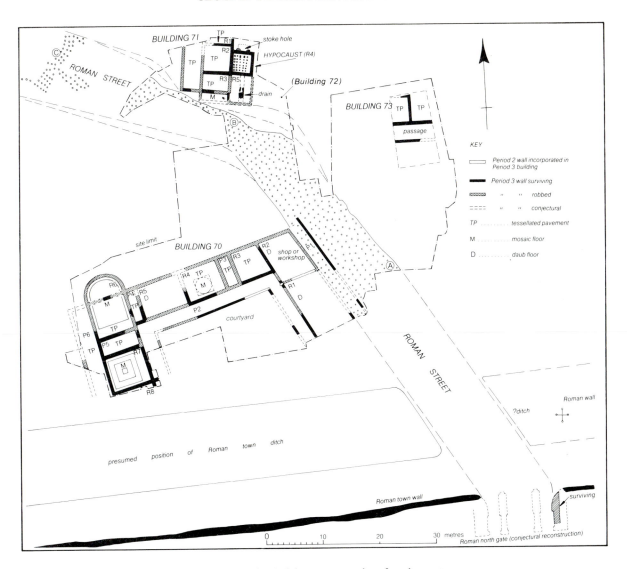

FIG. 17   Extramural houses at Middleborough, Colchester, second to fourth century.

standard of housing is remarkably high. A possible link with the nearby legionary fortress at Caerleon has been hinted at before now and is supported by the early-third-century honorific inscription to Ti. Claudius Paulinus.[84] The simplest explanation is that the city became a retirement centre for the army, but it could equally have provided residential accommodation for merchants or traders operating army contracts. Dedications to Mars Lenus Ocelus, one by a junior officer, indicate connections with both the Rhineland and the army.[85]

A group of buildings just inside the eastern fortifications at Cirencester carries the clear implication that farms existed in towns.[86] The two main dwellings of mid-fourth-century date strongly resemble countryside villas, while one of the ancillary buildings is a typical example of an aisled barn or farmhouse (Fig. 15). An iron coulter and possible evidence for smithing, together with four bone tablets for weaving and a ready-to-use stack of roofing slates in the yard might be taken to suggest the existence of a self-contained agricultural estate, farming land both inside and outside the city walls, repairing its own buildings and equipment and producing its own cloth. Support for this hypothesis comes from the animal bones recovered from the site, which show the presence of whole carcases, presumably of animals slaughtered on the premises.

In a series of very extensive excavations at Colchester, notably at Lion Walk and Culver Street,

84.   *RIB* 311.
85.   *RIB* 309, 310.
86.   A. McWhirr, *Houses in Roman Cirencester* (Cirencester, 1986).

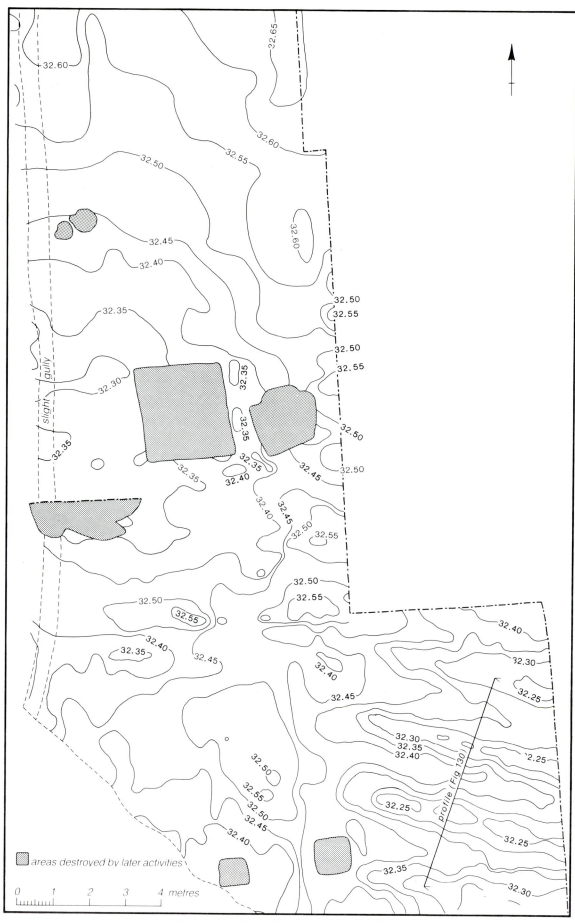

FIG. 18   Contours of the allotments at Balkerne Lane, Colchester.

a great deal of evidence has been gathered about the developed housing of, presumably, the descendants of the original veterans.[87] The layout of a number, situated along street frontages from which they were usually separated by covered pedestrian pavements, suggest that some may have had commercial connections. Such was the mid-second-century Building 20 in Lion Walk (Fig. 16). Although a substantial courtyard house, at least two of its rooms fronting a street had been workshops. Just south of it, another even larger courtyard house, Building 19, was similarly dated. It had possessed a kitchen containing a sequence of ovens. Towards the end of the third century or early in the fourth, among several other alterations, at least two mosaics were inserted, both in rooms to the rear of the house. Although they were both badly damaged, enough remained of one to show that it was based on a concentric circle pattern of a design not hitherto seen in Britain; the other, of which even less survived, contained a lion set in a semicircle and accompanied by a basket of leaves or fruit.

Colchester has also produced a good deal of evidence for extensive suburbs containing respectable buildings with mosaics and painted wall-plaster, although as in Lion Walk some of the houses seem to have been connected with shops or workshops.[88] One which lay west of the main road just after it had emerged from the north gate, had possessed two good quality mosaics of unusual design; the central panel of one of them contained a pair of wrestling cupids (Fig. 17). An additional feature of interest was found outside the Balkerne Gate over the demolished remains of a building, and dating to the second and on probably into the third century. It consisted of some nine raised beds of topsoil which had been most likely used for cultivation; each bed was some 2m wide (Fig. 18). What was grown in them is not known; vines and, or, asparagus were two suggestions made by the excavator. But they would have been perfectly suitable for growing most types of vegetable or herbs, or even fruit bushes.

A good deal of attention is at present being focused on environmental remains from urban sites. The almost unique – for its time – list of plant remains from the early excavations at Silchester has now been supported by the collection of further macro-samples and pollen from Fulford's work. This has shown that much of the landscape around the city was occupied by open heath, pasture or arable, crossed at intervals by small valley bogs containing some plant species which today are extinct in the area. Colchester has produced carbonised date-stones, presumably imported from the Mediterranean,[91] while what was probably a crate of cucumbers had been dropped in the river beside the London quay.[92] London has also contributed a lengthy list of plant remains, which include fig and mulberry.[93] There are other isolated recordings such as the stump and roots of a tree which had survived as a series of voids beneath the north range of the forum at Leicester.[94] Animal remains feature high on most sites and provide information not only on husbandry and diet but also on butchery techniques.[95]

THE FUTURE

Despite the considerable advances which have been made in both discovery and synthesis over the past two or three decades, much remains to be done. No town or city in Roman Britain is so well known that we can say with confidence that excavations are no longer needed. Yet it is also true that some sites are in greater need of exploration than others, and, in these days of limited

87.   P. Crummy, *Excavations at Lion Walk, Balkerne Lane, and Middleborough, Colchester, Essex* (Colchester, 1984).
88.   ibid.
89.   Usefully summarised by G.C. Boon, *Silchester, the Roman Town of Calleva* (Newton Abbot, 1974).
90.   M. Fulford, *Silchester Defences, 1974–80* (London, 1984), 212–23; *Guide to the Silchester Excavations: The Forum Basilica 1982–84* (Reading, 1985), 33–7.
91.   op. cit. (note 87), 40.
92.   *Journ. Arch. Science* (1977), 279.
93.   e.g. C. Hill, M. Millett, and T. Blagg, *The Roman Riverside Wall and Monumental Arch in London* (London, 1980), 78.
94.   *Britannia* iv (1973), 19.
95.   e.g. at Cirencester. J. Wacher and A. McWhirr, *Early Roman Occupation at Cirencester* (Cirencester, 1982), 211–27.

resources, somehow a middle course has to be steered between the two extremes. Many of the priorities have recently been identified and published.[96] But perhaps the most pressing need and ultimate aim is for the re-creation of the 'total' landscape of each and every city, which must include not only its visual appearance and the appearance of the surrounding countryside, but also the people who inhabited it and their way of life; they were as much a part of the landscape as the buildings which they used. Most cities in the Roman world would have been busy, noisy, dirty and smelly, despite the considerable advances that had been made in drainage and personal hygiene, and in the provision of fresh water. Disease was probably part of everyday life and life-expectation was never very great. Nor must we forget religious beliefs, local politics and the maintenance of law and order, all essential parts of the fabric of civilised urban life. Sadly, archaeology is not by itself equipped to provide all this information, especially in Britain, because of the restrictions caused by the lack of survival of certain types of evidence. But that seems to the present writer a very poor reason to ignore completely a whole range of knowledge that made up the total human condition of Romano-British cities, even if it means the creation of models after the manner of prehistory, which is but another way of saying imaginative interpretation. That is something which Roman scholars such as Haverfield, Collingwood, Richmond and Frere have been doing since long before New Archaeology was thought of. But, with the wealth of information available from the whole Roman Empire on which to draw in order to create these models, they should at least be more accurate, and altogether more dependable, than those artificially constructed by prehistorians.

96. The Roman Society, *Priorities for the Preservation and Excavation of Romano-British Sites* (London, 1985); op. cit. (note 3), 27–45.

THE ROMANO-BRITISH COUNTRYSIDE

By David Miles

It is just over half a century since R.G. Collingwood produced his elegant synthesis of the history and archaeology of Roman Britain. He summed up the countryside: '. . . by far the largest part of the inhabitants of Roman Britain were country-folk living either in villages or in isolated farm-houses, large or small, which are called villas . . . we should not be far wrong if we reckoned that at no time during the Roman period did agriculture occupy less than two thirds of the inhabitants of Britain'.[1]

Building on the work of Francis Haverfield, whose 1905 lecture to the British Academy 'The Romanization of Britain' launched a thousand undergraduate essays, Collingwood, as much as anyone, set the agenda for Romano-British studies.

The countryside has not, however, occupied centre-stage in Romano-British studies. The concern with Romanization and the Romans in Britain has led to greater emphasis on military affairs and urbanization. When archaeologists have turned to the Romano-British countryside it has usually been to the security of the well-heated, stone-founded country house, the Roman villa.

There has, nevertheless, been an enormous increase in the outpourings of data from the Romano-British countryside and remarkably the flow continues: from aerial photography, field survey and scores of excavations. It is now a commonplace that the Romano-British countryside is everywhere. The pace of discovery has brought a loss of innocence to Romano-British archaeology; an increasing awareness that the Romano-British landscape is a confusing and complex place where we are only beginning to find our way.

Collingwood did not overemphasise the importance of agriculture; in fact he probably underestimated the proportion of people engaged in farming. Even in the late 18th century it required nineteen farmers to support one town-dweller. By Collingwood's own day nineteen farmers could support fifty six town-dwellers, and now, as everyone knows, one farm worker can feed over fifty others and still accumulate a grain mountain. In Roman Britain the proportion of people engaged in primary food production was probably over ninety percent.[2] The Roman peasant ate most of what he (or she) produced, and produced most of what he ate.

Only a very small proportion of farmers would have lived in the thousand or so villas whose locations we currently know. Collingwood put the peasants in villages which, from a modern English view point, seems a not unreasonable place for them. The Romano-British village has undergone an interesting transformation, which is itself a lesson in archaeological interpretation. In 1877, during the construction of the Oxford University Examination Schools, a lunar landscape of small holes was excavated. Contemporary photographs label this as 'Ancient British Village'. Haverfield's villages, like that under the Examination Schools, were, in fact, clusters of pits (not 'pit dwellings') which Gerhard Bersu, at Little Woodbury, showed to be underground silos principally for the storage of corn. The village went out of fashion with the discredited pit

---

1. R.G. Collingwood and J.N.L. Myres, *Roman Britain and the English Settlements* (1936), 208.
2. K. Hopkins, *Conquerors and Slaves* (1978), 15.

dwelling. In the 1960's the Romano-British village began to re-emerge in the archaeological literature.[3] Aerial photography, in particular, appeared to show agglomerations of village-like settlements. Too often, however, assumptions have been made which lack definition and precision.[4]

Villages remain remarkably elusive in the Romano-British landscape. In fact in a recent book on the subject, with the possible exception of some roadside settlements, convincing villages are notable for their absence.[5] Although it is true in settlement studies that disorder is reality, nevertheless more careful classification, integrated into problem-orientated survey and excavation, is still required to tackle the vexed question of Romano-British settlement types.

Romano-British studies have been accused of being stuffy; most vividly and recently by Barry Cunliffe who conjured up a picture of *Britannia* as: 'an aged, cossetted old lady, sitting immobile in an airless room reeking of stale scent, fawned upon by a bevy of tireless, dedicated servants.'[6]

It is true that Romano-British archaeologists have been slow to adopt the ways of their prehistoric colleagues. A gruff broadside was delivered against the purveyors of abstract and mechanistic models of the New Geography which belatedly attempted to intrude in the 1970's.[7] Nevertheless it would be Luddite to ignore the lessons of the new 'ologies' which have encouraged archaeology to become more rigorous and wide-ranging. Ironically, however, the theoretical pendulum has in some ways swung back towards the traditional approaches, with the re-emergence of interest in the individual[8] and 'thick description' of unique events.[9]

The later 70's and 80's have also seen the emergence out of New Archaeology of 'Middle Range Theory',[10] the most useful aspect of which is the explicit attempt to understand the formation processes of the archaeological record. There is a need for this in landscape archaeology where only recently (in contrast to palaeobiology) has a debate begun about the quality of data and the means of its survival, collection and interpretation. The growth of interest in this aspect of archaeology is perhaps reflected in the move away from chronologically orientated research questions to categories of evidence which make up the subdivisions of the most recent general policy statement from the Council for British Archaeology (for example aerial archaeology and historic buildings).[11]

Aerial archaeology has provided us with the most prolific, albeit sometimes confusing, view of the Romano-British countryside. In the 60's and early 70's, Professor St Joseph and his colleagues in Cambridge produced an endless flow of magnificent photographs in the pages of *Antiquity*. These were mostly in the form of impressive site portraits; they told us little of the wider context

3. S.J. Hallam, 'Villages in Roman Britain: some evidence', *Antiq. Journ.* xliv (1964), 19–32. H.C. Bowen and P.J. Fowler, 'Romano-British rural settlement in Dorset and Wiltshire', in C. Thomas (ed.), *Rural Settlement in Roman Britain* CBA Res.Rep. 7 (1966), 43–68.
4. S.S. Frere and J.K.S. St. Joseph, *Roman Britain from the Air* (1938), 201, 205.
5. R. Hanley, *Villages in Roman Britain* (1986). B.K. Roberts, *Rural settlement in Britain* (1979), 83. Referring to medieval and post-medieval villages 'although villages generally possessed churches, smithies, and specialist tradesmen and craftsmen not found in hamlets, all had a basic dependence on the land'.
6. B. Cunliffe, 'Images of Britannia', *Antiquity* lviii (1984), 175–78.
7. S.S. Frere, 'The Origin of Small Towns', in W. Rodwell and T. Rowley (eds.), *Small Towns in Roman Britain* BAR 15 (1975), 4. For a more recent summary of geographical approaches to settlement studies see R.W. Paynter, 'Expanding the Scope of Settlement Analysis', in J.A. Moore and A.S. Keene (eds.), *Archaeological Hammers and Theories* (1983), 233–275.
8. I. Hodder, *Reading the Past* (1986), 6–11.
9. B.G. Trigger, 'Archaeology at the Crossroads: What's New?', *Annual Rev. Anthrop.* xiii (1984), 275–300. J. Bintliff, 'A Review of contemporary perspectives on the 'Meaning' of the past', in J. Bintliff (ed.), *Extracting Meaning from the Past* (1988), 25–26.
10. L.R. Binford, 'Meaning, inference and the archaeological record', in C. Renfrew and S. Shennan (eds.), *Ranking, Resource and Exchange* (1982), 161: 'I would suggest that the accuracy with which we can infer the past is directly related to the degree that our uniformitarian assumptions are justifiable. Concern with the justification of such assumptions and with the development of strongly warranted means of giving meaning to our contemporary observations made on the archaeological record is what I have called middle range research'.
11. C. Thomas (ed.), *Research Objectives in British Archaeology* (1983). M. Morris, 'Changing Perceptions of the Past: the Bronze Age – A Case Study', in J. Bintliff (ed.), *Extracting meaning from the Past* (1988), 76.

of the sites they revealed. The geographical mapping approach pioneered by Major Allen in the Thames valley fifty years ago[12] was largely neglected in the post-war period. The major research emphasis was on military archaeology.[13]

The most important advance in the use of aerial reconnaissance for the study of the Romano-British countryside was the appearance in 1970 of the Royal Geographical Society's study of the Roman Fenland.[14] For the first time this revealed the extent of the impact of farming and settlement on the landscape in the Roman period. Largely uncluttered by earlier or later occupation, well preserved, rich in organic remains, it is not surprising that C.W. Philips believed 'the only obstacle to clearing up the whole question of the Roman occupation of the Fens was the sheer magnitude of the task'. Unfortunately the archaeological response was belated; concerted research on a substantial scale has followed only in the wake of extensive destruction by ploughing and drainage.

In the 1970's the mapping of aerial photographic evidence became the norm with a series of surveys of the Thames valley and the volumes by the Royal Commission for Historic Monuments (England), notably in Northamptonshire.[15] The same period saw the emergence of a nationwide series of county or regional Sites and Monuments Records. These also promoted the mapping of aerial data.

In addition to the Fens there have been other achievements of particular significance for Romano-British rural studies. In south Yorkshire and north Nottinghamshire Derrick Riley's aerial surveys have revealed apparently planned systems of fields on a massive scale.[16] The most common and distinctive fields – the so-called brickwork plan – are made up of ditched strips 50 to 100 m wide, subdivided into areas of 0.5 to 2.8 ha. Small-scale excavations indicate that these were farmed in the later Roman period. Their date of origin, presumed to be in the Roman period, is, however, uncertain. (Fig. 1).

Another major breakthrough has been the discovery of complex settlement patterns in the Solway Plain region of north-west England and south-west Scotland.[17] In the drought summers of 1975 and 1976 two hundred previously unknown sites were found from the air in north Cumbria south of Hadrian's Wall. In the following two years about 70 further sites were located north of the Solway. At the local level it is now possible to see a fort such as Old Carlisle in the context of its *vicus*, road and trackway systems, and surrounding farmsteads. On a larger scale, comparisons can be made between settlement types and densities north and south of Hadrian's Wall, opening up fascinating areas of research into the impact of Rome's northernmost frontier on the native communities.

Both of these exercises in systematic aerial reconnaissance show the dangers of assumptions based on negative evidence. The valleys of the Highland zone have often been portrayed as forested or liver-fluke infested, avoided by the Romano-British farmers who clung to their supposedly preferred fell-slopes.[18] The new evidence indicates that all suitable sites in the Solway

12. G.W.G. Allen, 'Discovery from the Air', *Aerial Archaeology* x (1984), fig. 17.
13. Frere and St. Joseph, op. cit. (note 7). The emphasis on military archaeology is reflected in the contents: 125 pages devoted to military sites, 34 to towns and 32 to the countryside. Similarly in Maxwell and Wilson's survey of recent aerial reconnaissance in Roman Britain (*Britannia* xviii (1987), 1–48) 40 pages are devoted to military sites and 2 to rural settlement.
14. C.W. Phillips (ed.), *The Fenland in Roman Times* (1970).
15. D. Benson and D. Miles, *The Upper Thames Valley* (1974). T. Gates, *The Middle Thames Valley* (1975). R. Leach, *The Upper Thames Valley in Gloucestershire and Wiltshire* (1977). C. Taylor, 'Roman settlements in the Nene Valley: the impact of recent archaeology', in P.J. Fowler (ed.), *Recent Work in Rural Archaeology* (1975), 107–120.
16. D.N. Riley, *Early Landscape from the Air: Studies of Crop Marks in South Yorkshire and North Nottinghamshire* (1980).
17. N. Higham and B. Jones, *The Carvetii* (1985). South of the Wall the authors record sites at the rate of 1 per 3.6 km². North the sites are more heavily defended, sparser at 1 per 10.5 km² and less frequently associated with fields. The mid 1970's also saw major increases in data even in supposedly well known areas. There was for example a 30% increase in cropmarks between 1972 and 1976 in the Upper Thames Valley.
18. Collingwood, op. cit. (note 1), 177–78, for the supposed valleyward shift of population from the primary zones on higher ground.

FIG. 1 "Brickwork" plan of fields at Babworth, Nottinghamshire. (D.N. Riley, 5 viii 1977)

Plain and valleys of the Annan and Nith, notably the sand and gravel ridges, were in fact occupied. These are also the most favourable areas for agriculture; hence earthworks are obliterated by subsequent generations of ploughmen as in the valleys of Midland and Southern England.

Aerial photography has also contributed to the study of surviving earthwork sites, particularly in north and south-west Britain. At Eller Beck, for example, at about 200m above the Lune Valley an extensive Romano-British landscape of settlements and fields spreads across 60 hectares. Irregular paddocks are superimposed on rectilinear fields at Eller Beck.[19] This kind of evidence has generated interesting hypotheses about the extension of arable farming on to marginal land, promoted by the demands of local military garrisons. After the high tide mark of second-century cultivation, pastoralism may have increased.

The simple, albeit persistent, concept of the Highland/Lowland zone has increasingly been brought into question.[20] The widespread belief that the garrisons of the pastoral north were supplied with grain by the breadbasket of the lowland south was challenged by Manning[21] on the grounds of military logistics. Recent discoveries support the view of the north and west as a more complex mosaic of upland and lowland resources with mixed farming strategies adapting to the pressures of population growth and trading networks. In reaction to the Roman-orientated interests of the older generation of archaeologists there is a trend to see the impact of Romanization on the natives as shallow and short-lived.[22]

In contrast to the south, chronology remains a major problem in the rural archaeology of the north and west. George Jobey, the pioneer of northern settlement studies, has emphasised the point, which is reiterated in several recent major reviews. When is Roman not Roman?[23] In other words how can pre- and post-Roman Conquest trends and changing settlement patterns be analysed in the absence of precise dating techniques? The validity of stone querns as a reliable dating-aid has been successfully challenged.[24] At Thorpe Thewles, Cleveland, a welcome, but rare, example of large-scale excavation, the majority of the nineteen querns were shown to derive from secondary contexts or have secondary uses.[25] Thorpe Thewles has also produced a rare example of independent dating (thermoluminescence) in an area where radiocarbon determinations from settlement sites are sparse, and a period where accuracy of this technique is questionable.

Aerial archaeology, then, has launched rural studies in the Roman north and west into one of its potentially most exciting phases. It has encouraged archaeologists to perceive the past on the scale of the geographer. The trend is not new, witness the work of Sir Cyril Fox, O.G.S.

19. N. Higham, *The Northern Counties to AD 1000* (1986), 203–4.
20. C. Fox, *The Personality of Britain* (1943). For more recent discussion see P.J. Fowler, 'Lowland landscapes: culture, time and Personality', in S. Limbrey and J.G. Evans (eds.), *The effect of Man on the landscape: the lowland zone* CBA Res.Rep.21 (1978), 1–12.
21. W.H. Manning, 'The Economic Influences on land use in the military areas of the Highland Zone during the Roman period', in J.G. Evans, S. Limbrey and H. Cleere (eds.), *The effect of Man on the landscape: the highland zone* CBA Res. Rep. 11 (1975), 112–6. For a view of the economic backwardness of the Highland zone see A.L.F. Rivet, 'The Rural Economy of Roman Britain', in H. Temporini and W. Haase (eds.), *Aufstieg und Niedergang der römischen Welt* (1975), 328–363.
22. J.C. Chapman and H.C. Mytum (eds.), *Settlement in North Britain 1000 BC – AD 1000* BAR 118 (1983) see page VII, and for the contrasting views of the 'Roman interlude' see paper by Jones and Walker (185–204) and Bennet (209).
23. G. Jobey, 'Between Tyne and Fourth: some problems', in P. Clack and S. Haselgrove (eds.), *Rural Settlement in the Roman North* (1982), 10. For an overview of settlement in Wales see M. Lloyd-Jones, *Society and Settlement in Wales and the Marches 500 BC to AD 1100* BAR 121 (1984). The problems of settlement analysis in the South West are discussed in N. Johnson and P. Rose, 'Defended settlement in Cornwall: an illustrated discussion', in D. Miles (ed.), *The Romano-British Countryside* BAR 103 (1982), 151–207. Recent overviews are provided by N. Higham, op. cit. (note 19), esp. 145–234. M. Todd, *The South-West to AD 1000* (1987), 151–235.
24. D.H. Heslop, 'The Study of Beehive Querns', *Scottish Arch. Rev.* v.1.2 (1988), 59–65.
25. D.H. Heslop, *The Excavation of an Iron Age Settlement at Thorpe Thewles, Cleveland, 1980–1982* CBA Res.Rep. 65 (1987).

Crawford and Cecil Curwen in the 1920's and 30's.[26] However, there has been a resurgence of interest in wider regional strategies. The trend has, in part, been fertilised by ideas from the United States, Binford's argument that 'the methodology most appropriate to the task of isolating and studying processes of cultural change and evolution is one which is regional in scope and executed with the aid of research designs based on the principles of probability sampling'.[27] Binford's argument, supported by the examples of geographers and British landscape-archaeologists,[28] has influenced the approach of English Heritage (HBMC) to rescue archaeology funding and the work of many younger archaeologists.

The growth of interest in area survey has complemented aerial reconnaissance. For political and logistical reasons survey has been a particularly important aspect of Classical archaeology in the Mediterranean.[29] In Britain such surveys are more difficult owing to heavier soils, the problems of access to private land, extensive pastoralism and the lower visibility of much cultural material. In addition, co-ordinated surveys as part of an explicit regional policy are hampered by the divisions and lack of coherent structure in British archaeology itself.

Nevertheless, there has been some interesting, albeit relatively small-scale work in this field: the stratified random sampling organised by Shennan in east Hampshire, the Maddle Farm Project around a Roman Villa on the Berkshire Downs, the surveys of Roman landscapes in the Fens and the north west Essex.[30] Such surveys are helping to overcome the bias of the 'honeypot' approach to Roman Britain, the attraction to highly visible, high-status sites with substantial buildings and the neglect of the minor sites which are an integral part of the complex rural landscape. In particular so-called 'off-site archaeology' is promoting the investigation of activity areas and fields beyond the confines of the site itself.

It is only through such surveys, combined with aerial photography and a problem-orientated strategy of excavation, that the important questions about the Romano-British countryside can be tackled. The exponential increase in sites discovered in the past twenty years has already led to drastic revisions in the estimates of the population of Roman Britain – from three hundred thousand to four million or more.[31] But as Sir Mortimer Wheeler said in 1930, 'One guess is as bad as another'. Jones has provided a powerful theoretical argument for a proposed increase of population in later Roman Britain. Better structured fieldwork, combined with cemetery and settlement studies, is required if research into the fundamental problem of population is to progress.

Excavations have always played a major part in the study of Roman Britain. In the past twenty years they have become bigger, more complex and more numerous. Unfortunately they often remain unpublished. They are also difficult to synthesise, in part because of the lack of agreed research strategies and sampling design.

---

26. C. Curwen, *Prehistoric Sussex* (1929). C. Fox, *The Archaeology of the Cambridge Region* (1923). For a fuller discussion of the development of field archaeology see P. Ashbee, 'Field Archaeology: its origins and development', in P.J. Fowler (ed.), *Archaeology and the Landscape* (1972), 58–74.

27. Lewis Binford's influential paper 'A Consideration of Archaeological Research Design' was originally delivered in 1963 and published in *American Antiquity* xxix (1964), 425–441. It became more widely available to British audiences in L.R. Binford, *An Archaeological Perspective* (1972), 135–162.

28. For a minority British response see J.F. Cherry, C. Gamble and S. Shennan (eds.), *Sampling in Contemporary British Archaeology* BAR 50 (1978).

29. O.R. Keller and D.W. Rupp, *Archaeological Survey in the Mediterranean Area* BAR Int. Ser. 155 (1983).

30. S. Shennan, *Experiments in the Collection and Analysis of Archaeological Survey Data: the East Hants Survey* (1985). See pages 79–87 for the Roman period, which responded best to surface survey owing to the durability of pottery which is also relatively well dated. V. Gaffney and M. Tingle, 'The tyranny of the site: method and theory in field survey', *Scottish Arch. Rev.* iii.2 (1984), 135–140. eidem, 'The Maddle Farm (Berks) project and micro-regional analysis', in S. Macready and F.H. Thompson (eds.), *Archaeological Field Survey in Britain and Beyond* (1985), 66–73. T.M. Williamson, 'The Roman Countryside: settlement and agriculture in North West Essex', *Britannia* xv (1984), 225–30. For a more recent account of this work see *Essex Arch. and Hist. Journ.* xvii (1987). C. Haselgrove, M. Millett and I. Smith (eds.), *Archaeology from the Ploughsoil: studies in the collection and interpretation of field survey data* (1985).

31. For references on the subject of population see M.E. Jones, 'Climate, Nutrition and Disease: a hypothesis of Romano-British population', in P.J. Casey (ed.), *The End of Roman Britain* BAR 71 (1979), 251, note 81.

The fascination of the Romano-British archaeologist with the villa has often been criticised as an example of over-compartmentalising the subject.[32] However, changes of approach have led to important advances. These were signalled by Graham Webster's agenda for villa studies in 1969.[33] Webster listed four main aspects: regional surveys, using aerial photography to show the spatial relationship to other villas, farms and fields; the restudy of earlier excavation reports; a long-term programme of total excavation of villas of different type and background; the study of continuity from the Late Iron Age and into the Anglo-Saxon period. The thrust of research has proved to be very much in these directions, with in addition the powerful assistance of palaeobiology.[34]

It is now customary to see the Romano-British villa as part of an operating agricultural system. The archaeologist's view has largely shifted from the house to the surrounding landscape. Nevertheless the villa as architecture has generated interesting research. D.J. Smith's work on mosaics has set many villas within a framework of regional styles and influences and emphasised their prosperity in the fourth century.[35]

The study of villa plans has also generated a healthy and persistent interest in the social aspects of Romano-British rural settlement. J.T. Smith, for example, has argued that 'the transformation of Celtic material culture through the adoption of Roman methods produced types of house-plan which expressed existing social relations, and it can be assumed that social relations were closely linked to land tenure'.[36] This Celtic joint-proprietorship can be seen, Smith argues, in the mirror-image architecture or multiple houses of 'Unit-system villas' such as Chedworth or Bignor. In the face of increasing prosperity and Romanization, Celtic joint-proprietorship, it can be argued, breaks down in the fourth century. In contrast J.T. Smith's more modest Hall-villas have been seen as a reflection of Gallic immigration in the late third or fourth century on the basis of architectural parallels with Gallia Belgica.[37]

Attempts have also been made to relate Romano-British social structure to the Welsh system codified in the tenth-century *Hwyel Dda*, in particular the system of *tir gwelyawg*, associated with free tribesmen and their families and *tir cyfrif*, which related to bondsmen and the township community.[38]

Mr Stevens has himself said 'You can dig up a villa but you cannot dig up its land-tenure'. Nevertheless analogy and model-building on the basis of literary evidence remain a valid and stimulating, if often controversial, aspect of Romano-British rural studies.

Villa excavation reports often seem particularistic, with a strong emphasis on badly sampled artefacts. Nevertheless, as Webster argued, detailed individual studies are required if patterns and processes are to emerge. In the Chilterns, for example, a group of villas in the hinterland of Verulamium has been investigated which show continuity from the pre-Conquest period (Gorhambury and Park Street) and a high level of Romanization by the later first century

32.   G. Webster, 'The Future of Villa Studies', in A.L.F. Rivet (ed.), *The Roman Villa in Britain* (1969), 217–249.

33.   See Jones, below, pp. 127–34.

34.   D.J. Smith, 'The Mosaic Pavements', in A.L.F. Rivet (ed.), *The Roman Villa in Britain* (1969), 71–125.

35.   J.T. Smith, 'Villas as a key to social structure', in M. Todd (ed.), *Studies in the Romano-British Villa* (1978), 149–185.

36.   J.T. Smith, 'Villa plans and social structure in Britain and Gaul', *Bulletin de l'Institute Latine et de Centre de recherches A. Piganiol* 17 (1982), 321–36. K. Branigan, 'Gauls in Gloucestershire', *Trans. Bristol Glos. Arch. Soc.* xcii (1973), 82–95. Though against this argument see M. Todd, 'Villa and Fundus', in K. Branigan and D. Miles (eds.), *The Economies of Romano-British Villas* (1988), 17.

37.   C.E. Stevens, 'The social and economic aspects of rural settlement', in C. Thomas (ed.), *Rural settlement in Roman Britain* (1966), 108–128. M. Lloyd-Jones, op. cit. (note 23), 194–203.

38.   For an argument against C.E. Stevens' poor man's villas, economically restricted by *tir gwelyawg*, see K. Branigan, 'Pavement and Poverty – the Chiltern Villas', *Britannia* ii (1971), 109–116. For the same view 'Archaeology of course cannot provide answers about property relations' but accompanied by a valuable attempt to relate literary and physical evidence see C.R. Whittaker, 'Rural labour in three Roman provinces', in P. Garnsey (ed.), *Non-Slave Labour in the Greco-Roman World* Cambridge Philological Society suppl. Vol.6 (1980), 73–99.

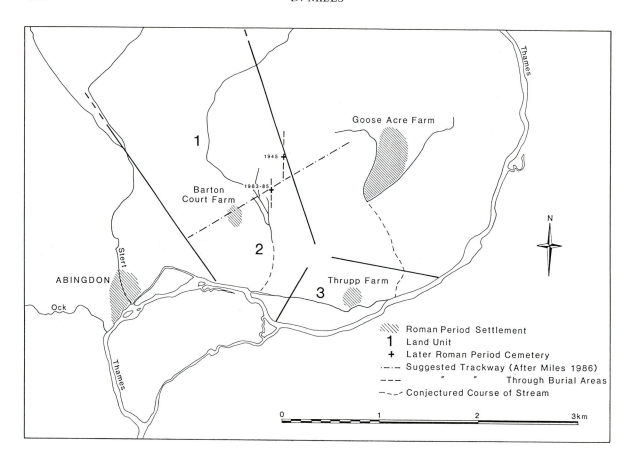

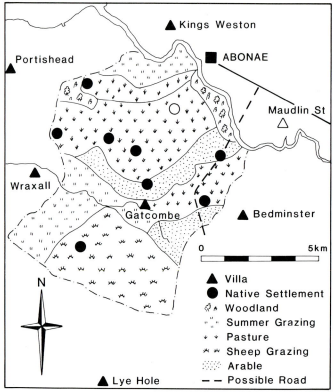

FIG. 2   Hypothetical Romano-British estates at Barton Court (Oxon.) and Gatcombe (Avon).

(Gadebridge Park, Boxmoor) with further expansion of villa building in the second century (Latimer, High Wycombe).[39]

In other areas such as Kent, Essex and Sussex, Roman villas appeared at an even earlier date in the first century A.D., in the 60's and 70's, notably spectacular buildings such as Fishbourne, Eccles and Southwick. It has been suggested that these may have been founded with capital brought from outside Britain, whether for the benefit of allied local aristocracy or by *negotiatores*, organising trade with the new province.[40]

Throughout south-eastern Britain villas achieved their greatest prosperity in the fourth century. This can best be explained in terms of agricultural success and slowly accumulating capital. However, villas were not exclusively agricultural; other activities such as quarrying, brick, tile and pottery manufacture, shale production, fish farming and iron-working have been identified. Gadebridge Park, with its huge swimming pool, may have even for a short period been a health farm or spa.[41]

Nevertheless, agriculture was the basis of the villa economy and increasingly it has taken centre-stage in Romano-British research. Landscape studies, aided by environmental sampling and experimental archaeology have increased the sophistication of model building of agricultural systems.[42] Such approaches were pioneered by Applebaum[43] using the evidence that was then available, notably and contentiously, the buildings themselves. Studies of the land exploited by villas at Shakenoak (Oxon.) Gatcombe (Avon) and Barton Court Farm (Oxon.), have integrated multi-disciplinary approaches to generate models of hypothetical estates[44] (Fig. 2). It would be naive to believe that a villa's land necessarily coalesced in one block. However, these studies clarify our assumptions and allow them to be tested against data which otherwise looms with overwhelming complexity.

Larger scale approaches to Roman landscapes, both through survey and excavation, also inevitably clarify the questions of continuity which Graham Webster advocated. Traces of Late Iron Age buildings are well known under villas such as Park Street. However, investigations on a massive scale at Claydon Pike (Gloucs.) and Stanwick (Northants.) are producing much more coherent evidence about the extensive nature of Late Iron Age farming.[45] The strategy behind such regional projects is to investigate the full range of settlement types within a variety of landscapes. At Claydon Pike, for example, native settlements and fields, Romanized farms, estate centres, roads, cemeteries and shrines were integrated into the micro-topography of marshes, streams, dry islands, woodland and pasture. (Fig. 3)

Similar projects are taking place in the North at Holme-on-Spalding Moor, an area in which rural industry is important, and on the Yorkshire Wolds, where the relationship between

39.   D.S. Neal, *The Excavation of a Roman Villa in Gadebridge Park, Hemel Hempstead 1963–68* (1974). idem, 'The growth and decline of villas in the Verulamium area', in M. Todd (ed.), *Studies in the Romano-British Villa* (1978), 33–58. K. Branigan, *Latimer* (1971). idem, *The Catuvellauni* (1985), 103–10.

40.   M. Todd, 'Villas and Romano-British Society', in M. Todd (ed.), *Studies in the Romano-British Villa* (1978), 220–202. B. Cunliffe, *Excavations at Fishbourne 1961–69* (1971).

41.   K. Branigan, 'Specialisation in Villa Economies', in K. Branigan and D. Miles, *Economies of Romano-British villas* (1988), 42–50.

42.   P.J. Reynolds, *Iron Age Farm: the Butser Experiment* (1979). P.J. Reynolds and J.K. Langley, 'Romano-British corn-drying ovens: an experiment', *Arch. Journ.* cxxxvi (1979), 27–42. Work at Butser has revealed the spectacular grain yields possible to farmers using Iron Age and Romano-British technology. Corn-drying ovens are interpreted as used for malting barley. It is still possible, however, that grain parching prior to threshing was a function of these areas.

43.   S. Applebaum, 'Roman Britain' in H.P.R. Finberg (ed.), *The Agrarian History of England and Wales* (1972). idem, 'Some observations on the economy of the Roman Villas at Bignor, Sussex', *Britannia* vi (1975), 118–32.

44.   S. Applebaum, 'The Agriculture of Shakenoak Villa' in A.C.C. Brodribb, A.R. Hands and D.R. Walker, *Excavations at Shakenoak* V (1978), 186–200. G. Barker and D. Webley, 'An integrated economy for Gatcombe', in K. Branigan, *Gatcombe Roman Villa* (1979) BAR 44, 198–200. M. Jones, 'Towards a model of the villa estate', in D. Miles (ed.), *Archaeology at Barton Court Farm* CBA Res. Rep. 50 (1986), 38–42.

45.   For Claydon Pike see: D. Miles, 'Romano-British settlement in the Gloucestershire Thames Valley', in A. Saville (ed.), *Archaeology in Gloucestershire* (1984), 197–203. The Stanwick excavations in D. Neal, *Britannia* xx (1989).

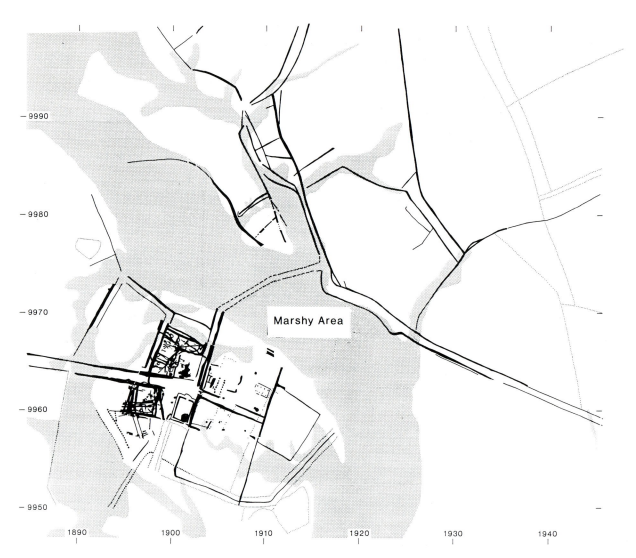

FIG. 3   Claydon Pike, Lechlade, Gloucestershire: the Romano-British complex of the late first/early second century.

ladder-shaped settlement and later villas such as Rudston is being clarified.[46] Opportunities for intensive landscape studies are also provided by new towns. At Milton Keynes a series of Roman sites have been excavated close to Magiovinium including the extensive villa at Bancroft and lesser farmsteads at Wymbush and Stantonbury.[47]

The Roman countryside is constantly producing new types of site. One of the most spectacular is the unique tower-like building at Stonea in the Fens, part of a complex which was probably central to the Roman organisation of the surrounding peasant landscape.[48] The Fenland project, like many others, is increasingly revealing the Iron Age roots which lie behind the Roman colonization of the second century. Nevertheless the Roman impact on the landscape is impressive. While there were few major improvements in technology, the scale of farming, its

46.   M. Millett and P. Halkon, 'Landscape and Economy: recent fieldwork and excavation around Holme-on-Spalding Moor', in J. Price and P.R. Wilson (eds.), *Recent Research in Roman Yorkshire* BAR 193 (1988), 37–47. H.G. Ramm, 'Aspects of the Roman Countryside in East Yorkshire', also in Price and Wilson, 81–88. H.G. Ramm, 'Native Settlements East of the Pennines', in K. Branigan (ed.), *Rome and the Brigantes* (1980), 28–40.

47.   D.C. Mynard, *Roman Milton Keynes: Excavation and Fieldwork 1971–82* Bucks Arch. Soc. Monograph Ser.1 (1987). For Bancroft see also *Britannia* xvii (1986), 399 and *Britannia* xviii (1987), 326–27, fig. 14.

48.   For Stonea see T. Potter, 'A Roman Province: Britain AD 43– 410', in I. Longworth and J. Cherry, *Archaeology in Britain* (1986), 110, fig. 57, and below, pp. 160ff. *Antiquity* lxii (1988), 312. For the evidence of Iron Age colonization op. cit. p. 321

organisation and specialization certainly increased. The wetlands, in particular, offered new opportunities to Romano-British farmers. (below, pp. 147–73).

The most recent discovery of such colonization is in the Wentlooge Level of south-east Wales between Cardiff and Caerleon.[49] This massive drainage scheme, involving the construction of a sea bank, 12 km long, would have created some 325 km² of reclaimed land. Such a large undertaking may well have been carried out by and for the benefit of the Second Legion.[50]

There have been major advances in the study of Romano-British fields since the pioneering work of Colin Bowen.[51] Riley's aerial discoveries have already been noted. On the Berkshire Downs small-scale excavations have dated extensive field systems to the Roman period. Around villas such as Barnsley Park (Gloucs.) and Winterton (Lincs.), fields and enclosures have been planned and excavated. In north-west Essex detailed field survey and the plotting of pottery scatters have generated a pattern of dispersed farmsteads close to the better quality soil surrounded by manured infield and less frequently ploughed outfield.[52]

Alluvial and colluvial deposits in southern and central Britain illustrate the impact of Romano-British arable farming. Ten years ago Roman field systems in the Thames Valley were virtually unknown. Since then they have been identified in several locations in the valley bottom and soil, mollusc, insect and plant studies have shown a changing pattern of pastoral and arable farming and the presence of hedges. It is only in the Roman period in the Thames valley that there is evidence for the cultivation of hay, at the same time as long scythes appear in the archaeological record.[53]

Such work emphasises that if we are to discover the uses to which the fields were put, the quality of the archaeological record is paramount. Buried soils and waterlogged deposits provide more useful information than multiple re-cut ditches packed with residual material. Of particular importance to the potential study of river valleys has been the discovery near Reading and Abingdon in the past year of Roman fields surviving as earthworks, but sealed beneath Roman and Medieval alluvial deposits. These have been discovered as a result of trenching as part of systematic archaeological assessment, funded by developers seeking planning permission. This change in archaeological politics and funding will focus attention even further on sampling strategies and regional research designs.

The tyranny of historical barriers is gradually disintegrating in rural archaeology. Large-scale excavations and regional studies are encouraging archaeologists to examine the processes of change rather than simply events. In the countryside A.D. 43 rarely registers. The persistent question of Romanization can only be approached via the Iron Age foundations of Roman Britain. It is clear that the pace of change had quickened in the late Iron Age and many of the elements of 'Romanization' were already underway. But the pattern and rate of change was not uniform across the country.[54]

The question of continuity is equally relevant at the end of the Roman period. The archaeology of the later fourth and fifth centuries is, however, bedevilled by the difficulties of precise dating,

49. J.R.L. Allen and M.G. Fulford, 'The Wentlooge Level: a Romano-British Saltmarsh reclamation in south east Wales', *Britannia* xvii (1986), 91–117.

50. For a discussion of legionary *prata*, land whose main function was to provide grazing and fodder for the legions' animals see D.J.P. Mason, '*Prata Legionis* in Britain', *Britannia* xix (1988), 163–189.

51. H.C. Bowen, 'Ancient Fields', in H.C. Bowen and P.J. Fowler, *Early Land Allotment* BAR 48 (1978)

52. P.J. Fowler, 'Continuity in the Landscape', in P.J. Fowler (ed.), *Recent Work in Rural Archaeology* (1975), fig. 8.6 for a plan of Barnsley Park. R. Goodburn, Winterton, 'Some villa problems', in M. Todd (ed.), *Studies in the Romano-British Villa* (1978), 93–101. T. Williamson, 'Settlement, Hierarchy and Economy in North West Essex', in K. Branigan and D. Miles, *The Economies of Romano-British Villas* (1988), 73–82.

53. S. Rees, 'The Roman scythe blade', in G. Lambrick and M. Robinson, *Iron Age and Roman riverside settlements at Farmoor, Oxfordshire* (1979), 61–64.

54. For a view of the contrasting degree of Romanisation of native communities in north, south-west and south-east Britain, see the relevant volumes of the Longmans Regional History of Britain, N. Higham (1986), op. cit. (note 19), M. Todd (1987), op. cit. (note 23), 189–236 and D. Prewett, D. Rudling and M. Gardiner, *The South-East to AD 100* (1988), 178–245. A collection of papers which deals with the impact of Rome as an imperial power on Britain is B.C. Burnham and M.B. Johnson (eds.), *Invasion and Response: the case of Roman Britain* BAR 73 (1979).

even in the materially rich South. The shift from catastrophe to continuity was stimulated by Professor Finberg's historical and geographical analysis of Withington in the Cotswolds.[55] In the 1970's many Romano-British settlement excavations produced traces of Anglo-Saxon occupation.[56]

Unfortunately, archaeology has not produced direct evidence to explain the decline of the relatively prosperous rural farms of the mid-fourth century. And the presence of Saxon pottery or huts means little in terms of explanation. Philip Rahtz has attempted to define continuity more closely in relation to the project at Wharram Percy in East Yorkshire. At the least it implies 'continuous exploitation of resources in a given area' whether this is a field or a building.[57] Arguments have polarised between what Rahtz refers to as 'functional continuity' and 'ethnic continuity'. Peasant communities are by their very nature relatively stable. There is no doubt, however, that the fifth century witnessed, in the more Romanized South at least, a substantial economic and probably demographic collapse.

In the Upper Thames Valley, for example, late Romano-British settlements occurred approximately every kilometre along the edge of the floodplain in the Lechlade area of Gloucestershire. They were supported by a drainage system which had originally been dug seven centuries before. By the mid-fifth century all these settlements had disappeared and the drainage ditches became infilled. The land was not, however, abandoned to a 'natural' state. Instead it was utilized as pasture, and eventually as meadow in the early medieval period. By the eleventh century alluvium generated by intensive ploughing of the slopes was being deposited. Nearby on the higher second gravel terrace, settlement continued almost uninterrupted in the fifth century in the form of sunken featured buildings. These light soils were first occupied by Neolithic farmers and were the site of the Romano-British villa of Roughground Farm. Similar patterns of retreat from marginal land and from land requiring a relatively large labour input have been observed elsewhere in the Thames Valley.

The small villa or farmstead of Barton Court Farm, also on the second terrace, was demolished in the early to mid-fifth century. While its enclosure ditches were still open people using 'Anglo Saxon' pottery occupied the site and constructed timber buildings in the open spaces.[58] Waterlogged deposits in their wells indicate a lessening of intensity in farming practices. Cattle and horses declined in favour of sheep, but in many respects the agriculture was similar to that of the previous century. An apparent decline in the number of humans encouraged wild animals, including the white-tailed eagle, to thrive. On the lower ground the Romano-British settlements and drainage ditches were abandoned.

What such evidence tells us is that it is unwise to generalise from the evidence of a single site, even to its immediate hinterland. The past is knowable, but it takes much effort, and persistence, using different techniques in different circumstances, and asking the right questions, if we are to discover the answers.

55. H.P.R. Finberg, *Roman and Saxon Withington: a study in continuity* (1959).

56. It is now customary, if not particularly helpful, to point out that Britons could perfectly well dress as Anglo-Saxons and use hand-made pots. With this proviso, Anglo-Saxon material has been found on many Romano-British sites e.g. Orton Hall Farm, D.F. Mackreth in M. Todd (ed.), *Studies in the Roman Villa* (1978), 209–223. Rivenhall, Essex, W.J. and K.A. Rodwell, *Rivenhall: investigations on a villa, church and village (1950–77)* Pt.1 C.B.A. Res. Rep. 50 (1984), 30–37, 51–53. For general discussion: S. Haselgrove, 'Romano-Saxon Attitudes', in P.J. Casey, *The End of Roman Britain* BAR 71 (1979), 4–13.

57. P.A. Rahtz, 'From Roman to Saxon at Wharram Percy', in J. Price and P.R. Wilson (eds.), *Recent Research in Roman Yorkshire* (1988), 130, fig. 8.6. The Wharram Percy project began over 35 years ago as an investigation of a deserted medieval village. The aims of the project have changed as the complexity of the prehistoric and Romano-British landscape became apparent.

58. op. cit. (note 56.)

AGRICULTURE IN ROMAN BRITAIN: THE DYNAMICS OF CHANGE

By Martin Jones

INTRODUCTION

In studies of the environment of Roman Britain and its provision of natural resources, the impact of the Roman presence has variously been seen as involving the expansion of farming into new areas, the introduction of new agricultural methods, the exploitation of an existing agricultural system, and various combinations of the three. The various constructions are based partly upon speculation about what 'must have been' in order for the imperial machine to operate, and partly upon analyses of archaeological data supplemented by fragments of epigraphy. In the second case the inferences drawn have depended greatly on the quality and chronological precision of that data.

In this paper I aim to review evidence that has arisen from the last two decades of fieldwork and research, with two foci: the nature of the British environment when the province was incorporated into the Roman Empire in the first century A.D.; and the nature of the impact of the Roman presence on British agriculture in the three aspects outlined above, expansion, introduction, and exploitation.

THE ENVIRONMENT AT THE TIME OF CONQUEST

We must start by disposing of two surprisingly durable misconceptions about the agrarian landscape that the Roman administrators inherited; first that it was static, and second that it was populated by self-sufficient farmers.

The analysis of both pollen and valley sediments bears witness to the substantial environmental changes taking place in the centuries running up to and continuing after the conquest, and the associated clearance of wildwood on an unprecedented scale.[1] Within that period the number of farmsteads detectable across the landscape is much greater than in any preceding period. The developed nature of the agriculture practised within them is evident from environmental analyses from sites both in the South, for example the Ashville settlement in Oxfordshire, and in the North, for example Thorpe Thewles in Cleveland.[2]

On the question of self-sufficiency, the artefactual, historical, and biological evidence all indicates the existence of a mobilised agricultural surplus. While there are sites, particularly in the North and West, without evidence of imported commodities of any kind, such items as imported pottery, metalwork, quernstones and salt-containers are widespread on Iron Age farmsteads, and

---

1. J. Turner, 'The vegetation,' M. Bell, 'Valley sediments and environmental change', and J. Turner, 'The Iron Age,' in M. Jones and G. Dimbleby (eds.), *The Environment of Man* BAR 87 (1981).
2. M. Parrington, *The excavation of an Iron Age settlement, Bronze Age ring ditches and Roman features at Ashville Trading Estate, Abingdon* CBA Res. Rep. 28 (London, 1978); D. Heslop, *The excavation of an Iron Age settlement at Thorpe Thewles, Cleveland, 1980–82* (Cleveland, 1987).

a number of late Iron Age coins have been found in association with small farming settlements.[3] The best known written evidence of agricultural surplus is Strabo's list of exports from late Iron Age Britain, which includes corn and cattle. The archaeological plant remains themselves reflect a great deal of crop movement between sites, and, in the case of the hillfort of Danebury, of communal storage and processing.[4]

In any consideration of the surplus extracted to support the Roman Imperial machine, it is clearly essential to take account of the surplus that was already being mobilised to support indigenous non-producers.

Moving to the specific character of the inherited environment, analyses of pollen and macrofossils indicate a managed landscape of woodland, grassland and moor, and arable fields. Each of these was in the process of continuing change at the time of conquest.

Woodland

As well as diminishing throughout this period, we can envisage the continuing conversion of virgin woodland into a managed state. The work of the Somerset Levels Project has demonstrated the considerable antiquity of woodland management practices such as coppicing and pollarding, going back at least to the neolithic. By the 1st millennium B.C., the ring pattern of timbers from 'standard' trees establishes the existence of cyclical plot felling, a practice that continued to supply Britain's wood throughout the historic period.[5]

It has sometimes been suggested that the fuel needs of such expanding industries as pottery and metal production would diminish woodland by the removal of trees. The repeated removal of stems, however, rejuvenates rather than kills trees in the case of the majority of British species, and a more reasonable expectation is that growing fuel use would affect the growth form rather than the extent of British woodland.[6]

The proliferation of roundhouses across the late prehistoric landscape itself implies extensive availability of managed roundwood. While rectangular structures may be built in various ways, and the 'log-cabin' for example may be constructed from virgin trees, it is difficult to imagine the conical roofed roundhouse based on anything other than the long springy poles derived from woodland management.

Grassland and Moor

A challenging case has been made that hay-meadows were a Roman introduction to Britain.[7] The argument, based on archaeobotanical evidence from the Thames Valley, raises fundamental questions about the overwintering of livestock in prehistory. There is indeed evidence for a range of grassland types from the neolithic period onwards, from the closely grazed chalk grassland around Avebury to the rough pasture on Dartmoor.[8] These, however, would provide limited nutrition over winter months, and how animals survived remains open to question.

The expansion of grass and heather moor in the uplands was a continuing process its inception predating the neolithic period. By the time of the Roman conquest much existing moorland was already established and agriculturally marginal, then as now.[9]

3. D. Allen, 'Excavations at Bierton, 1979,' *Records of Bucks.* (1986); D. Miles, *Archaeology of Barton Court Farm, Abingdon, Oxon* CBA Res. Rep. 50 (1986).
4. M.K. Jones, 'The plant remains', in B. Cunliffe (ed.), *Danebury: an Iron Age hill-fort in Hampshire* CBA Res. Rep. 50 (London, 1984), 483–95; idem, 'Archaeobotany beyond subsistence reconstruction', in G. Barker and C. Gamble (eds.), *Beyond domestication in prehistoric Europe* (London, 1985), 107–28.
5. O. Rackham, 'Neolithic woodland management in the Somerset Levels: Garvin's, Walton Heath and Rowland's tracks,' *Somerset Levels Papers* iii (1977), 65–75; R.A. Morgan, 'Tree-ring studies in the Somerset Levels: the Meare Heath track 1974–80,' *Somerset Levels Papers* viii (1982), 39–45.
6. O. Rackham, *Ancient woodland: its history, vegetation and uses in England* (London, 1980).
7. G.H. Lambrick and M.A. Robinson, 'The development of floodplain grassland in the Upper Thames valley', in M. Jones (ed.), *Archaeology and the flora of the British Isles* (Oxford, 1988), 55–75.
8. J.G. Evans, *Land snails in archaeology, with special reference to the British Isles* (London, 1972); S.C. Beckett, 'Pollen analysis of the peat deposits', in K. Smith et al., 'The Shaugh Moor project: 3rd. report', *PPS* xlvii(1981), 205–73.
9. I.G. Simmons and M.J. Tooley, *The environment in British prehistory* (London, 1981).

Arable land

Ard-cultivation for a broad range of cereal and legume species, but principally spelt wheat and hulled six-row barley was widespread by the time of conquest.[10] In the south, there is recurrent evidence of soil nitrogen depletion from the weed species found, and of extensive soil erosion from river alluvium. The pressure on land is further evident in the form of weed-species indicative of marginal land cultivation. In the South, the wetland plant *Eleocharis palustris* (spike rush) occurs as a weed of cereals, as does the heathland grass *Sieglingia decumbens* in the North and West. The very occasional appearance of *Anthemis cotula* in Iron Age contexts suggests the cultivation of heavy clays.[11]

There is some evidence of agricultural innovation in the late pre-Roman Iron Age. Balanced sickles appear for the first time, enabling more labour- intensive harvesting. More settlements appear in areas with heavy clay soils, and excavation and survey both suggest an extension of artificial field drainage in this period.[12]

EXPANSION OF THE AREA UNDER CULTIVATION

The premise that demand automatically stimulates production has in turn stimulated the idea that the presence of a large resident army, and an improved network of communications, necessarily led to enhanced agricultural output. The evidence drawn upon to support this has been pioneer landscapes, ideally centuriated landscapes, accompanied by new innovative farms and in some cases backed up by biological evidence.

The chronology of landscapes is far more difficult to establish than the chronology of settlements within them. The major epoch of physical land division in Britain would appear to be the second millennium B.C., but such landscapes continue to be reworked in subsequent millennia.[13] Attempts either to compress all prehistoric land enclosure into the second millennium B.C., or to isolate subsequent periods of extensive enclosure, have not stood the test of time.[14] We must envisage a continuous reworking of an ancient structured landscape, some of which is to be located in the late prehistoric and Roman periods.[15] On the question of centuriation, despite some ambitious speculation no patterns have been discerned within the contemporary British landscape that approach anywhere near the pronounced rectilinearity of centuriated landscapes found elsewhere in the Empire; nothing resembling the ordered patterns recovered from more southerly parts of the Empire survives in the British landscape.

As for new farms, the appearance of villas has frequently been discussed in the context of changes in production. The evidence we have from the earlier British villas, in the form of architecture and artefacts, reflects consumption rather than production.[16] The linkage of the two is the consequence, not the test, of the premise outlined above; that the evident wealth of villas automatically implies the stimulation of agricultural production to support it. Not only is this an unnecessary assumption in the context of societies already producing and mobilising a surplus, but, in addition, we lack evidence that any of the *early* Roman villas are associated with a tangible change in the agrarian base. This may in part be due to the shortage of environmental evidence

10. M.K. Jones, 'The development of crop husbandry', in Jones and Dimbleby, op. cit. (note 1), 95–127; S. Rees, *Agricultural implements in prehistoric and Roman Britain* BAR 69 (1979).
11. M.K. Jones, *The ecological and cultural implications of carbonised seed assemblages from selected archaeological contexts in southern Britain*, unpubl. D.Phil. thesis, Oxford (1984); G.C. Hillman, 'Interpretation of archaeological plant remains: the application of ethnographic models from Turkey,' in W. van Zeist and W.A. Casparie (eds.), *Plants and ancient man* (Rotterdam, 1984), 1–41; M. van der Veen and C.C. Haselgrove, 'Evidence for pre-Roman crops from Coxhoe, Co. Durham,' *Arch. Ael.*[5] xi (1983), 23–5.
12. Jones, op. cit. (note 10).
13. H.C. Bowen and P.J. Fowler (eds.), *Early Land Allotment* BAR 48 (1978).
14. A. Fleming, 'Coaxial field-systems: some questions of time and space,' *Antiquity* lxi(1987), 188–202.
15. D.N. Riley, *Early landscapes from the air* (Sheffield, 1980); T.M. Williamson, 'The Roman countryside: settlement and agriculture in N.W. Essex,' *Britannia* xv(1980), 225–30.
16. M.J. Millett, *The Romanization of Britain* (Cambridge, in press)

from such sites, but neither is there artefactual nor structural evidence from such sites to indicate changes in agricultural *production*. There is, however, clearer evidence of farming expansion during the Roman period in some of the more marginal areas, of which two examples are discussed here.

The first is the northern frontier region. West of the Pennines numerous sites are known from aerial photography in the Eden Valley and in the north-east is a series of stone-built upland sites stretching from the Cheviots to the Upper Tees.[17] In each case, the attribution to the Roman period rests heavily on assumed tight association between site morphology and date, but, in the case of the north-eastern sites, a series of pollen analyses with radio-carbon estimates links them with agricultural expansion running into the Roman period.[18]

From these we can infer that, in the coastal lowlands beneath the Pennines, agriculture was well established and of great antiquity by the time of the conquest. There are extensive arable clearances going back to second millennium B.C., and in the first millennium BC, the farmstead at Thorpe Thewles[19] reflects an agricultural development directly comparable with contemporary sites in the agricultural heartlands of the South.

In terms of the Carbon 14 estimates from the east Pennine pollen cores, the zone of late Iron Age agricultural expansion is the middle valleys and in the Roman period the zone of agricultural expansion is more marginal still, in the middle and upper Dales.[20] Here, the early Roman expansion relates to a progressive intake of land that is marginal rather than central to agricultural production. Rather than being a single episode, this marks the continuation of a trend that began in prehistory and continued into the modern period.

The second example is the brackish regions around the North Sea basin, in many cases linked to salt-working. The best known area of Roman exploitation is the Fenland, and the overall picture is currently being greatly expanded by rescue work along the Essex coast.[21] The extent of potential adaptation to brackish lowlands in this period has been demonstrated in the study of a contemporary settlement on the far coast of the North Sea, at Feddersen Wierde in Northern Germany. Even within a landscape dominated by seasonally inundated salt marsh, a wide range of spring-sown crops, barley, oats, gold of pleasure, flax and horsebeans, was successfully raised in the immediate vicinity of the settlement mound.[22]

While the British evidence is not directly parallel, the Hullbridge Basin survey in Essex[23] has brought to light the links between agriculture and saltworking in sites such as Canvey Island, where the coarse sievings from the agricultural processing of spelt wheat were used to temper clay in the salt-working process.

In both the examples cited above, we would not expect the extension of farming in marginal areas to have a significant impact on total agricultural surplus. The appearance of such farming activity may instead be led by a growing response to the industrial rather than the agricultural potential of these areas.

17. N. Higham, 'The Roman impact upon rural settlement in Cumbria', in P.A.G. Clack and S. Haselgrove (eds.), *Rural settlement in the Roman north* (Durham, 1981), 105–22; idem, *The northern counties to AD 1000* (London, 1986).
18. D.D. Bartley, C. Chambers and B. Hart-Jones, 'The vegetational history of parts of south and east Durham', *New Phytologist* lxxvii(1976), 437–68; A.M. Donaldson and J. Turner, 'A pollen diagram from Hallowell Moss, near Durham City', *Journ. Biogeography* iv(1977), 25–33; B.J. Roberts, J. Turner and P.F. Ward, 'Recent forest history and land use in Weardale, northern England', in *Quaternary Plant Ecology*, 14th. symposium of the British Ecological Society (Oxford, 1973), 207–21.
19. Heslop, op. cit. (note 2).
20. Roberts *et al.*, op. cit. (note 18).
21. T.J. Wilkinson and P.L. Murphy, 'Archaeological survey of an intertidal zone: the submerged landscape of the Essex coast, England', *Journ. Field Arch.* xiii, 2, (1986), 177–94; eidem, *The Hullbridge Basin Survey. Interim Report No.6* (Chelmsford, 1986).
22. U. Körber-Grohne, *Geobotanische Untersüchungen auf der Feddersen Wierde, in Feddersen Wierde, die Ergebnisse der Ausgrabung der vorgeschichtlichen Wurt bei Bremerhaven in den Jahren 1955–63*, Band I (Wiesbaden, 1967); idem, 'Crop husbandry and environmental change in the coastal area of the Feddersen Wierde, near Bremerhaven, northwest Germany', in Jones and Dimbleby, op. cit. (note 1).
23. Wilkinson and Murphy, op. cit. (note 21).

INTRODUCTION OF NEW METHODS

The timescale of innovation

A major result of the increased chronological precision of recent data collection is the feasibility of relating innovations to particular centuries or parts of centuries, rather than to the 'Roman period' in general. This has allowed us to observe that innovation in the techniques of grain production does not coincide with the conquest itself. It either precedes it, as in the case of improved drainage, new harvesting tools and new crop strategies, or postdates it, as in the case of plough technology and horticulture. I have argued elsewhere that the conquest heralds a period of stagnation, in terms of the methods of grain-production, that lasts through to the later third century.[24]

The same cannot be said of hay-production. As outlined above, evidence of neither the tools of hay-collection, nor the hay itself, has been found before the conquest. Yet in the early decades after the conquest, scythes suitable for hay-cutting appear in association with military sites,[25] plant communities of hay-meadow are detectable in the Thames valley, and direct macrofossil evidence of hay appears in military contexts at Lancaster, Papcastle, York, and Carlisle,[26] in direct association with stabling facilities in the latter three sites. It may be that, like many other supposed introductions, hay-production will be back-dated, but the necessary evidence is currently lacking. It should be stressed that we lack not only the biological evidence for prehistoric hay, but also artefactual evidence of a prehistoric implement suitable for the effective cutting of large quantities of grass.[27]

We might expect industrial growth to have an impact on another plant resource, underwood. Just as extensive coppicing in earlier periods is reflected by high hazel counts in contemporary pollen diagrams,[28] the same might be anticipated of Romano-British pollen evidence. The hazel counts in contemporary cores from regions known to have considerable industrial activity do not, however, noticeably peak in this period.[29] A major study of woodland management is being undertaken for Roman Carlisle.[30] Here, much of the exploitation of underwood by the army reflects short term opportunism rather than longer term management.

Turning to the latter part of the Roman period, from the late third century onwards, innovation is directly evident in the sphere of arable production, particularly in the extensive use of metal in ploughs and harvesting equipment, and the appearance of deep cultivation and mouldboard ploughing, evident from coulters and asymmetrical shares respectively.[31]

The progression of the Roman period also sees growing evidence for horticulture in one form or another. There is a greater occurrence of 'garden' and 'orchard' crops, planting-trenches and digging-holes appear both in rural and urban settings,[32] and cultivated soils in small plots become increasingly evident as the 'dark earths' of Roman towns, perhaps the best preserved of which occurs at Culver Street in Colchester.[33] The innovations outlined above relate in the main to the

24. Jones, op. cit. (note 10).
25. Rees, op. cit. (note 10).
26. J. Huntley and A. Hall, pers. comm.
27. Rees, op. cit. (note 10).
28. S.C. Beckett and F.A. Hibbert, 'An absolute pollen diagram from the Abbot's Way,' *Somerset Levels Papers* ii (1976), 24–7.
29. P.V. Waton, *A palynological study of the impact of man on the landscape of central southern England*. Unpubl. Ph.D. thesis (Southampton, 1983).
30. J. Huntley, pers. comm.
31. Rees, op. cit. (note 10). Jones, op. cit. (note 10); idem, 'Crop production in Roman Britain', in D. Miles (ed.), *The Romano-British countryside* BAR 103 (1982), 97–107.
32. J. Wacher, *The towns of Roman Britain* (London, 1975); D. Webster, H. Webster and D.F. Petch, 'A possible vineyard of the Romano-British period at North Thoresby, Lincolnshire,' *Lincs. History and Arch.* ii (1967), 65–61.
33. R. Macphail, 'Soil and botanical studies of the "Dark Earth",' in Jones and Dimbleby, op. cit. (note 1), 309–31; P.J. Murphy, *Culver Street, Colchester. Environmental studies* (HBMC Lab. Reports, London, 1985).

valley bottoms. Here we see three elements of a 'new lowland agriculture': the intensive and deep cultivation of clays and clay loams with a growing emphasis on bread-wheat; the creation of hay-meadows; and the development of orchards, allotments, and perhaps market-gardens within towns as well as in the country.

In other words, we see major elements of the valley-bottom landscapes of the historic period emerging between the late Iron Age and late Roman periods. What they emerged from is less clear, as much of our information on earlier landscapes is largely from higher terraces and high ground generally. Farmoor in Oxfordshire[34] and Lechlade in Gloucestershire[35] provide two of the more comprehensive environmental analyses of transitions between prehistoric and historic period valley-bottom landscapes. In each case, their middle Iron Age predecessors were occupied by small-scale pastoralists labouring opportunistically within an uncontrolled seasonally flooded landscape dissected by numerous stream channels, in contrast to the drained and structured landscapes that superseded them. We can see the agrarian innovations taking place between the late Iron Age and late Roman periods in terms of the successive manipulation of these valley bottoms through intensive use of labour, first to achieve adequate drainage, and subsequently for intensive exploitation. The ability to intensify in this way relates in turn to access to biological and technological economic resources. That brings us to consider the economic context of such innovations.

The context of innovation

The possibilities of increased chronological definition are not as yet matched by those of increased contextual definition, so that we can easily examine variations between farmsteads in a single region. Where that is possible, as in the case of Iron Age and Romano-British farmsteads around Abingdon, Oxfordshire,[36] variations in agricultural production are visible in relation to variations in economic contacts. Thus at Barton Court Farm, the settlement expands in both layout and material wealth during the period in question, on the basis of a broad crop repertoire including intensive valley-bottom crops such as bread-wheat and flax. At the same time its near-neighbour, the Ashville site, apparently contracts in the context of much lesser material wealth and a conservative crop repertoire with weeds that reflect progressive soil starvation. However, data-sets with sufficient detail to allow such comparisons are still rare; the consequent tendency to generalise excessively from individual 'type-sites' to a total regional economy is still great.

One form of data which may pick up the spatial patterning of innovation is the record of crops associated with intensive farming, in particular, bread wheat (*Triticum aestivum*). Today, no other species, besides rice, contributes as much to the global human diet. Its early historic transition from a secondary to a major crop, is therefore, of some significance, and the context of an important part of that transition is temperate Europe in the Roman period. A revealing aspect of that transition is its piecemeal progression. Rather than occurring as a single episode or wave, records of the crop appear at different times in different places, forming a growing mosaic that merges into a continuum by the end of the first millennium A.D..[37] As a crop suited to labour-intensive and resource-intensive farming, we can also follow the appearance of the artefacts of deep cultivation and weeds of the associated soil-types through temperate Europe, and find that these too follow the same piecemeal progression.[38] This is not the simple and even diffusion of a new resource from its point of origin, but the complex and variable breakdown of barriers to the exploitation of an age-old resource. The nature both of the overall transition, and of such contextual information as exists, suggests that variation in the economic options open to

34.   G.H. Lambrick and M.A. Robinson, *Iron Age and Roman settlements at Farmoor, Oxfordshire* CBA Res. Rep. 32 (London, 1979).

35.   S. Palmer and D. Miles, *Figures in a landscape: archaeological investigations at Claydon Pike, Fairford Lechlade, An interim report* (Oxford Arch. Unit, 1982).

36.   Parrington, op. cit. (note 2). Miles, op. cit. (note 3).

37.   Jones, op. cit. (note 11).

38.   Jones, op. cit. (note 10). Rees, op. cit. (note 10).

farmers sharing a particular environment is a significant and principal limiting factor in the process of innovation.

In this light, it is possible to understand why the rise to prominence of bread-wheat, well suited to the 'rich' farmer intensively cultivating fertile soils, is broadly accompanied by the parallel rise of rye and oats, equally well suited to the 'poor' farmer manually or shallow-cultivating depleted soils. The parallel rise of these three can be seen in terms not so much of increased overall economic potential, as of increased economic disparity. The appearance of such disparity brings us to the third possible aspect of Romano-British agriculture.

EXPLOITATION OF EXISTING PRODUCTION

The radio-carbon estimates that exist for pollen diagrams in the frontier zone support the argument that the northerly wave of agricultural clearance precedes rather than follows conquest by a number of generations, and establishes the economic basis for successful conquest.[39] This is borne out by evidence incidentally preserved in the construction of the Hadrianic and Antonine Walls. Recent excavations have shown how the former overlies cultivated land surfaces on many parts of its length,[40] while in contrast, turves from the construction of the latter reflect a pastoral landscape further to the north, with little or no evidence of arable farming. In addition, there is indication of soil depletion during the first century A.D., leading to the expansion of heather moor.[41]

The depletion evident in these turves may be part of a wider pattern of Roman impact in the frontier region. On another frontier zone, at the Dutch site of Noordbarge, van Zeist notes that a relatively short military presence, about 15 years, coincides with a marked shift towards the cultivation of rye.[42] Such a shift is just what might be expected from a short-term military presence in a landscape of small-scale farmers. The loss of even a single seasons's crop, seedcorn, or of a draught-animal could be sufficient to force a farmer down the ladder of intensification, from ox-cultivation of wheat to hand-cultivation of rye, for example.

Such a transition can be placed in a broader context of space and time. In the Iron Age, the crops I have suggested are markers of intensive and non-intensive cultivation; bread-wheat, rye and oats, occur in small numbers and relatively evenly through the temperate European crop record.[43] By the historic period the numbers are greater and the evenness has disappeared. A far clearer regional segregation of crops is visible, with bread-wheat in the core agricultural areas, rye together with millett most prominent in the east, and oats together with barley most prominent in the north.[44]

In retrospect we may relate this development to adaptions to the different environments of Europe. However, the process of transition itself may be seen in the context of particular historic and economic episodes, such as the Roman military presence. Not only do the turves from the Antonine Wall and the crops at Noordbarge provide evidence of depression in the agricultural landscape at particular sites along the military zone, but, in addition, the transect that provides the most comprehensive and continuous existing crop record across the *limes*, running through northern Germany and the Low Countries, shows a more widespread correlation between

39. M. van der Veen, 'Evidence for crop plants from north-east England: an interim overview with discussion of new results', in N.R.J. Fieller, D.D. Gilbertson and N. Ralph (eds.), *Palaeobiological investigations: research design, methods and data analysis* BAR S266 (1985), 197–219.

40. e.g. D.J. Breeze, 'Plough marks at Carrawburgh on Hadrian's Wall,' *Tools and Tillage* ii (1974), 188–90.

41. W.B. Boyd, 'Environmental change and Iron Age land management in the area of the Antonine Wall, a summary,' *Glasgow Arch. Journ.* ii (1975), 75–81.

42. W. van Zeist, 'Plant remains from Iron Age Noordbarge, province of Drenthe, the Netherlands,' *Palaeohistoria* xxiii (1981), 169–93.

43. U. Willerding, 'Zum Ackerbau in der jüngeren vorrömischen Eisenzeit', in *Festschrift Maria Hopf* (Cologne, 1979), 309–30.

44. U. Willerding, 'Anbaufruchte der Eisenzeit und des frühen Mittelalters, ihre Anbauformen, Standortsverhält-nisse und Erntemethoden,' in H. Beck and H. Jankuhn (eds.), *Untersuchungen zur eisenzeitlichen und frühmittelalter-lichen Flur in Mitteleuropa und ihrer Nutzung* (Göttingen, 1980), 126–96.

emerging crop specialisation and the frontier itself. In data that Körber-Grohne collated for this region, rye and oats only reach proportions of 5% or more on or beyond the *limes*, while records of bread-wheat lie without exception within the *limes*. Neither pattern is apparent in the pre-Roman data.[45]

CONCLUSION

The evidence drawn upon in this paper accommodates neither a simple demand-led stimulation of indigenous agriculture, nor an equally simple exploitation of an unchanging productive base. A key feature of Romano-British agriculture is that, as emphasised at the outset, the Roman occupation took place in the context of much longer term change in the agrarian landscape. A trend is visible in Britain and other parts of temperate Europe towards agricultural intensification, involving a new balance of crop species, changing methods of cultivation, and new developments in horticulture and hay production. While the evidence supports the idea of a principally exploitative Roman presence, diverting the existing crop production, this exploitation is by no means without impact on that process of change. That impact can be seen to have two aspects. In the early period of Roman occupation of lowland Britain, and in parts of the frontier zone at all stages, the Roman presence would appear to halt or even reverse intensification of arable production, even while the technology of storage and distribution is being enhanced. In the later Roman period by contrast, the impact is quite different, and we see in places the culmination of a process of agrarian change of much longer duration than the Roman presence itself.

45. U. Körber-Grohne, 'Pflanzliche Abdrücke in eisenzeitlicher Keramik – Spiegelbild damaliger Nutzpflanzen?' *Fundberichte aus Baden-Württemberg* vi (1981), 165–211.

ANIMALS IN ROMAN BRITAIN*

By Annie Grant

As a source of information for understanding the husbandry of domestic animals, their economic and ritual significance, and the exploitation of the wild animal resources of the Romano-British countryside, we have primarily the animal bone remains that have been recovered during archaeological excavation. Documentary evidence, which can be extremely detailed and illuminating for the central, Mediterranean regions of the Roman Empire, is rarely helpful for the more distant and climatically temperate areas. In fact, some of the small number of direct references to Britain, although often quoted, may well be inaccurate. For example, Caesar's assertion[1] that the Britons regarded the consumption of the flesh of domestic fowl and geese as tabu must be set against the archaeological evidence of finds of chicken bones mixed in with the food remains from the larger domestic animals.[2]

Animal bone remains are frequently amongst the most numerous classes of evidence recovered from excavations, and while in the past many excavators have chosen to ignore their potential, more recently there has been an increased investment of both time and money in their study. Indeed, in terms of the numbers of sites from which animal bones have been investigated, the Roman period in Britain has perhaps received far more attention than any other, earlier or later. Several reviews of Romano-British archaeozoological evidence have been made within the last ten years.[3] King's survey lists over 197 different contexts within Britain from which animal bones have been studied. Many other sites have been published since this review was completed, now over four years ago, and these have been looked at in some detail for this article. There would now appear to be a sufficient quantity of Romano-British faunal assemblages to begin to approach some of the important questions that we might expect such evidence to answer, but close examination shows that quality is frequently lacking. Firstly, some of the bone material, particularly from those regions of the country with acidic soils, is poorly preserved. Thus we have very little information for the upland regions of the country.[4] Secondly, there are very few sites that have produced sufficiently large faunal assemblages for detailed analysis to be either appropriate or possible. Of the 197 contexts listed by King, only three have produced even 5000

* I would like to thank Mike Fulford and Graeme Barker for their comments on the earlier drafts of this paper.

1. *De Bello gallico*, v,12.
2. For example, J. Coy in B.W. Cunliffe (ed.), *Danebury, an Iron Age Hillfort in Hampshire* (London, 1984), 530.
3. A.C. King, 'A comparative survey of bone assemblages from Roman sites in Britain.' *Bull Instit Arch. Univ. London* 15 (1978), 207–32; A.C. King in T.F.C. Blagg and A.C. King (eds.), *Military and Civilian in Roman Britain* (Oxford, 1984), 187–217; M. Maltby in M. Jones and G. Dimbleby (eds.), *The Environment of Man: the Iron Age to the Anglo-Saxon Period* (London, 1981), 155–203; R.-M. Luff, *A Zooarchaeological Study of the Roman North-Western Provinces* (Oxford, 1982); J. Coy and M. Maltby, *Archaeozoology in Wessex*. Report to the Science Panel of the Department of the Environment, Ancient Monuments Board (unpublished, 1984).
4. King (1984), op. cit. (note 3), fig. 5.

bones. In order to be able to understand complex, urban settlements and to be able to look in detail at animal management we need to have far more large and well-preserved bone samples. Thirdly, the archaeological dating of faunal assemblages is frequently insufficiently precise. Collections of bones that have accumulated over several centuries, while the status or size of the settlement may have radically altered, are of little value for answering any but the most basic of questions. Fourthly, a lack of standardization in the methods of analysis used by archaeozoologists has made much comparative study difficult or even impossible.

With these caveats in mind, in the rest of this paper I would like to take some aspects of the economic, social and religious life of Roman Britain and look at the contribution that has been made to their understanding by the study of animal remains.

First of all it is helpful to take a very general look at Romano-British domestic animal management against the background of that of the preceding centuries.

A review of the evidence for animal husbandry in the Iron Age in Central Southern Britain has pointed to the prime importance of sheep rearing at this period.[5] At many settlements on the chalk uplands, proportions of sheep bones (or, more accurately, sheep and/or goat bones) are as high as seventy per cent, but even in the lowland areas, in environments more suitable for raising cattle, the proportion of sheep bones rarely falls below one third. In general, cattle are less numerous, although at settlements on lower ground their greater suitability as animals to keep on damp, heavy soil is reflected in higher percentages of their bones.

In order to understand the causes of and reasons for change, it is essential to examine the role of the domestic animals in the farming system as a whole and not just as providers of meat. Our knowledge of the animal-rearing strategies of the past is largely dependent on an assessment of the age at which animals were killed. For example, when animals are raised primarily to provide meat, many will be killed when juvenile or sub-adult, with only sufficient adult animals kept to ensure the maintenance of the herds.

Despite the dominance of sheep-rearing in some regions, the Iron Age economy was clearly mixed, not only in respect of the species of animals kept, but also in terms of the management strategies adopted. Many of the sheep were killed and eaten only when quite elderly, suggesting that the sheep-management strategy aimed to produce not only meat and perhaps milk, but also wool. This interpretation of the sheep mortality at many sites is supported by the very common occurrence of spindle whorls, loom weights and other tools connected with spinning and weaving. Cattle mortality suggests that these animals were as necessary for their pulling-power as for the food they yielded, as many were quite elderly when they died.

King's summary of the animal bone evidence for the Roman period shows clearly that the proportion of cattle remains was in general far higher than in the Iron Age, and increased over the period of Roman occupation.[6]

In the absence of many very large samples of animal bones, we have little or only very imprecise information for age at death. However, the dominant impression is that at many Roman sites, the majority of cattle were killed when they were fully mature, as in the Iron Age, implying their use for other purposes in addition to the provision of meat.

Sheep were, therefore, proportionally much less important in the Roman period than in the Iron Age, and it is possible that there was a shift in emphasis in their husbandry.[7] From some sites of the later period we have evidence that meat production had become more important, although this seems to have been balanced with wool production, rather than totally replacing it.

We can then, detect, differences between Iron Age and Romano-British animal management. However, the beginnings of the change to a predominantly cattle- rather than sheep-dominated husbandry are, in fact, evident prior to the Roman conquest. In the late pre-Roman Iron Age, while the proportion of sheep bones rises at some chalkland settlements, at others on lower

5. A. Grant in B.W. Cunliffe and D. Miles (eds.), *Iron Age Communities in Central Southern Britain* (Oxford, 1984), 164–73.
6. King (1978), op. cit. (note 3).
7. Maltby, op. cit. (note 3), 175.

ground, it is cattle-rearing that appears to increase. However, the sites where there is a greater concentration on sheep-rearing are often those whose occupation ceases before or shortly after the Roman conquest. At other sites, particularly those in lowland areas or on heavier soils, occupation continues, and the increased importance of cattle is maintained into and throughout the Roman period.[8] The movement of population centres from hilltops with light soils to valley bottoms must be an important factor in accounting for the rising importance of cattle, but again this too began in the late Iron Age. Clearly the initial impetus for the changes in both settlement patterns and in animal husbandry was not the Conquest itself.

This then is a part of the very general picture. However, we are discussing a period of over four centuries, in a country with a great diversity in its natural environments, using evidence from human settlements of different size, complexity and status. I shall now attempt to examine the evidence in more detail, although this can be an extremely frustrating exercise: the inadequacies of the currently available archaeozoological evidence are all too evident here.

An important consequence of the Roman Conquest was an increase in the numbers of people who were consumers but not producers of agricultural products. First among these were the military, who needed food, both vegetable and animal, and a range of animal products, particularly leather and wool. One possible response to a demand for more meat is to increase pig production. Given sufficient food resources – for example, local scrub- or woodland or plentiful cereal waste – the fecundity of this animal can be exploited to increase rapidly the amount of available meat. More intensive pig production may indeed have been seen as at least a partial solution to the problem of increasing meat supply; percentages of pig bones at early military sites such as Sheepen, Caerleon, Exeter, Leicester, Cirencester and Fishbourne are certainly a great deal higher than in many Iron Age settlements.[9] The apparent increase in pig-rearing seems to be part of a fairly general phenomenon, and not just a solution to feeding military personnel. At some sites, such as Sheepen, Fishbourne, and Leicester, where the initial military occupation was followed by a civilian one (though of a rather different character in each case) the high percentages of pig bones were maintained or dropped only very slightly. Several pre-Roman oppida, such as those at Silchester and Braughing also have particularly high percentages of pig bones.[10] The increase in the importance of this animal cannot then be seen to be entirely due to a Roman impetus, although, as King has pointed out, at several of these sites, finds of a range of imported goods demonstrate contact with the Roman world.

While the frequently cited equation of pigs with woodland has been shown, for the medieval period at least, to be much too simplistic a way of viewing the husbandry of this animal, environmental factors must have played a significant role in the shaping of local animal husbandry; but they were clearly not the only forces determining the response to the problems of food provision.[12]

By the end of the Roman period, pigs seem to have declined in importance; at the late forts such as Portchester and Burgh Castle the proportions of pig bones were very similar to those found at many Iron Age chalk downland sites, while at Vindolanda pig remains were quite rare in fourth-century contexts.[13]

8. Grant, op. cit. (note 5).
9. R. Luff in R. Niblett, *Sheepen: an early Roman Industrial Site at Camulodunum* (London, 1985), 143–9; T. O'Connor in J.D. Zienkiewicz, *The Legionary Fortress Baths at Caerleon* (Cardiff, 1986), 225–48; M. Maltby, *The Animal Bones from Exeter 1971–1975* (Sheffield, 1979); A. Brown in P. Clay and J.E. Mellor, *Excavations in Bath Lane, Leicester* (Leicester, 1985) 79–83; B. Levitan in A. McWhirr, *Houses in Roman Cirencester* (Cirencester, 1986), 133–52; A. Grant in B.W. Cunliffe, *Excavations at Fishbourne 1961–1969* (London, 1971), 377–88.
10. A. Grant (in preparation); R. Ashdown and C. Evans in C. Partridge, *Herts. Arch.* v (1978), 22–108; R. Ashdown and C. Evans in C. Partridge, *Skeleton Green* (London, 1981), 205–235; P. Croft in C. Partridge, *Herts. Arch.* vii (1979), 28–132.
11. King (1984), op. cit. (note 3).
12. A. Grant in G. Astill and A. Grant, *The Countryside of Medieval England* (Oxford, 1988), 159.
13. A. Grant in B.W. Cunliffe, *Excavations at Portchester Castle. Volume 1: Roman* (London, 1975), 378–408; A. Grant in J.S. Johnson, *East Anglian Arch.* 20 (1983), 108–11; G. Hodgson in R.E. Birley, *Arch. Ael.* xlviii (1970), 150–5.

The largest contribution to the meat diet at many of the early forts must have been made by cattle, but the military sites seem to have been like other sites of the period, and most of the cattle were eaten when mature. There is certainly no evidence to suggest that the establishment of military settlements fundamentally changed the nature of local cattle husbandry by encouraging a shift in emphasis to meat production. They may have made considerable demands on the local cattle herds, but these demands seem to have been satisfied mainly by animals that had already fulfilled their other roles in the rural economy as breeding animals and providers of traction or milk.

In fact, it is the crucial importance of cattle within the agricultural system as a whole that must be considered when assessing the impact of the military occupation of Britain, and also that of the growing population, in particular the growing urban population. Cereals were almost certainly the basis of the diet, whether military or civilian.[14] Granaries are often a feature of military sites, and attempts have been made to estimate their storage capacity and from this to calculate the area of land that must have been cultivated. For Longthorpe, an area of at least 592 ha. has been suggested.[15] It is important to remember that the cultivation of cereals relied heavily on animals – on cattle for pulling- power for ploughs and harrows and the carts for transport, and on all three of the domestic animals discussed here for manure. While cattle were essential on the predominantly light soils that were exploited in the Iron Age, the ploughing of heavier soils in the Roman period must have greatly increased the demand for traction. The steady increase in the importance of cattle throughout the Roman occupation may reflect the needs of an expanding population requiring larger or more intensively cultivated areas of land.

A further demonstration of the relationship between cattle and cereal growing can be shown by the scatters of Roman pottery that often cover a wide area around agricultural settlements.[16] These are assumed to have derived from the mixing of domestic refuse with manure from animals stalled in or near the settlements. Stock-enclosures are a feature of many farmsteads and villas, as are buildings that have been interpreted as cattle byres.[17]

A feature of several first-century settlements is the reduced contribution of sheep to the diet in comparison with the preceding period. This is again not solely a characteristic of military sites, but also found in towns and *vici*. However, unlike the cattle, many of the sheep that were eaten in the early military settlements, were fairly young, suggesting that they had been reared specifically for their meat, although older animals were also eaten. The reduced importance of sheep and the general nature of their husbandry is maintained throughout the Roman occupation. In fourth-century deposits at the Saxon shore fort of Portchester, the majority of the sheep were killed before they were fully mature, in contrast to the late Saxon period at the fort, when a much larger proportion of mature sheep suggests an increased emphasis on wool production.[18]

The land around forts was in some cases cultivated by the soldiers themselves, but military sites are very unlikely to have been entirely self-supporting agriculturally, and the food, both vegetable and animal, that was consumed by the soldiers may have been requisitioned or purchased from civilian farmers.[19] Possible evidence that military sites were supplied with food from a number of local farmers, exploiting different environments, has been found in the variability in sheep tooth-wear from Roman Portchester, thought to reflect the feeding of sheep on different terrains, or genetic differences between individual flocks. In the late Saxon period, wear patterns were much more consistent.[20]

14.   R.W. Davies, *Britannia* ii (1971), 122–24.
15.   G.B. Dannell and J.P. Wild, *Longthorpe The Military Works Depot: an Episode in Landscape History* (London, 1987), 67.
16.   For example, V. Gaffney and M. Tingle in F.H. Thompson and S. McReady (eds.), *Archaeological Field Survey in Britain and Abroad* (London, 1985), 67–73.
17.   S. Applebaum in H.P.R. Finberg (ed.), *The Agrarian History of England and Wales: AD43 – 1042* (Cambridge, 1972), 5–282; P. Morris, *Agricultural Buildings in Roman Britain* (Oxford, 1978).
18.   A. Grant in B. Wilson, C. Grigson and S. Payne (eds.), *Ageing and Sexing Animal Bones from Archaeological Sites* (Oxford, 1982), 91–108.
19.   Davies, op. cit. (note 14), 123.
20.   Grant, op. cit. (note 18).

In order to understand the way that the demands of the army and indeed of the towns for food and animal products was fulfilled, we need to look at the rural settlements too. At some of these sites sheep bones predominate, and the suggestion has been made that this is a characteristic of 'unromanized' settlements.[21] However, the position is far from clearcut: although cattle bones outnumber those of sheep at the majority of military and urban settlements, and this is the case at a much lower proportion of unromanized settlements, cattle bones are still in the majority at over half these sites listed in King's survey. Particularly in the south and east of England, the regions from which we have most information, no agricultural settlement is likely to have operated in total isolation from the prevailing economic and political system, even if their buildings and material remains showed little obvious sign of Roman influence. Even in the Iron Age, it is unlikely that any farmsteads in these regions were totally self-sufficient. Wool was a marketable product, both in the Iron Age and Roman period, and a concentration on wool production may have been, in some situations, the best strategy to benefit from the new Roman system. Other settlements may have chosen cattle-rearing, perhaps together with more intensive cereal cultivation. One should perhaps be somewhat cautious of interpreting faunal assemblages as merely reflecting dietary trends, particularly in rural contexts. Such data as we have do indeed suggest that an important aim of the management of sheep was the production of wool, with a good proportion of animals kept until maturity, but young animals, perhaps surplus males and infertile females could have been culled from the flocks and sold for meat to the urban or military settlements.

The farmstead at Odell in Bedfordshire provides an example of animal management at a settlement which was perhaps largely self-supporting and unromanized.[22] The animal husbandry of the first-century B.C. Iron Age occupation was based on the raising of cattle and sheep, in apparently similar numbers, with a small but significant amount of pig-rearing. Over the period of Roman occupation, there is a gradual but steady increase in the importance of cattle, and a decline in the amount of sheep and pig rearing; by the fourth century, two thirds of the bones are those of cattle.

Unfortunately, the bone sample was rather small for detailed comparison of the evidence for the age at death of the animals from different periods, but there was certainly no evidence for major changes in animal management. Some cattle were killed when juvenile, but many were mature at death, and the use of at least some of these for pulling heavy loads is suggested by traces of osteo-arthritic conditions on several bones from the lower limbs.[23] The very limited evidence for the sex of the animals suggests that there was a slight predominance of males. In contrast, metrical analysis of the cattle bones from Exeter and Portchester indicates that the cattle here were mainly female.[24] Both these latter sites are likely to have received at least part of their food supply from other settlements. While it is recognised that we are contrasting three sites that are widely separated geographically, it is tempting to suggest that the mature cattle sold on the urban and military market may have been predominantly females that were no longer good breeders, while the castrates and bulls were retained on the farms until they had reached the end of their working lives.

Buildings excavated at Silchester and interpreted as cattle byres suggest an alternative, or additional explanation.[25] Some cattle could have been kept within towns to supply milk, at least for part of the year.[26] Other interpretations of these buildings are of course possible. Cattle would have been very important for the transport of heavy loads and they may well have been stalled within towns.

There are parallels to be drawn with the medieval rural economy, particularly that of the

21. King, op. cit. (note 3), 190.
22. A. Grant in B. Dix, *Excavations at Harrold Pit, Odell, Bedfordshire, 1974–1978* (forthcoming).
23. See J. Baker and D. Brothwell, *Animal Diseases in Archaeology* (London, 1980), 117.
24. Maltby, op. cit. (note 9); Grant, op. cit. (note 13).
25. G. Boon, *Silchester, the Roman Town of Calleva* (Newton Abbot, 1974).
26. See Grant, op. cit. (note 11), 259.

twelfth and thirteenth centuries. Mature cattle and younger sheep tend to dominate medieval urban bone assemblages, while mature sheep are more common at rural settlements. In the later medieval period, an increasing proportion of juvenile cattle was being killed to supply the urban market. Maltby has noted an increase in the slaughter of immature cattle at Exeter in the late Roman period, but there is as yet no corroborating evidence to show that there was a widespread change in cattle management at this time.[27] Cattle in fourth-century deposits at Potchester were mostly mature.[28]

It is interesting to note the differences in cattle and sheep management. While there seems to have been a good market for even quite elderly cattle, the mature sheep were more frequently eaten by those that raised them. The market value of a cow would clearly be much greater than that of a sheep, largely because of their size difference. However, there may have been another factor involved: the value of cattle carcasses lies not only in their meat but also in their hides, and it is the hides of mature animals that are the most valuable. It is difficult to find any unambiguous evidence for leather production, although groups of pits have sometimes been interpreted as tanning-pits,[29] but one might speculate that the processing of leather may have been a centralized, often urban craft, in contrast to wool production which may have been a local, rural activity. The tanning process requires space and a good supply of raw materials, and produces rather noxious waste, so while it is possible to process leather locally, it is much more efficient and profitable on a larger scale. A demand for hides may have been another important factor in determining the way in which the rural economy was organised in order to satisfy its own needs as well as those of the urban or military market.

While we can only speculate that tanning may have become a specialized activity, there is stronger evidence that other cattle products were the basis of urban crafts or industries. Collections of cattle horn cores, with cut-marks suggesting the removal of the horn, have been found in several urban contexts, and may be the waste from hornworking.[30] At Exeter horn cores were rare finds, but cut-marks found on the skulls suggested that the horns had been removed to be worked elsewhere in the town.[31] However, the processing of animal byproducts was clearly not exclusively an urban occupation and deposits of horn cores have also been found in rural contexts.[32]

Our understanding of the nature of the relationship between the urban and the rural economies is hampered by the small amount of good faunal evidence from urban sites. Exeter, where nine different sites were excavated between 1971 and 1975, has produced the largest published urban Roman assemblage, but Maltby's study has highlighted the amount of variation that exists between the bones from different parts of the town.[33] In general, urban bone assemblages are similar to those of the military settlements with mature cattle frequently the best represented animals.

Evidence for an organized marketing of animals, particularly of cattle, is seen in the nature of some of the bone deposits from urban sites. While at most rural settlements all parts of the animal skeletons are fairly well represented, some urban deposits are dominated by a limited range of skeletal elements. Concentrations of cattle skull fragments and limb extremities have been found, for example, in first-century contexts at Silchester, Exeter and London and in early-second-century contexts at Baldock.[34] These have been interpreted as the waste from the preliminary

27. Maltby, op. cit. (note 9).
28. Grant, op. cit. (note 13).
29. Boon, op. cit. (note 24), 291.
30. For example, M. Maltby in M. Fulford, *Silchester Defences 1974–80* (London, 1984), 199–212.
31. Maltby, op. cit. (note 9), 38.
32. B. Wilson, *Oxoniensia* xli (1976), 67–8.
33. Maltby, op. cit. (note 9).
34. Maltby, op. cit. (note 28); Maltby, op. cit. (note 9); P. Armitage in D. Jones and M. Rhodes, *Excavations at Billingsgate Buildings 'Triangle', Lower Thames Street* (London, 1980), 149–56; R.E. Chaplin and McCormick in I.M. Stead and V. Rigby, *Baldock, the Excavation of a Roman and Pre-Roman Settlement, 1968–72* (London, 1986), 396–415.

butchery of the animals, and suggest a centralized slaughter of animals as part of a well organized supply of meat from outside the towns. From the very limited evidence so far available, such deposits are rather rarer in late urban contexts. For example, at both Silchester and Exeter the late deposits generally have a much more even representation of bone elements.[35] O'Connor has also noted a change from an 'orderly' approach to meat distribution during the military occupation at Caerleon to a more 'relaxed' system following the military withdrawal.[36] It is possible that there were changes in the ways that food supply was organized in the late Roman period but more evidence is needed before this can be fully investigated.

The nature of the butchery practice itself is another informative aspect of the organization of food supply in the Roman period which has begun to be investigated. At the late Roman fort at Portchester the study of the cut-marks on the cattle bones showed that the butchery of these animals was by no means haphazard, but was carried out in a rather consistent manner.[37] Subsequently other authors have noted similar butchery marks at other Roman sites. While certain aspects of any butchery tradition are dictated by anatomical considerations and may thus show some broad similarities, distinct traditions can be detected in present-day practise and in the past from archaeological evidence. The Roman tradition of butchery is quite distinct from that of the Iron Age. The careful separation of bones by the cutting of ligaments, often using only a sharp knife, is replaced by a technique that frequently utilizes heavier chopping tools to separate the carcass into joints by cutting through the bones. These differences cannot entirely be explained by changes in tool technology.[38]

This 'Roman' method of butchery appears to have been used at some of the earliest military sites[39] and may thus have been a technique that was brought in by the Roman armies from Italy, as part of a military tradition of food preparation. One of the very few studies of Roman butchery in Italy showed a very similar method being used in the third century B.C..[40] A very distinct butchery practise is perhaps more likely to emerge where the killing and cutting up of the animal carcasses was centralized rather than where animals were butchered by those who raised them, as and when they were needed. It, therefore, would not be surprising if such a tradition emerged in a military context. However, if this method of butchery was initially a military one, it eventually seems to have had a wider influence. At Odell, the butchery marks on the bones from the late Iron Age and the early Roman occupation levels had usually been made with knives in the Iron Age tradition. In the later Roman phases there was evidence of new techniques, suggesting changes in the manner of food preparation.[41] Culinary traditions are very much culturally determined, so we may be seeing here a 'romanization' of the farm's inhabitants with the adoption of new cooking methods.

Odell was a modest farmstead, and the material remains suggest a modest standard of living for its inhabitants. Other rural sites suggest a far more luxurious way of life, with the adoption of Roman fashions and habits clearly demonstrated in the layout and construction of the buildings, their internal fittings and the material remains left behind by their occupants. These are the villas, often the centres of large estates. They may be expected to give us two different sorts of information. Firstly, the bone remains should reflect the dietary habits of the wealthy of high status, and secondly they should give us some indication of the way in which the economy of the estates was managed. In practice, it is of course rather difficult to isolate these two elements, and this problem is exacerbated by the way that many villas were excavated in the past, when excavations focussed on the unravelling of the structural sequences of the main buildings. Few, if any, excavations have specifically attempted to look for the refuse dumps associated with the

35.   Maltby, op. cit. (note 28); Maltby, op. cit. (note 9).
36.   O'Connor, op. cit. (note 9), 241.
37.   Grant, op. cit. (note 12), 390.
38.   A. Grant in J.-D. Vigne (ed.), *La Découpe et le Partage du Corps à Travers le Temps et l'Espace* (Paris, 1987), 53–8.
39.   For example, Luff, op. cit. (note 3), 102.
40.   J. de G. Mazzorin in *L'Alimentazione nel Mondo Antico* (Rome, 1985), 87–93.
41.   Grant, op. cit. (note 22).

main phases of villa occupation, which should be amongst the richest sources of information for subsistence and economic reconstruction.

A feature of several bone assemblages from villas is the apparent importance of pig in the diet. This is particularly marked at the palace at Fishbourne where pigs were the best represented animals in all phases of occupation, but above average percentages of pig bones have been reported, particularly in third- and fourth-century contexts at other villas too.[42]

With the predominance of pork in the recipes of the Classical world[43] the apparent importance of this meat in the diet at villas can be viewed as evidence for the adoption of Roman dietary habits. It may also imply an increased proportion of meat in the diet and may be as much an indication of wealth and power as a desire to ape Roman habits. A recent review of animal husbandry in the medieval period in England has shown that pigs provided a much larger proportion of the diet of those of high status than of those living in towns or ordinary rural settlements.[44] It was suggested that while increased culling of young cattle or sheep for meat could have had a disastrous impact on the agricultural economy, with sufficient resources to feed the pigs, meat production could be increased without such harmful effects; and it was the rich that had control of the necessary food, be it access to woodland areas, cereal waste or even cereals themselves.

It is tempting, and perhaps not entirely inappropriate, to draw parallels here between the medieval and Roman periods. However, there are also some important differences in the ways in which the population of the Roman and medieval periods fed itself. These are particularly apparent in the use of wild animals, which are discussed below.

While some villa faunal assemblages seem to reflect the status of their occupants, in others we have indications of how the estate economies were organized. The cattle bones recovered from the extensive excavations of the villa at Barton Court include a large proportion of mature animals, but the majority of these animals were male. Wilson has suggested that male animals may have been bought in from neighbouring sites, but it is also possible that the females had been sold off, as has been suggested for some of the smaller farmsteads.[45] The sheep mortality pattern was also similar to that seen at many small farmsteads, with mature animals in the majority. The large villa estates were operating in the same economic climate as the small farms. They too had to provide for themselves as well as producing surplus items for sale, and it seems that in some cases at least they adopted similar animal management strategies.

The discussion so far has centred on the ways in which the domestic animals were managed in the Roman period, but the archaeological evidence for the size and form of the animals themselves can also be extremely informative. The domestic animals of the late Iron Age were very small and slight, particularly by modern standards.[46] In the Roman period, although they were still considerably smaller than modern animals, there is evidence for much larger cattle and also a much greater range of size, with animals as small as those of the earlier period still present even in late Roman contexts. Maltby has suggested that there are regional variations in cattle size, with large cattle absent in some areas, but the pattern appears to be complex, with the full range of sizes represented at many settlements.[47]

At Portchester, for example, the large variation in cattle size could reflect the provisioning of the fort from a range of different local farms, in different environments (see above). However,

42. Grant, op. cit. (note 9). For example, Dicket Mead, King (1984), op. cit. (note 3); Bradwell, B. Westley in M.J. Green, *The Bradwell Roman Villa* (Milton Keynes, 1975), 5–6; Chalk, A. Eastham in *Britannia* iii (1972), 141–2; Shakenoak, L. Cram in A.C.C. Brodribb, A.R. Hands and D.R. Walker, *Excavations at Shakenoak Farm, near Wilcote, Oxfordshire* (Oxford, 1978), 117–78; Frocester, B. Noddle in *Trans. Bristol Glos. Arch. Soc.* xcvii (1979) 51–61.
43. For example, Apicius, B. Flower and F. Rosenbaum, *The Roman Cookery Book: a critical translation of The Art of Cooking, by Apicius, for use in the study and the kitchen* (London, 1958).
44. Grant, op. cit. (note 11), 158, 181.
45. B. Wilson in D. Miles (ed.), *Archaeology at Barton Court Farm, Abingdon, Oxon* (Oxford, 1984), fiche 8:A1–G14.
46. See, for example, A. Grant in B.W. Cunliffe, op. cit. (note 2), 496–549; P. Armitage, *The Ark* ix, 57.
47. Maltby, op. cit. (note 3).

there was also a significant increase in the average but also in the range of cattle size from the Iron Age to the Roman period at the farmstead at Odell.[48]

There is some disagreement about the causes of the improvement of Romano-British cattle. Maltby's review shows evidence for the presence of large cattle in some areas of Britain in the early part of the Roman period, and suggests the likelihood of importation of cattle, as well as improvements to native stock in some regions.[49] Armitage strongly refutes the importation explanation – 'all the skeletal remains I have examined so far indicate that the larger of the Romano-British cattle probably arose from the upgrading of existing British cattle. . .'.[50] The horn cores of the cattle of Britain were, like those of the Iron Age, mainly short horned, with some small and medium horned animals. Long horned animals are not found in Britain until the Middle Ages, but appear in Italy at least as early as the first century A.D.. Changes in animal form would constitute good evidence for animal importation. Without this we would be safer to assume that other factors, and in particular improved nutrition, may have been responsible for the size increase.[51] Movement of settlement to areas of lower ground may have made available better quality pasture, and more intensive cereal cultivation could have increased the amount of fodder for supplementary feeding.

However, we also have indications that suggest that developments were being made in the understanding of animal breeding. This is shown not only in the many new types of dogs that appear in this period (see below) but also in the find of a mule bone in a second-century context.[52] If it is not clear whether the animals involved were, initially at least, imported, the improved knowledge of breeding may well have been.

Sheep also seem to have increased in size over the Roman period, although there are rather fewer metrical data available for this animal. There is also evidence for changes in sheep morphology – hornless sheep have been reported from several sites, and occasionally four-horned animals have been found. However, these characteristics can arise as a result of genetic mutation, and since their occurrence is only spasmodic, they do not in themselves constitute secure evidence for importation of new types of sheep. The Roman farmers were probably less interested in the size of their sheep than in the quality of the wool that they produced, and there is evidence for improvement here.

Preserved textile remains from Roman Britain include a variety of types, including the primitive hairy pigmented ones but also the fine true wools. These latter appear for the first time in the Roman period and may be from imported animals, but the possibility of local evolution is not discounted.[53] Britain seems to have lagged behind the continent in the improvement of wool quality as the preserved textiles recovered here have included a higher proportion of pigmented and hairy wools[54] but by the fourth century at least British woollen goods were being exported and commanding high prices.[55]

The animals discussed so far have been the three most common domestic animals, cattle, sheep and pigs. However, the exploitation of other animals also contributed to the Roman economy. The introduction to Britain of the domestic chicken took place in the late Iron Age, but at this period their bones are rare finds. Fowl are far more frequently reported from Roman sites, both military and civilian, and of all periods. They are often found with smaller numbers of duck and goose bones. Although fairly ubiquitous, the bones of domestic birds usually occur in very small numbers and can have only provided a very small part of the diet. However, they appear to be slightly more common on military sites and in towns than on rural settlements, including villas,

48. Grant, op. cit. (note 22).
49. Maltby, op. cit. (note 3).
50. Armitage, op. cit. (note 44).
51. B. Noddle in M. Jones (ed.), *Integrating the Subsistence Economy* (Oxford, 1983), 212; Grant, op. cit. (note 11), 177.
52. P. Armitage and H. Chapman, *London Arch.* iii (1979), 339–46.
53. M. Ryder, *Sheep and Man* (London, 1983), 178.
54. Ryder, op. cit. (note 50), 178.
55. J.P. Wild in D. Miles (ed.), *The Romano-British Countryside* (Oxford, 1982), 120.

although the Fishbourne palace has rather high percentage of bird bones.[56] Raising chickens seems to have been part of the solution to the problem of feeding the non-productive population, the army and the town-dwellers, who may have raised them within the towns and the military settlements. They do not seem to have been very common farmyard animals. In this context it is interesting to note the finds made during the excavation of the fortress baths at Caerleon. Most of the bones found in the first- and second-century *frigidarium* drain were from domestic fowl. These have been interpreted as the remains of 'light snacks' served to the bathers.[57]

Faunal assemblages from Romano-British sites also include the bones of a range of wild animals which appear to have been a part of the diet. The study of the exploitation of fish has been hampered by the small amount of attention that has been given to adequate recovery techniques for their very small bones and quantifying the contribution of fish to the diet is an almost impossible task. The indications are that the consumption of fish increased in comparison with that of the Iron Age, but the fishing seems to have mainly been of fresh, estuarine and coastal waters rather than the deep sea. Very intensive exploitation is not indicated.

Parker list 94 species of wild birds from 86 Romano-British sites,[58] and the bones of the two native species of deer (red and roe) and of hare are frequently found, at sites of all types and all periods. The range of wild bird species is considerably larger than has been reported for the Iron Age, and slightly larger although similar to that of the medieval period. However, any similarity in the range of wild species exploited in the Roman and medieval periods is belied by the considerable difference in their importance in the diet. On Romano-British sites, with very few exceptions, the bones of wild animals occur only in very small numbers. In the medieval period the archaeological evidence suggests that wild animals sometimes made a substantial contribution to the diet. Wild birds were eaten in the towns and in the countryside, and marine fish were eaten even in landlocked regions.[59] Although deer were legitimately a food resource only for the upper classes, and their bones are rarely found in towns, their presence in the rubbish of rural settlements attests their contribution to the peasant diet too. This intensified exploitation of wild animal resources can be viewed as a response to the problems of feeding an expanding population in a period when agricultural productivity was not similarly increasing.[60]

For the Roman period the scarcity of wild animal remains may be a testament to the efficiency of the agricultural system, which was adequately feeding the population, and producing a surplus with which to pay the taxes demanded by the Roman administration and to participate in local and international trade. It has been suggested that where there is evidence for increased exploitation of wild animals on Romano-British sites, we may have an indication of times of stress or difficulty in producing food and we can draw parallels with the medieval period here.[61] However, in the Roman period such times seem to have been rare and localized; in the later period the problems were far more fundamental. Nor do we have for our period any clearcut evidence for an association between increased percentages of deer bones and settlements of high status, although proportions of deer remains at Shakenoak villa were rather high.[62] The prime importance of deer for our period seems to have been as a source of antler as a raw material. Most of the deer remains that have been reported are not bones but antler fragments, and it seems that in the majority of cases, the antlers were collected after they had been shed, and not removed from slain animals.[63]

This paper has concentrated on the animals that were used for food in Britain in the Roman period, although it has emphasized that many of the domestic animals may have been as

56.   Grant, op. cit. (note 9).
57.   O'Connor, op. cit. (note 9), 227.
58.   A.J. Parker, *Oxford Journ. Arch.* vii (1988), 197–226.
59.   Grant, op. cit. (note 11), 172.
60.   Astill and Grant, op. cit. (note 11), 213ff.
61.   A. Grant in M. Jones and G. Dimbleby (eds.), *The Environment of Man: the Iron Age to the Anglo-Saxon Period* (Oxford, 1981), 205–13.
62.   Cram, op. cit. (note 40).
63.   Grant, op. cit. (note 12).

important when alive as when dead. The remains of some other animals, whose uses were slightly different, have also been found. Horses and dogs are the most common of these, and their bones are found at most settlements, although they are rarely very common. This is not surprising since most excavated deposits containing animal bones are refuse, usually food refuse deposits, and neither of these animals was normally used as food for human consumption. Cut-marks have been reported on some horse bones, but some of these appear to have been the result of the skinning of the carcasses rather than the removal of meat. Since it seems unlikely that they were used for pulling heavy loads at this period, horses must have been mainly used as riding animals, and to have been particularly important for the army. However, their bones seem to have been rather rarely recovered at many military settlements. We may here be seeing the results of an orderly attitude to rubbish disposal, but it is also possible that horses were only of use in a military context when in optimum condition. Once past their prime they may have been sold to civilians.

The majority of the bones from deposits in the Silchester amphitheatre were those of horses, and this has suggested that these animals may also have been used in performances.[64] A bear mandible was recovered at Sheepen but this was a very exceptional find.[65] Most of the wild animals that were popular in the spectacles staged in Italy were not available in Britain and customs no doubt had to adapt to local conditions.

The most interesting aspect of the dog remains is the great variety in form and size that they display. There is relatively little variation in Iron Age dogs, and yet Roman dog bones come from animals whose sizes range from those of toy poodles to alsatians and include animals with distinctly bowed legs.[66] The regular occurrence of animals of small size and distorted form suggests not only an increasing understanding of breeding but also a fundamental change in attitude to animals. We see the emergence of animals kept not for their usefulness, but merely as man's companions, as pets. The influence of the classical world may have been powerful here.

Finally, and very briefly, mention must be made of the role of animals in ritual and religion. There is considerable evidence for the importance of animals in Iron Age ritual.[67] Whole animals, or parts of animals, sometimes associated with stones, appear to have been deliberately deposited in pits within settlements and in wells. Some continuity of this practice throughout the Roman period is demonstrated by unusual collections of bones, particularly in wells, but occasionally in pits too. Skulls of horses, cattle, sheep and dogs, and red deer remains have all been reported from wells, and in some instances they may have been associated with human infant burials. Parker has discussed the possible religious significance of birds, and has noted that ravens are particularly frequent on Roman sites.[68] Ravens are also amongst the most frequent of birds found on Iron Age sites, and there is evidence to suggest that they had some special or religious significance here.[69]

Other animal deposits result from different practices that demonstrate more profound changes in ritual and religion. Animals or parts of animals are sometimes found with inhumations in graves, a phenomenon not usually encountered in Iron Age ritual, although they do occur with cremations in late Iron Age contexts. The remarkable collection of animal remains from the temple site at Uley more clearly demonstrates a new religious practise in Britain. The majority of the bones, particularly in the second- to fifth-century contexts, were those of male goats and chickens, animals that are rather rare at other Romano-British sites.[70] These animals are almost certainly sacrificial victims, and seem to be associated with the Roman god Mercury. The important contrast with Iron Age ritual is that the animals seem to have been butchered, and

64. A. Grant in M. Fulford, *The Silchester Amphitheatre: Excavations of 1975–85* (London, 1989).
65. Luff, op. cit. (note 9), 148.
66. R. Harcourt, *Journ. Arch. Science* i (1974), 151–176; R. Harcourt in B.W. Cunliffe, op. cit. (note 13), 406–8.
67. G.A. Wait, *Ritual and Religion in Iron Age Britain* (Oxford, 1985).
68. Parker, op. cit. (note 54).
69. A. Grant in P. Meniel (ed.), *Animal et Practiques Réligieuses: les Manifestations Materielles* (Paris, in press).
70. B. Levitan in A.D. Woodward and P.J. Leach, *Uley Shrines* (London, in press).

presumably eaten, whereas those ritual deposits that have been detected from the Iron Age are usually of unbutchered animals. An important aspect of the ritual of animal sacrifice in the Classical world was the butchery and division of the carcass, which was specified in sacred laws.[71]

CONCLUSIONS

The impact of the Roman conquest and occupation of Britain on animal husbandry is perhaps most evident in the change from a sheep- to a cattle-dominated husbandry, although the beginnings of this change can be detected before the Conquest. It has been suggested here that the main causes of this change are linked to a need to intensify agricultural production, particularly cereal cultivation. The increase in non-productive elements of society, mainly the army and the developing urban population, clearly put pressure on the existing agricultural system to produce more food. But the demand was also for other animal products, particularly wool and leather; the army and the towns provided not only the main market for these goods, but also the necessary organization for their exchange. The continuity of occupation of many of the rural farming settlements, be they villa estates or more modest farmsteads, together with the very small reliance on wild animal resources can be viewed as a testament to the successful adaptation of British animal husbandry to the changing situation.

The period of Roman occupation also saw considerable changes in the animals themselves. There were size increases in both the cattle and the sheep populations, with an improvement of wool quality demonstrated for the latter. There is, as yet at least, no clear indication of whether these improvements were due to importations of new breeding stock, or the result of better understanding of animal nutrition and animal breeding. The most marked changes were seen in the greatly increased range of variation in the dog population. Some of these dogs 'were too small to have served any useful purpose . . . or to have survived without human shelter'[72]; they were in fact pets. This perhaps demonstrates beginnings of the development of a fundamental change in attitude to the animal kingdom.

Changes in religious or ritual attitudes to animals can also be demonstrated for this period, with the influence of the classical world clearly apparent in the nature of animal sacrifices. And the 'romanization' of the diet is perhaps most apparent in the butchery practises used, which suggest that new cooking methods were gradually adopted.

The evidence for any differences in the diet that can be related to status is slight, but a higher proportion of pork seems to have characterized the diet of those who lived in villas, while chickens were more commonly eaten by the army and those who lived in towns.

What this discussion clearly lacks is a detailed temporal and regional dimension. The limitations of the available archaeozoological evidence have already been discussed above, and these inhibit the possibility of such analyses. However, this is not a reflection of the potential of the animal bone studies. Methodological advances have been made that allow for example, the possibility of examination of mortality patterns in order to be able to understand the nature of husbandry practices, and whether assemblages from individual settlements represent closed herds or suggest import or export of parts of the herds. Trace element analysis, and even examination of tooth-wear may be able to suggest where and how animals have been grazed.

If we wish to understand the nature of subsistance, and the way that it was organized, we need to adopt different excavation strategies, ones that are *specifically* designed to recover faunal assemblages of the appropriate quality. We also need to be able to look in detail at large numbers of sites within single *regions*, so that we can understand how settlements of differing size and status were related economically. The work of some of the best of our archaeological units is beginning to make such approaches possible. We look to the future for enough material of appropriate quantity and quality to allow the potential of the study of bone remains to be expressed in an increased and valued contribution to mainstream archaeology.

---

71.   J.-L. Durand in Vigne, op. cit. (note 36), 58–66; J. Svenbro in Vigne, op. cit. (note 36), 59–66.
72.   Harcourt (1974), op. cit. (note 62), 164.

THE ROMAN FENLAND: A REVIEW OF RECENT WORK*

By T.W. Potter

The current vogue for 'landscape archaeology' is amongst the most positive lines of present-day research. The intensive examination of individual sites has for long been a profitable line of enquiry; but, if undertaken in spatial (and chronological) isolation, rarely has so much to offer as a more broadly based study. The point is well made by Leveau's sensitive investigation of Iol Caesarea, modern Cherchel in northern Algeria, and its *territorium*.[1] By use of field survey, combined with epigraphical and archival research, he has been able to define the intricate relationship between the city and its hinterland in remarkable detail, resulting in some hypotheses of far-reaching importance. The conclusion may not always provoke consensus, but there is no doubt of the validity of the approach.

In Cambridgeshire, landscape studies were put on a firm footing as early as 1923, with Fox's magisterial survey of the archaeology of the Cambridge region.[2] Although this only considered the southern part of the Fens, the evidence that he collected demonstrated a rich concentration of Bronze Age material, a notable sparsity of Iron Age finds, extensive occupation in the Roman period and a much more limited number of Anglo-Saxon sites. A settlement model was thus framed, which was endorsed and expanded during the 1930s.[3] Aerial photography rapidly emerged as an invaluable tool for locating and plotting Romano-British settlements, field systems and drove roads, while pedological and environmental studies, combined with excavation, established a relative chronology for the layers of silt, peat and clay which fill the Fenland basin.

The immediate post-War years are sometimes depicted as a period of neglect in Fenland studies, but this is far from being the case. Bromwich was surveying the southern skirtlands, and Hallam the south Lincolnshire silts (in 1950–52); Clark excavated the Car Dyke at Cottenham in 1947 and St. Joseph carried out repeated aerial reconnaissance.[4] From 1956, the writer and his brother were also at work in the March area, first with field survey and then with excavation, and

*   I am grateful to Peter Salway and Malcolm Todd for their comments on this paper; to Simon James for making available the plan of Estover; to Stephen Crummy who drew all save one of the line drawings; and, above all, to the Trustees, and my colleagues, at the British Museum for supporting the work at Stonea, especially my co-director, Ralph Jackson.

1. Ph. Leveau, *Caesarea de Maurétanie. Une ville romaine et ses campagnes* Collection de L'Ecole française de Rome 70 (Rome, 1984).
2. C. Fox, *Archaeology of the Cambridge region* (Cambridge, 1923).
3. C.W. Phillips in W.F. Grimes (ed.), *Aspects of archaeology in Britain and beyond* (London, 1951), 258–73.
4. J. Bromwich and S. Hallam in C.W. Phillips (ed.), *The Fenland in Roman Times* RGS Research Memoir 5 (1970), 22–126; J.G.D. Clark, *Antiq. Journ.* xxix (1949), 145–63; J.K. St. Joseph, *JRS* xliii (1953), 96 and *JRS* xlv (1955), 90.

other groups were active in regions such as the Fen edge near Peterborough.[5] There was also an investigation in 1957 of a temple complex at Leylands Farm, Hockwold, and three excavations in advance of the Great Ouse Cut-Off channel, at Denver (1960), Little Oulsham Drove, Feltwell (1962 and 1964), and at Grange Farm, Hockwold (1961–62).[6] Thus, when Salway took on the onerous task in 1960 of assembling the data into a single volume, there was much on which to build. Published in 1970, the result – which included substantial contributions by Hallam, Bromwich and others – was a masterly synthesis, which set out a series of stimulating hypotheses, and laid a solid foundation for future work.[7]

As it happens, it was during the 1950s and 1960s that most of the last well-preserved major Romano-British settlements, with earthworks fossilised in pasture, were broken up for arable farming. It is particularly unfortunate that, with the exception of Grandford,[8] none of these sites received attention before they were ploughed (and we shall turn later to an assessment of the consequences); and that the publication of *The Fenland in Roman Times* did not immediately prompt a programme of excavation. Indeed, it was not until 1976 that a new initiative was taken when David Hall began a pilot field survey in Cambridgeshire, funded by the Department of the Environment.[9] This multi-period examination of the Fenland landscape rapidly produced important new evidence, including a Roman stone building at Stonea Grange, and in 1981 a major project was set up to extend the survey into the Fenland areas of Norfolk, Suffolk and Lincolnshire.[10] Funding was also available for new environmental investigation, and both projects are now reaching completion.[11] About the same time, several new major excavations were initiated. Between 1979 and 1981, Pryor and French examined crop-mark sites at Maxey, in the lower Welland valley,[12] thus continuing Pryor's remarkable work on the prehistoric landscapes at Fengate, to the east of Peterborough;[13] since 1980, Hodder and Evans have been carrying out a multi-period investigation of sites near Haddenham;[14] and between 1980 and 1984, the British Museum excavated a substantial area at Stonea Grange and also made a brief study of Stonea Camp.[15]

The British Museum excavations were the direct outcome of the writer's work on the publication of his earlier investigations in the March area.[16] The Museum's programme fitted harmoniously with the aims of the Fenland Project and led additionally to a very small excavation at Field Baulk, March in 1982[17] and to an investigation, funded by HBMC and directed by Simon James, at Estover, March, in 1985.[18] Both were sites of exceptional interest since they

5.   T.W. Potter, *Britannia* xii (1981), 79; G. Fowler, *Proc. Cambs. Antiq. Soc. (PCAS* below) xliii (1949), 7–20; B.R. Hartley and E. Standen, *PCAS* lii (1959), 21–2; G.F. Dakin, *PCAS* liv (1961), 50–67; A. Challands, *Durobrivae* 6 (1978), 32–4.

6.   D. Gurney, *Settlement, religion and industry on the Fen-edge: three Romano-British sites in Norfolk* East Anglian Archaeology 31 (1986); P. Salway, 'Excavations at Hockwold-cum-Wilton,' *PCAS* lx (1967), 39–80.

7.   Phillips (ed.), op. cit. (note 4).

8.   T.W. Potter and C.F. Potter, *A Romano-British village at Grandford, March, Cambs.* Brit. Mus. Occ. Pap. 35 (1982); *PCAS* lxx (1980), 75–112. Cf. D.N. Hall, *Fenland landscapes and settlement between Peterborough and March* East Anglian Archaeology 35 (1987), 65 on the few grass sites that do survive. Cf. *Britannia* vi (1975), 250 for work on the Fen edge at Earith in 1974.

9.   D.N. Hall, 'Elm: a field survey', *PCAS* lxviii (1978), 21–46.

10. cf., *inter alia*, J.M. Coles and D.N. Hall, 'The Fenland project,' *Antiquity* lvii (1983), 51–2; D. Hall, 'Survey work in eastern England' in S. Macready and F.H. Thompson (eds.), *Archaeological field survey in Britain and abroad* Soc. Antiq. Lond. Occ. Pap.6 (1985), 25–44. See also now *Antiquity* lxii (1988), 305–80.

11. M. Waller, 'The Fenland Project's environmental programme,' *Antiquity* lxii (1988), 336–43; Hall, op. cit. (note 8).

12. F.M.M. Pryor, C. French *et al.*, *Archaeology and environment in the lower Welland Valley* East Anglian Archaeology 27 (1985).

13. cf. especially F.M.M. Pryor, *Excavations at Fengate, Peterborough: the Third Report* (Toronto and Northampton, 1980); idem, *The Fourth Report* (Toronto and Northampton, 1984).

14. cf. summary reports in *Fenland Research* i–iv (1983– 87).

15. T.W. Potter and R.P.J. Jackson, *Antiquity* lvi (1982), 111–20.

16. T.W. Potter, 'The Roman occupation of the central Fenland,' *Britannia* xii (1981), 79–133.

17. So far unpublished except in T.W. Potter, *Roman Britain* (British Museum, 1983), 28 and fig. 25.

18. S. James, *Fenland Research* iii (1985–86), 29–30.

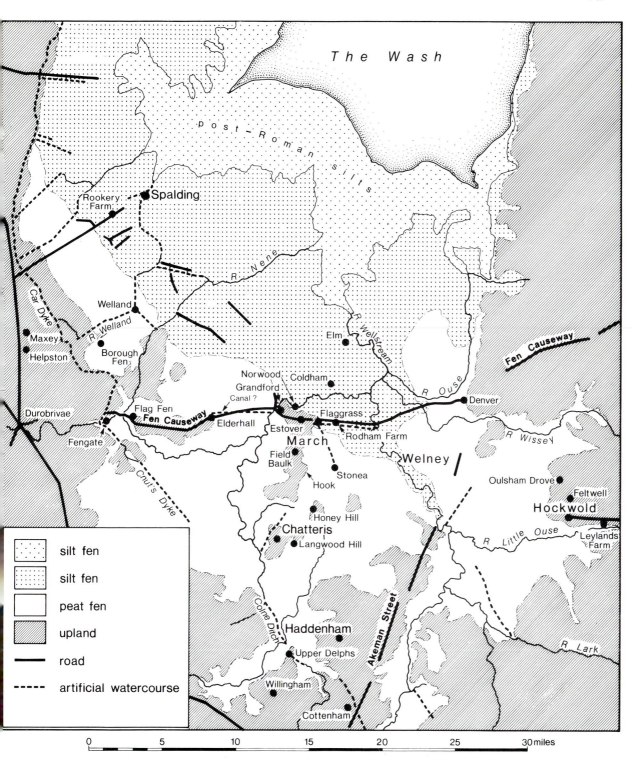

FIG. 1   General map of the Fenland, showing places and features mentioned in the text.

were in occupation about the time of the Roman conquest, a period that hitherto had been ill-represented in the archaeological record of the Fenland.

The cumulative result of this great investment of resources into the Fens is that the body of data has grown enormously over the last decade or so. It is therefore a timely moment to take stock, especially as the first two Fenland Project volumes have recently been published,[19] as have some of the older excavations on the eastern margins of the region.[20] The monograph on the work at Stonea is still in preparation, due to the enormous quantities of material that were recovered; but much has been done and the picture of the site's evolution (if not its interpretation) can now be considered well established.

THE PRE-ROMAN BACKGROUND

One of the great revelations of the recent Fenland survey has been the discovery of a prodigious number of prehistoric settlements, implying sustained exploitation of the marginal environment of the Fens. The disclosure of those earlier landscapes must in part be due to the fact that, in some areas at least, the plough is now breaking through into much older deposits, which are rich in prehistoric finds.[21] The process is particularly clear on the eastern side of the Fenland, in areas such as Hockwold-cum-Wilton, but can also be demonstrated in the central part of the region. At Flaggrass, for example, huge collections of pottery were collected when the southern part of the site was first ploughed in 1956, and over the following few years. Nothing was found which dated before the late first century A.D.. Now, however, Hall reports a quantity of late Iron Age pottery, including butt-beakers and *terra nigra*, which presumably derive from layers that were untouched until fairly recently.[22] By contrast, in the west and south-western Fens, there are many pre-Roman sites which have been masked by alluvium and, in some cases, still remain completely buried. Here, systematic study of freshly cleaned dyke sections has proved most informative, leading to remarkable discoveries like the late Bronze Age settlement at Flag Fen and the Iron Age ringwork at Borough Fen.[23]

Hand-in-hand with the work of field survey, there is a continuing programme to refine our understanding of the highly complex geological and environmental changes that have taken place within the Fenland basin since the end of the last glaciation.[24] This is not the place to review these studies in detail; however, two broad conclusions seem to emerge from the current investigation. One is to underline still further the precarious balance between human occupation and the environment in the Fenland region, where very slight physical changes can have drastic consequences. The value of wetlands as a major resource was well recognised in antiquity, not least by the Romans. The bounteous nature of the Po Plain, for example, with its huge production of wheat, millet and grapes, and its celebrated woollen goods, was clearly appreciated by writers such as Pliny and Strabo, who laid particular emphasis upon its commercial value.[25] However, it was equally recognised that only careful management of the landscape, through the use of dykes and canals, could ensure that this bounty continued, and even then vines died young and cities, like Spina and Ravenna, could become wholly land-locked. Wetlands, therefore, were well worth exploiting, but this took time, trouble and, above all, organisation, skill and manpower – as, indeed, the recent history of Fenland drainage clearly shows.[26]

19. Pryor and French, op. cit. (note 12); Hall, op. cit. (note 8).
20. Gurney, op. cit. (note 6).
21. cf., for example, B. Sylvester, *Antiquity* lxii (1988), 327.
22. Hall, op. cit. (note 8), 40, 43 and microfiche.
23. C. French, 'The southwest fen dyke survey project,' *Antiquity* lxii (1988), 343–8; Pryor *et al.*, 'Flag Fen, Fengate, Peterborough,' *PPS* lii (1986), 1–24; for Borough Fen, Pryor in *Northants. Arch.* xviii (1983), 167, and Hall, op. cit. (note 8), 26f.
24. I. Shennan, 'Flandrian sea-level changes in the Fenland,' *Journal of Quaternary Science* i (1986), 119–79; Waller, op. cit. (note 11).
25. e.g. Pliny, *Nat. Hist.* III, xvi; Strabo, V, 1, 12.
26. cf. T.W. Potter, 'Marshland and drainage in the classical world,' in R.T. Rowley, (ed), *The evolution of marshland landscapes* (Oxford, 1981), 1–19; K.D. White, *Roman farming* (London, 1970), 146f.

The other feature to emerge from the current environmental work is to demonstrate the enormous degree of variation in the local sequences of deposits. For instance, the deposition of the great bed of Fen Clay – once thought to represent a single episode of marine flooding – now appears to vary in date by a thousand years or more from one area to another, implying that local factors were paramount in its distribution.[27] It follows that many of the judgements about the nature of the environment, at any one time and in any one region, need careful appraisal, a matter to which we shall return below. A break-down in the local drainage system (which, as the Fengate excavation shows, was organised from at least as early as the second millennium B.C.)[28] would certainly lead to severe agricultural problems, and a loss of production. Were resources insufficient to restore the situation, then the inhabitants would rapidly have found difficulty in meeting any demands over and above subsistence living: in the more complex societies of the later prehistoric and Romano-British periods, when taxation was doubtless a factor, this may well have generated considerable difficulties and perhaps altered the pattern of land exploitation and, indeed, settlement.

Organisation of the Fenland landscape extends far back into prehistory. This much is clear from the excavations at Haddenham[29] and Maxey,[30] both of which seem to have emerged as important ritual centres during the Neolithic; and from the work at Fengate, with its field systems and drove-roads.[31] Moreover Stonea, a site in the heart of the Fens, has yielded traces of what appears to have been a cursus, as well as much other evidence for prehistoric occupation. It may also have been selected as a 'central place' early in the development of the region, and the same may well be true of some of the other large 'islands' in the southern and central Fens, all of which have produced substantial quantities of Neolithic and Bronze Age material.

The interpretation of the Neolithic and Bronze Age landscapes of the Fens is not a matter for detailed discussion in these pages. On the other hand, the newly revealed evidence for Iron Age settlement is of considerable relevance, since it furnishes a background to the Roman occupation that was not available until recently. It must be said at once that the picture is still relatively blurred, and will remain so until greater focus is achieved by means of further excavation, especially within the Fens. However, it is now established that there was occupation during some of the Iron Age on many of the Fen islands, and also on the marine clays in the Spalding-Crowland area of southern Lincolnshire.[32] The Lincolnshire sites yield pottery that is primarily of Middle Iron Age type, but whether this is a true reflection of their date-range is impossible to say; what is not in doubt, however, is that a high proportion is associated with saltern debris, anticipating the major concentration upon the winning of salt that characterises the Romano-British period in this region.[33]

Most of the pottery so far recovered from the southern Fen 'islands' seems to belong primarily to the earlier part of the Iron Age. But the collections are not particularly large, and, as in the Lincolnshire Fens, may not provide a very sensitive indication of the period of settlement. Two notably large settlements are known from the Chatteris island, while at Stonea excavation disclosed part of a settlement of late Bronze Age/early Iron Age date. This was sealed beneath 70 cm of flood silts, into which were cut pits containing pottery of the early to mid-first century

27.   Waller, op. cit. (note 11), is the most recent statement. Cf also *Fenland Research* iv (1984), 11–17, and H. Godwin, *Fenland: its ancient past and uncertain future* (Cambridge, 1978), 62f.
28.   Pryor, op. cit. (note 13), especially *The Fourth Report*, 206f.
29.   D. Hall, C. Evans, I. Hodder and F. Pryor, 'The Fenlands of East Anglia,' in J.M. Coles and A. Lawson (eds.), *European Wetlands in prehistory* (Oxford, 1987), 169–202; interim reports in *Fenland Research*, vols. i–iv (1983–84f.).
30.   Pryor and French, op. cit. (note 12).
31.   Pryor and French, op. cit. (note 12). For a Neolithic causewayed enclosure at Etton, near Maxey, see Pryor, French and Taylor in *Antiq. Journ.* lxv (1985), 275–311.
32.   T. Lane, 'Pre-Roman origins for settlement on the Fens of south Lincolnshire,' *Antiquity* lxii (1988), 314–21.
33.   S. Hallam, 'The Romano-British salt industry in south Lincolnshire,' *Lincs. Architect. and Arch. Soc., Reports and Papers* n.s. viii (1959–60), 35–75, and Addendum, ibid ix (1961), 88; idem in Phillips, op. cit. (note 4), 67–70. See also E. Birley, *Roman Britain and the Roman Army* (Kendal, 1953), 88f. for possible state-owned salt-works in Britain.

A.D.. The base of these silts lay at a height of *c.* 3m AOD, clearly attesting the onset of much wetter conditions. Diatoms from these silts point to the type of conditions that prevail towards the head of an estuary, suggesting that the flooding was not a localised phenomenon.[34]

Some pits and ditches of early to middle Iron Age date were found in the area to the north-east of the main excavation at Stonea, cut through another, quite different, deposit, seemingly of alluvial type; but too little was examined to cast much light upon the nature of the settlement. Nevertheless, there are hints here that the occupation at Stonea, however affected by flooding, may have continued throughout the Iron Age, a conjecture that receives some support from the metalwork recovered from the site.

Elsewhere in the Fens, the evidence for a wet and inclement environment during the Iron Age is correspondingly strong. At the Upper Delphs near Haddenham, a three-year-long programme of excavation has brought to light the impressive remains of a Middle Iron Age landscape with enclosures and field boundaries that cover 5 ha.[35] The complex lies on a gravel terrace, 2.50 m AOD, which juts into the fen, and one enclosure was almost totally excavated. Ard marks beneath the bank attest some arable cultivation, but the animal bones, although dominated by sheep (63%) and cattle (24%), included a remarkable number of typical wetland species, especially beaver and waterfowl. Indeed, the site was eventually covered by alluvium, its abandonment dating to the late Middle Iron Age.

The Fengate site of Cat's Water, which lies at about 3m AOD on the Fen edge to the west of Peterborough, was also founded in the Middle Iron Age.[36] It carried on in occupation down to the period of the Roman Conquest, when it comprised a settlement of about ten buildings, some of which housed animals. Cattle were here marginally more numerous than sheep, but waterfowl and fish again attest exploitation of the fenland. Cereals seem to have been of minor importance, and may well have been imported to the site. Further north, in the Maxey area, sustained activity is attested throughout the Iron Age, although it is apparently late in the period that large-scale field systems were laid out, pointing perhaps to the need for much more systematic land management.[37]

It would be very premature to press our few data for the Iron Age settlement of the Fens and its margins into a firm model. However, it is clear that, despite a steady deterioration of the environment, and especially of the local drainage conditions, the resources of the marshlands were exploited for much of the Iron Age. There may well have been a quite considerable permanent community within parts of the Fenland, and it is intriguing to wonder how it was organised. The Borough Fen ring-work, which encloses 3.8ha and may be of Middle Iron Age date, hints at a more complex social structure within the region than might first be supposed, and other comparable sites may yet come to light.[38] Part of a large undated enclosure, *c.*300m in diameter (Fig. 1), is now known from Stonea, and we shall see below that a modern urban landscape such as March (which itself, as with other Fenland towns, lies in a position of prime topographical importance) can conceal sites of remarkable, and unexpected, interest. A hierarchy of settlements within the Fens is therefore by no means impossible. However, environmental considerations do seem to imply that there was little stability of settlement and, given the value of marshland as a resource, political factors may also have played a part in the fortunes of individual sites, as they were often to do later on.

34. Identification of the diatoms by A. Alderton. The flooding might belong to the so-called Terrington inundation of the late Iron Age date: see note 39.

35. C. Evans and D. Serjeantson, 'The backwater economy of a Fen-edge community in the Iron Age,' *Antiquity* lxii (1988), 360–70.

36. Pryor, op. cit. (note 13, *The Fourth Report*).

37. Pryor and French, op. cit. (note 12).

38. For the Borough Fen ring work, cf. note 23.

THE LATE IRON AGE AND EARLY ROMAN PERIOD

The weight of the evidence now available suggests that large parts of the silt lands of Cambridgeshire, which were so extensively colonised in Romano-British times, were being laid down in final form around the time of the Roman Conquest. This marine incursion may have begun late in the Iron Age, representing the culmination of a long period of deteriorating conditions.[39]

The southern Fens were not directly affected by this inundation, and increasingly appear to have supported a quite considerable population. To what extent this was the result of a steady development from earlier in the Iron Age (as at Fengate and the lower Welland Valley) is quite unclear; but there is an apparent expansion in settlement during the first part of the first century A.D., which hints at the emergence of more complex societies. Political boundaries certainly changed during this period in south-east England, and populations may well have been rising.[40] Marshlands, however precarious a place in which to live, had a particular value, and there may have been competing interests from the Iceni, Catuvellauni and Coritani (or Corieltauvi)[41] in this area.

The site of Stonea (Fig. 2) is of considerable importance for our understanding of the period, although its prominence may be exaggerated due to the survival of a single monument, namely Stonea Camp, and because of the intensity of recent work there. On the other hand, the island seems to have been singled out as a 'central place' far back in prehistory, and the 'Camp' and the exceptional Roman settlement that succeeded it may be an echo of a longstanding pre-eminence.

The 'Camp' itself is a complex feature, probably with three phases of construction (Fig. 3). A notional first phase comprises an approximately circular enclosure, with a single bank and ditch, and an internal area of c.4.3 ha. This was subsequently enlarged to the north and west, and also in the north-east corner, bringing the enclosed area up to about 8 ha, a layout that is reminiscent of some oppida in southern England.[42] Finally, the defences were radically modified by the construction of a double arc of ramparts and ditches, stretching from river to river, and thus reducing the enclosed area to about 3.2 ha. It was the latest phase of defences that were sectioned in 1980.[43] These had been slighted soon after they were constructed, although the botanical evidence from the deposits in the ditch is consistent with a surrounding landscape that was cleared and partly cultivated, but with pockets of oak, willow and alder in wetter areas.[44]

The pottery from Stonea Camp indicates activity from about A.D.40 to c.A.D.60, after which it was effectively abandoned. This date is corroborated by a group of brooches, and also by a single coin of Gaius and three of Claudius. However, excavation, aerial photography and geophysical survey have yielded no evidence for buildings or pits, and (without here arguing the case in detail) we are now inclined to see it as some sort of tribal centre, which might have been finally modified in response to the tumultuous events of A.D.47 or A.D.60–61.[45]

A picture of Stonea Camp as a type of 'port of trade', perhaps combined with a religious function, is heavily influenced by finds of coins and high-status metalwork from the area immediately to the north and north-east. The coins are of particular interest. They include both

39. *Britannia* xii (1981), 81. For radiocarbon dates from the contact between underlying peat and the silts (the so-called Terrington Beds) near Wisbech, see Waller, *Antiquity* lxii (1988), 338–9; the dates are 2120 ± 60 b.p., Q–2519; 2100 ± 50 b.p., Q–2511; 2010 ± 50 b.p., Q–2508, which support a late date for the flooding.

40. cf. *interalia*, B. Cunliffe (ed.), *Coinage and society in Britain and Gaul: some current problems* CBA Res. Rep. 38 (Dorchester, 1981); B. Cunliffe and D. Miles (eds.), *Aspects of the Iron Age in central and southern Britain* Univ. Oxford Comm. Arch. Monograph 2 (Oxford, 1984).

41. cf. R.S.O. Tomlin, *Antiq. Journ.* lxiii (1983), 353– 5 for the Corieltauvi.

42. e.g. B.W. Cunliffe, 'The origins of urbanisation in Britain,' in B. Cunliffe and T. Rowley (eds.), *Oppida in barbarian Europe.* BAR S11 (Oxford, 1975), 135–62 and fig. 5.

43. T.W. Potter and R.P.J. Jackson, *Antiquity* lvi (1982), 111-20.

44. Report by A.M. Blackham, D.G. Gilbertson and M. van der Veen.

45. Later coins are recorded as being from the site, including issues of Hadrian (3), Antoninus Pius (1), Commodus (1) and 13 coins of the third and fourth centuries (identified by D.C.A. Shotter).

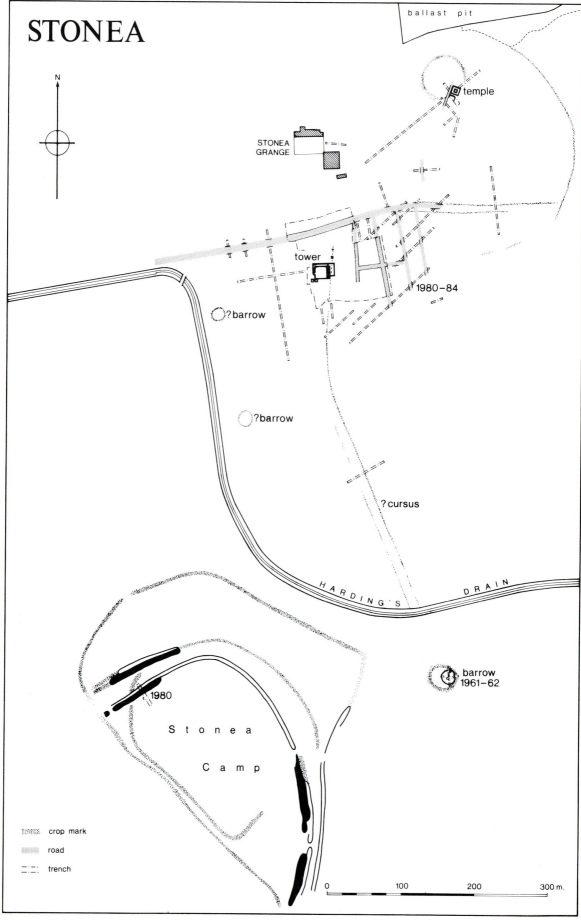

FIG. 2 Overall plan of Stonea and its environs, showing excavations and principal features.

STONEA CAMP; possible sequence

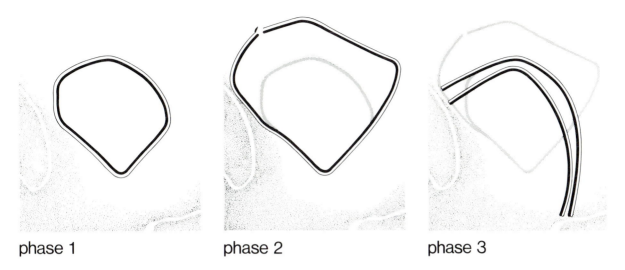

phase 1   phase 2   phase 3

FIG. 3   Stonea Camp: possible sequence.

hoard material and some casual losses, and are dominated by issues of the Iceni. This recalls the hoard of Iceni coins, with 'Ed', 'Symbols' and 'Aesu' issues, reported first by Evans;[46] although it is sometimes, and erroneously, associated with Stonea Camp, it does seem certain that it was found somewhere on the island. If so, it supports the case for regarding Stonea as an Icenian centre, a view that is further reinforced by other coin hoards from the March area, which will be referred to below. Allen had long ago shown how the Iceni were divided into a number of *pagi* which probably remained autonomous well into the first century A.D..[47] Antedios may have been the first leader to assume overall control, and it was his successor, Prasutagus, who struck coins with the tribal legend ECE or ECEN. We may perhaps regard the Fenland finds as, therefore, marking a western *pagus* of the Iceni, especially as some finds, such as Dressel 1 amphorae, suggest that occupation may go back well before the Roman Conquest.

Indeed, the coins from Stonea include issues which are not Icenian, and which are in some cases older. These finds include two Gallic potin coins, attributable to the Sequani, which might take occupation back to the period before Caesar; a gold stater of the Coritani; and a Trinovantian bronze, attributable to Addedomaros.[48] Numerous finds have also reportedly been made by people using metal detectors. These are said to have included a hoard with gold coins of Cunobelin and silver issues of the Coritani and Iceni; a second hoard with silver coins of the Iceni, as well as *denarii*; and a hoard of *aes* with Claudian issues. Very many individual coin finds are also reported, especially of the Iceni, but also including early *denarii* and potin coins. Whilst we can place only very limited reliance upon these ill-documented discoveries, they would be broadly consistent with known coin-finds from the site, and should probably be seen as amplifying, rather than distorting, the general picture.

The presence of non-Icenian coinage from Stonea is an interesting hint of more long-distance connections, which may further underline its possible role as a 'port of trade'. Saham Toney, which lies close to the Icknield Way, in west-central Norfolk, provides a not dissimilar pattern,

46.   J. Evans, *The coins of the ancient Britons* (London, 1890), 586–7.
47.   D.F. Allen, 'The coins of the Iceni,' *Britannia* i (1970), 14f.; see now the discussion in T. Gregory and D. Gurney, *Excavations at Thornham, Warham, Wighton and Caistor St. Edmund, Norfolk* East Anglian Archaeology 30 (1986), 35; and A.L.F. Rivet, 'The first Icenian revolt,' in B.R. Hartley and J.S. Wacher (eds.), *Rome and her northern provinces* (Gloucester, 1983), 202–9.
48.   Identified by A.M. Burnett.

with a large number of Icenian coins, and also issues of the Trinovantes, Catuvellauni, Cantii, Atrebates and Durotriges.[49] A central Fenland site at Langwood Hill, Chatteris also yielded a comparatively wide range of coins: six Iceni (AR), two of Tasciovanus (AU, AR) one of (?)Cunobelin (AE), as well as four Republican coins (of 118B.C., 109B.C., 83B.C. and 42–40B.C.), two of Augustus and one of Tiberius.[50]

Other hoards of Iron Age coins from the central Fens, several of which have come to light in recent years, tend to consist exclusively of Icenian coins. An old find from March comprised 40 to 50 issues; 54 were found on three separate occasions on Stonea Grange Farm; a hoard was allegedly found at West Fen, March; and a major group came to light in 1982 at Field Baulk, March.[51]

The Field Baulk find consisted of 860 Icenian coins, buried in a globular beaker, imitating Camulodunum form 91, and datable to the Neronian/Flavian period.[52] The coins comprised Pattern/Horse (1), Pig/Horse (34), Head/Horse (170), Antedi (194), Ecen and copies (267), Ece (159), Aesu (10), Saenu (15) and ten uncertain.[53] On Allen's chronology, this would indicate that the hoard was buried about the time of the Boudiccan revolt. Fortunately, it was possible to establish the context of the find by excavation. The pot and coins had been set into the side of a circular ditch, which contained late Iron Age pottery. Early Roman material was also found, suggesting that the site was in occupation from about A.D.40–60; one post-hole was identified, and the ditch may have enclosed a building. This is of particular interest since, together with the discoveries at Stonea, it suggests a phase of settlement in the central Fens which considerably predates the Flavian and main Hadrianic 'colonisation'.

This view is further strengthened by James' excavation at the Estover site, on the north side of March (Fig. 4).[54] The site, which then lay under pasture at a height of 3.2m AOD, conserved a stretch of Fen Causeway, a trackway and the low banks of a number of enclosures. It emerged that the trackway, which shares an alignment with some of the enclosures, was laid out in the late Iron Age or very early Roman period; at its intersection with the Fen Causeway, it was shown that the trackway ditches were backfilled at this point, and the Roman road laid out over it. As elsewhere along the Fen Causeway, the finds are consistent with an early Roman date for this road.[55]

The pottery from the enclosure ditches at Estover suggests that they silted up in the mid- to late-Roman period, but the presumption is that this system extends back to the period of the Conquest, if not before. There was no evidence, however, for domestic occupation, and they should probably be regarded as stock-enclosures or paddocks. Indeed, they might relate to surface evidence for late Iron Age settlement at Flaggrass, just over one km to the east. At the very least, they imply a much more organised late Iron Age/early Roman landscape on the northern side of March than was once supposed.

The net result of chance finds, systematic excavation and metal-detector survey (legal and unauthorised) is to demonstrate a quite unexpected density of settlement in the central Fens between c.A.D.40 (and perhaps well before) and c.A.D.60. It is not unlikely that much more remains to be discovered, perhaps including relatively 'high status' sites. Moreover, it is striking that none of these settlements have yielded any appreciable quantity of Flavian pottery. The aftermath of the Boudiccan Revolt was perhaps severe in this region, adding some credence to the suggestion that Grandford originated as a Roman fort, and explaining the impoverished nature of the few Flavian sites that are known, such as Coldham.[56]

49.   R.A. Brown, 'The Iron Age and Romano-British settlement at Woodcock Hall, Saham Toney, Norfolk,' *Britannia* xvii (1986), 8.
50.   Identified by T.R. Volk; information via A.M. Burnett.
51.   March hoard: *Num.Chron.* (1839), 89; Stonea Grange hoard: unpublished (identified by A.M. Burnett); Field Baulk hoard: illustrated in T.W. Potter, *Roman Britain* (British Museum, 1983), fig. 26.
52.   Identification by V. Rigby.
53.   Identification by J.P.C. Kent.
54.   S. James in *Fenland Research* iii (1985–86), 29–30. For earlier work on the site see *Britannia* xii (1981), 116.
55.   See *inter alia Britannia* xii (1981), 131f.
56.   *PCAS* lviii (1965), 12–37.

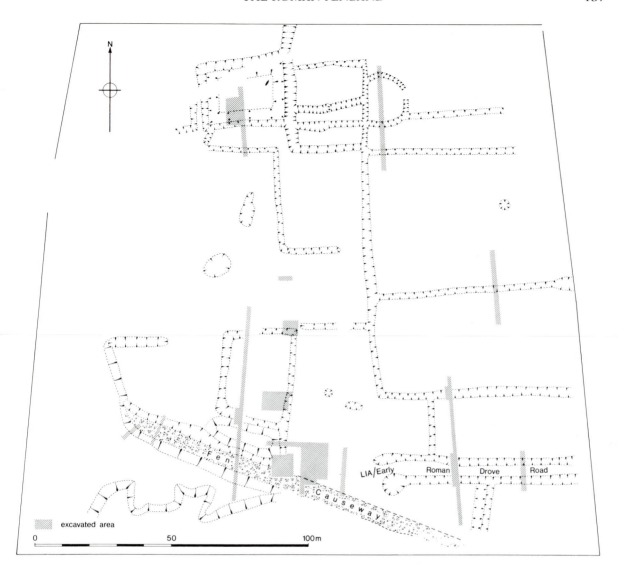

FIG. 4 Plan of the site at Estover, March (Cambs.). (By kind permission of S. James).

THE ROMAN DEVELOPMENT OF THE FENS

The Fenland Project Survey has now covered vast tracts of the region, and has begun to provide a detailed distribution map of sites, and especially their relationship to the surface geology.[57] It has also prepared rough plots of the drove-roads, field systems and other features on aerial photographs and soilmark data.[58] Once blank areas, such as the Norfolk Fens, have been filled in, and major sites like that at Stonea Grange have been discovered. Overall, the maps of the Roman Fenland have therefore been much improved.

Nevertheless, it must also be said that the quality of the surface collections has deteriorated sharply over recent years. An examination in 1983 of Flaggrass, for example, yielded only a small sample of comminuted sherds, which is in stark contrast to the very large and numerous pieces collected in 1956–58. At Grandford, Hall's survey in 1983 yielded material of the late second to late fourth centuries A.D., whereas the excavated assemblage began as early as the Neronian period – an encouraging indication that the plough has yet to bite into the lowest levels, even

57. e.g. Hall, op. cit. (note 8).
58. R. Palmer, 'Applications of air photo-archaeology,' *Antiquity* lxii (1988), 331–5.

though the site has been regularly ploughed since 1967.[59] Similarly, at Norwood, March, an excavated saltern site with prodigious quantities of briquetage (including, in 1959–61, much on the surface of the ploughed field adjoining the excavated area), the present survey located no saltern debris.[60] Even at Stonea Grange, where ploughing has cut deeply into the sub-soil, the surface finds do not properly reflect the history of the settlement.

The conclusion must be that the results from the field survey, however well conducted, may not always be representative of anything more than the broad history of a site. This is a matter that has been much debated in Mediterranean archaeology, where sites can be totally erased by a few years of ploughing.[61] It follows that over-refined analysis of surface data, especially from intensively farmed landscapes, may tend to somewhat misleading impressions; the size and quality of the surface assemblage is here of paramount importance, as is repeated reconnaissance of the same landscape.

That said, there is still no reason to dispute the long-standing view that the main development of the Fens took place under Hadrian.[62] Even in southern Lincolnshire, where salt-winning was apparently a well-established activity in the Iron Age, there seems to be something of a gap in occupation during the first century A.D., so that the second-century development of the region was effectively *de novo*.[63] This immediately brings into question the subject of the Fen Causeway, which is usually dated to the first century A.D.. This is now supported by the results of James' work at Estover, March (*supra*); by Gurney's detailed publication of Charles Green's excavation at Denver, which suggests a Neronian date for the road;[64] and by Pryor's demonstration of two phases of metalling at Fengate, the later associated with late-first- or early-second-century pottery.[65] Indeed, Pryor has now demonstrated at Flag Fen that parts of the western stretch of the road was surfaced not with gravel but with limestone, further underlining its importance as a carefully built east-west route of communication.[66]

Recent work has not elucidated further the complex situation to the east of Flaggrass, March, where the Rodham Farm canal appears to take the place of the road for some six km although the north levee was later surfaced with gravel. Similarly, Hall now believes following, in fact, a suggestion of Evans,[67] that, to the west of March, the Fen Causeway also replaced a canal that ran for seven km across the peat between the Romano-British settlements of Eldernell and Grandford; he also thinks that there was a second (and perhaps earlier) waterway that crossed the same stretch of fen to join the River Nene a kilometre to the south-west of Grandford. It is unfortunate that these hypotheses are in no way documented, especially as they seem to be in contradiction with a published photographic section of the Causeway (which does not show a canal roddon);[68] without proper evidence, these ideas must therefore be regarded as speculative, although they are well worthy of proper investigation through excavation.

Military involvement with the digging of canals, both to achieve better communications and flood prevention, is well attested, as the works of Drusus, and later of Corbulo, at the mouth of the Rhine, remind us.[69] Thus, while the Fen Causeway may still plausibly be seen as a route

59. Hall, op. cit. (note 8), 43; for the site, Potter and Potter, op. cit. (note 8).

60. Hall, op. cit. (note 8), Site 27 (microfiche); for the site, cf. also T.W. Potter, *Britannia* xii (1981), 104–16.

61. Cf. for examples the essays in D.R. Keller and D.W. Rupp (eds.), *Archaeological survey in the Mediterranean area* BAR S155 (Oxford, 1983); also A.J. Ammermann and M.W. Feldman, 'Replicated collection of site surfaces,' *American Antiquity* xliii (1978), 734–40.

62. Salway in Phillips, op. cit. (note 4), 9f; idem, *Roman Britain* (Oxford, 1981), 189–90.

63. T. Lane, *Antiquity* lxii (1988), 320; see also S. Hallam in Phillips op. cit. (note 4), 44–5.

64. Gurney, op. cit. (note 6), 134.

65. Pryor, *The Third Report* (see note 13), fig. 89, no. 7, and 151f.

66. Pryor, op. cit. (note 23). See also Hall, op. cit. (note 8), pl.X.

67. R. Evans, 'The early course of the River Nene,' *Durobrivae* vii (1979), 19–21; Hall, op. cit. (note 8), 41–2, unfortunately does not discuss Evan's interesting suggestion of a canal which ran from the Flaggrass Waterway across to near Grandford. See also Salway in Phillips, op. cit. (note 4), 218–9.

68. *Britannia* xii (1981), pl.VIIIA.

69. Drusus: Tacitus, *Ann.* II,8; Suetonius, *Claudius* I. Corbulo: Tacitus, *Ann.* II, 20; Cassius Dio lx, 30,6. See also L. Bonnard, *La navigation intérieure de la Gaule à l'époque Gallo-romaine* (Paris, 1913).

constructed for military purposes in the aftermath of the Boudiccan revolt, it is by no means impossible that it was begun earlier; certainly the available dating evidence would suit this view. In that case, the legionary force based at Longthorpe, which lies on the western end of the road, may well have been responsible for the work.[70] By this time, the northern silt-lands were beginning to dry out, and the construction of canals can only have hastened this process. It is puzzling that Flavian settlement in the Fens proceeded – on present evidence – so slowly; but, as we hinted above, the Boudiccan revolt may well have influenced such matters. Equally, the conquest of the North will have deprived the region of military resources, while the absence of any nearby urban centres (*Durobrivae* developed only in Flavian-Trajanic times) may have rendered futile any extensive investment of resources. It is probably significant in this respect that the reclamation of the wetlands bordering the Severn Estuary seems to be intimately linked with the growth of civilian centres at Gloucester and Caerwent.[71]

The enormous scale of the Hadrianic colonisation of the Fens, especially the silt-lands, still stands in sharp contrast with the sporadic settlement of the previous half century. The arrangement of the Hadrianic landscape requires, however, much more detailed study. Palmer's acute analysis of aerial photographs of Thorney, for example, has disclosed an organised agricultural system, which points to a high degree of planning.[72] Much the same is true of the rectilinear enclosures which cover one hundred hectares or so of the silts to the north and east of Flaggrass.[73] Although somewhat irregularly laid out, in the manner of most Fenland sites, they suggest a largely coeval system of paddocks, and perhaps arable fields, which implies an advanced level of land management. Still more remarkable is the very precisely planned farmstead, *c.*58 by 75m, at Rookery Farm near Spalding; it is linked to the main road by a straight ditched *diverticulum*, some 60m in length, and there is a similar side road, leading to a more irregularly laid-out settlement, a short distance to the north. The finds from Rookery Farm are predominantly of the second century, and its regularity of design may point to a farmer of quite different origins from the majority of the Fenland population, perhaps a veteran. It is a prime site for investigation.[74]

It has long been argued that the massive development of the Fens in the Hadrianic period was the result of Imperial intervention on state-owned land. Indeed, now that a case can be made for the southern Fenland being Icenian territory, it seems possible that these lands came under Imperial ownership after Prasutagus' death. Hadrian, as is well known, had a particular interest in the reclamation and administration of marginal land. He reorganised the system of procurators, with important consequences for, *inter alia*, Egypt;[75] assigned land in Latium;[76] carried out works in Africa[77] and in the Copais Basin in Greece (where canals were dug to cope with the problem of upland-runoff of water, generated by the melting of the winter snow);[78] and, it would seem, gave the impetus to develop the Fenland, a region that he presumably saw on his visit to Britain in A.D.122. Salway lays emphasis upon the contemporary reorganisation of both the northern frontier and the Fenland, suggesting a close economic link between the two;[79]

70. cf. S.S. Frere and J.K. St. Joseph, 'The Roman fortress at Longthorpe,' *Britannia* v (1974), 1f. and fig.1.
71. J.R.L. Allen and M.G. Fulford, 'The Wentlooge Level: a Romano-British saltmarsh reclamation in south-east Wales,' *Britannia* xvii (1986), 91–117; 'Romano-British settlement and industry on the wetlands of the Severn estuary,' *Antiq. Journ.* lxvii (1987), 237–89.
72. Palmer, op. cit. (note 58).
73. cf. Phillips, op. cit. (note 4), Map 13, which is more detailed than Hall, op. cit. (note 8), fig. 23; also Potter, *Britannia* xii (1981), fig. 3.
74. *JRS* xlv (1955), pl.XX; S.S. Frere and J.K. St. Joseph, *Roman Britain from the air* (Cambridge, 1983), pl.133 and 251; Phillips, op. cit. (note 4), pl.XIIB.
75. D. Crawford, 'Imperial Estates,' in M.I. Finley (ed.), *Studies in Roman property* (Cambridge, 1976), 53.
76. Crawford, op. cit., citing the *Liber Coloniarum*, 233.
77. *CIL* viii, 25943, 26416.
78. J.M. Fossey, 'The cities of the Kopais in the Roman period,' in H. Temporini (ed.), *Augstieg und Niedergang, Principat* vii (1979), 549–91 and references.
79. Salway, op. cit. (note 62), 189.

certainly a productive Imperial estate (or estates) could have done much to facilitate the provision of supplies to the units based on the Wall, especially given the wide range of materials and foodstuffs that was required, as the Vindolanda tablets imply.[80]

STONEA GRANGE (Fig. 5)

The site at Stonea Grange is here of particular interest. Situated only some 500m to the north of Stonea Camp, it was extensively excavated between 1980 and 1984; over five campaigns, more than a hectare was completely investigated and a further seven hectares were sampled by means of machine-cut trenches. It should immediately be stressed that as a proportion of the total area of the island – some 300 ha – this represents a very small sample. However, the other sites at Stonea appear to belong to the normal type of Fenland farm and village, whereas the complex at the Grange presents a number of quite different features.

There is evidence for a little sporadic activity in the area of Stonea Grange during the first century A.D., but it was essentially a virgin site that was taken over in the Hadrianic period, probably in the 130s. Earlier ditches and hollows were levelled with clay, and measures were taken to drain the wetter parts, especially on the north side of the site. A carefully planned settlement, covering some 150 by 200m, was then laid out. The north side was demarcated by a great gravel-metalled road, 8 to 10m wide, running approximately east–west. Curiously, the road does not take the exact alignment of the rest of the settlement, but this may be due to local topographical factors. Its course to the east was traced by aerial photographs and excavation for nearly 250m, (Fig. 5) while to the west it heads down into the fen, along the line of the modern farm track. Its destination was surely the high ground of Hook, on the eastern side of the March island, a distance of one kilometre.

Hall's supposition that Stonea was not linked to the March island by a road is therefore clearly incorrect; however, he has collected some important evidence to suggest that the island was connected by canals to the March uplands. One, he believes, ran from the Rodham Farm canal, near Flaggrass, down to the northern tip of the Stonea island, while the other crossed the fen between Stonea and Wimblington. Detailed documentation is again lacking, but the notion is an attractive one.[81]

At the Grange site, the area on the south side of the road was divided up into a series of blocks by gravelled streets (Fig. 5). Two alignments are apparent, a western and an eastern, so that two blocks are not perfectly rectangular. This may suggest an expansion eastwards from the original nucleus, which entailed some modification to the first 'blue-print'. At least one east-west street was identified, as well as three north-south, and there may have been a second east-west street, which went out of use at an early stage.

The principal building lay in the most westerly block (Fig. 6). It sat on a slight natural eminence, and consisted of a rectangular foundation, one metre deep, made up of successive rafts of pitched stone and concrete. This carried footings 1.20m thick. To the east was a vestibule or portico, while to the west there was a large apse, set a little off-centre. Overall the building measured 17 by 20m, and was clearly intended to stand to a considerable height. It was provided with a hypocaust, heated by a *praefurnium* near the south-west corner, and had a tessellated floor and walls decorated with painted plaster, including an imitation of cipollino marble. Large quantities of window-glass and tile were also found.

This unusual and elegant building, which must have been visible from a considerable distance in the flat Fen landscape, has aroused much discussion as to its purpose. A full consideration of the alternatives must be deferred to the final report, and it must suffice here to observe that we believe it to be a 'prestige building', designed for official purposes; indeed, it is remarkable that

---

80.   A.K. Bowman and J.D. Thomas, *Vindolanda: the Latin writing-tablets* Britannia Monograph 4 (Gloucester, 1983); idem, *Britannia* xviii (1987), 125–42. See also footnote 124.

81.   Hall, op. cit. (note 8), 42 and fig. 23.

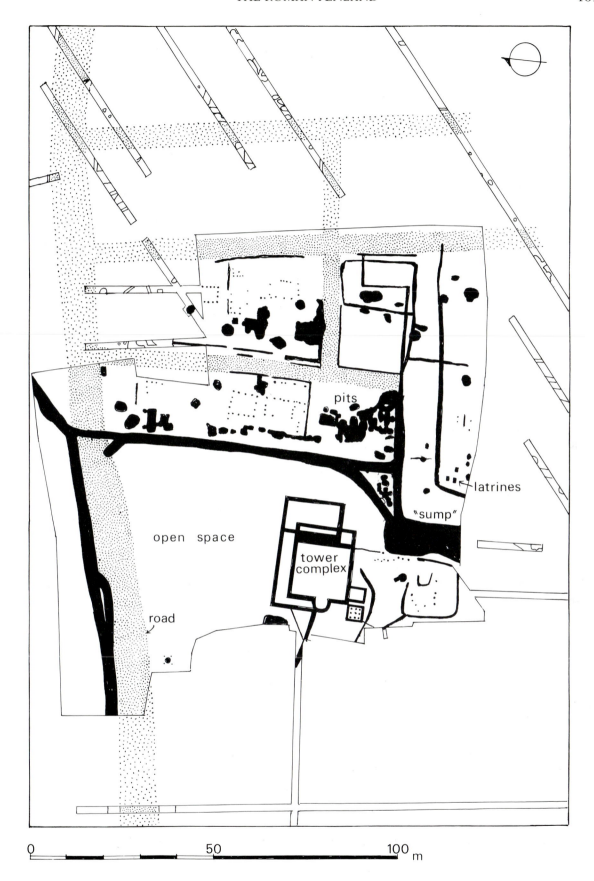

FIG. 5   Stonea Grange in the second century.

FIG. 6   Stonea Grange: the tower complex, looking east.

the closest analogies lie not in the northern provinces, but in Hadrianic-Antonine structures from the vicinity of Rome itself.[82]

To the north of the stone building lay a large reserved space, measuring some 45m by 35m. Its surface was metalled, and there was a boundary fence (later made into a ditch) to the east, and the main road to the north. No demarcating line was found to the west, an area where no buildings or pits were identified, and with very little occupation debris. We suppose that this closely defined space was a public zone, which may have been intended as a market, although many other activities are of course possible.

Behind the tower-like structure to the south, was a fenced enclosure, which probably contained a wooden building and which adjoined an enormous sump-like feature (Fig. 7). Its purpose is quite unclear, but it yielded a very considerable array of organic material, including much constructional material: a wooden spade, parts of a bucket, a long plank and much wood-working debris. There were also three tablets of the wax kind, one bearing manifest traces of lines of writing.[83] (Fig. 8)

The stone building was soon modified by the addition of a large stone hall-like structure, measuring 14 by 7m internally, to the east, and further rooms to the north and west, one with a hypocaust. This would seem to have altered the position of the main entrance from the east to the north, so that it faced onto the 'square' in front. It is hard to understand why the main building

82.   T.W. Potter and D.B. Whitehouse, *World Archaeology* xiv (1982), 218–23.
83.   Currently being studied by Dr A. Bowman; it may be a letter, but the script is extremely hard to decipher.

FIG. 7   Stonea Grange: the 'great sump', looking south.

FIG. 8   Writing-tablet from the 'great sump' at Stonea Grange.

FIG. 9   Stonea Grange: general view of the excavations of 1984, looking south down one of the streets. Deep plough- and pan-breaking ruts are visible.

(which must originally have faced east, given the position of the apse) and the 'square' were not more closely integrated from the start; but the archaeological evidence for a substantial change of design of the stone 'tower' is unambiguous.

The area to the east of the 'tower block' presents a remarkable contrast, in that it was tightly packed with buildings and pits, although these were again distributed in an ordered manner. The streets were four metres wide, and there are hints throughout the site that it may in part have been laid out in units of 25 and 50 feet. Lining the streets were wooden fences (many of which were later converted into drains or gutters), again conveying the impression of a careful allocation of properties. The buildings themselves were entirely constructed of wood, although their post-holes proved particularly difficult to identify in all cases. However, the structures do not seem to have been very large (c.7 by 10m.), and there may have been several buildings in each block. There were also discrete clusters of wells, rubbish pits and latrines (an unsalubrious but consistent combination), and also one, perhaps communal, area of rubbish pits, covering 8 by 25m; quite untypically for the site, they contained very little domestic refuse, and may have been used for the disposal of organic matter. There was, in addition, one isolated group of latrines, which might again have been for communal purposes.

The total number of buildings can only be guessed at; but, given that its overall limits have been established, there is room for thirty to forty houses, perhaps implying a population of one or two hundred. However, the site is remarkable in that there is no evidence for any industrial activity at all; it was, in effect, a consuming rather than a producing community. Van der Veen's study of the plant remains also tends to support this view.[84] She finds that the seeds from the second-century deposits are dominated by a variety of weeds, rather than by cereals and chaff. This suggests that grain (primarily spelt) was brought to the site in a ready threshed state, although not in large quantities: there is no botanical (or archaeological) evidence for a grain storage area. Some nearby cultivation of cereals is not out of the question, but never on a large scale in this period. Interestingly, there are also some exotic imports, especially figs and lentils, which normally occur only on major sites, and were apparently not cultivated in Britain.[85]

In a material sense the community of Stonea Grange was relatively affluent. This is demonstrated in many ways: by an abundance of coinage; by a very large collection of metalwork, including fine rings, brooches and other jewellery; by high-quality glass; and by the pottery. Cameron's study of the ceramic evidence is particularly revealing, since the assemblage stands in considerable contrast to those from other Fenland sites; although dominated by Nene Valley products (including some exotic decorated pieces, and a remarkable collection of beakers embellished with phalli), it is particularly rich in imported vessels, including Continental colour-coated wares and Spanish wine amphorae.[86] There are also numerous flagons and, untypically for the Fens, some Black Burnished pottery. Samian ware is also very common.

Whilst a few items of metalwork from the Grange site have possible military associations, the great bulk are unmistakably civilian. Remarkably, they include nothing with obvious religious associations, one reason for which emerged in 1984. Aerial photography then disclosed the crop-mark of a circular enclosure, c.40m across, which lay some 200m to the north-east of the Grange site. A street led into the enclosure from the main road, described above. Two structures were exposed, one being a building that had been floored with large *tesserae*; close to it was a typical Romano-Celtic temple, probably of third-century date. (Fig. 10) It succeeded several earlier structures on the same alignment, the oldest of which appears to date to the late Iron Age. It would seem, therefore, that this was a long-established sanctuary which, if a pipe-clay figurine of a horse is any guide, might have included Epona amongst the deities that were worshipped. It is also worth recalling, however, the prevalence of equine motifs upon the coinage of the Iceni, and

84. Van der Veen's study will be published in the final volume on the excavations. The report on the animal bones (by S. Stallibrass) is incomplete, but points to a 'high-status' site, with little evidence for specialised rearing of livestock.

85. Van der Veen, forthcoming in the Stonea report.

86. F. Cameron in Hall, op. cit. (note 8), 68–9; her full report will appear in the volume on the Stonea excavations.

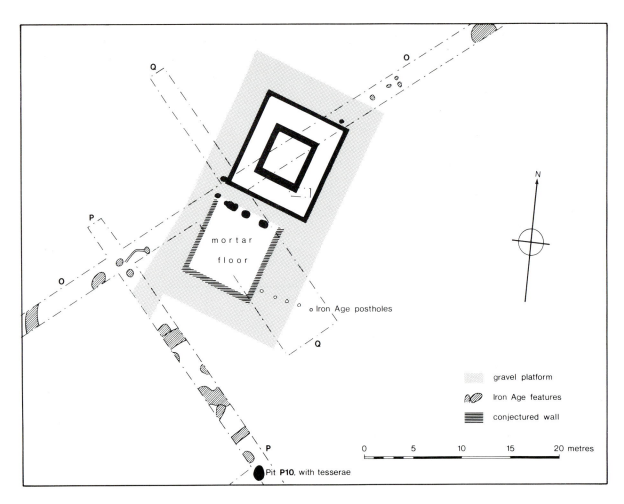

FIG. 10   Stonea Grange: the temple complex.

the ubiquity of 'horse and rider' brooches in East Anglia.[87] To infer a link is tenuous but has its attractions.

This does not entirely resolve the question of religious sanctuaries at Stonea, since there is also an abundance of evidence that points to the existence of a temple to Minerva.[88] None of the relevant objects can be associated with the newly located cult centre (which, rather surprisingly, yielded no metal votive items), and it may be that another temple awaits discovery – perhaps in an area to the south-east, close to Stonea Camp, where, according to persistent reports, very large numbers of Roman coins have been recovered through metal-detecting.

It is worth noting that recent work has provided documentation for a number of religious sanctuaries in the region, especially around the Fen margins. Gurney has now published the Leylands Farm cult centre (which yielded the 'Wilton' crowns and diadems from a late-Roman context),[89] and Johns the Hockwold Treasure, this being a set of silver cups of first-century date, which may have been buried for votive purposes.[90] There was another nearby temple at Sawbench,[91] while a fourth religious site in the Hockwold-cum-Wilton area has also been

87.   Gurney, op. cit. (note 6), 89–90.
88.   *Britannia* xii (1981), 101f.; *Antiquity* lvi (1982), 115.
89.   Gurney, op. cit. (note 6), 49–92; the crowns are in the British Museum, accession numbers P1956 10–11, 1–2; P1957 2–6, 1–29.
90.   C.M. Johns, 'The Roman silver cups from Hockwold, Norfolk,' *Archaeologia* cviii (1986), 1–14.
91.   Gurney, op. cit. (note 6), 92.

postulated.[92] Along the south-western Fen edge, finds from a temple have been recorded at Cottenham,[93] a possible temple has been photographed from the air at Willingham,[94] and an octagonal shrine constructed on one side of a barrow has been excavated at the Upper Delphs, Haddenham.[95] This last site is of particular interest; built in the late first or early second century, the centre of the shrine included the burial of a complete sheep or goat. There were also a number of sheep/goat mandibles, with horses placed on either side and, in two cases, a coin in the mouth. Four other sheep/goat burials, each with a pot, lay within a rectangular *temenos*, as well as a boar's skeleton. Evans has suggested a link between this remarkable shrine, and the well-known Willingham hoard, which was found only a short distance away.[96]

A shrine-like structure has also been excavated at Maxey,[97] but within the Fens themselves (Stonea apart) religious sanctuaries have so far proved elusive. Antiquarian records indicate the possibility of a temple at Elm,[98] and major sites such as Whaplode have also been suggested as likely religious centres,[99] but the temples themselves have not been susceptible to aerial photography (somewhat surprisingly), even though their existence can hardly be doubted. Gurney has made the interesting suggestion that the temples on the Norfolk fen edge may have served as centres for periodic fairs and festivals, thus providing the opportunity for commercial transactions.[100] In support of this, he cites the lack of nucleated villages in the area, and the contrast between the coin-rich temples and the dearth of coins from the settlements. The coin assemblages from the sanctuaries tend, however, to be dominated by late-Roman issues, and a votive purpose is probably to be preferred. Even so, the idea remains attractive and requires further investigation.

Such speculation returns us to the question of the role of the settlement at Stonea Grange. It, too, is very rich in coins, although a bias is introduced into the excavated sample by the fact that, despite precautions, the site was plundered by treasure-hunters at the beginning of each of the final three seasons. Shotter's analysis of the coins, here presented very simplistically, is as follows:[101]

TABLE 1: COINS FROM STONEA GRANGE

	excavation	casual finds
First century	12	19
Second century (Trajan to Severus)	39	179
Third century (Caracalla to A.D.294)	4	314
Fourth century (Diocletian to Arcadius)	5	338
	60	850

92. Gurney, op. cit. (note 6), 92.
93. A. Taylor *et al.*, *PCAS* lxxiv (1985), 1f.
94. *PCAS* lxxiv (1985), 48.
95. *Britannia* xv (1984), 298.
96. C. Evans, 'A shrine provenance for the Willingham Fen hoard,' *Antiquity* lviii (1984), 212–14.
97. Gurney in Pryor and French, op. cit. (note 12), 100f.
98. Phillips, op. cit. (note 4), 324; D. Hall, *PCAS* lxviii (1978), 40.
99. Phillips, op. cit. (note 4), 302.
100. Gurney, op. cit. (note 6), 148.
101. The full report will be published in the volume on the Stonea excavations.

Leaving aside detailed analysis, it is nevertheless quite clear that this was a coin-using site from the time of its foundation in the Hadrianic period. As such, it stands in considerable contrast to the few other Fenland settlements for which we have evidence. Coldham[102] and Hockwold[103] yielded no coins, and the Golden Lion Inn, Stonea[104] only one (a surface find): all three sites were abandoned by the early third century. Large-scale work at Maxey brought to light only five coins, dismissed as 'irrelevant' by Reece,[105] while even Grandford produced only eight second-century issues (although the site as a whole is numismatically fairly rich).[106] When taken in conjunction with other data, we might conclude that, for the second century at any rate (but probably not for the fourth), many Fenland communities were using little, if any, coinage.[107] In the central Fens, only Stonea Grange and perhaps Grandford and Flaggrass, all of them major sites, stand out as exceptions.

Assessing the role of the Stonea Grange site remains, however, problematic. If it is accepted that the Fens were partially or wholly Imperial property, then it is the most obvious candidate so far identified for a centre of administration. The tower complex, however eccentric a design, has all the appearances of a public, rather than private, construction, and might have been suited to administrative purposes, especially in its modified form. The apse was presumably intended to house a statue, perhaps of the emperor, and the upper stories may have provided accommodation, and even storage: Pliny kept both wine and grain on an upper floor in his Laurentian villa, a building in which he had a three-storey tower.[108]

The apparent absence of large-scale storage facilities is otherwise somewhat puzzling, if Stonea was really intended to receive taxes in kind. None of the excavated buildings has the appearance of a warehouse, nor is there any evidence for a barrack block for the estate guards that one might expect.[109] On the other hand, it may well be either that such structures lie outside the excavated area or, indeed, that we are mistakenly predicting the nature of a settlement-type for which we have no real evidence.

Much the same difficulties apply to the definition of its status. It may be that it should be called a *principia*, as on the famous Combe Down inscription, set up by the procurator's assistant, Naevius.[110] Alternatively, the grid of streets, the 'square', and the imposing stone-built complex might point to the official creation of a more urban-like community. In Republican Italy, *fora* were not uncommonly founded as market and administrative centres on main roads. An inscription from Forum Popillii in Campania, on the important route between Capua and Reggio Calabria, records how 'I made the road . . . set up bridges. . . here I made a market-place and public buildings (*forum aedisque poplicas heic fecei*)'.[111] Festus, writing of *fora* in the later second century A.D., notes that they 'often exist even on private property and on roads and estates'. Sherwin-White concludes that 'as a form of municipality they were rudimentary. . .; although they might have *magistri*, and even a local council, they lacked the broad basis of municipal life, the *territorium*. . .'.[112]

Most *fora* were Republican foundations, but a few which date to the Imperial period are known, such as *Forum Triani* in Sardinia,[113] and *Forum Hadriani* (Arentsburg in Holland).[114] The

102. T.W. Potter, *PCAS* lviii (1965), 12–37.
103. P. Salway, *PCAS* lix (1967), 57; Phillips, op. cit. (note 4), 12.
104. T.W. Potter, *PCAS* lxvi (1975–76), 23f.
105. In Pryor and French, op. cit. (note 12), 164.
106. D.C.A. Shotter in Potter and Potter, op. cit. (note 8), 91f.
107. Denver yielded only 4 coins (Gurney, op. cit. (note 6), 107). See also D.C.A. Shotter, *Britannia* xii (1981), 120f.
108. Pliny, *Letters* 2, 17.
109. Crawford, op. cit. (note 75), 52 and footnote 80 (p.179), listing evidence for Italy, Africa, Belgica and the East.
110. *RIB* 179.
111. Dessau, *ILS* (1892), no.23 = *CIL* x, 6950.
112. A.N. Sherwin-White, *The Roman citizenship* (Oxford, 1973), 75, and citing Festus, S.V. 'forum' and 'vici'. See also E. Ruoff-Väänänen, *Studies on the Italian fora* (Wiesbaden, 1978).
113. *Notizie degli Scavi* (1888), 175; ibid (1903), 469.
114. cf. *inter alia* J.E. Bogaers, 'Forum Hadriani,' *Bonner Jahrbücher* clxiv (1964), 45–52; idem, 'Civitates und Civitas-Hauptorte in der nördlichen Germania inferior,' *B.J.* clxxii (1972), 310–32. Hadrian's interest in promoting urban development in Britain may be generally relevant (J.S. Wacher, *The towns of Roman Britain*, (London, 1975), 375f.).

latter is of particular interest from the point of view of Stonea. In the first place, it occupied a low-lying position beside a Roman canal (perhaps Corbulo's *fossa*). Secondly, it was granted the *ius nundinarum* in Hadrian's reign, shortly before the foundation of the settlement at Stonea. Thirdly, its plan is similarly unusual, with a military-like layout, including buildings which resemble barracks, and no conventional civic centre. Prior to the award of the *forum* title, it was the capital of the *civitas Cananefatum*,[115] and not, therefore, a *de novo* foundation, unlike Stonea Grange. However, it should be remembered that the evidence from Stonea as a whole does suggest the existence of a major centre in the late Iron Age and early Roman periods, so that the history of the two sites in the first century A.D. is not wholly dissimilar.

Whatever interpretation of the Stonea Grange settlement is favoured, its eventual fate is not in doubt. About A.D.200, the entire tower complex was demolished and most of the stone removed, leaving a great pool on the site of the sunken raft. Large numbers of whole pots, bearing only very slight damage, were thrown into the eastern boundary ditch and some of the pits, conveying the impression of a systematic emptying of the stores, and the disposal of all but the perfect goods. Some of the wooden buildings were also demolished, although to what extent this was total remains to be worked out.

Prior to this event, there had been some changes on the site. Some boundaries were obliterated by pits, suggesting alterations in the division of properties, while many others were replaced by ditches or drains. We infer that generally wetter conditions began to prevail in the second half of the second century, a conclusion supported both by French's study of the molluscs[116] and by deposits of water-laid silt in a few of the hollows. Whether, however, this was a deciding factor in the decision to demolish the 'official' buildings on the site is perhaps more debatable, and is a matter that we shall return to below.

THE FENLAND ECONOMY

Emphasis has already been laid upon the economic benefits that a carefully controlled wetland environment can yield, and it was clearly to the Roman advantage to exploit these as fully as possible. Much work remains to be done, however, before the question of the economy is properly resolved. In part, this is a reflection of the continued dearth of excavations upon Roman-period sites, for it is only through the recovery of properly stratified data that significant advances can be made. Some useful evidence for the western margins of the Fens has been obtained from Pryor's sensitively conducted, large-scale investigations at Fengate and in the lower Welland valley.[117] The main Fengate Roman settlement has been largely destroyed, but we know that the low-lying Cat's Water site was reoccupied about A.D.140, after being abandoned in the early post-Conquest period. A drove-road was identified, but structural evidence proved more elusive: however, there is no archaeological reason to suppose that the main economic base, namely the rearing of livestock (especially cattle and sheep), had altered from Iron Age times. Arable farming continued to play a minor role, and the site was abandoned about A.D.200, after which it was covered with alluvium.

At Maxey, by contrast, the Romano-British settlement was comparatively well preserved. Although only 3.5km from a villa at Helpston (occupied from the early second to the fourth centuries),[118] the inhabitants of Maxey lived at a very rudimentary level. The buildings were mainly circular in plan, and the economy was also firmly rooted in Iron-Age tradition. Sheep predominated over cattle and, interestingly, were slaughtered young: wool production was not, therefore, a primary aim, although numerous loomweights do suggest some weaving (perhaps of wool brought in from the central Fens). Cereals were attested in the deposits, but appear to have been processed elsewhere, although nearby areas seem to have been manured, perhaps for

115. Tacitus, *Ann.* 11, 20.
116. For the final report on the site.
117. See notes 12, 13.
118. A. Challands, *Durobrivae* iii (1975), 22–4.

the cultivation of vegetables. Chronologically, the site starts early, *c*.A.D.50, and may have developed directly from the late Iron Age settlement; it expanded considerably towards A.D.100, but seems to have been largely abandoned around the beginning of the third century, although there was sporadic (perhaps seasonal) reuse of the area in the late third and early fourth centuries.

Maxey and Fengate, therefore, stand out as comparatively unromanised communities, whose inhabitants lived close to the land, probably not far from subsistence level. There is a seeming lack of specialisation in the economy, although at Maxey, with the Helpston villa so near, one might wonder whether there could have been tenurial or contractual links between the estate and the 'native' farm. While the agricultural strategy of these Fen-edge sites may have been dictated by the proximity of the adjoining wetlands, it seems likely that, in organisational terms, they fell within the *territorium* of *Durobrivae*, and are thus in some senses to be regarded as separate from the main development of the Fens.[119]

Within the Fenland itself, the economic models that were evolved by Salway, Hallam and others have been little changed by recent work.[120] No significant body of new evidence has been brought forth to support (or refute) the hypothesis that the production of wool was a primary area of specialisation,[121] although survey work has revealed many scatters of saltern material (now in a much abraded state).[122] In the Elm area, for example, only four of the thirty-eight sites that were examined did not yield briquetage,[123] a remarkable comment on the importance of the industry. The majority of the sites lie beside once tidal watercourses, and are surrounded by paddocks, enclosures and drove-roads. An intimate link between the winning of salt and the rearing of livestock is evident, the salt being a prerequisite for the preservation of meat (and also fowl and oysters) and the preparation of hides, as well as for other purposes.[124]

Gurney has provided an admirable analysis of salt-producing at Denver, a site flanking the Fen Causeway excavated by Charles Green in 1960.[125] He adduces convincing evidence to show that it was probably a seasonal activity, and lays emphasis upon the typological diversity of briquetage in the Fenland: we must beware, perhaps, of inferring too organised a structure of salt-production and, without further pointers, certainly question Hall's designation of sites like Flaggrass as 'industrial villages'.[126] Interestingly, the production of salt at Denver does not seem to extend beyond the third century (the main period of occupation, although there is earlier material). This conforms with previous views that the industry as a whole was primarily a phenomenon of the earlier Roman period, for as yet no saltern site can be shown to have been operative in the fourth century.[127] If this is really the case, then it may have considerable implication for changes in the local economy in late Roman times. Norwood, a site with second-century salterns and third- to fourth-century occupation, is an obvious place to examine the question further.[128]

119.   cf. Pryor and French, op. cit. (note 12), fig. 204.
120.   In Phillips, op. cit. (note 4). For the important sample of animal bones from Grandford, see S. Stallibrass in Potter and Potter, op. cit. (note 8), 98–122.
121.   T.W. Potter, *Britannia* xii (1981), 129f. See also J.P. Wild 'Wool production in Roman Britain,' in D. Miles (ed.), *The Romano-British countryside* BAR 103 (Oxford, 1982), 109–22.
122.   See Hall, op. cit. (note 8), fig. 24, and Gurney, op. cit. (note 6), 68.
123.   Hall, *PCAS* lxviii (1978), 26.
124.   cf. the interesting letter from Vindolanda recording the gift of 50 oysters: Bowman and Thomas, op. cit. (note 80), 135–6.
125.   Gurney, op. cit. (note 6), 138f.
126.   Hall, op. cit. (note 8), 44. Hallam in Phillips, op. cit. (note 4), stresses the lack of organisation, although Norwood (*Britannia* xii (1981), 104f. and fig. 11) looks like a large site. Hall (43) claims to recognize turburies, covering as much as 60 ha, but does not publish aerial photographs.
127.   Hallam in Phillips, op. cit. (note 8), 57, 70.
128.   *Britannia* xii (1981), 104f.

CHANGES IN THE LATER ROMAN PERIOD

The apparent decline of the salt industry in the third century and the abandonment of the 'official' complex at Stonea Grange about A.D.200 hint at a significant reorientation in the organisation of the Fenland. This also coincides with a lengthy period when many sites experienced difficulties with flooding, and an overall fall in the size of the population is probable. It may well be that, when a sufficiency of evidence is available, it will become clear that the flooding was not as chronologically restricted as is sometimes thought;[129] but there is no doubt that, whatever the causes and nature of the waterlogging, insufficient measures were taken to control the problem. There is thus an implied lack of resources and organisation which is consistent with the removal of key foci such as the Stonea Grange site.

It is germane at this juncture to consider the form and reasons for these organisational changes. Salway has already provided ample documentation for the broad relevance of Severan activities elsewhere in the province for the Fenland region;[130] indeed, in some parts of the Empire it can be shown that this involved some restructuring of the procuratorial system on Imperial Estates.[131] It is immediately tempting, therefore, to link the demise of a site such as Stonea Grange to political factors, generated at a senior level. However, local factors may also have played a significant part. We have already described the signs of waterlogging that affected the settlement at Stonea, albeit on a modest scale, in the later second century, and have laid emphasis upon the absence of evidence for industry and manufacturing. Despite some manifestations of wealth, the settlement does not seem to have attracted the investment of private resources that was so crucial for its successful development.[132] It remained, one would suppose, a modest administrative centre throughout the second century.

By contrast, some sites on the periphery of the Fenland became very prosperous during this period, most notably *Durobrivae*. Although only a *vicus*[133] (at any rate for the earlier part of its history), it had the solid agricultural and commercial base to become one of the wealthiest regions of Roman Britain. The excellent farm land in the *territorium* was extensively exploited, there was a considerable building industry (which provided both stone and tile for the Stonea settlement), iron-working was practised on a large scale, and there was an enormous production of pottery. It is particularly striking to see the huge quantities of Nene Valley coarse- and table-ware that turn up on every Fenland site; the emergence of this huge new market must have been a major factor in the development of *Durobrivae's* wealth.[134]

C.E. Stevens long ago suggested that *Durobrivae* may have been promoted to the status of a *civitas* capital in the later Roman period, a notion that still carries conviction.[135] The idea would gain further weight were we to suppose that the main administrative role for the Fens devolved upon the town in the early third century. As Mackreth has pointed out, this might explain the eventual construction of palatial buildings such as the enormous Castor *praetorium*, which has the appearance of an official, rather than a private, residence.[136] Indeed, Mackreth has drawn attention to a large complex within the heart of the town which, he feels, could represent an administrative centre.[137]

129.   The notion of a mid-third-century flood was first proposed by Bromwich in Phillips, op. cit. (note 4), 114f. Further evidence was presented in *Britannia* xii (1981), 132. No traces of flood deposits were found on the eastern fen edge by Gurney (op. cit., (note 6), 148), although it is well attested at Fengate (Pryor, op. cit. (note 13) *The Fourth Report*, 201).

130.   Salway in Phillips, op. cit. (note 4), 16.

131.   Crawford, op. cit. (note 75), 53.

132.   cf. B. Ward-Perkins, *From classical antiquity to the Middle Ages. Urban public building in northern and central Italy* (Oxford, 1984) for a most useful discussion; also R.P. Duncan-Jones in F. Grew and B. Hobley (eds.), *Roman urban topography in Britain and the western Empire* (London, 1985), 28–33.

133.   J.P. Wild, 'Roman settlement in the lower Nene Valley,' *Arch. Journ.* cxxxi (1974), 147.

134.   idem., 140–69 surveys the economy.

135.   C.E. Stevens, 'Gildas and the civitates of Britain,' *Eng. Hist. Review* lii (1937), 193–203.

136.   D. Mackreth, *Durobrivae* ix (1984), 22–5; *Britannia* xiv (1983), 303–5.

137.   D. Mackreth, *Durobrivae* vii (1979), 19–21.

It seems unlikely, however, that the bureaucratic structure that was necessary to administer a vast region such as the Fens was entirely based in one place. Todd maintains that collectors of the *annona militaris* may have resided in the small towns,[138] and it is interesting in this respect to note Green's discovery of a basilica-like building of official appearance, constructed in the early third century, in the Roman town at Godmanchester.[139] Wacher infers that this may have been a centre for tax collection, although whether it relates to the town's immediate environs or was linked with the adjacent Fenland is as speculative as the proposed identification of the building's function.[140]

Within the Fens, we can still say comparatively little about the nature of settlement in the third century. The Fenland Project survey has begun to refine our knowledge of the complex shifts in the settlement of the flood-prone regions of southern Lincolnshire;[141] but, elsewhere the picture remains poorly understood. The site at Stonea Grange seems to have escaped serious flooding, and a provisional interpretation envisages some occupation throughout the third century; but its nature remains somewhat obscure. However, there do seem to have been significant developments around A.D.300. The robbed-out foundations of the tower were filled in, and a substantial building using some stone was laid out over it. Ploughing had destroyed most of the footings and the plan of the structure cannot be reconstructed; but the totality of evidence from the site is for a relatively prosperous community, probably of some considerable size.

This picture accords well with earlier views, which envisaged a series of affluent communities both within the Fens and along its fringes. Salway has attempted to draw a distinction between the *vicani* of the village-like settlements that seem to characterise the margins of the Wash in the late Roman period and *coloni*, tied to villa-estates around the southern Fen edge.[142] The recently published fourth-century villa at Little Oulsham Drove, Feltwell might be taken to typify such villas.[143] However, with the evidence of Grandford, Flaggrass, Stonea, Coldham and Honey Hill now before us,[144] it can be seen that villages were as much a part of the southern Fenland landscape as in the northern Fens. Moreover, we might infer that the stone-built late Roman cottages (if that is a suitable term), best exemplified at Grandford,[145] were perhaps the residences of the *conductores*, or similar officials, who were charged with the collection of rents and taxes, and who also carried out supervisory duties on the estates.[146] This does not rule out the existence of a tied colonate around the Fen edges, (where lands, Salway now thinks, may in some instances have come into the ownership of the Church);[147] but it does help to separate off the heartland of the Fens from the topographically distinct units around its margins, with their seemingly different systems of land management.

It is not intended to discuss here the increasingly complex evidence for the demise of Romano-British settlement, and the emergence of Saxon communities. Much has been learnt from the recent programme of field survey about this important period of transition, but is only provisionally published;[148] while analysis is still in progress on the series of Saxon buildings which were constructed over part of the Roman site at Stonea Grange. They appear to span the period between the later fifth and seventh centuries, and raise a series of intriguing questions about the way in which some late Roman settlements may have been utilised in early Saxon

138. M. Todd, 'The small towns of Roman Britain,' *Britannia* i (1970), 126.
139. H.J.M. Green 'Godmanchester,' in W. Rodwell and T. Rowley (eds.), *The 'small towns' of Roman Britain* BAR 15 (Oxford, 1975), 183–210.
140. J.S. Wacher, *Roman Britain* (London, 1978), 98.
141. P.P. Hayes, 'Roman to Saxon in the south Lincolnshire Fens,' *Antiquity* lxii (1988), 321–5.
142. Salway in Phillips, op. cit. (note 4), 17.
143. Gurney, op. cit. (note 6), 1–48. See also T. Gregory, 'Romano-British settlement in west Norfolk,' in D. Miles (ed.), *The Romano-British Countryside* BAR 103 (Oxford, 1982), 351–76.
144. *Britannia* xii (1981), 129.
145. Potter and Potter, op. cit. (note 8).
146. See A.H.M. Jones, *The later Roman Empire* (Oxford, 1964), 388f., 412f.; also Crawford, op. cit. (note 75), 50–1 on the use of *vilici* as supervisors.
147. P. Salway, *Roman Britain* (Oxford, 1981), 730.
148. Hayes, op. cit. (note 141).

times. Here, if anywhere, recent survey work promises to extend considerably our understanding of a period of Fenland history which has hitherto remained nebulous.[149]

SOME CONCLUSIONS

The last decade has witnessed a remarkable investment of resources in the archaeology of the Fens. The main field to benefit has unquestionably been that of prehistoric studies, especially through a series of spectacular excavations, usefully backed up by field survey (which has itself disclosed some major sites such as Flag Fen and the Haddenham barrows). The unexpected demonstration that Iron Age communities did exploit the Fenland is of particular interest, as is the recovery of early Saxon sites: Fox's model has here been substantially modified.[150]

For the Roman period, the most notable achievement has been the identification, by D.N. Hall, of the Stonea Grange settlement, and its subsequent excavation. However the site is interpreted (a matter that will doubtless remain controversial), it is clearly exceptional in the context of the Fenland. Its Hadrianic date, highly unusual stone-built complex and its regular layout all point to an official creation which, in turn, lends further support to the hypothesis that much of the Fens was Imperially owned. Equally, the work at Stonea, combined with other discoveries from elsewhere on the islands, especially March, strongly suggests that the Hadrianic settlement was the heir to an Icenian centre, perhaps for a western *pagus* of the tribe. This revelation of a substantial pre-Flavian presence in the central Fens (mainly, as it happens, through chance finds,) is quite novel and largely unpredicted.

As far as the recent programme of field survey is concerned, the detailed picture of the distribution of Romano-British settlement has not been greatly modified from that advanced in 1970. Its particular value would seem to lie in the greatly enhanced understanding of the geology and soils that we now have; in the much more comprehensive list of sites with saltern debris; and in the acquisition of a broader chronological perspective in which to set the Roman evidence. As with many field surveys, however, the quality and range of the evidence that is now available from the surface of the Fens restricts the conclusions to comparatively generalised statements, which have to be refined by excavation. The work at Stonea Grange illustrates some of the possibilities, but we can still only speculate on the results that, for example, well-placed sections across the canals at Flaggrass or large-scale examination of a major salt-producing site such as Norwood, might divulge. Whilst the potential for organic survival on these (and most) Roman sites is likely to be limited,[151] there is a huge amount that is still to be learnt about the settlement patterns, history and economy of the Fens in this period. Until such excavations are carried out, our conclusions must remain correspondingly tentative.

---

149. *Britannia* xii (1981), 132–3; C.C. Taylor, *The Cambridgeshire Landscape* (London, 1973), 45f.
150. Fox, op. cit. (note 2).
151. Roman organic material from excavations in the central Fens is confined to material from the great 'sump' and a few wells at Stonea Grange.

THE ECONOMY OF ROMAN BRITAIN★

By Michael Fulford

INTRODUCTION

Our understanding of the economy of Roman Britain has surged so far ahead over the last ten to fifteen years that it has become practicable to attempt a synthesis for the first time. This is due to a number of factors, the first of which has been a general rise in interest in the economic affairs of the Roman world.[1] This has had a particular value for our assessment of the British situation, for it has not only generated models which can be tested against the British evidence, but it has also offered a central perspective on ideas developed in isolation on the basis of British data alone. Secondly, there has been an overall improvement in field-techniques and expansion in the scale of excavations which have produced quantities of artefacts and environmental data which have demanded attention. The study of the latter, representing a third area of development, has been profoundly influenced by the behavioural and natural sciences as well as by mathematics and computer-studies.

We can examine now the conceptual framework in which these new data are being set. Broadly, there are two themes; first, the relationship between the imperial government (the centre) and Britain and the extent to which economic activity was shaped by policy and the institutions of the army and civil administration, rather than by indigenous developments. Determining the relative influences of Roman and native becomes important from as early as the first century B.C.. Fundamental to this theme is the debate as to how much the development of the physical fabric of Roman Britain and the mechanisms which maintained it was due to a net inflow of capital from the centre, rather than to resources generated within Britain. A.H.M. Jones' theory that 'the raising and spending of the imperial revenue effected a certain redistribution of wealth between the provinces . . . the greater part of it (*sic* the revenue) was spent on the army which was stationed in poorer and underdeveloped areas such as Britain, the Rhineland and Danubian provinces. This expenditure stimulated the development of these backward areas, and in particular the growth of towns in them'[2] is pivotal to this debate. A development of Jones' idea is Hopkins' model that the tax-consuming frontier areas like Britain demanded a higher volume of goods than could be satisfied by local production and that this outward flow of trade to the periphery was paid for by a reverse flow of the money originally paid out to the provincial army.[3] This money then returned as tax to the treasury from the

★ I am grateful to Jane Timby for drawing FIGS. 2–4 and 6 and to Brian Williams for FIGS. 1, 5 and 7.

1. e.g. M.I. Finley, *The Ancient Economy* (London, 1973, rev. ed. 1985); A.H.M. Jones (ed. P.A. Brunt), *The Roman Economy* (Oxford, 1974); K. Hopkins, *JRS* lxx (1980), 101–25; P. Garnsey, K. Hopkins and C.R. Whittaker (eds.), *Trade in the Ancient Economy* (London, 1983); K. Greene, *The Archaeology of the Roman Economy* (London, 1986); P. Garnsey and R. Saller, *The Roman Empire: Economy, Society and Culture* (London, 1987), 43–103.
2. Jones, op. cit. (note 1), 127.
3. Hopkins, op. cit. (note 1).

producers and manufacturers in the Mediterranean provinces. It has been argued that the massive debasement of the silver coinage from the later second century combined with the levying of taxes in kind, destroyed this cycle of trade and reciprocal money-flow.[4] The second theme is the debate over the character of the economy within Roman Britain. How and when (if at all) did economic activity evolve to become independent of pre-Roman social institutions and how far did the use of cash and independent price-fixing markets develop?[5] This particular argument can be seen in the context of a wider discussion about the character of the ancient economy as a whole and the extent to which the government and related institutions rather than individual entrepreneurs were the generators and controllers of economic activity.[6] This question has particular importance regarding the complexity of economic activity within Roman Britain. It is only possible here to sketch briefly recent developments in our understanding of the Romano-British economy. The mass of data allows us to survey these chronologically, rather than thematically. In this respect, the subject of Britain's regional and long-distance trade has been treated elsewhere.[7]

PRE-ROMAN IRON AGE

We may begin with the pre-Roman situation and the development of contacts between Britain and the Roman world. These can be broadly divided into three periods, each of which shows evidence of progressively more intense relations. In the first period, before Caesar's invasions, we have two principal forms of artefactual evidence, whose distributions are almost mutually exclusive. First, there is evidence for Roman and/or Gallic traders making or developing contact with southern Britain west of the Isle of Wight. The recent excavations at Hengistbury Head reveal both the long-distance elements of this contact, as exemplified by the finds of Italian Dressel 1A wine amphorae dating from about the mid-second century, and the more regional, as evidenced by the finds of Breton pottery.[8] Second, from south-east Britain there is the evidence for the importation of precious metal north Gaulish coinage peaking in the late second/early first century B.C.. Associated with this, and probably stimulated by its importation, is evidence for the production of a native potin coinage which Haselgrove believes circulated alongside the gold and also served a prestige role.[9] The production of British gold coinage began in earnest during the second quarter of the first century B.C., mainly within the area served by the imported currency.

The explanation for these early contacts remains elusive. On the one hand, trade with raw materials like tin as the principal reciprocal seems a satisfactory explanation for the south-western imports and has limited support from written sources.[10] On the other, the coin evidence has invited wider-ranging speculation as to its origin. Allen's original idea[11] that importation might be connected with the arrival of Gallic immigrants has found less favour in recent years,[12] but has not yet been entirely discarded.[13] Caesar's *de Bello Gallico* offers us a variety of possibilities

4. ibid.
5. I. Hodder, 'Pre-Roman and Romano-British Tribal Economies' in B. Burnham and H. Johnson (eds.), *Invasion and Response: The Case of Roman Britain* BAR 73 (1979), 189–96.
6. cf. Finley, op. cit. (note 1); C.R. Whittaker, 'Late Roman trade and traders', in Garnsey *et al.*, op. cit. (note 1), 163–80; P. Middleton, 'The Roman Army and Long-Distance Trade', in P. Garnsey and C.R. Whittaker (eds.), *Trade and Famine in Classical Antiquity* (Cambridge, 1983), 75–83; C.R. Whittaker, *OPUS* iv (1985), 49–75.
7. M. Fulford, 'Britain and the Roman Empire: the evidence for Regional and Long Distance Trade', in R.F. Jones (ed.), *Britain in the Roman Period* (Sheffield, in press).
8. B. Cunliffe, *Hengistbury Head, Dorset Vol. 1: The Prehistoric and Roman Settlement, 3500 B.C. – A.D. 500* (O.U.C.A., Oxford, 1987).
9. C. Haselgrove, *Iron Age Coinage in South-East England: The Archaeological Context* BAR 174 (1987), Ch. 9.
10. Recently reviewed by M. Todd, *The South West to A.D. 1000* (London, 1987), 185–8.
11. D.F. Allen, *Archaeologia* xc (1944), 1–46.
12. e.g. M. Todd, *Roman Britain 55 B.C. – A.D. 400* (London, 1981), 28–30.
13. W. Rodwell, 'Coinage, Oppida and the rise of Belgic Power in South-Eastern Britain', in B. Cunliffe and T. Rowley (eds.), *Oppida in Barbarian Europe* BAR Supp. Ser. 11 (1976), 181–366.

including trade and the recruitment of help from Britain by the Belgae, the latter in the context of the Gallic wars themselves.[14] If we cannot distinguish between the range of possible mechanisms on the ground, we can at least be certain that the precious metal coinage circulated only among the élite and thus that the beneficiaries of these cross-channel transactions were few in number. What returned across the channel remains clear in outline, but vague in detail. We are very dependent on written sources such as Caesar and Strabo, the latter writing in the time of Augustus. His well-known observation, that Britain exported corn, cattle, slaves, gold, silver, hides, slaves and hunting-dogs,[15] is notoriously difficult to verify in the archaeological record, either because the commodities in question are difficult or impossible to characterise or have a poor survival record. Curiously Strabo does not mention tin in this passage, although Diodorus Siculus implies that this was sought after by Mediterranean merchants.[16] Early imports, whether Roman or Gaulish are altogether rare and it is too early yet to determine what impact this first phase of trade had on southern British society generally.

The Gallic wars seem to have intensified cross-channel contacts; thanks to the work of Scheers[17] on the Gallic coinage and of Kent[18] and Haselgrove[19] on the British material, it is clear that the wars were responsible for an influx of gold (representing payment for mercenaries or the wealth of refugees, etc.) into the South-East which stimulated further British coin production within the South-East, extending it into East Anglia and Lincolnshire. Apart from precious metal coinage, there is little other evidence of imports – some Dressel 1B amphorae and a small amount of metalwork – in the period between Caesar's invasions and the last ten or twenty years of the first century B.C..[20] Cross-channel contacts seem to be firmly related to socio-political ties, based on common ethnicity, marriage and alliances among élites and their clients in north-west Gaul (Pas-de-Calais, Somme basin and Seine region), the Atrebates representing one such common link.

The consolidation of Gaul by Augustus and the start of campaigning across the Rhine in 16 B.C. re-introduced direct Roman links with southern Britain and the volume of cross-channel activity undoubtedly increased. This is not only evident in the changing character of the British coinage, but in the wide range of material imports of a Gaulish and Mediterranean origin now found in southern Britain. (Fig. 1) Until the publication of Skeleton Green,[22] we were largely dependent on Camulodunum[23] for our appreciation of material culture at the end of the Iron Age. Research on the material from these and related sites (Baldock,[24] Ower[25] and now Silchester[26]) has greatly enlarged our appreciation of the volume and diversity of imports: Italian and Spanish amphorae, Italian and south Gaulish sigillatas, central and north Gaulish table and coarse wares, Italian and Gaulish metalwork, glass, etc. These finds tend to occur on a small number of high status nucleated settlements (oppida) in the South-East whose initial occupation within the second half

14. Reviewed by Haselgrove, op. cit. (note 9), 190–3.
15. Geography IV, 5, 2.
16. History, V, 22.
17. S. Scheers, Traité de Numismatique Celtique II: la Gaule Belgique (Paris, 1977).
18. J.P.C. Kent, 'The origins of coinage in Britain' in B.W. Cunliffe (ed.), Coinage and Society in Britain and Gaul C.B.A. Res. Rep. 38 (London, 1981), 40–2.
19. C. Haselgrove, 'Romanisation before the Conquest: Gaulish precedents and British consequences', in T.F.C. Blagg and A.C. King, Military and Civilian in Roman Britain BAR 136 (1984), 5–63.
20. A.P. Fitzpatrick, Oxford Journ. Arch. iv (1983), 305–40 (amphorae); I.M. Stead, 'The earliest burials of the Aylesford culture', in G. Sieveking, I. Longworth and K. Wilson (eds.), Problems in economic and social archaeology, (London, 1976), 401–16 (metalwork).
21. e.g. C. Haselgrove, above, pp. 1–18.
22. C. Partridge, Skeleton Green: a late Iron Age and Romano-British site Britannia Monograph 2 (London, 1981).
23. C.F.C. Hawkes and M.R. Hull, Camulodunum Res. Rept. Soc. Antiq. Lond. 15 (London, 1947).
24. I.M. Stead and V. Rigby, Baldock: the excavation of a Roman and pre-Roman settlement 1968–72 Britannia Monograph 7 (London, 1986).
25. P.J. Woodward, 'Excavations at Ower and Rope Lake Hole', in N. Sunter and P.J. Woodward, Romano-British Industries in Purbeck (Dorchester, 1987), 44–124.
26. M. Fulford, Guide to the Silchester Excavations: the Forum Basilica 1982–4 (Reading, 1985).

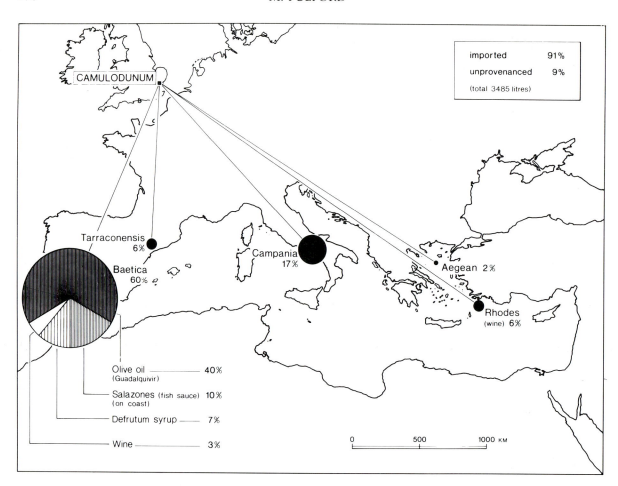

imported   91%
unprovenanced   9%
(total 3485 litres)

CAMULODUNUM

Tarraconensis
6%

Baetica
60%

Campania
17%

Aegean 2%

Rhodes
(wine) 6%

Olive oil ——————— 40%
(Guadalquivir)

Salazones (fish sauce) 10%
(on coast)

Defrutum syrup ——— 7%

Wine ——————————— 3%

0   500   1000 KM

FIG. 1   The principal sources of the contents (estimated total of 3485 litres) of a sample of the amphorae supplied to
Camulodunum (Sheepen) between AD 43 and 61. (Source: Fulford (note 7) and Sealey (note 45))

of the first century B.C. appears to be more or less contemporary. Alongside this, we have the
evidence of the precious metal coinages – predominantly gold in the South-East, predominantly
silver in the south.[27] Clearly some of this coinage relates to a recycling of earlier imported coin,
but we may reasonably assume that this pool continued to be supplemented. How? It is often
assumed that British mineral resources were responsible,[28] but, to any great extent, this seems
unlikely. Not only is there very little precious metal of this date in the West where such minerals
are to be found, but in the case of silver we have to assume a derivation from lead, which in
Britain had low concentrations of silver. There is precious little evidence for the working of lead
before the conquest and none for the extraction from it of silver.[29] Tylecote is sceptical whether
the extraction of silver from British lead was ever carried out, even in the Roman period,
although there is some evidence for the small-scale cupellation of silver-containing copper.[30] The
silver was imported, as was the gold. The mutually exclusive character to the circulation of these
metals in Britain probably relates to the different routes of access to the island; the Atlantic route
from Spain on the one hand, the short, north Gaul/south-east Britain channel-crossing on the
other. Alongside trade, some of the imported wealth evident in pre-Claudian Britain may have
arrived in the form of diplomatic gifts.

27.   Haselgrove, op. cit. (note 9); R.P. Mack, *The Coinage of Ancient Britain* (3rd ed., London, 1975).
28.   e.g. P.R. Sealey, *PPS* xlv (1979), 165–78.
29.   cf. P. Northover in Cunliffe, op. cit. (note 8), 191.
30.   R.F. Tylecote, *The Prehistory of Metallurgy in the British Isles* (London, 1986), 54–80.

THE ROMAN CONQUEST

While it is not the intention to consider all the implications of pre-conquest contacts, it is appropriate to reassess the economic value of Britain to the Roman world. All surveys of Roman Britain have attached a greater or lesser importance to the economic gains of conquest, with political motivation usually in first place.[31] These ideas are based on the written sources – Tacitus' 'gold and silver as the reward of victory'[32] – whose rhetorical flavour undermines their value as historical evidence. In contrast we have the remark of Strabo (of Augustan date) which indicated that more revenue could be gained from customs' dues than from tribute, given the costs of maintaining a garrison army.[33] A straightforward review of our evidence is not at first sight encouraging; on the one hand we have unquantified remarks from the ancient written sources, while on the other we have a range of imported artefacts whose relationship with the original imported cargoes it is now impossible to evaluate. One way out of the impasse is to compare the British evidence of pre-invasion relations with that from elsewhere around the periphery of the empire. If we consider those areas of Europe with which Rome maintained economic relations after the Augustan consolidation of the opportunistic conquests of the Republic, only Dacia with its wealth of imported material from the Graeco-Roman world emerges as remotely comparable to Britain.[34] Elsewhere relations were determined by long-distance and widespread (but low volume) luxury trades in slaves and luxury commodities such as amber and furs. These were sustained by exchanges of metalwork and other prestige items which had a limited circulation among the élite.[35] Britain was able to respond to the 'knock-on' demands of the Romanisation of Gaul and the German wars in a way which other trans-frontier regions were unable to do. While this still does not help us to quantify the economic importance of the island (which the Romans themselves could not do), it does serve to show that the invasion was likely to meet with a more supportive agricultural infrastructure than might be met elsewhere. Indeed, recent experimental and theoretical work has suggested how productive Britain *might* have been.[36] Although it may not have been perceived in this way at the time, the post-Augustan conquests of Britain and Dacia had an economic rationale which was absent in Augustus' German strategy; expectations therefore could well have been different.

ARMY SUPPLY

Attractive and (comparatively) productive as Britain was, the realities of conquest were different. The invasion army was some four times larger than that which Strabo thought might be sufficient and it is clear from the archaeological record that insular resources were inadequate to maintain this force. Harvest fluctuations, the ravages of warfare on crops as Roman territory expanded, the need to maintain adequate reserves of grain (two-years' supply), all contributed to the problem of supporting the invading army. Demands were also different in kind. The demand for beef which, it has been shown, was a characteristic of early military garrisons must have been

---

31. e.g. S.S. Frere, *Britannia: a history of Roman Britain* (3rd ed., London, 1987), 45-6; P. Salway, *Roman Britain* (Oxford, 1981), 65–72; Todd, op. cit. (note 12), 60–4.
32. *Agricola*, xii, 6.
33. *Geography* IV, 5, 3.
34. I. Glodariu, *Dacian Trade with the Hellenistic and Roman World* BAR S8 (Oxford, 1976).
35. e.g. H.J. Eggers, *Der römische import im freien Germanien* (Hamburg, 1951); L. Hedeager, 'A quantitative analysis of Roman imports in Europe north of the limes (0–400 A.D.) and the question of Romano-Germanic exchange', in K. Kristiansen and C. Paludan-Müller (eds.), *New Directions in Scandinavian Archaeology* (Copenhagen, 1977), 197–276; M. Fulford, 'Roman material in barbarian society', in T.C. Champion and J.V.S. Megaw (eds.), *Settlement and Society* (Leicester, 1985), 91–108.
36. P. Reynolds, 'Deadstock and livestock', in R. Mercer (ed.), *Farming Practice in British Prehistory* (Edinburgh, 1981), 97–122; M. Millett, 'Forts and the Origin of Towns: cause or effect?' in Blagg and King, op. cit. (note 19), 65–74.

difficult to accommodate without inflicting serious damage to existing herds.[37] The rebellion of Boudicca brought destruction to the heart of the province; loss of harvest in 60/61 and the years immediately following reduced the province to famine.[38]

Demonstration of the island's dependence on external supplies comes from both direct and indirect sources.[39] The deposit of imported cereals in pre-Boudiccan London is an example of the former;[40] the volume of imported artefacts, notably pottery as containers (amphorae) and tableware and glass in the pre-Flavian period, serves as an example of the latter. Although romanised communities had to look outside Britain for familiar consumer durables, it seems likely that the volume of importation of goods attested from distant sources could only have been sustained if it was carried, or effectively subsidised, by a high volume of requisitioned foods and other essentials. As others have pointed out, the overall distribution of major consumer durables like South Gaulish sigillata (where much of the output is found across Gaul to Germany and Britain, rather than southwards to the Mediterranean) makes no economic sense, unless their transport was underwritten by the carriage of other supplies.[41] The fact that Britons sometimes had to buy back requisitioned grain from army granaries in the time of Agricola is itself an indication of its shortage.[42]

The importance of a cross-channel lifeline is implicit in the location of early fortresses on navigable river estuaries. Although communications around the coasts of Britain were ensured, the number and range of imported artefacts points to the importance of the strategic link. In a civilian context, the spectacular growth of pre-Boudiccan London also demonstrates the importance of maritime links with Britain. The presence of imported cereals in Caerleon on the R. Usk shows that these strategic considerations were still important in the early second century.[43] As quantified data from pre-Flavian Kingsholm (the predecessor to the legionary fortress at Gloucester) show, the range and volume of imports were considerable;[44] comparable, but only partially quantified data (amphorae) from Camulodunum (Sheepen) offer a point of comparison (Fig. 1).[45]

Whereas the South and South-West could be supplied directly by sea, the inland fortresses of Lincoln and Wroxeter were land-locked. London's role as the hub of a supply system established in the Neronian–early Flavian period finds support in the distribution of Verulamium region pottery of which mortaria are the best known product. Stamped examples have been traced across the province to the northern frontier, clearly indicative of a land-based supply system where it would be perverse to see them as the sole item carried.[46] One explanation for the origin of the road network centred on London can be sought in its role in the system of supply in the first century A.D..

37. A. King, 'Animal bones and the dietary identity of military and civilian groups in Roman Britain, Germany and Gaul', in Blagg and King, op. cit. (note 19), 187–217.
38. Tacitus, *Annals*, XIV, 38.
39. M. Fulford, 'Demonstrating Britannia's dependence in the first and second centuries', in Blagg and King, op. cit. (note 19), 129–42.
40. V. Straker in, P. Marsden, *The Roman Forum Site in London* (London, 1987), 151–3.
41. P. Middleton, 'Army supply in Roman Gaul: an hypothesis for Roman Britain', in Burnham and Johnson, op. cit. (note 5), 81-97; A. King, 'The decline of samian ware manufacture in the North-West provinces: problems of chronology and interpretation', in A. King and M. Henig (eds.), *The Roman West in the Third Century* BAR S 109 (1981), 55–73.
42. Tacitus, *Agricola*, xix.
43. H. Helbaek, *The New Phytologist* lxiii (1964), 158–64.
44. H.R. Hurst, *Kingsholm* (Gloucester, 1985).
45. P.R. Sealey in R. Niblett, *Sheepen: an early Roman industrial site at Camulodunum* CBA Res. Rept. 57 (London, 1985), 98–111.
46. S. Castle, *Arch. Journ.* cxxix (1972), 80, fig. 7.

TAXATION

The needs of the army probably remained paramount throughout the first and second century and it is appropriate now to consider the mechanisms of supply within Britain and the possible links with the way in which the province was taxed. In the course of campaigning, we can assume that there was much forcible requisitioning and plundering, but we also need to consider how the army was regularly supplied in this formative period. The only direct source for Britain is Tacitus where he describes the abuses which were corrected by Agricola in the way the grain was supplied to the army by the native population.[47] The provincials were being forced to supply more than was required, and then having to buy back at higher prices to meet their own needs. At the same time they were responsible for delivery to specified destinations. Although it is dangerous to read too much into one piece of evidence, it is a reasonable deduction, as we have seen, that there was not enough grain to satisfy everybody's requirements. On what basis was the grain supplied? One might assume from this text that grain was being exacted as tax in kind. An alternative might be that the army, via the procurator and using cash raised from taxation simply purchased its needs at a low price.[48] The question is more important than it may at first seem, because if taxation, as organised by the procurator, consisted of the provision in kind of the *annona* for the army, there would have been no place for money-taxes.

The importance of money-taxation as a mechanism for encouraging the development of markets and a monetised economy has been stressed by several writers.[49] If money-taxation was present in early Roman Britain, it ought to be reflected in the pattern of coins lost in the province. Reece has drawn attention to the comparatively low proportion of early Roman coinage among site-finds that he has studied.[50] More recently, on the basis of his study of the coins from the sacred spring at Bath – a group which represents the largest single assemblage from Britain – Walker has advanced the idea that there was no systematic introduction of bronze coinage into circulation in Britain until A.D. 96.[51] Prior to this there had been sporadic, but massive injections of bronze coinage, first in the invasion period of A.D. 43–52, then 64–67, and on three occasions in the Flavian period, 71–73, 77–78 and 86–87.[52] Alongside the official currency the Claudian period saw the large-scale production of copies (certainly with official sanction and probably carried out by army units) to offset the dearth of regular supplies from the official mint. Preliminary work on the dies suggests that while some of this coinage was imported from Gaul, much was produced and circulated locally.[53] Very little early Roman coinage is known to have circulated in the countryside. Native coinages continued to play their part, although the coins were not accepted as legal tender by the Roman authorities.[54] In the client kingdom of the Iceni, coinage continued to be struck up to the time of the Boudiccan revolt; in the client kingdom of Cogidubnus there is evidence for the continued circulation of currency up to the Flavian period, but little to point to the striking of fresh coinage after A.D. 43.[55] What does all this add up to? While it is debatable how much can be deduced from the behaviour of bronze coinage, the erratic nature of its official or semi-official supply seems to imply limited monetization of the province, with money-using markets confined to the major towns, fortresses and forts, as is implied by the

47. Tacitus, *Agricola*, xix.
48. Strabo, *Geography* III, 4, 20; D. Breeze, 'Demand and Supply on the Northern Frontier', in R. Miket and C. Burgess (eds.), *Between and Beyond the Walls* (Edinburgh, 1985), 264–86.
49. e.g. Hopkins, op. cit. (note 1).
50. R. Reece, *Britannia* iii (1972), 269–76; ibid, iv (1973), 227–41.
51. D. Walker, 'The Roman Coins', in B. Cunliffe, *The Temple of Sulis Minerva at Bath Vol. 2. The Finds from the Sacred Spring* (O.U.C.A. Oxford, 1988), 281–358.
52. ibid, 286–8.
53. G.C. Boon, 'Counterfeit coins in Roman Britain', in J. Casey and R. Reece (eds.), *Coins and the Archaeologist* (2nd ed., London, 1988) 118–24; R. Kenyon in N. Crummy (ed.), *Colchester Archaeological Rept. 4: The Coins from Excavations in Colchester* (Colchester, 1987), 24–41.
54. R. Reece, 'Roman monetary impact', in Burnham and Johnson, op. cit. (note 5), 211–17.
55. Haselgrove, op. cit. (note 9), 204–8.

pattern of circulation of the Claudian copies. We do not know very much about the circulation of silver which would very probably have been the main medium for the payment of taxation. If the collection of the *annona* was independent from that of taxes, the failure of the latter to stimulate local markets suggests that the responsibilities for payment were jealously guarded by the tribal, landowning elite. They extracted the surplus from their clients and estates and arranged for its sale, so restricting access to the market on the part of the dependent peasantry. The implication of this is that the social organisation of the pre-Claudian period was perpetuated into the early Flavian period in southern Britain. A corollary of this picture of limited change is the lack of evidence for significant increases in the specialisation of labour before the end of the first century.

CIVIL DEVELOPMENTS

The erratic way in which money was supplied to Britain in the first century contrasts with the received picture of rapid urban growth in the Flavian period. There is no reason for associating any of this money supply with civilian developments, although the Neronian bronze may have played a part in paying for the labour involved in the building and re-building of the cities after Boudicca. However, the Flavian bronze is inextricably linked with the conquest of the North. Material evidence apart, there are two reasons for supposing a spate of urban development; on the one hand, we are told by Tacitus that Agricola encouraged the building of temples, market-places and private houses;[56] on the other, the conquest of the North is assumed to have left an administrative vacuum which could only be filled by the establishment of autonomous *civitates peregrinae*. The archaeological evidence for the physical fabric of late-first-century towns still remains elusive and there is reason to be cautious in assuming a Flavian date for the earliest phases of public building unless the dating evidence is unequivocal (above, p. 75ff.). In Leicester and Caistor-by-Norwich the evidence does point to a gradual development up to the mid-second century.[57] In the South the continued use of wood for the Flavian forum-basilica at Silchester also urges caution in our interpretation of older excavated evidence from monumental masonry buildings.[58] Nevertheless, there were developments and this is reflected in the appearance of small urban industries to satisfy the new demands. The growth of the Verulamium region potteries on the one hand and Pollard's study of the Roman pottery of Kent reveal the changes of the later first century when the potteries at Canterbury were first established and the first British fine wares circulated at a regional level.[59]

Urban development could not be plucked out of the air; it required a supply of both skilled craftsmen (carpenters, masons, smiths, etc.) and unskilled labour. We can trace the start of stone-quarrying in the South from the Neronian-early Flavian period. The freestones used in the Neronian phase of the Fishbourne 'palace' originated from a number of localities including Gaul (Caen), the Weald and Gloucestershire and were supplemented by decorative marble veneers and *opus sectile* from Purbeck and continental sources.[60] The temple of Bath can now be dated to the late Neronian/early Flavian period and is direct witness to the operation of the Bath limestone quarries.[61] Elsewhere, such as distantly at Colchester, we can find evidence of the early use of limestone from quarries from along the Jurassic system between Avon and Northamptonshire. In Cirencester, as in Bath, it was the obvious material to use. However, despite the availability of such stone, timber continued to remain a most important building material well into the second century. At Silchester, for example, a town within seven or eight miles of unlimited flint, timber was selected for use in the successive Neronian and Flavian fora and in the Neronian or early Flavian amphitheatre;[62] only in the contemporary bath-house can we be certain that flint was

56. *Agricola*, xxi.
57. J. Wacher, *The Towns of Roman Britain* (London, 1975), 226–38; 335–57.
58. M. Fulford, *Antiq. Journ.* lxv (1985), 39–81.
59. R.J. Pollard, *The Roman Pottery of Kent* (Maidstone, 1988), 58–80.
60. B. Cunliffe, *Excavations at Fishbourne 1961–1969* Vol. II (Leeds, 1971), 1–42.
61. T.F.C. Blagg, *Britannia* x (1979), 101–7.
62. Fulford, op. cit. (note 58).

used right from the start. In Verulamium, although the Flavian forum-basilica was of masonry, timber continued to be used widely in shops and houses until after the fire of 155/60.[63] In London, too, masonry seems largely to have been limited to major public buildings, like the 'proto-forum' and its successor.[64]

REORGANISATION OF NORTHERN FRONTIER AND ARMY SUPPLY IN THE SECOND CENTURY

In the early second century a number of phenomena is visible in the archaeological record which seems to mark a major change in the organisation of the economy. These observable patterns coincide with the massive restructuring of the northern frontier under Hadrian and the two may well be connected. The first phenomenon provides evidence for the integration of the whole province (except the frontier zone) in the supply of food and certain raw materials to the North and Welsh garrisons. The changes in the distribution of Dorset BB 1 provide the clearest evidence for this. Originally limited to the south-west peninsula, by the second quarter of the second century BB1 is found commonly on the northern frontier, in Wales and on civil sites across the province.[65] In the South-East stamped tiles show the involvement of the *Classis Britannica* in the exploitation of Wealden iron and inscriptions attest to the presence of detachments of the fleet on Hadrian's Wall during its construction.[66] One implication here is that the fleet was involved in the carriage of supplies, which included iron, to the North. The pottery evidence can be interpreted as indicating the movement of general supplies around the coasts to the frontier garrisons;[67] the pattern contrasts markedly with that for the Flavian period described above.

These internal developments are reflected in the pattern of long-distance trade and supply; the first quarter of the second century represents something of a lacuna between the demise of the trade in or supply of South Gaulish sigillata and the rise of Central and, to a lesser extent, East Gaulish wares. That gap is only partly filled by the increasing recognition of Central Gaulish Martres de Veyre sigillata of Trajanic date.[68] The period of reorientation of supplies also corresponds with a low in the size of the British garrison. *Legio II Adiutrix* was transferred to the Danube under Domitian and it seems likely that *Legio IX Hispana* was moved out of Britain a few years before A. Platorius Nepos brought *Legio VI* into the province early in the reign of Hadrian. A period when the volume of imports declines coincides with reductions of the garrisons and comes to an end with the evidence for the restructuring of supply within and without of Britain during the second quarter of the second century. The Vindolanda writing-tablets[69] are beginning to provide a valuable insight into the organisation of supply to an auxiliary unit at the beginning of the century, contrasting with the archaeological evidence for the organisation of supply from Hadrian onwards.[70]

The ceramic evidence for change outlined above is not really susceptible to close dating, but it seems to come somewhat later than an interesting development in the coin supply to the

---

63. S.S. Frere, *Verulamium Vol. I* (London, 1972); Vol. II (London, 1983), for military use of timber see W.S. Hanson, *Britannia* ix (1978), 293–305.
64. Marsden, op. cit. (note 40).
65. D.F. Williams, 'The Romano-British Black-Burnished Industry: An Essay on Characterization by Heavy Mineral Analysis', in D.P.S. Peacock (ed.), *Pottery and Early Commerce* (London, 1977), 163–238.
66. H.F. Cleere, 'The Classis Britannica', in D. Johnston (ed.), *The Saxon Shore* CBA Res. Rept. 18, (London, 1977), 16–19.
67. M.G. Fulford, 'Roman Pottery: towards the investigation of economic and social change', in H. Howard and E.L. Morris (eds.), *Production and Distribution: A ceramic viewpoint* B.A.R. Int. Ser. 120 (Oxford, 1981), 195–208.
68. G. Marsh, 'London's samian supply and its relationship to the development of the Gallic samian industry' in A.C. and A.S. Anderson (eds.), *Roman Pottery Research in Britain and North-West Europe* BAR S 123 (1981), 173–238.
69. A.K. Bowman and J.D. Thomas, *Vindolanda: The Latin Writing-Tablets* (London, 1983); *Britannia* xviii (1987), 125–42.
70. cf. J.P. Gillam, 'Sources of Pottery found in Northern Military Sites', in A. Detsicas (ed.), *Current Research in Romano-British Coarse Pottery* CBA Res. Rept. 10 (London, 1973), 53–62.

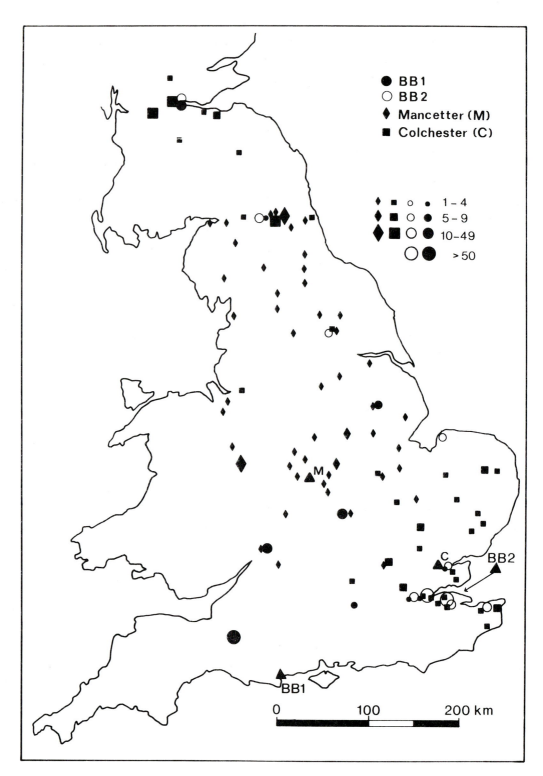

FIG. 2   The 'pull' of the Northern Frontier: aspects of supply in the Antonine period. The figures for Colchester and
Mancetter are based on *numbers* of mortaria stamps; those for BB1 and BB2 are based on the *ratio* of those
wares to the rest of the appropriate assemblage. (Source: author and Hartley (note 73))

province. On the basis of the evidence from Bath,[71] complemented by Reece's survey,[72] it seems that from 96 through to the end of the second century bronze coinage was supplied to Britain on a regular basis. Does the first date mark the approximate moment when the southern *civitates* began to contribute a money-tax regularly, with recourse to the market for sale of agricultural produce and other goods? With foodstuffs coming to market regularly, the organisation of the *annona* from British resources, rather than overseas, would have become a more attractive proposition. However, we should be cautious about assuming too radical a change, since the volume of coinage in absolute and relative terms still remained low.

By the third quarter of the second century, the evidence for provincial integration in the supply of the northern and western garrisons is convincing. With the establishment of the Antonine frontier, we can detect the use of east coast routes in the extended distribution of Colchester mortaria, BB2 and other wares from the South-East.[73] The almost bi-partite character of these distributions reflects the ability of the army to mobilise resources far from the immediate neighbourhood of its establishments. (Fig. 2) Indeed the local economic effect of the army on native communities outside the *vici* seems to have been negligible.[74] These maritime patterns of supply, with BB1 and Severn Valley ware[75] continuing to characterise the western sea-route to the North, are complemented by the expansion in the middle decades of the second century of pottery industries in the Midlands: mortaria from the Hartshill/Mancetter potteries reach the northern frontier during the third quarter of the second century as does pottery from the Nene Valley.[76] These types of pottery can be regarded as tracers of the source areas and routes of supply in general, not simply of the movement of pottery.

CIVIL DEVELOPMENTS IN THE SECOND CENTURY

Further evidence for the spread of a monetized market economy among the *civitates* can be seen in rural settlements which were gaining access to a wider range of manufactured goods. Once again the diversity of ceramic types of regional manufacture complemented by diversity among metalwork is an indication of this phenomenon. Pollard has shown that it is by the second century in Kent that rural settlements begin to share with the nearest large towns both the same complexity in the variety of ceramic assemblages and in the coarseware fabrics themselves.[77]

Developments within Britain were not of such vigour as to remove totally a reliance on imported consumer goods. In the second century these originated almost entirely from the provinces of Gaul, Germany and Spain (Fig. 3). From the latter came olive-oil in the ubiquitous Dressel 20 amphorae and fish-sauce from the region of Cadiz, while from Gaul came wine (in Gauloise 4 amphorae and barrels) and fine pottery (Central Gaulish sigillata, north Gaulish fine wares) and from the German provinces, wine (barrels), fine pottery (East Gaulish sigillata) and glass (Cologne). A small volume of luxury goods continued to arrive from further afield,[78] but essentially Britain in the second century was enmeshed within a network embracing the north-west provinces and Spain (Baetica). Demands were not engendered by purely market

71. Walker, op. cit. (note 51), 288–300.
72. Reece, op. cit. (note 50).
73. K.F. Hartley, 'The Marketing and Distribution of Mortaria', in Detsicas, op. cit. (note 70), 39–51, fig. 7; Williams, op. cit. (note 65), 207–13; J. Monaghan, *Upchurch and Thameside Roman Pottery: a ceramic typology, first to third centuries A.D.* BAR 173 (1987).
74. cf. N. Higham and B. Jones, *The Carvetii* (Gloucester, 1985), 68–120.
75. P.V. Webster, *Arch. Ael*[4] 1 (1972), 191–203 and, 'Severn Valley Ware on the Antonine Frontier', in J. Dore and K. Greene (eds.), *Roman Pottery Studies in Britain and Beyond* BAR S 30 (1977), 163–77.
76. Hartley, op. cit. (note 73), fig. 1.
77. Pollard, op. cit. (note 59), 80–117.
78. D.P.S. Peacock and D.F. Williams, *Amphorae in the Roman Economy* (1986); for the range of pottery imports to second-century London, see C. Green in D.M. Jones, *Excavations at Billingsgate Building 'Triangle', Lower Thames Street, 1974* (London, 1980), 39–85 and Pollard, op. cit. (note 59), 80–7 describing the imports found in rural and urban Kent; See also Fulford, op. cit. (note 7).

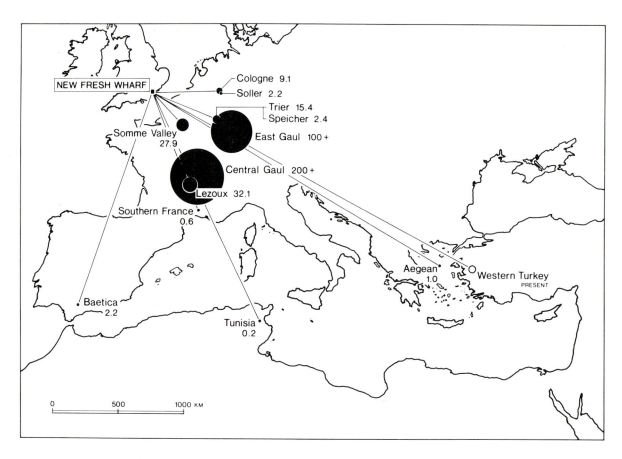

FIG. 3   The sources and relative importance of imported pottery of late-second- and early-third-century date found in
the London waterfront at New Fresh Wharf and dated *c.* 225–45. Quantification by EVE's (estimated vessel
equivalents). (Source: Miller *et al.* (note 116))

forces; the distribution pattern of Central Gaulish sigillata and its prevalence within Britain in
comparison with the nearer sources of East Gaulish wares suggest strongly that non-market, i.e.
military, supply factors were still important. The British frontier was active for much of the second
century; the establishment of Hadrian's Wall, followed on rapidly by the advance of Antoninus and
construction of the new frontier, the withdrawal under Aurelius and the wars of Commodus
provide a context where British resources were inadequate to meet all demands.[79] The German
provinces were quiet by comparison and able to meet their needs very largely from local resources.
This is the implication of the relative lack of long-distance traded goods there except for those, like
olive-oil, which could not be locally produced. Unlike in Britain, manufactured goods such as
pottery (the growth of East Gaulish sigillata industries, for example) and glass (Cologne, etc.) were
very largely of local origin. Britain does appear to be different from its neighbouring provinces in
the degree to which it depended on imported goods in the second century.

The development of towns, both major and minor, which continues to show evidence of
growth throughout the second century, ought to be intimately related to the agricultural
economy and the way that food was marketed. Unfortunately archaeological evidence does not
yet allow us much insight into changes in food production and marketing. There is some
evidence from the age of death of sheep in urban deposits that these animals were being killed
young, the implication being that they were being deliberately raised for the meat market. Cattle,
on the other hand, were relatively mature animals when they were slaughtered.[80] The evidence

79.   Appian, *Praef.* 5.
80.   A. Grant, above, pp. 135–46; M. Maltby, 'Iron Age, Romano-British and Anglo-Saxon Animal Husbandry: a
review of the Faunal Evidence', in M. Jones and G. Dimbleby (eds.), *The Environment of Man: The Iron Age to the
Saxon Period BAR* 87 (1981), 155–203.

from crops is not so helpful at this period; we have an idea of the range of cereals being grown, but not of the way in which farmers responded to changing demands. Although Jones regards the early Roman period as one of stagnation, there is some evidence of intensification of existing practices.[81] We can look to the physical evidence from the countryside and note that the second century sees the widespread appearance of 'villas', by which we must understand Romanised residences in the countryside. Although it is tempting to see changes in the physical fabric of the buildings in the countryside as reflecting the profits from marketing agricultural surplus, we should remember that buying land was a traditional form of investment in the ancient world and that the capital behind rural villas need not have come directly off the land. That is why it is important to see villas in a wider landscape context in order to relate, where possible, changes in the physical fabric of the villa to changes in farm-buildings and the wider estate (provision of granaries, byres, wells, date and character of associated field-systems etc.). Specific evidence for intensification from the second century is so far elusive. An interesting example is that of the Maddle Farm villa in west Berkshire where extensive field survey has been carried out over about 1800 hectares in the vicinity of the villa and an adjacent settlement. The presence of pottery in small quantities over much of this territory is interpreted as evidence of the spreading of manure from stalled cattle; much of the material is difficult to date, but the collection seems to belong between the late first/early second and fourth centuries, with a slight emphasis on the earlier period.[82] Coupled with this there is evidence from field-systems nearby that the formation of their lynchets seems to date from the late first/early second century A.D., rather than from the prehistoric period as was previously thought.[83]

Problems of interpretation surround the well-known reclamations of the second century. Evidence of the partial drainage of the Cambridgeshire, East Anglian and Lincolnshire Fens from the early second century is usually regarded as a response to the growing demands of the province, but we still know very little of the way that the land was exploited. Furthermore, it is now becoming evident that Iron Age settlement on the Fens was more extensive than has previously been thought, so that Roman settlement and exploitation may not be so different from what went before (see above, pp. 147–73). Widespread finds of briquetage attest that salt-making was clearly an important activity (at least as far as the late second or early third century) to complement the grazing of livestock (notably sheep). Apart from the Fens of East Anglia, we now know that large tracts of the wetlands bordering the Severn wetlands were reclaimed from perhaps as early as the second century. Here there is definite evidence for the building of sea-banks.[84] Yet, until we know more of the way that the land was exploited, it would be premature to assume that it was growth in the demand for food, rather than other motives, which prompted settlement. Similar doubts must relate to the evidence for the deforestation of the North, the acceleration of which begins in the first millennium B.C..[85] The need for wood for building and fuel on the part of the northern garrisons and their *vici* probably accounts for much of the increased demand, but there is little evidence to support a massive extension of arable in the wake of the clearances.

Were any of the natural resources of the province coming under pressure in the second century? The availability of suitable timber for structural purposes and for fuel perhaps comes into question. As we have seen, the North provides us with a generalised picture of depletion,

81. M. Jones, 'The Development of Crop Husbandry', in Jones and Dimbleby, op. cit. (note 80), 95–127; also 'Crop Production in Roman Britain' in D. Miles (ed.), *The Romano-British Countryside* BAR 103(i) (Oxford, 1982), 97–107 and above, pp. 127–34.

82. V. Gaffney and M. Tingle, 'The Maddle Farm (Berks.) Project and Micro-Regional Analysis', in S. Macready and F.H. Thompson (eds.), *Archaeological Field Survey in Britain and Beyond* (London, 1985), 67–73; *The Maddle Farm Project: an integrated survey of Prehistoric and Roman landscapes on the Berkshire Downs* BAR 200 (1989).

83. M. Bowden, S. Ford, V. Gaffney and G. Mees, *Britannia* xix (1988), 401–4.

84. J.R.L. Allen and M.G. Fulford, *Britannia* xvii (1986), 91–117; *Antiq. Journ.* lxvii (1987), 237–89.

85. J. Turner, 'The Vegetation', in Jones and Dimbleby, op. cit. (note 80), 67–73; *Journ. Arch. Science* vi (1979), 285–90; P.A.G. Clack, 'The Northern Frontier: Farmers in the Military Zone', in Miles, op. cit. (note 81), 377–402.

but more specific examples can be adduced from the South. The expansion of the Wealden iron industry is reckoned by Cleere to have had a major impact on the forest; indeed the expansion of ironmaking sites inland may well have been determined by the availability of timber.[86] We do not know whether any kind of wood husbandry, such as coppicing, was practised and there are no environmental data to set beside the spatial patterning of the industry. Among the towns which relied heavily on timber for building and fuel up to the middle decades of the second century, the strain on local resources must have been considerable. Various strands of evidence from Silchester provide some insights. In the mid-second century the amphitheatre was partly rebuilt and a new arena wall provided. This was made of numerous closely-spaced small-diameter timbers in contrast to the original first-century retaining-wall which was composed of fewer, more massive oaks. The timber used to underpin the earthen rampart of *c.* A.D.200 at the south-east gate consisted of oak with a felling age of 29–37 years and alder 20–30-years-old when felled.[87] Pollen contemporary with the earthen rampart points to an open, largely pastoral landscape around the town.[88] Given that the town is situated in an area where there was abundant clay for brick-making and which, historically, supported forest, the changeover to the use of stone as the preferred building material takes on an added interest. This is most conspicuous in the early- to mid-third-century rebuilding of the arena wall and the slightly later (260–280) town-wall where bricks were not even used for bonding and stone was imported from as far away as Bath (80 km).[89] Where the town-wall passes over wet areas, such as by the south-east gate, piles of oak and alder 25–40-years-old when felled were employed. While individually these pieces of evidence are not conclusive, collectively they do point to pressure on the woodland and this may have been one of the factors underlying the general trend towards masonry rather than timber construction in the south of Britain from the mid second century onwards. The evidence from the third-century waterfront in London, where massive, mature forest oaks were used, need not be regarded as conflicting with the above picture.[90]

As stone became more widely used, the preference continued to be for local materials wherever possible. Thus in the Midlands and the South, flint from the chalk and limestone from the Jurassic were popular materials. Surprisingly little detailed work has been done on the sources of building stone, but at Lincoln it has been shown that the limestone used in the second-century *colonia* wall probably came from quarries within about 2 km from the town.[91] In London the preferred general-purpose stone was Kentish Rag, a greensand which was probably quarried from the Medway Valley, but Northamptonshire and Lincolnshire limestone were used for major architectural purposes, such as for the recently discovered second- or third-century monumental arch.[92] As the Blackfriars wreck shows, the ragstone was brought by river to the capital, where it was extensively employed in the early third-century city wall.[93] In Leicester millstone grit was used as a freestone in second-century public buildings and was brought from the Pennines about 48 km distant.[94] One of the most important building stones was Bath limestone. Not only was this employed locally, but it was also exported up to 80 km to be used for columns and capitals in the Antonine forum-basilica at Silchester and, as unworked blocks, in the late third-century town wall. Across the Severn it is found as a worked freestone in the *basilica principiorum* at Caerleon.[95] The most widely exported British stone remained Purbeck marble

86.   H. Cleere, *Arch. Journ.* cxxxiii (1976), 177.

87.   R. Morgan in M. Fulford, *Silchester: Excavations on the Defences 1974–80* (London, 1984), 212–15.

88.   D.M. Keith-Lucas in Fulford, op. cit. (note 87), 215–221.

89.   B.W. Sellwood in Fulford, op. cit. (note 87), 229–30.

90.   G. Milne, *The Port of Roman London* (London, 1985), 65–7.

91.   M. Fenton, 'The Roman city wall: building materials and techniques'. in M.J. Jones, *The Defences of the Upper Roman Enclosure* Arch. of Lincoln vii(1) (London, 1980), 37–9.

92.   F.G. Dimes in C. Hill, M. Millet and T. Blagg (T. Dyson ed.), *The Roman Riverside Wall and Monumental Arch in London* London and Middlesex Arch. Soc. Special Pap. 3 (London, 1980), 198–200.

93.   P.R.V. Marsden, *A Roman Ship from Blackfriars, London,* (London, 1965).

94.   Wacher, op. cit. (note 6), 338.

95.   G.C. Boon, *Silchester: The Roman Town of Calleva* (Newton Abbot, 1974), 108–20; Fulford, op. cit. (note 58), 49–52; Sellwood, op. cit. (note 89), G.C. Boon, *Isca* (Cardiff, 1972), 73.

which continued to be used decoratively for opus sectile, cornicing, dados and inscriptions, as in, for example, Caerleon, Fishbourne (Chichester), London, Silchester, Verulamium and as far north as Chester.[96]

Except for the Wealden iron industry (see below) little substantial progress has been made recently in furthering our understanding of mineral extraction in the province. Nevertheless the second century appears to have been the period of greatest exploitation. Dolaucothi remains the only gold source for which there is reasonable evidence for Roman mining.[97] However this has not gone unchallenged; the very nature of the surface remains combined with the lack of datable material means that it will always be difficult to distinguish between Roman and medieval or early modern phases of working.[98] In any case the output and duration of working appear to have been slight. Apart from iron, lead remained the principal mineral extracted in the province and it is a reasonable assumption that all areas that have produced evidence of Roman working were active in the second century. Our best source for appreciating output remains the lead pigs since little work has been done on the actual production sites themselves. However, there are no dated lead pigs later than the reign of Marcus Aurelius.[99] The end of the stamping of such pigs probably relates to the organisation of production, with mines being leased out to private individuals and declining procuratorial control. The recent discovery of a wreck carrying lead pigs of British origin off the coast of Britanny gives some hint of the scale of exports, previous discoveries being limited to chance finds of single pigs.[100] The demand for lead continued, as is best evidenced by the supply of pewter in the later Roman period. However, recent analytical work suggests that the earliest examples of this alloy would seem to date from the second or early third century.[101] Assuming the tin to be British, this provides an earlier date for the resumption of tin-mining in the South-West. The assumption that Spain remained the principal source of tin until the later third century rests on the evidence for the abundance of coinage of that and later date in the South-West.[102] In fact the south-western finds can best be regarded as part of a provincial pattern of coin loss and deposition and not as an indication of intensified activity. Rural finds of early Roman coins are rare across the province. It is not unlikely that production continued from the Iron Age throughout the Roman period.[103]

Fieldwork and excavation in the Weald has seen the greatest expansion in our knowledge of any of the metal industries of Roman Britain (Fig. 4). Cleere has defined the main period of working as the first to mid-third centuries with the greatest output between about 100 and 250 with approximately 700–750 tonnes of iron produced per annum.[104] The estimated scale of production suggests that a proportion was exported from Britain. The association of stamped tiles of the *Classis Britannica* with iron-making sites in the eastern Weald implies very strongly that the fleet was responsible for the organisation of production from the late first or early second century. Sites in the western Weald which have not produced epigraphic evidence were probably leased out to individuals. Although the Weald is the only area to provide evidence for the organised and large-scale production of iron in the second century, we still know little about the operation of the Forest of Dean at this time (Fig. 4). To complement the Weald, sufficient evidence has accrued from settlements in Northamptonshire, Lincolnshire and Norfolk to show a

96. Cunliffe, op. cit. (note 60); F. Pritchard, *Britannia* xvii (1986), 169–89; Boon, Silchester, op. cit. (note 95), 115, Caerleon, op. cit. (note 95), 103; Frere, op. cit. (note 63), I, 156; Chester, *RIB* 463.

97. G.D.B. Jones and P.R. Lewis, *Antiq. Journ.* xlix (1969), 244–72.

98. D. Austin and B.C. Burnham, *Bull. Board Celtic Stud.* xxxi (1984), 304–12.

99. Tylecote, op. cit. (note 30), 61–70.

100. M. L'Hour, *Rev. Arch. Ouest* iv (1987), 113–31.

101. R.S.O. Tomlin in Cunliffe, op. cit. (note 51), 82–3.

102. C. Thomas, 'The Character and Origins of Roman Dumnonia', in C. Thomas (ed.), *Rural Settlement in Roman Britain* CBA Res. Rept. 7 (London, 1966), 91–2.

103. Todd, op. cit. (note 10), 231–33.

104. H. Cleere and D. Crossley, *The Iron Industry of the Weald* (Leicester, 1985), 57–86.

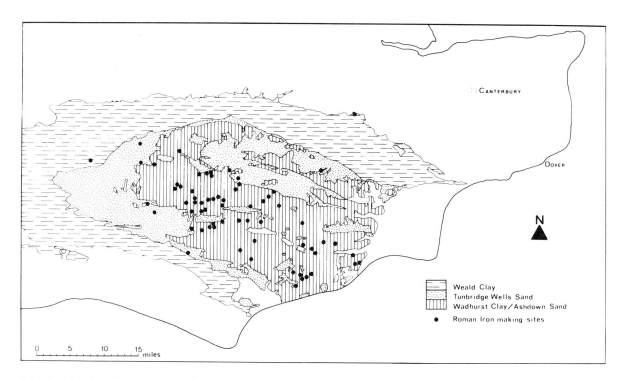

FIG. 4   The distribution of Roman iron-making sites in the Weald, first to third centuries. (Source: Cleere and
Crossley (note 104))

widespread exploitation of local ironstone, but in conjunction with farming, rather than as
specialist activity.[105]

When we come to consider the evidence for the production and consumption of manufactured
goods, we are hampered by the quality of the archaeological record; either artefacts do not
survive or they are difficult to trace to source. Because of its abundance and durability,
considerable attention has focussed on pottery. Peacock has characterised the different levels of
pottery production from household manufacture to manufactories of the scale that produced the
major sigillatas in Gaul and Italy.[106] The evidence from Britain is particularly good for tracing the
development of this industry and it is in the second century that we can trace the emergence of a
number of major nucleated 'industries' each producing a range of specialised vessels for regional
or provincial markets.[107] Unlike small workshops the nucleated 'industry' will have produced
evidence of a number of kilns in close proximity sometimes accompanied by evidence of related
structures and features. Their organization and ownership remains unclear, but each 'industry'
represents a concentration of resource and effort directed at producing products with shared
characteristics. Many of these 'industries' continued to remain important until the late Roman
period. We have already seen how the seaborne supply of the northern frontier and Wales served
to stimulate the Black-burnished industries of south Dorset and the Thames estuary; similar
factors may lie behind the growth of Colchester, the Nene Valley and Hartshill/Mancetter at this
time. By virtue of their size these 'industries' involved large workforces, perhaps numbering in
the low hundreds, but were there enterprises of comparable size in other specialisms where the
preservation is poor or the evidence is difficult to detect, such as textiles, leatherworking,
glass-making or metalworking? The demand for clothing must have been great and Peacock's
model for pottery might not be inappropriately applied to textile manufacture. However, the

105.   e.g. M. Todd, *The Coritani* (London, 1973), 106–10; D.A. Jackson *et al.*, *Britannia* ix (1978), 115–242; *Northants.
       Arch.* xiv (1979), 31–7; D. Hall, 'The Countryside of the South-East Midlands and Cambridgeshire', in Miles,
       op. cit. (note 81), 338–41, fig. 1.
106.   D.P.S. Peacock, *Pottery in the Roman World* (London, 1982).
107.   V.G. Swan, *The Pottery Kilns of Roman Britain* R.C.H.M. Supp. Ser. 5 (London, 1984), 91–112.

majority of industrial activity was carried out alongside farming. This seems to be the case with iron-making in Northamptonshire/Lincolnshire[108] as well as for salt-making in the Fenland.[109] Recent work on the Isle of Purbeck has revealed evidence for a hierarchy of specialisation; salt-making and the working of simple shale artefacts, like bracelets, in small rural settlements, while the more sophisticated working of shale as well as Purbeck marble and other stones took place in the larger, central settlement at Corfe.[110] Altogether the second century reveals consistent evidence of growth in both non-agricultural and agricultural activities.

THE THIRD CENTURY

The third century has been seen as a period of difficulty for Britain. From the point of view of economic change the 'difficult' period is sandwiched between the revolt of Albinus of 196–197 and the surge of activity represented by the evidence for building in town and country in the last three or four decades of the third century. The earlier period is characterised by significant changes in two forms of material, coins and imported sigillata. These can be considered in their own right as indicators of economic activity, but they are both of crucial importance for dating, and their rarity or absence has obvious implications for establishing continuity between the late second and the late third centuries.

Let us consider the evidence of the coins first. By 194/5 the silver denarius had been debased to a silver content of about 55%; the reduction in fineness was accompanied by a massive increase in output.[111] Under Severus the denarius was virtually the only form of coin imported to Britain. Without new bronze, second-century and earlier issues continued to circulate until the middle of the third century. Bronze was deliberately not supplied to Britain, even when it was being minted in quantity in Rome, and very few attempts were made locally to produce counterfeits. If, as Walker suggests, we should see this as evidence of a lack of demand for low-value currency we can follow him in concluding that the level of monetization in Britain in the third century was very low indeed, with transactions limited to gold and silver.[112] The implications of this will be considered further below. This situation changes with the Gallic Empire when, from 259/60, large quantities of very debased antoniniani entered into circulation.[113]

In the case of sigillata, it has been argued that supplies of Central Gaulish ware ceased to enter Britain after 196/7, the factories being closed as part of the measures taken against the supporters of Albinus.[114] In fact the evidence is not so clear-cut and importation seems to have continued through the first quarter of the third century.[115] However, a lack of independently dated horizons and stylistic stagnation makes it difficult to arrive at a clear appreciation of developments of decoration, potters' marks and typology from the later Antonine period onwards. East Gaulish sigillata continued to be imported until the middle of the third century, but it was never as widely distributed as Central Gaulish ware and groups dating to the second quarter of the third century are rare, the large deposit dated to the 240's at New Fresh Wharf (London) being exceptional.[116] (Fig. 3). The decline in the importation of sigillata does not appear to be a response to local, Romano-British competition. The production of Colchester samian, for example, does not appear to outlive the end of the second century and the widespread production of red-slipped wares from the Nene Valley, New Forest and Oxfordshire potteries, which plainly copy sigillata forms but are not so well produced, does not begin until the mid-third century whence it

108.   op. cit. (note 105).
109.   op. cit. (note 83).
110.   op. cit. (note 25).
111.   D.R. Walker, *The Metrology of the Roman Silver Coinage III* BAR Int. Ser. 40 (Oxford, 1978), 59, 126.
112.   Walker, op. cit. (note 51), 300–1.
113.   Reece, op. cit. (note 50).
114.   J.A. Stanfield and G. Simpson, *Central Gaulish Potters* (Durham, 1958), XL-XLIII.
115.   King, op. cit. (note 41).
116.   J. Bird in L. Miller, J. Schofield and M. Rhodes (T. Dyson ed.), *The Roman Quay at St Magnus House, London* (London, 1986), 139–98.

gradually increases in importance to reach maximum output in the first half of the fourth century.[117] The end of the importation of sigillata is accompanied by a corresponding decline in the trade of amphorae. The olive-oil carrying Dressel 20 from Baetica and the wine amphora, Gauloise 4, from Narbonensis are conspicuous elements of second-century pottery assemblages which continued to be imported in small quantities in the first half of the third century.[118]

Since it has been argued that the highly visible import trade of the first and second centuries is a product of the spending to support the army of Britain, it follows that its end reflects the end of high military expenditure. The implications of this are either that purchasing for the army in Britain was radically overhauled and expensive overseas contracts terminated but that the size of the army establishment remained the same, or that the volume of goods required had fallen because of reductions in the military establishment. Present opinion seems to favour the latter with a substantial cut in the size of the British garrison in the third century, presumably following the Severan campaigns.[119]

A further possibility can be explored: as the debasement of the coinage partly parallels the decline in long-distance trade to Britain, it may have induced a loss of confidence among merchants and to this extent may be partly responsible for the decline. Hopkins has observed that there appears to be a widespread reduction in long-distance trade from the end of the second century on the basis of the fall in number of recorded Mediterranean shipwrecks.[120] He believes that this is a consequence of the debasement. However, the shipwreck evidence is very regional in character and the area which shows the greatest change is limited to the coasts of southern France and Spain.[121] Undoubtedly long-distance Mediterranean traffic did continue to flourish in the third and fourth centuries, as is evidenced, for example, by the remarkably widespread distributions of African amphorae and African Red Slip ware.[122] We take the view that the long-distance traffic between Britain and the rest of the empire in the first and second centuries was exceptional, resulting from the need to support an army which could not or would not rely on local resources. The demise of this long-distance traffic, therefore, reflects a change in policy which radically altered the pattern of public spending within the empire.

Further support for a reduction of the British garrison can be adduced from internal trade-patterns. It was pointed out above that, for the second century, the whole province seemed to have become involved in the supply of the northern frontier. By the mid-third century less reliance was placed on the east coast supply route when BB2 and Colchester pottery ceased to form a significant component of assemblages. Instead, wares from further north, such as Derbyshire ware, and, later in the third century, Dales ware from Humberside along with the already established Nene Valley and Hartshill/Mancetter pottery are found on the northern frontier.[123] These suggest that the South-East was no longer an important source of supply. The decline of the Wealden iron industry can also be associated with this period. Southern and south-western Britain, as exemplified by the distribution of BB1, continued to be drawn on until the later fourth century. Overall, however, the hinterland of the frontier garrisons within Britain had shrunk significantly by the mid-third century.

A significant reduction in the garrison of Britain seems an attractive explanation for the decline in trade and the lack of bronze circulating in the island in the early third century may be connected with both of these phenomena. One problem with the latter, however, is that the

117. M.D. Howe, J.R. Perrin and D.F. Mackreth, *Roman Pottery from the Nene Valley: A Guide* (Peterborough, 1981); M.G. Fulford, *New Forest Roman Pottery* BAR 17 (Oxford, 1975); C.J. Young, *Oxfordshire Roman Pottery* BAR 43 (Oxford, 1977).

118. Peacock and Williams, op. cit. (note 78), for the London (New Fresh Wharf) material of this date see C.M. Green in Miller *et al*, op. cit. (note 116), 100–5, 134–5.

119. S. James, 'Britain and the late Roman army', in Blagg and King, op. cit. (note 19), 161–86.

120. Hopkins, op. cit. (note 1), 105–6.

121. A. Parker in K. Muckelroy (ed.), *Archaeology under Water: An Atlas of the World's Submerged Sites* (New York & London, 1980), 50–1.

122. Peacock and Williams, op. cit. (note 78), fig. 82; J.W. Hayes, *Late Roman Pottery* (London, 1972).

123. Gillam, op. cit. (note 70), 60–2; N. Loughlin in Peacock, op. cit. (note 65), 85–146.

cessation of supplies of bronze can be traced back to before the Severan campaigns and why this should have been so is not clear. In the case of Severus and Britain, when demands for military material would surely have increased, a possible explanation is that reliance was placed on the (debased) silver or on requisition in kind. Hopkins has suggested that the debasement of the coinage precipitated a move towards taxation in kind and the institution of the *annona militaris*.[124] If this was the case (and there is little proof of it), it would have served to depress market activities and the demand for bronze, because this form of taxation made the market redundant.

Such a combination of circumstances may help to explain why the first half of the third century seems to be a period of stagnation or 'recession'. This view is reinforced by the consequences of a lack of dating evidence, so that the material of the late second century, when datable artefacts were relatively abundant, generally provides a *terminus post quem* for sequences that might extend well into the third century.[125] Frere's excavation of town-houses at Verulamium has provided an alternative view. After the Antonine fire rebuilding in masonry appears slow and a combination of coin and ceramic evidence would place much of this activity in the first half of the third century.[126] Corroborative evidence comes from London where, not only was the building of the city wall completed by the end of the first quarter of the century,[127] but the construction of a new and massive waterfront can be placed within the first or second quarter of the century.[128] The recently discovered monumental arch is also tentatively dated to the early third century.[129] Nevertheless, elsewhere, without the rare coin or epigraphic evidence or a closely argued relative sequence, it is inevitable that there will be an upward trend to dates so that they appear earlier than they really are.

Circumstances change dramatically with the Gallic Empire and the proliferation of very debased antoniniani and their imitations. This coinage circulated widely across Britain in both rural and urban settlements, providing proof for the first time of the involvement of all levels of the settlement and social hierarchy (particularly in lowland Britain) in a coin-using economy. We should remember that this is a low-value coinage and, recalling the medieval period when silver coin was used, does not necessarily preclude the widespread use of coin earlier. That phenomenon has simply become much more visible. How did this coin get into circulation so rapidly? As with central imperial coinage earlier, its use for the payment of soldiers and officials as well as for official supplies can be postulated. One implication of its widespread distribution and volume is that official supplies for the army were no longer sought in kind. Official and unofficial radiates of Gaulish origin are supplemented in large numbers by British imitations from the 270s. The discovery of moulds, blanks and other manufacturing debris as well as the study of die- and style-links point to the production of coin in a number of rural and urban localities but with a western British emphasis.[130] The quality of coins was very poor, but this does not seem to have prejudiced their desirability! At all levels – the imperial and provincial (Gallic and whatever administrative arrangements prevailed in Britain), the *civitas*, the landowner and, perhaps, the merchant – coin was produced to pay for goods and services.

Whatever official links were restored with Britain following the suppression of the Gallic empire by Aurelian, the increasing isolation of the island implicit in the proliferation of British copying in the 270s provided some foundation for Carausius' usurpation in 284. The duration of the rebellion surely indicates that by this time the island and its garrison was self-supporting. It was outside intervention and not poverty-stricken troops which brought the downfall of Allectus. The self-confidence of the Carausian interlude finds expression in his coinage which

124. Hopkins, op. cit. (note 1), 115–16.
125. H. Sheldon, *London Arch.* ii(11) (1975), 278–84; ii(13) (1975), 344; 'London and South East Britain', in King and Henig, op. cit. (note 41), 363–82.
126. Frere, op. cit. (note 63), Vol. II.
127. J. Maloney, 'Recent work on London's defences', in J. Maloney and B. Hobley (eds.), *Roman Urban Defences in the West* CBA Res. Rept. 51 (London, 1983), 96–117.
128. Miller *et al.*, op. cit. (note 116).
129. Hill *et al.*, op. cit. (note 92).
130. J.A. Davies, *Num. Chron.* cxlvi (1986), 107–18.

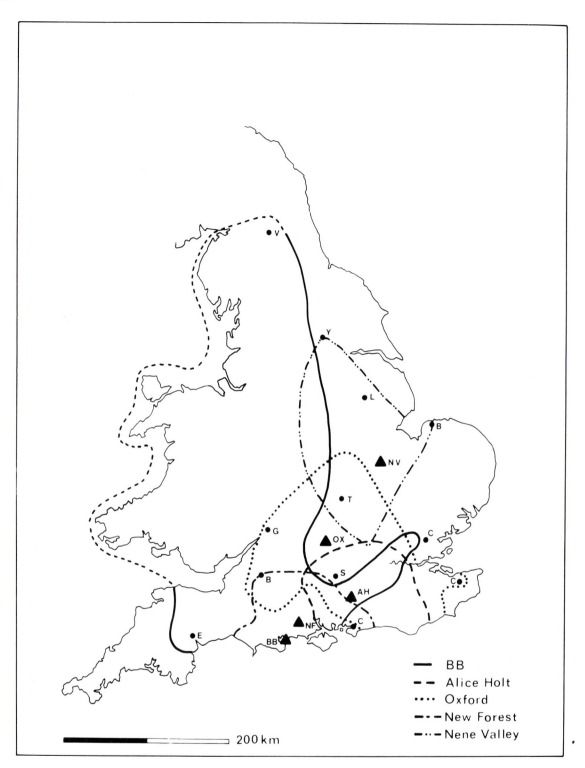

FIG. 5   The principal marketing areas of five major late Roman potteries in the period of *c*. 300–350. The lines have
been drawn around sites where the ware in question accounts for 10% or more of their pottery assemblages.
(Source: author)

was produced on the Aurelianic standard but which was accompanied at the same time by issues of high grade silver and aurei.

Whether or not the stimulus of public spending on, for example, Shore forts and town walls was primarily responsible, the late third century provides evidence for a resurgence which is particularly marked by the growth of villas in the countryside. The possibility that some of this development was fostered by the capital of landowners fleeing from unsettled Gaul has not found favour.[131] In fact the evidence of relative prosperity is present throughout the settlement hierarchy until the middle decades of the fourth century. If we are right to ascribe the initial stimulus to public expenditure, it was maintained by other means thereafter. Growth in fabric was accompanied by increased specialisation – at one end builders and carpenters, the mosaic specialists, at the other, the craftsmen who turned out the small durables which are such a feature of later Roman assemblages. Pottery is particularly visible and we might single out as representative of the growth of this period the industries which characterise the late period in the Midlands and the South: Alice Holt, Hadham, Nene Valley, New Forest and Oxfordshire.[132] (Fig. 5) All of them have their origins much earlier, but all display distinctive developments in the range and scale of output between the late third and mid-fourth century. Increased specialisation is inextricably linked with increased marketing and it is in the late Roman period that the 'small towns' appear to attain their greatest complexity and reach their largest size.[133] At a general level, this is supported by their coins; late coins are much more prolific than early issues on these sites when compared with the ratios from the civitas capitals and other ranked towns.[134] However, this growth is not at the expense of the larger towns which themselves show evidence of development and suburban expansion until the later fourth century.[135]

There has been some debate about the character of the larger towns in the later Roman period. While there is evidence of change, particularly in the state of public buildings and the emergence of more spacious town-houses with masonry foundations at the expense of smaller and more tightly distributed timber-framed buildings, there is no compelling evidence for them having lost their prime function as the administrative centres of *civitas* or province, responsible for the raising of taxation and the administration of law and order. Such evidence as we have for the role of the larger towns in small-scale manufacturing shows no diminution in production in the later period. It has to be said that our evidence is not good for any period but 'pewter-making' involving stone moulds serves as one example of an 'industry' which took place at large and small towns alike in the late period.[136] The range of metalworking activities in the forum-basilica at Silchester or in later fourth-century Winchester provides further evidence.[137] Only with larger, fuel-hungry concerns like pottery and brick-making do we see a shift away from these towns. This move takes place from the end of the second or early third century, as the decline of such industries as the Canterbury, Colchester and Verulamium region potteries exemplifies.[138] This shift in emphasis is not, however, to the small towns, but to rural locations. Only where a major industry had become established close to a small town in the second century, as at Water Newton with pottery and iron or Mancetter with pottery, is there continuity as well as expansion away from the town.

131. D.J. Smith in A.L.F. Rivet, *The Roman Villa in Britain* (London, 1969), 114 and *contra*, J.T. Smith, *Oxford Journ. Arch.* ii (1983), 239–46.

132. op. cit. (note 117); M.A.B. Lyne and R.S. Jefferies, *The Alice Holt/Farnham Roman Pottery Industry* CBA Res. Rept. 30 (London, 1979).

133. R.F. Smith, *Roadside Settlements in Lowland Roman Britain* BAR 157 (1987); W. Rodwell and T. Rowley (eds.), *The Small Towns at Roman Britain* BAR 15 (1975).

134. Reece, op. cit. (note 50).

135. S. Esmonde-Cleary, *Extra-Mural Areas of Romano-British Towns* BAR 157 (1987).

136. M. Fulford, 'Town and Country in Roman Britain – a parasitical relationship', in Miles, op. cit. (note 81), 403–419, fig. 5.

137. Fulford, op. cit. (note 58), 53–5; M. Biddle, *Proc. British Acad.* lxix (1983), 112.

138. M.G. Fulford, 'The location of Romano-British Pottery Kilns: Institutional Trade and the Market,' in J. Dore and K.T. Greene (eds.), *Roman Pottery Studies in Britain and Beyond* BAR Int. Ser. 30 (Oxford, 1977), 301–16; Swan, op. cit. (note 107), 19.

THE FOURTH CENTURY

The interdependence of large and small and indeed of rural settlement in the 'lowland zone' can be seen if we examine the evidence for marketing. Our most useful tool for gaining insight here is pottery. If we look at the distributions of certain of the major industries of the South – Dorset BB1, Nene Valley, New Forest pottery, Oxfordshire – we can see how widely and abundantly these wares circulated. Excluding its high representation on the northern frontier, BB1, for example, accounts for 5–10% of pottery assemblages over more than half of the urbanised zone of Britain; Nene Valley and Oxfordshire wares cover a comparable area at the same level. Large areas of southern Britain had ready access to two or three specialist wares.[139] (Fig. 6) It is this regional and inland patterning to distributions of southern British pottery which distinguishes the late Roman from the second-century pattern, when there was an emphasis on British regional wares having coastal or midland–northern distributions. Inland, settlements were dependent on local cooking-wares and imported fine pottery, leavened with a small proportion of British specialist wares, notably the Verulamium region flagons and mortaria which travelled some distance (above, p. 180). We may extrapolate from this pattern of interlocking, regionally-produced pottery to suggest a similar pattern in the distribution of agricultural produce and other goods (merchants did not only travel in pottery). No doubt the bulk of agricultural produce was consumed locally, but the demands of military and overseas consumers would have led to the satisfaction of a wider market. This evidence for a sophisticated and integrated market economy in lowland Britain finds support in the coin evidence, not only in its ubiquity, but also in the speed and distance over which it circulated. Ryan has shown that there is homogeneity among the coin finds of all types of urban and rural sites up to about 350.[140] These two strands of evidence point to a period of confidence and prosperity from the later third century which continued until the mid-fourth century. The signs of strain evident thereafter will be examined below.

The army continued to play a major role in economic affairs in the later Roman period, despite the case for a drop in the numerical strength of the garrison. We can see this in the way that its supply continued to extend distribution networks from east Yorkshire, the Midlands and the South-West. East Yorkshire pottery (Crambeck and calcite-gritted) provided the major component of northern frontier pottery supplies in the fourth century;[141] from the east midlands, Nene Valley pottery continued to be important, while Dales Ware and Derbyshire ware are consistently represented in the North; BB1 remained a major component in western and northern assemblages until the mid to late fourth century.[142] With the exception of the latter, it would seem that the reduced garrisons of the North could very largely be satisfied with supplies from the North and Midlands, a contrast with the second-century situation.

What happened then to the southern surplus? We have already seen that it was supporting increased specialisation and larger non-agricultural communities than before, but there is also a case for the South exporting agricultural surplus to the continent as well as meeting the needs of the Saxon Shore and the field army of Britain. The evidence for the export to the continent of cereals rests on the reporting of a decision of Julian to send British grain to help restore a ravaged Rhineland. The problem with the passages concerned is that there is no positive indication that this had been or became a regular supply,[143] albeit on a smaller scale. Determining the extent of Britain's relations with the continent in the late Roman period is difficult. With the production of volume consumer goods of similar quality on both sides of the Channel there is little traded material evidence to go on. Nevertheless, the combined evidence of numismatic, pottery and

139.   M. Fulford, 'La Céramique et les Echanges Commerciaux sur la Manche à l'Epoque Romaine', in L. Rivet (ed.), *Actes du Congrès de Caen, 28–31 Mai 1987*, S.F.E.C.A.G. (Marseille, 1987), 95–106.

140.   N.S. Ryan, *Fourth-Century Coin Finds from Roman Britain: A Computer Analysis* B.A.R. 183 (Oxford, 1987).

141.   J. Evans, *Crambeck: The Development of a Major Northern Pottery Industry*, Y.A.S. monograph (forthcoming).

142.   Gillam, op. cit. (note 70), 61–2; Williams, op. cit. (note 65), 204–7.

143.   Frere, op. cit. (note 31), 339.

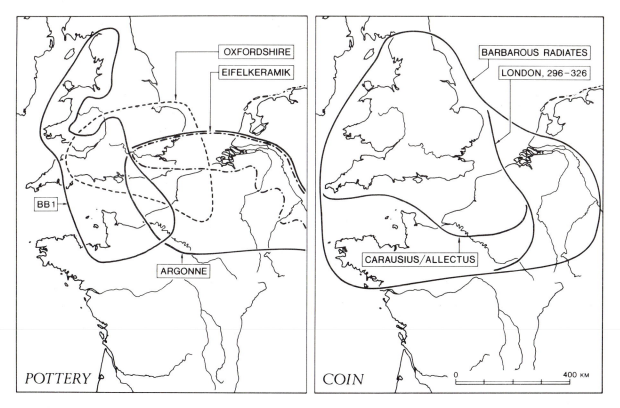

FIG. 6   The interdependence of Britain and north-west Gaul in the later Roman period based on the main areas of supply and circulation of certain coin and pottery types. (Source: Fulford (note 7))

other artefactual evidence points to regularised links between north and west Gaul and south-east Britain (Fig. 6). The use of the Rhine–Thames axis, presumably exploited by Julian, is evidenced by *Eifelkeramik* as a regular find in urban and rural settlements either side of the Thames estuary. Connections with Aquitania are supported by finds of 'céramique à l'éponge' in southern Britain.[144] The numismatic evidence is also suggestive for the integration of southern Britain with north and west Gaul, particularly in the first half of the century. Although there can be little disagreement about the role of the government in the minting and initial distribution of bronze coin as pay to army, civil servants, suppliers, money-changers, etc., it is clear that trade must have played a considerable part in the circulation of coins throughout the settlement hierarchy of the lowland zone to account for the great variety of issues from different mints in site assemblages. Coins from eastern mints regularly account for up to about 5% of these collections.[145] This can best be seen in the early fourth century when British coin circulated in some volume in the north-west of Gaul, while at the same time considerable quantities of coin of continental origin circulated in Britain.[146] An alternative explanation is that the diocesan administration drew varying amounts of coin from at least two mints before releasing them into circulation.[147] We do not know the location or number of those directly served by the treasury. That there was, at times, a huge demand for coin in the fourth century, is indicated by the size of copying at moments of shortage of official money. The enormous copying of issues in the 340s and, later, between 354 and 364 particularly in Britain, but also in northern Gaul and Germany

144.   Fulford, op. cit. (note 139); M. Fulford, 'Pottery and Britain's Trade in the later Roman Period', in Peacock, op. cit. (note 65), 35–84.
145.   R. Reece, 'Bronze coinage in Roman Britain and the western provinces, A.D. 330–402', in R.A.G. Carson and C.M. Kraay (ed.), *Scripta Nummaria Romana: essays presented to Humphrey Sutherland* (London, 1978), 124–42; M.G. Fulford, *Arch. Journ.* cxxxv (1978), 67–114.
146.   Fulford, op. cit. (note 144), fig. 10.
147.   Ryan, op. cit. (note 140), 148–50.

serves to demonstrate this.[148] Had the desire to extract the residual silver been the only motive, then the recoining of bronze need not have followed unless there was a demand for it. In conclusion, the late Roman period lacks the evidence for a large volume of goods moving into Britain, on the back of which travelled those manufactured articles which are so conspicuous earlier in the archaeological record. Nevertheless, the scale of traffic between Britain and the continent was not inconsiderable, perhaps bearing comparison with the volume and character of trade in the medieval period. In the absence of the scale of demand for supplies that characterised the early Roman military occupation of Britain which began to have beneficial economic effects within Britain from the early second century, overseas exports offered some compensation in the later Roman period. It is this aspect of the later Roman economy which may account for the continued growth in prosperity which is such a feature of lowland Britain up to the middle decades of the fourth century.

We have noted changes in the location of the pottery industries in the later Roman period. The iron-making industry also appears to offer similar evidence of a shift in locational emphasis. The industry which is centred on the exploitation of the ores of the Forest of Dean has been poorly researched and much of what we know about it comes from settlements on the fringes and beyond the Forest. Dating evidence is sparse but such as there is points to the later Roman period as the time when output was at its greatest. Several sizable settlements appear to have depended on iron-making as their principal raison d'être. Besides Ariconium (Weston under Penyard), there was Blestium (Monmouth) on the Wye and, as an outlier, Worcester, upriver on the Severn. Although other, non-Forest ores, were probably worked, Worcester draws attention to the role of the Severn in the distribution of raw materials and finished products. Preliminary reconnaissance and excavation of riverside settlements between Gloucester and Cardiff/Avonmouth suggests that iron-making, as attested by the presence of bloomery slag, was widespread along the estuary in the later Roman period (Fig. 7).[149] Dean ore was considerably richer than its Wealden counterpart and this, combined with the attractiveness of the river for transporting materials, probably accounts for both the dispersed and intense character of its production. Very probably the iron was feeding into the trade routes around western and south-western Britain attested by the distribution of BB1. The industry seems to be the single most important source of iron in Britain in the late Roman period.

Of other mineral extraction in the later Roman period, we can say little except that the prevalence of pewter table-ware and the number of lead sarcophagi imply the continuing extraction in the South-West of tin and lead,[150] the latter probably also deriving from a number of different sources including north Wales. In all cases, we can find no evidence for direct imperial involvement in the organisation of extraction, but can assume that mines were leased to entrepreneurs.

THE END OF ROMAN BRITAIN

Economically the province seems to die very rapidly at the beginning of the fifth century. The origins of this demise appear to lie in the second half of the preceding century. In the absence of detailed regional settlement histories, the behaviour of the low-value coinage provides a valuable insight into the economy. Charting the pattern of activity in detail is made more complicated by the lack of official coinage between 341 and 346/7, 348 and 363 and 375 and 387. In the first two periods shortage is made up by profuse imitations of the official issues and the demand implicit by this copying points to continuing stability and prosperity within Britain. However, Valentinianic coinage is not as abundant as that of the preceding periods and this is most evident at villas and rural buildings where total coin losses are not as great as earlier in the fourth century. If we were to see this as an indication of the decline of the market economy within Britain, it

148.   R.J. Brickstock, *Copies of the Fel Temp Reparatio Coinage in Britain* BAR Brit. Ser. 176 (Oxford, 1987).
149.   Allen and Fulford, op. cit. (note 84),
150.   Tylecote, op. cit. (note 30), 47–50; Todd, op. cit. (note 10), 231–2.

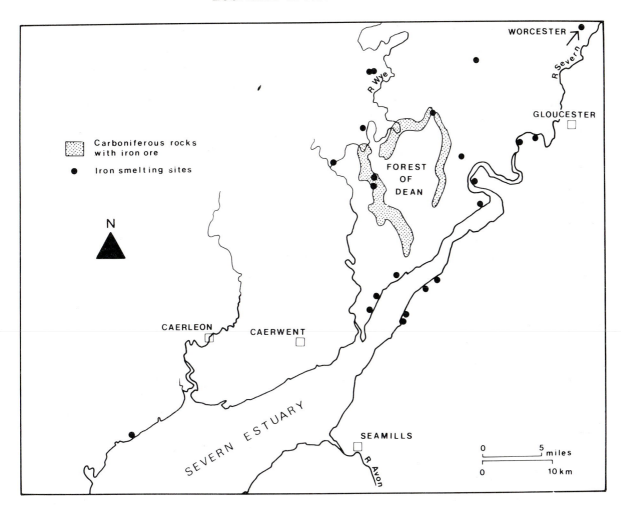

FIG. 7   The distribution of late Roman iron-making sites using Forest of Dean ore. (Source: author)

would gain support from the scarcity of evidence for copying in the period of 375–387 and from the rarity of Theodosian issues, both in general and, in particular, from the countryside. Part of the explanation for this may lie in the fact that Valentinianic and later bronze coinage no longer had even a trace of silver, but this factor cannot be so relevant as the general fall in the volume of coin in circulation.[151] It is not easy to explain this trend and attempts to associate rural decline with the 'Barbarian Conspiracy' of 367 have failed because of the lack of new coin between 348 and 363 and the rarity of finds to fill the short intervening period. Thus we should not confuse disengagement from the market with the possible end of occupation caused by barbarian invasion. Besides decline in absolute numbers after the mid fourth century, there is greater variation among sites in patterns of deposition although the significance of this is not yet clear. Valentinianic coins are lost in greater numbers at temple sites than in other rural settlements.[152] Coins issued after 388 are rare altogether outside towns; only a small number of rural sites in Gloucestershire and Oxfordshire have such issues.[153]

Evidence for decline in the countryside can be complemented by the evidence from the towns. Once again, if we start with the coin evidence, this reveals a shift in emphasis from the South-East towards the west and, in particular, to the Cotswolds with the western towns, like Cirencester, producing higher ratios of later-fourth-century coinage.[154] Physical evidence from

151. Reece, op. cit. (note 50); Ryan, op. cit. (note 140), 151–5.
152. A. Ravetz, *Num. Chron.* iv (1964), 201–31; Ryan, op. cit. (note 140), 151–5.
153. Ryan, op. cit. (note 140), 152.
154. R. Reece, *Herts. Arch.*, viii (1982), 63; 'The Coins' in S.S. Frere, *Verulamium III* (O.U.C.A., Oxford, 1984), 3–17.

the suburbs provides evidence of their shrinkage over the last quarter of the century, although this trend is not universal.[155] Within some towns there is evidence of significant change among the town-houses with evidence of demolition at Colchester,[156] Verulamium[157] and Winchester.[158] The latter has also produced evidence for iron-working on the site of these abandoned properties. On the other hand there is still evidence for the residence of élites either from townhouses, as at Verulamium (Insula XXVII),[159] or from the cemeteries, as at Dorchester (Poundbury)[160] and Winchester (Lankhills) in the later fourth century.[161] However, the latest group of graves in the Lankhills cemetery is comparatively small, perhaps hinting at a declining population.

Among industrial concerns, such as pottery manufacture, one can see signs of decline in the repertoire of forms, as in the New Forest and Oxfordshire potteries,[162] and in the volume of production, as in the New Forest, in the second half of the century.[163] BB1 appears no longer to be widely distributed in the later fourth century.[164] Clarke has argued that the fall-off in the variety and number of grave-goods as a whole associated with the later burials in the Lankhills cemetery is also a sign of declining manufacture and not just a change in burial practice.[165]

There is, therefore, a background to the collapse of the first decade of the fifth century whose origins pre-date the 'Barbarian Conspiracy' of 367. The run-down of the military establishment with troops leaving to serve pretenders intending to establish their claim on the continent from Magnus Maximus to Constantine III can have only had a depressing effect on demand. The sense of insecurity engendered by these episodes and the interruption of links with continental authorities can only have exacerbated problems. What chance had the bureaucracy to collect taxes in these times? Breakdown of any one of the inter-related phenomena such as the market, the collection of taxation and the imperial establishment (military and civilian) would have had consequential effects on other parts of the system. The departure of Constantine in 407 left an empty treasury in London and an island without official forces; the continuation of administration was left to the towns but there was no controlling force to ensure that responsibilities were discharged. It has often been argued that the economic collapse of Roman Britain was slow, extending towards the mid-fifth century, but the loss of confidence which sustained the prosperity of the early fourth century had evaporated and collapse must have been swift. Apart from its bullion value, there was no authority to guarantee the coinage and the coin-using economy disintegrated; the only bond between town and country was that which linked landowners owning urban residences with their country estates.

The negative evidence for the economic state of Roman Britain at the beginning of the fifth century is powerful. The lack of evidence for the continuity of production of the majority of the artefact classes present in 350 is compelling. Striking, too, is the lack of evidence for residual wealth in Roman Britain after 410. The practice of clipping silver coin after 395 hints at a diminishing pool of precious metal.[166] Apart from stunning collections like the Mildenhall treasure, the size and value of hoards deliberately hidden in late Roman Britain is quite small.[167]

155. Esmonde-Cleary, op. cit. (note 135), 197–200.
156. P. Crummy, *Excavations at Lion Walk, Balkerne Lane and Middleborough, Colchester, Essex* Colchester Arch. Rept. 3 (Colchester, 1984).
157. Frere, op. cit. (note 63), Vol. II.
158. Biddle, op. cit. (note 137).
159. Frere, op. cit. (note 63), Vol. II.
160. C.J.S. Green, 'The Cemetery of a Romano-British Christian Community at Poundbury, Dorchester, Dorset', in S.M. Pearce (ed.), *The Early Church in Western Britain and Ireland* BAR 102 (Oxford, 1982), 61–76.
161. G. Clarke, *The Roman Cemetery at Lankhills* Winchester Studies 3(2) (Oxford, 1979).
162. Young, op. cit. (note 117).
163. Fulford, op. cit. (note 144).
164. Williams, op. cit. (note 65), 204–7.
165. Clarke, op. cit. (note 161), 345–6.
166. A. Burnett, *Britannia* xv (1984), 163–68.
167. S. Archer, 'Late Roman gold and silver in Britain: a gazetteer', in P.J. Casey (ed.), *The End of Roman Britain* BAR 71 (Oxford, 1979), 29–64.

Are these hoards typical of the wealth of Roman Britain or were there more collections like Mildenhall and Water Newton which had either been dissipated earlier or had disappeared abroad with their owners? The lack of precious metal in post-Roman Britain raises interesting questions; certainly there was no charismatic leader and no central source of wealth or armed force to which he could gain access in order to establish control over Britain. The petty tyrant, Vortigern, settled his mercenaries not with cash, but with land. The economic end of Roman Britain was rapid; nothing was left upon which a unified authority could be built.

ART AND ARCHITECTURE

By T.F.C. Blagg

ART

The Nature of Romano-British Art

In 1961 the Society for the Promotion of Roman Studies celebrated its fiftieth anniversary with an exhibition of 'Art in Roman Britain' at the Goldsmiths' Hall in London. The catalogue of the two hundred exhibited items was written by Jocelyn Toynbee, who already had in preparation her much fuller treatment of *Art in Britain under the Romans*.[1] The exhibition and publications were a landmark in the study of Romano-British art, and provide a particularly appropriate point with which to begin a review of developments in the subject in recent years.

Toynbee's intention was 'to set the art of Roman Britain firmly in its proper context – that of imperial art as a whole'.[2] Her approach was that of a classical art historian and archaeologist, whose range of learning was firmly and centrally based on Rome itself. In that, she contrasted with R.G. Collingwood, whose view of Romano-British art was very differently moulded. Collingwood's interests extended well beyond the metaphysical philosophy in which he held the Oxford chair, and included the philosophy and theory of art as well as his extensive writing about the archaeology of Roman Britain. He regarded his chapter on Art in *Roman Britain and the English Settlements* as one which 'I would gladly leave as the sole memorial of my Romano-British studies'.[3]

Collingwood's thesis essentially saw Romano-British art in terms of opposition between representational Greco-Roman art and abstract curvilinear Celtic art, and as related to the concept of Romanization. 'The artistic romanization of Britain is therefore a melancholy story, not because Rome failed to impose her standards . . . nor because Britain lacked artistic aptitude . . . but because teacher and pupil were at cross-purposes'.[4] A genuine Romano-British art failed to develop: 'the badness of Romanizing British Art, as I say, was notorious.'[5]

Toynbee was not concerned to judge Romano-British art in such an explicit way. Indeed, it may seem surprising that in both her books there is only one occasion when she directly confronts Collingwood's view; significantly that is in relation to the Gorgon pediment at Bath, a key element in his argument, from which she dissented.[6] In her view, art in Roman Britain was basically classical throughout, and much influenced by copybooks.[7] Nevertheless, she recognised a variety of ways in which Celtic (British) artists responded to the challenge of the classical

---

1. J.M.C. Toynbee, *Art in Roman Britain* (London, 1962); eadem, *Art in Britain under the Romans* (Oxford, 1964).
2. op. cit. (note 1), (1964), 14.
3. R.G. Collingwood, *An Autobiography* (Oxford, 1939), 144; R.G. Collingwood and J.N.L. Myres, *Roman Britain and the English Settlements* (Oxford, 1936).
4. Collingwood and Myres, op. cit. (note 3), 254–5.
5. Collingwood, op. cit. (note 3), 144.
6. op. cit. (note 1), (1964), 138.
7. op. cit. (note 1), (1962), 16; (1964), 10.

'tradition' in such aspects as the rendering of eyes, hair, and drapery, and the expressive quality of their approach, and she took a much more favourable view of the results.

The distinction between Classical and Celtic thus remained an important part of Toynbee's viewpoint, and one problem arising from it is that of confusion between the style of an object and the identity of the artist responsible. Oversimplified, it assumes that the most classical works were produced by mediterranean craftsmen; if they are rather provincial, they suggest a craftsman from Gaul; if very provincial or 'Celtic' looking, a native Briton is to blame.[8] By this *reductio*, no Romano-Briton could ever produce 'good' romanizing British art.[9]

Given the great sympathy and insight with which Toynbee discussed individual works of art, it is rather a pity that she did not attempt any broader synthesis than the relatively short introductory chapters to her two books. Collingwood's views have been influential, particularly on those whose interests have been more generally in Romano-British society than its art as such, and there are those who still share Collingwood's opinion.[10] Few of Collingwood's successors among the general historians of Roman Britain in the last thirty years have had much or anything to say about Romano-British art, with the notable exception of Frere, who considered that Collingwood completely underestimated its achievements.[11]

A second problem arising from the Classical/Celtic dichotomy is that of defining what 'Celtic' means in that context. It is not enough for it to be 'unclassical', in terms of proportions, or the stylisation of natural forms. That is a feature of the art of other provinces of the Empire, not ethnically Celtic; it is also a feature, defined by Bianchi-Bandinelli (1971) as 'popular', or 'plebeian', which is characteristic of the artistic products of Roman Italy which did not conform to the hellenised tastes of the aristocracy.[12] Lindgren's attempt to identify the 'Celtic' mutations of classical art forms failed for lack of a satisfactory definition of the Celtic.[13] More productive was Phillips' essay, in which he examined some aspects of 'popular' sculpture against the classical tradition.[14] That was in a volume of conference papers under the title *Roman Life and Art in Britain*,[15] the only publication since Toynbee to deal at all widely, if selectively, with the subject as a whole. Some of its other papers will be mentioned below. The main advances, however, have been in the publication of articles and monographs on particular classes of material: mosaics, wall-painting, sculpture and the decorative arts of jewellery and metalwork.

Mosaics

The systematic study of Romano-British mosaics has been pioneered by Dr David Smith, notably in his identification of four regional schools of mosaic-workers active in the fourth century, mainly in villas.[16] These were based in the areas around Dorchester, Dorset (the Durnovarian School), Cirencester (Corinian), Water Newton (Durobrivan) and Brough on Humber (Petuarian). In addition to these, Johnston proposed a broadly contemporary Central-Southern school operating between Silchester, Winchester and Chichester.[17] The distinguishing features of these schools include aspects of design, the repertoire of motifs and the style of

8. cf. Toynbee, op. cit. (note 1) (1964), 5–9.
9. cf. E.J. Phillips, 'The classical tradition in the popular sculpture of Roman Britain', in J. Munby and M. Henig (eds.), *Roman Life and Art in Britain* BAR Brit. ser. 41 (1977), 35–49, esp. 35–6.
10. e.g. R.M. Reece, 'The badness of British art under the Romans', *ANRW* II, 12.4, (forthcoming); I thank the author for letting me see the typescript of his article, which has long awaited publication.
11. S.S. Frere, *Britannia, a History of Roman Britain* (London, 1967), 315–22. = (3rd edn., 1987), 306–11.
12. R. Bianchi Bandinelli, *Rome, the Centre of Power* (Rome, 1971).
13. C. Lindgren, *Classical art forms and Celtic mutations* (Park Ridge, N.J., 1980); cf. review by T.F.C. Blagg, *Britannia* xiv (1983), 365–6.
14. op. cit. (note 9).
15. Munby and Henig, op. cit. (note 9).
16. D.J. Smith, 'Three fourth-century schools of mosaics in Roman Britain', in *La Mosaïque Greco-Romaine* (Paris, 1965), 95–115; idem, 'The mosaic pavements', in A.L.F. Rivet (ed.), *The Roman Villa in Britain* (London, 1969), 71–125.
17. D.E. Johnston, 'The central southern group of Romano-British mosaicists', in Munby and Henig, op. cit. (note 9), 195–215.

FIG. 1   Mosaic from the villa at Brantingham (N. Humberside). (RCHM England)

execution. They represent a revival of, maybe even a fresh start to, the craft, since there are very few mosaics datable to the third century, particularly its second half.[18] The correspondence between geometric patterns on the Woodchester pavement, the finest of the Corinian School, and those from the Constantinian Palace at Trier is so close as to make it virtually certain that the same craftsmen were responsible. The question of which came first is very relevant to the origins of the fourth-century British Schools of which the Corinian seems to be the earliest, but despite Smith's preference for seeing Woodchester as the earlier, it cannot be conclusively decided.[19]

There has also been some confusion between the concept of a 'school' and that of a workshop.[20] Cookson has studied the different levels of stylistic affinity which might be used to define them more precisely.[21] He argued that during the second century more localised workshops were in operation, which would help explain why in that period only one school of mosaicists (working in Colchester and Verulamium) has been proposed with any confidence.[22] Neal's observations of the techniques of laying mosaics, made in the course of preparing his meticulous coloured drawings, (published with a catalogue of 88 mosaics in the first *Britannia* monograph) have also indicated distinctions between different *officinae* within the schools which Smith defined.[23] Both Neal and Cookson discuss the techniques of construction and design, though from different aspects.

Significant new discoveries of mosaics in the past three decades include: the Fishbourne Palace, where mosaics, mainly black and white geometric, are among the earliest in Britain, laid *c.* A.D. 75, the figured mosaics from the villa at Brantingham, Lincolnshire (Fig. 1) and the Christian pavement of the Durnovarian School from Hinton St. Mary, Dorset.[24] D.J. Smith has discussed the mythological subject matter of figured mosaics, which is of particular interest for the light it throws on the literary culture of Roman Britain, notably its familiarity with Virgil and Ovid. It also led him to question whether pattern books were as influential as Toynbee had claimed in transmitting classical ideas and motifs.[25]

Wall-paintings

Three decades ago, systematic study of wall-painting in Britain had barely begun. Two major discoveries had created awareness of its potential, and the problems of lifting and restoring fallen wallplaster; these were at the Lullingstone villa in 1949, and in Frere's excavations at Verulamium in 1955 and later. Both were exhibited at the 1961 Exhibition,[26] though full restoration of the more fragmentary Lullingstone Christian paintings has only recently been completed. The measure of difference between the state of knowledge at that time, and how much has been gained since, may be seen from comparing Liversidge's chapter in Rivet's *The Roman Villa in Britain*, albeit restricted to the decoration of villas, with the *Britannia* monograph by Davey and Ling.[27]

The painted plaster found in several houses at Verulamium remains the most extensive collection for any single British site. It includes walls painted with a variety of architecturally based schemes, including representations of columns and marble panelling, floral scrolls, and also

18. D.J. Smith, 'Roman mosaics in Britain before the fourth century', in *La Mosaïque Greco-Romaine* II (Paris, 1977), 269–90.

19. Smith, op. cit. (1965), 114.

20. See D.S. Neal, *Roman Mosaics in Britain* Britannia monograph I (London, 1981), 114.

21. N.A. Cookson, *Romano-British Mosaics. A reassessment and critique of some notable stylistic affinities* BAR Brit. ser. 135 (1984).

22. Neal, op. cit. (note 20), 19 and 72.

23. op. cit. (note 16), (1969).

24. B. Cunliffe, *Excavations at Fishbourne, 1961–1969* Soc. Antiq. London Res. Rep. 27 (1971), I, 145–50; Neal, op. cit. (note 20), nos. 12 and 61.

25. D.J. Smith, 'Mythological figures and scenes in Romano-British mosaics', in Munby and Henig, op. cit. (note 9), 105–93. Toynbee, op. cit. (note 1), (1964), 10–11.

26. Toynbee, op. cit. (note 1) (1962), nos. 169–72 and 175–6.

27. J. Liversidge, 'Furniture and interior decoration', in Rivet, op. cit. (note 16), 127–72. N. Davey and R. Ling, *Wall-painting in Roman Britain* Britannia monograph 3 (London, 1982).

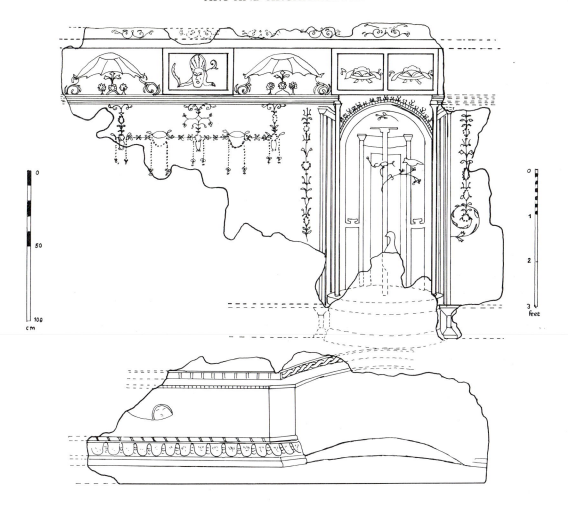

FIG. 2   Wall painting from a second-century house at Leicester.

plaster from vaulted ceilings. Outstanding among major new discoveries was that of the Painted House at Dover in 1971, where plaster painted to imitate architectural features in perspective was found still attached to walls up to a height of two metres.[28]

A second-century house at Leicester (Fig. 2), the early fourth-century legionary *principia* at York and the villa at Rudston have produced the other most significant new discoveries of plaster painted to imitate architectural perspective in the Pompeiian manner (Fig. 2); notable, if more fragmentary, remains of figural painting of quality have been found in villas at Sparsholt, Tarrant Hinton and Winterton and a mausoleum at Poundbury, Dorchester. Detailed comparison with continental wall-painting has to be made with caution, particularly in relation to dating.[29] Generally, however, the publication of recent conference papers,[30] including several contributions on Britain, indicates the increasing interest in Roman wall-painting in the western provinces, and provides a wider context to which British developments may eventually be related.

Sculpture
In 1963, an ambitious international scheme was established to produce a comprehensive and fully illustrated catalogue of the sculpture of the Roman Empire, *Corpus Signorum Imperii Romani*. It is divided into national volumes with regional fascicules. Six of the intended twelve on sculpture

28.   Davey and Ling, op. cit. (note 27), no. 14.
29.   ibid., 30.
30.   J. Liversidge (ed.), *Roman Provincial Wall-painting in the Western Empire* BAR S140 (1982); A. Barbet (ed.), *La Peinture Murale Romaine dans les Provinces de l'Empire* BAR S165 (1983).

FIG. 3   Relief carving of a wind god, from the Screen of the Gods, London. (Museum of London)

from Roman Britain have been published,[31] and the others are in active preparation. With the exception of the Bath and Wessex fascicule, those published so far all deal with north Britain and Wales, where much of the sculpture was executed for a military clientèle. It is instructive to compare that with, say, Bath and Silchester, and to consider the variations in technical quality, in the degree of classical influence on style and subject matter, and the relative frequency of certain categories, e.g. funerary monuments or Corinthian capitals. When complete, *CSIR Great Britain I* will provide a full and well-illustrated source for more detailed studies of sculpture, and for comparison with material from other provinces.

By analogy with the studies of mosaics mentioned above, Phillips has defined a workshop of sculptors working in and around Carlisle, and the present writer has identified schools of architectural stonemasons.[32] Major new discoveries of sculpture have been surprisingly few, however, given the scale of archaeological excavation. A notable exception was the discovery in 1975 and 1976, during work on the riverside defensive wall of Roman London, of nearly fifty elaborately ornamented limestone blocks, reused in its foundations. They have been shown to have come from a Monumental Arch and a Screen, both decorated in relief with figures of deities,[33] (Fig. 3). An earlier discovery in London (1954), the finest in quality so far found in Britain, was the marble sculpture from the Walbrook Mithraeum, which included heads of Minerva, Serapis and Mithras, and statuettes of Mercury and a Bacchic group, all now definitively published by Toynbee. Most were of second-century date and, to judge from the techniques of carving, supported by the identifications of the marble as probably Carrara, are likely to have been carved in Italy; the Bacchic group, however, is more probably third-century and of Balkan origin.[34]

31.   *Corpus Signorum Imperii Romani, Great Britain I* (Oxford): 1. E.J. Phillips, *Corbridge, Hadrian's Wall east of the North Tyne* (1977); 2. B.W. Cunliffe and M.G. Fulford, *Bath and the rest of Wessex* (1982); 3. S. Rinaldi Tufi, *Yorkshire* (1983); 4. L.J.F. Keppie, *Scotland* (1984); 5. R. Brewer, *Wales* (1986); J.C. Coulston and E.J. Phillips, *Hadrian's Wall west of the North Tyne, and Carlisle* (1988).

32.   E.J. Phillips, 'A workshop of Roman sculptors at Carlisle', *Britannia* vii (1976), 101–8; T.F.C. Blagg, 'Schools of stonemasons in Roman Britain', in Munby and Henig, op. cit. (note 9), 51–70.

33.   C. Hill, M. Millett and T. Blagg, *The Roman Riverside Wall and Monumental Arch in London* London and Middx. Arch. Soc. Special Paper 3 (1980).

34.   J.M.C. Toynbee, *The Roman Art Treasures from the Temple of Mithras* London and Middx. Arch. Soc. Special Paper 7 (1986), esp. p.55.

FIG. 4   Onyx cameo from Barnoldby le Beck (Lincolnshire), showing a mime actor. (R. Wilkins)

Jewellery and Metalwork
The work of Martin Henig, in his published *Corpus* of Romano-British gemstones as well as in numerous reports on individual discoveries,[35] has demonstrated the importance of jewellery as a category of Roman art, one which was perhaps more accessible to the individual Roman Briton than any other. (Fig. 4) The outstanding recent discovery of this nature was that of the Thetford treasure in 1979, published with exemplary promptness and thoroughness.[36] The 81 items of gold and silver included bracelets, necklaces and 22 gold finger-rings, partly unfinished, and thought to have been the stock-in-trade of a late-fourth-century jeweller or merchant. The association of the inscribed silver spoons from the treasure with the cult of the god Faunus is discussed in Henig's contribution to this volume (p. 230). He also discusses (p. 227) the religious significance of the fourth-century silver treasure from Water Newton, found in 1975,[37] as being the earliest known Roman ecclesiastical silver. Artistically, however, its workmanship is not considered to be of the highest quality. The finest piece is a jug decorated in relief with foliage, though two cups are of interest in being inscribed with the donors' names. (pp. 227–8)

Another late Roman silver treasure with Christian associations was found at Canterbury in 1962, with further items coming to light in 1983.[38] Mainly it comprises duck-handled and straight-handled spoons, several of them paralleled in the Thetford and Kaiseraugst treasures. It also included four silver ingots of approximately one *libra* in weight, two of which bore stamps of the *officinae* of production, one being Trier.

The Thetford and Canterbury publications, combining art-historical and scientific analyses, mark a distinct advance towards answering such questions as, how much of this silverware was made in Britain or imported and, if the latter, was it by trade or plunder? Unfortunately, in the circumstances in which such treasures have often been discovered, by metal-detector or by chance during building work, archaeological evidence for the context of their original burial is rarely adequate.

That applies less to artistry in baser metals, for which more of the evidence comes from excavations. Moulds for the casting of metal dishes or shallow bowls, probably from pewter,

35.   M.E. Henig, *A Corpus of Roman Engraved Gemstones from British Sites* BAR Brit. ser. 8 (1978).
36.   C. Johns and T. Potter, *The Thetford Treasure* (London, 1983).
37.   K.S. Painter, *The Water Newton Early Christian Silver* (London, 1977).
38.   C. Johns and T. Potter, 'The Canterbury late Roman treasure', *Antiq. Journ.* lxv (1985), 315–52.

have been found in several towns, notably Gloucester and Silchester.[39] Despite the great number of copper-alloy brooches, perhaps the lowest common denominator of Romano-British artistic product, little has been discovered about the organization of their manufacture. One recent excavation report where something was made of this material is that on the settlement at Baldock.[40] Few of the 162 brooches found appeared to have been manufactured after A.D. 100, although the site continued to be occupied, suggesting a change in fashion from the pre-Roman style of dress. The first volume of M.R. Hull's long-awaited *Corpus* deals with pre-Roman bow brooches and is relevant to the interpretation of early Romano-British society and artistic production.[41] To date, however, the three volumes in which Hattatt has published his extensive personal collection, although not confined to Britain, come closest to the *Corpora* of wall-paintings, sculpture and gems, in providing an overall view of this aspect of provincial art.[42]

ARCHITECTURE

The fact that Britain was Roman is demonstrated more obviously and permanently by its architecture than by any other aspect of its material culture. The two generations of Britons which followed the conquest saw their surroundings transformed by types of building and methods of construction which were totally new to them. The process is epitomised by the passage in Tacitus' *Agricola* 21, referring to Agricola's encouragement of and assistance to the Britons' leaders in building temples, fora and town-houses during the winter of A.D. 79. It is unfortunate that Tacitus did not specify the nature of the assistance which was essential in view of native inexperience: it is likely to have included architects and surveyors from the legions in Britain or neighbouring provinces, and builders and masons from Gaul (above, p. 87). Excavations in recent decades, however, particularly on urban sites, have demonstrated that the formative stages of Romano-British architecture were rather more complex than may previously have been supposed. Important studies of individual buildings and of types of building (e.g. temples, villas) have also added greatly to our knowledge of its evolution and regional diversity. These aspects will be considered below, under the headings of public buildings, temples and domestic architecture. A final section will review the work which has been done on building materials, construction techniques and planning.

Public Buildings

In its main public building type, the forum, Britain contrasts with other western provinces. In Northern Italy and Gaul, the regular layout of the colonnaded forum courtyard had a basilica across one end, and a *capitolium* temple at the other.[43] In some cases, a cross-colonnade divided the forum into two precincts. All known British examples except Verulamium lack the temple as a primary feature, and so effectively consist only of the basilica-precinct; the forum entrance was placed in the middle of the side opposite the basilica.

The resemblance of this plan to that of the military *principia* led Atkinson to derive the former from the latter, though alternatively, they have been considered to be parallel evolutions from a common source.[44] Interestingly, partial excavations of fora at three cities which had previously

39. T.F.C. Blagg and S. Read, 'The Roman pewter-moulds from Silchester', *Antiq. Journ.* lvii (1977), 270–6.
40. I.M. Stead and V. Rigby, *Baldock, the Excavation of a Roman and Pre-Roman Settlement* Britannia monograph 7 (London, 1986).
41. M.R. Hull and C.F.C. Hawkes, *Corpus of Ancient Brooches in Britain: Pre-Roman Bow Brooches* BAR Brit. ser. 168 (1987).
42. R. Hattatt, *Ancient and Romano-British Brooches* (Sherborne, 1982): idem, *Iron Age and Roman Brooches* (Oxford, 1985); idem, *Brooches of Antiquity* (Oxford, 1987).
43. M. Todd, 'Forum and Capitolium in the early Empire' in F. Grew and B. Hobley (eds.), *Roman Urban Topography in Britain and the Western Empire* CBA Res. Rep. 59 (London, 1985), 56–66.
44. D. Atkinson, *Report on Excavations at Wroxeter (the Roman City of Viroconium in the County of Salop), 1923–1927* (Oxford, 1942); J.B. Ward-Perkins, 'From Republic to Empire: reflections on the early provincial architecture of the Roman West', *JRS* lx (1970), 1–19.

been legionary fortresses (Exeter, Gloucester and Lincoln) have shown that the fora did not necessarily correspond with the orientation or even the site of the *principia*,[45] suggesting that the broad similarity in plan does not imply a perceived interchangeability of function. Moreover, Fulford's re-excavation of part of the forum basilica at Silchester has shown that the masonry basilica was not built until after *c.* A.D. 125, and that it had a Flavian predecessor of timber.[46] With more sites known, variations in the detail of the planning, e.g. the shape of the forum courtyard and the layout of its porticos, are now more evident. That, indeed, is also the case with the legionary *principia*, among which the most notable recent addition is York's, found in excavations below the Minster. The suggestion that the Romano-British forum is the result of military influence is now too much of a simplification to be an adequate explanation.

The problems of discriminating between the army in Britain and architects and builders from Gaul and other provinces, as the influences upon early Romano-British urban architecture, is complicated by the fact that Romano-British military architecture was itself dependent initially, particularly for early construction in masonry, on the skilled resources of other provinces. That is exemplified by the resemblance of the legionary baths at Exeter, built *c.* A.D. 70, to those at the fortress of Vindonissa and the *colonia* at Avenches.[47] Another large-scale excavation of legionary baths, those first discovered at Caerleon in 1964 and now partly displayed to the public, has shown that they were in use *c.* A.D. 75–230; their publication has also examined their similar relationship to contemporary architecture in the early empire, notably Avenches.[48] Among well-preserved examples of smaller bath-houses excavated in recent years, are those of the forts at Bearsden, Binchester and Vindolanda, and the baths of the iron-working site at Beauport Park associated with the *Classis Britannica*, important for the large quantity of brick and tile discovered, and for the survival of its walls to window height.[49]

Such smaller bath-houses have a more compact and informal arrangement of rooms than the axial plan of the *Reihentyp*, or row-type. This, in addition to being the simplest form of fort or villa baths, is also the central element in most of the major urban and legionary baths. In addition to the basic linear arrangement of *apodyterium, frigidarium, tepidarium* and *caldarium*, early bath-houses in some cities, e.g. Silchester, and fortresses, e.g. Wroxeter, had a palaestra courtyard in front. At Caerleon, this basic plan was soon modified by the addition of a basilican exercise-hall, no doubt a concession to the British climate, and a regular feature of other legionary (e.g. Chester) and city (e.g. Leicester and Wroxeter) baths. Part of the inspiration for this idea may have come from the Flavian/early Neronian building of the hall over the Great Bath at Bath, where also the excavations of the reservoir of the hot spring have demonstrated the high degree of Roman engineering skill.[50]

These bath buildings are architecturally rather more impressive than the relatively simple structures of British theatres and amphitheatres. Before 1970, the only fully published examples in Britain were the theatre at Verulamium and the amphitheatre at Caerleon; there have since been significant new discoveries and publications. The mid-second-century theatre at Verulamium was of northern Gaulish type, with an almost circular arena in place of the normally semi-circular Roman orchestra. The theatres excavated in 1950–51 at Canterbury and in 1967 at the religious sanctuary at Gosbecks, near Colchester were both semi-circular in the plan of their seating, in their final phases, but neither was truly of classical type, since they lacked substantial stage-buildings and parodos entrances.[51] Nor, except for the radial and perimeter corridors in the

45. P. Crummy, 'The origins of some major Romano-British towns', *Britannia* xiii (1982), 125–34.
46. M.G. Fulford, 'Excavation on the site of the amphitheatre and forum basilica at Silchester, Hampshire: an interim report', *Antiq. Journ.* lxv (1985), 39–81.
47. P.T. Bidwell, *The Legionary Bath-house and Basilica and Forum at Exeter* (Exeter, 1979), 43–50.
48. J.D. Zienkiewicz, *The Legionary Fortress Baths at Caerleon* (Cardiff, 1986), 115–29.
49. G. Brodribb and H. Cleere, 'The *Classis Britannica* bath-house at Beauport Park, East Sussex', *Britannia* xix (1988), 217–74.
50. B.W. Cunliffe and P. Davenport, *The Temple of Sulis Minerva at Bath* (Oxford, 1985).
51. S.S. Frere, 'The Roman theatre at Canterbury', *Britannia* i (1970), 83–113; R. Dunnett, 'The excavation of the Roman theatre at Gosbecks', *Britannia* ii (1971), 27–47.

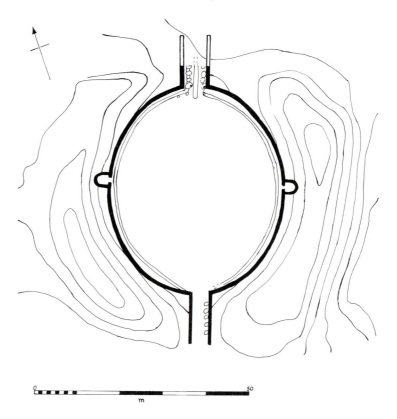

FIG. 5   Silchester amphitheatre: stone building.

early third-century rebuilding and enlargement of Canterbury, did they have vaulted substructures, so the seating is unlikely to have been of stone.

The seating of amphitheatres was also of wood, usually carried on earth banks, though that of the Phase I building at Chester was supported on scaffolding. The two known legionary amphitheatres, at Chester and Caerleon, differ from their urban counterparts in having a proportionately more elongated arena, with entrances on the short as well as the long axes and, when built of masonry, with buttressed outer walls. Excavation of the Silchester amphitheatre (since 1979) has shown that it was first built of turf and timber, with the walls facing the entrances and arena rebuilt in stone, probably mid-third century.[52] (Fig. 5). The raising in height of the seating bank preserved evidence for the terracing of the previous seating arrangement. The plan, with entrances on the long axis, and two small apsidal recesses in the arena wall on the short axis, has parallels at Augst and Martigny in Raetia. Other partly excavated amphitheatres (e.g. Cirencester and Maumbury Rings) are equally simple in their plan and structure. So far, in no town has both a theatre and an amphitheatre been found, and it may be that they were regarded as alternatives. The theatres are, however, situated in the central part of the towns (Canterbury, Verulamium and, recently located, one adjoining the temple of Claudius in Colchester), whereas amphitheatres are normally located outside the area of the street layout.

Temples

Britain had few temples of classical Roman type, i.e. standing on a podium, approached by a flight of steps at the front, and with a facade of columns and a pediment. The temple of Claudius at Camulodunum is usually supposed to have been classical, a view given some further support by Drury's reconsideration of the evidence for its development.[53] He also argues that it was rebuilt as a basilican hall, possibly a church, in the fourth century. The Temple of Sulis Minerva

52.   Fulford, op. cit. (note 46).
53.   P.J. Drury, 'The Temple of Claudius at Colchester reconsidered', *Britannia* xv (1984), 7–50.

at Bath has also been newly investigated and comprehensively published[54] (pp. 220–1). That it was a building of the Corinthian order, with a finely carved entablature and pedimental sculpture, has been known for two centuries. The difference now is that a coherent sequence of development of the temple, its surrounding precinct and associated buildings, has been proposed; and the date of its construction, based on archaeological stratigraphy and on the present writer's reconsideration of the architectural ornament, is now thought to be Neronian or early Flavian.

The more usual type of temple in both town and country in southern Britain is that named by Wheeler 'Romano-Celtic'. In plan, it has a square, or less commonly circular or polygonal, central cult room, with a concentric outer wall enclosing a passage-way all round it. Since the first comprehensive treatment of them,[55] there has been debate about the origins of the type, and how its appearance should be reconstructed. Wilson's seminal paper in which *inter alia* he observed how native ritual requirements, e.g. for processions around a sacred point, probably influenced that adaptation of Roman architectural ideas about shrines, has been followed by several relevant contributions among those presented to a conference on Romano-British religion in 1979.[56] Notably, Drury discussed the evidence which has slowly been accumulating for some sort of Iron Age predecessors in simple rectangular structures which appear to be shrines.[57] Some Romano-Celtic temple sites, e.g. Gosbecks and Frilford, have previous Iron Age occupation, though rarely is there clear evidence for previous religious function[58] (p. 223). At Hayling Island, however, a late Iron Age circular temple had a Roman successor, also circular, but of masonry.[59] (p. 220)

Older reconstructions show these temples with a portico of columns surrounding the tower of the cella. Muckelroy, however, showed that there was virtually no evidence for open porticos, and that most ambulatories were enclosed. He thought that this showed a British divergence from Gaulish practice, but Wilson has since argued that many Gaulish temples, too, may have had enclosed ambulatories.[60] There remains another contrast in practice, in that Britain does not have elaborate rural sanctuaries like Champlieu and Ribemont, where the temple, baths and a theatre were aligned along a central axis. Something of the idea of the complex, without the symmetrical planning, is present in some British rural sanctuaries which also have a theatre (Gosbecks) or amphitheatre (Frilford); Bath has it, but with a rectangular intersection of axes linking the temple, its altar, the reservoir, the great bath, and a monumental building (? a theatre) beneath Bath Abbey. In urban contexts, the theatre at Verulamium is axially sited in relation to the town's main Romano-Celtic temple, and it may be significant that at Canterbury and Colchester too there appears to be a close association between theatre and temple. Other relationships to topographical situation or features of the built landscape can be noted as factors in the architectural siting of temples.[61]

Domestic architecture

The volume of essays on the Roman villa in Britain edited by Rivet was a pioneer publication in the study of Romano-British houses.[62] The main architectural contribution to it was Richmond's

54.   Cunliffe and Davenport, op. cit. (note 50); see also Henig, this volume, p. 220–1.
55.   M.J.T. Lewis, *Temples in Roman Britain* (Cambridge, 1966).
56.   D.R. Wilson, 'Romano-Celtic temple architecture', *Journ. Brit. Arch. Assoc.*[3] xxxviii (1975), 3–27; W.J. Rodwell (ed.), *Temples, Churches and Religion: Recent Research in Roman Britain* BAR Brit. ser. 77 (1980).
57.   P.J. Drury, 'Non-classical religious buildings in Iron Age and Roman Britain', in Rodwell, op. cit. (note 56), 45–78.
58.   R. Hingley, 'Location, function and status: a Romano-British "religious complex" at the Noah's Ark Inn, Frilford (Oxfordshire)', *Oxford Journ. Arch.* iv.2 (1985), 201–14.
59.   R. Downey, A. King and G. Soffe, 'The Hayling Island temple and religious connections across the Channel', in Rodwell, op. cit. (note 56), 289–320.
60.   K. Muckelroy, 'Enclosed ambulatories in Romano-Celtic temples in Britain', *Britannia* vii (1976), 173–91; D.R. Wilson, 'Romano-Celtic temple architecture: how much do we actually know?' in Rodwell, op. cit. (note 56), 5–30.
61.   T.F.C. Blagg, 'Roman religious sites in the British landscape', *Landscape History* viii (1986), 15–25.
62.   op. cit. (note 16).

chapter on villa plans, in which, developing Haverfield's definition of the corridor and courtyard types, he proposed a fourfold classification of houses: the cottage; the winged corridor; the courtyard; and the aisled house. 'Cottage' is something of a misnomer for a house which typically consists of a range of five or six ground-floor rooms, 30–40 metres in overall length. The first three types can be seen, formally, as an evolutionary sequence, in that a 'cottage' might be enlarged by the addition of wing-rooms with a corridor between them; and a courtyard house might be formed by extending the wings as ranges of rooms on each side, with a cross-wall and gateway forming the fourth side of the courtyard.

Such a formulation was rarely followed so neatly in practice. There are also qualitative architectural differences. The winged corridor, by adding a symmetrical classical facade to the rectangular block of rooms, achieved a significantly greater level of Romanized display. Such courtyard villas as Bignor, Chedworth, North Leigh and Woodchester were designed for a grander and more three-dimensional spatial effect.

These features are not to be understood simply as permutations of Roman architectural forms. In his paper to a conference on villa studies at Nottingham University, J.T. Smith identified distinctive features in the plans of villas in the ethnically Celtic north-western provinces of the Empire.[63] He noted that many villas can be interpreted as constituting two or more separate architectural units, usually set at right angles to one another, and given the appearance of an ensemble by a continuous frontal corridor or portico; and also that repeated combinations of rooms within an apparently integral building might represent separate residential units. He interpreted these features as expressing indigenous traditions of landholding and inheritance through Roman architectural forms. Allowance must be made, however, for the possibility of the chronological evolution, both of the layout of a particular house, and also of the social institutions of those who lived in it. Frere's reinterpretation of Bignor in the light of selective new excavation, and Black's elucidation of the development of Darenth, indicate very different histories for two 'villas' of comparable size and plan.[64]

Domestic buildings are probably still the least well understood aspect of Romano-British architecture, but there has been progress in studies of houses in particular regions,[65] and through new excavations, particularly when accompanied by exercises in reconstruction, as in the publication of Gadebridge Park[66] (Fig. 6). The exploration at such sites of the buildings ancillary to the main residence, while also intended to give information about the economic functioning of the estate, has also aided understanding of overall planning and layout. At Rivenhall, the excavators detected a sophisticated geometry in the buildings' landscape setting, comparable with some Gaulish sites.[67] The larger of the two Rivenhall houses is one of the few substantial late first- or early second-century British villas. Most notable among them, indeed, exceptional for its size and the quality of its mosaics and marble furnishings, is the palatial villa at Fishbourne, built around four sides of a formal garden nearly 8000 m^2 in area, with a monumental entrance and several subsidiary suites of rooms arranged round inner courtyards.[68]

Haverfield's observation, that there was no special type of town-house, now has to be considered in the light of Walthew's paper in which, fortified by better datable evidence than was available to Haverfield, he argued that in the first century of Roman rule town-houses followed architectural precedents set by the villas, particularly the winged corridor type.[69] Excavations in

63. J.T. Smith, 'Villas as a key to social structure', in M. Todd (ed.), *Studies in the Romano-British Villa* (Leicester, 1978), 149–85.
64. S.S. Frere, 'The Bignor villa', *Britannia* xiii (1982), 135–95; E.W. Black, 'The Roman villa at Darenth', *Arch. Cant.* xcvii (1982), 159–83.
65. e.g. in Todd, op. cit. (note 63).
66. D.S. Neal, *The Excavation of the Roman Villa at Gadebridge Park, Hemel Hempstead, 1963–8* Soc. Antiq. London Res. Rep. 31 (London, 1974).
67. W.J. and K.A. Rodwell, *Rivenhall: Investigations of a Villa, Church and Village 1950–1977* CBA Res. Rep. 55 (London, 1985).
68. Cunliffe, op. cit. (note 24).
69. F. Haverfield, *The Romanization of Roman Britain* (Oxford, 4th edn., 1923). C.V. Walthew 'The Town House and Villa House in Roman Britain', *Britannia* vi (1975), 189–205. But see above, p. 108ff.

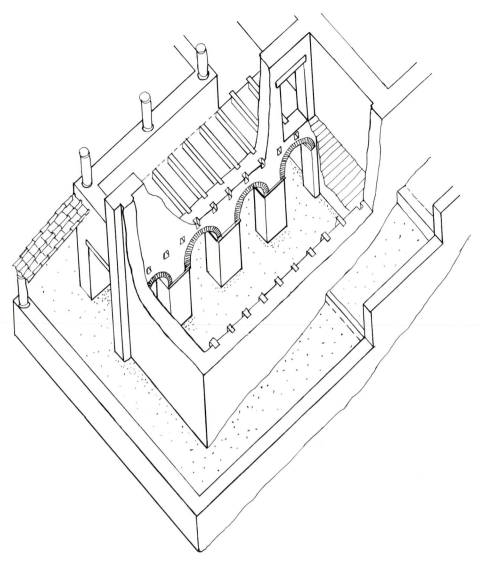

FIG. 6   Reconstruction of a wing in the Gadebridge Park villa (Hertfordshire).

the *coloniae* at Colchester and Gloucester, however, have shown that there the earliest houses were simple adaptations from barrack blocks. Courtyard houses made their appearance by the Antonine period, influenced, Walthew suggested, by military architecture, presumably the tribunes' houses of legionary fortresses, though the first-century courtyard houses in the south-east (e.g. those preceding the Flavian palace at Fishbourne) should be noted. The courtyard-type of town-house tends to be more compact in its planning than the equivalent third- and fourth-century villas, suggesting a separate line of development. Houses of that type, e.g. in Insula XXVII.2 at Verulamium, were still being built in the late fourth century.[70] So too, however, were winged-corridor type town-houses, e.g. Building XII.2 at Cirencester (Fig. 7); McWhirr's report on the houses at Cirencester illustrates the regular problem in achieving progress in understanding urban housing in Britain, that the remains, both in plan and in elevation, are usually very incomplete.[71] The function of rooms is rarely clear, and even the question of whether they, or villas, had more than one storey is usually in doubt. The aisled house which is being excavated at Meonstoke, where the collapsed gable-end wall has been found with windows still in position, is therefore all the more noteworthy.[72]

70.   S.S. Frere, *Verulamium Excavations* III (Oxford, 1984).
71.   A. McWhirr, *House in Roman Cirencester* (Cirencester, 1986).
72.   *Britannia* xix (1988), 476.

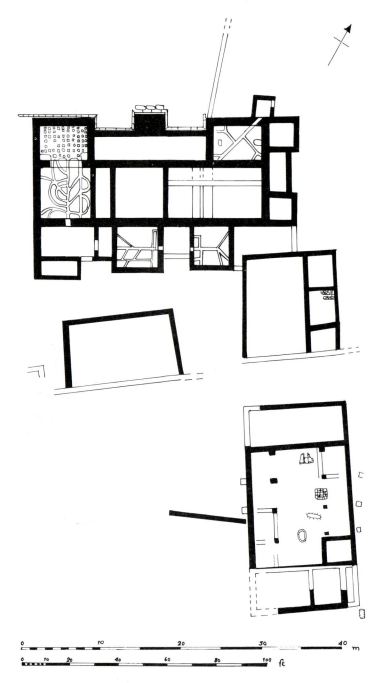

FIG. 7   House and outbuildings at Cirencester (Gloucester), Insula XII.2.

Planning, construction and building materials
The regularity of Roman rectilinear town and fort street plans, as well as of individual buildings, is often associated with the use of modular dimensions in both design and execution. Identification of the units of measurement employed in Britain is complicated by the existence of at least two standard lengths of foot, the *pes monetalis* (0.296 m) and the *pes drusianus* (0.333 m). Walthew's valiant attempts to discriminate between them in relation to the plans of individual buildings encountered statistical problems, but at a more general level of planning Crummy has been able to deduce something of the process of laying out towns and fortresses.[73]

73.   C.V. Walthew, 'Property boundaries and the sizes of building plots', *Britannia* ix (1978), 335–50; idem, 'Possible standard units of measurement in Roman military planning', *Britannia* xii (1981), 15–35; cf. M. Millett, 'Distinguishing between the *pes monetalis* and the *pes drusianus*: some problems', *Britannia* xiii (1982), 315–20; Crummy, op. cit. (note 45).

Detailed analysis of stone constructional techniques, e.g. those of Lincoln's defensive walls, has been increasingly important in elucidating the evolution of complex sequences of structures.[74] This has been assisted by studies of stonemasons' tools and techniques.[75] J.H. Williams has published surveys of the building materials used in the South-East and the South-West.[76] There have been relatively few studies of British quarries and building stones, however, though the use of foreign marbles has been examined, both in relation to such individual sites as Fishbourne and more generally.[77] Interest in both the production and the use of brick and tile has been marked by a conference on the subject in 1979 and by Brodribb's recent monograph.[78] Hanson's article on military timber supply has been one of the few general studies of building timber in Britain, but discoveries of such well-preserved waterlogged structures as London's riverside wharves have produced valuable new information about the construction techniques.[79]

The information from this research will assist the authenticity of reconstructions of Roman buildings for museum and site display. Such reconstructions have become increasingly important in presenting archaeology to a wider public. Experiments in building replicas of Roman structures, e.g. at the site of the fort at The Lunt, near Coventry, and the reconstructions of Hadrian's Wall in turf and stone at Vindolanda, have also provided useful insights into problems of methods and materials. Laser holograms and computer simulations, e.g. those of Roman Bath made for television presentation, are giving new technological opportunities for developing and testing theoretical reconstructions, in addition to their more popular appeal. Visual images are now of much greater importance educationally than they were thirty years ago, and the art and architecture of Roman Britain are of obvious importance in communicating new knowledge and ideas about the period.

74. M.J. Jones, *The Defences of the Upper Roman Enclosure* (Lincoln, The Archaeology of Lincoln VII.1, 1980).
75. T.F.C. Blagg, 'Tools and techniques of the Roman stonemason in Britain', *Britannia* vii (1976), 152–72; P.R. Hill, 'Stonework and the archaeologist including a stonemason's view of Hadrian's Wall', *Arch. Ael*[5]. ix, 1–22.
76. J.H. Williams, 'Roman building-materials in south-east England', *Britannia* ii (1971), 166–95; idem, 'Roman building materials in the south-west', *Trans. Bristol and Glos. Arch. Soc.* xc (1971), 95–119.
77. Cunliffe, op. cit. (note 24), II, 16–17; F.A. Pritchard, 'Ornamental stonework from Roman London', *Britannia* xvii (1986), 169–89.
78. A.D. McWhirr (ed.), *Roman Brick and Tile* BAR Brit. ser. 68 (1979); G. Brodribb, *Roman Brick and Tile* (Gloucester, 1987).
79. W.S. Hanson, 'The Roman military timber supply', *Britannia* ix (1978), 293–305; L. Miller, J. Schofield and M. Rhodes, *The Roman Quay at St. Magnus House, London* London and Middx. Arch. Soc. Special Paper 8 (1986).

RELIGION IN ROMAN BRITAIN

By Martin Henig

The past two decades have seen considerable growth in our understanding of religion in Roman Britain.[1] New, and sometimes spectacular, discoveries have accounted for much of this new knowledge which, inevitably, is not evenly distributed either in geography or theme. Much more is known about temples in southern Britain than in the north, and recent finds have favoured votive activity at 'Romano-Celtic' shrines rather than the organisation of the Imperial Cult, civilian religion rather than the cults of the army, and Christianity and late 'Paganism' rather than Mithraism. Fresh discoveries will undoubtedly correct such biases. A more fundamental gain arises from the publication of corpora of religious material (by Dr Miranda Green, one of the leading workers in this field) as well as of sculpture, wallpainting, mosaics and gemstones, all of great importance in the study of religious iconography.[2] Undoubtedly there is a new willingness amongst British scholars to note comparative material from other provinces and to study ancient texts and inscriptions. Nobody writing on this subject can afford to ignore the seminal contributions of social and religious historians such as Professor Peter Brown.[3]

Like the neighbouring provinces of the Gauls, Britain had a Celtic-speaking population and the native cults make a good starting point. Dr Anne Ross stimulated research into Celtic religion and iconography with her classic study *Pagan Celtic Britain* published in 1967. Her lead has been followed by a number of scholars, notably by Dr Green. She has published an important monograph on the Celtic sky god and on solar imagery (especially the wheel symbol) as well as a more general survey of Celtic religion.[4] It is apparent from these books, as it was from Ross, that most of the best evidence (religious sites, sculpture, inscriptions) is Roman in date.

The writer of this review does not dispute the local and often highly idiosyncratic nature of the cults discussed by Green, for religious practices were regional throughout the Ancient World and the Classic Olympian religion of popular imagination never existed. However the introduction of the Latin language as the language of the gods (in the making of vows and the setting up of inscriptions) was fundamental, as was the emergence of architecture and of representational art. Not for nothing did Tacitus specify the construction of *templa* (*Agricola* 21) as central to

---

1. This paper builds upon the foundation of my book, *Religion in Roman Britain* (London, 1984), as well as upon the varied contributions to W. Rodwell (ed.), *Temples, Churches and Religion in Roman Britain* BAR Brit. Ser. 77 (Oxford, 1980).

2. M.J. Green, *A Corpus of Religious Material from the Civilian Areas of Roman Britain* BAR Brit. Ser. (Oxford, 1976); eadem, *A Corpus of Small Cult-Objects from the Military Areas of Roman Britain* BAR Brit. Ser. 52 (Oxford, 1978); British Academy, *Corpus Signorum Imperii Romani Great Britain I*, fascicules 1–6 published between 1977 and 1988; N. Davey and R. Ling, *Wall-Painting in Roman Britain* Britannia monograph 3 (1982); D.S. Neal, *Roman Mosaics in Britain* Britannia monograph 1 (1981); M. Henig, *A Corpus of Roman Engraved Gemstones from British Sites* BAR Brit. Ser. 8 (Oxford, 1974, second edn. 1978). Cf. T.F.C. Blagg, pp. 203–17.

3. e.g. P. Brown, *The Making of Late Antiquity* (Cambridge Mass., 1978); idem, *The Cult of the Saints* (Chicago, 1981).

4. M.J. Green, *The Wheel as a Cult Symbol in the Romano-Celtic World* Coll. Latomus 183 (Brussels, 1984); eadem, *The Gods of the Celts* (Gloucester, 1986).

Agricola's policy of Romanisation. Thus it seems to me hazardous to reconstruct a mature Celtic system of religious belief in Iron Age times – any such system would be a product of Civilization in its proper sense – though this is an area where debate will continue. A recent contribution by Dr Graham Webster takes a central position, relating the cults which flourished in Roman Britain behind the names of deities both Celtic and Roman to human fears and needs. Certainly there was no fundamental ground for conflict between Celt and Roman.[5]

Links between pre-Roman practices and the religion of Roman Britain are best demonstrated through material evidence. Weapons, armour, horse-trappings and coins have been recovered from a number of Iron Age sites later occupied by Roman temples including Northney on Hayling Island (Hants.), Harlow (Essex), Wanborough (Surrey), and Uley (Glos.). At Hayling Island there was evidence for a Celtic precursor to the Roman temple and similar Iron Age shrines are suspected elsewhere.[6] However temples were not necessary to the Celtic (or for that matter the Roman) concept of a sacred place. The gods could live in a demarcated enclosure, a grove or a spring. For example at Bath (*Aquae Sulis*) finds of Celtic coins in the spring as well as the name of the goddess hint at continuity.[7] The nature of such features in the sacred landscape of Roman Britain owed more to patronage than to history and Bath is an extreme case of cult transformation.

The building of a major Roman temple was not a casual act: land made over to the gods had to be formally dedicated. In the case of the Temple of Divus Claudius at Colchester, the centre for the Imperial Cult in Britain in the first century at least, the Roman Senate seems to have provided the authorisation (Tacitus (*Ann.* XIV, 31) uses the verb *constituere*) on the death of that emperor.[8] The dedicatory inscription of the Temple of Neptune and Minerva at Chichester shows the like authority being exercised by the local client king.[9] In both cases much of the finance came from elsewhere. The British tribesmen who contributed to the Colchester temple could hardly empathise with the veneration of a dead Roman, but if the guild of smiths at Chichester consisted of Celts it is very likely that they were able to find native equivalents for the two Roman deities there commemorated. It is tempting to see the rebuilding in stone of the circular temple on Hayling Island as a contemporary event in the same client kingdom.[10]

The best place in Britain in which to explore the effects of patronage on religion is undoubtedly Bath where Professor Cunliffe's excavations have revolutionised our understanding of the site[11] (Fig. 1). The original focus of worship was presumably the hot spring, partially investigated in the nineteenth century, although the nature of the massive Roman enlargement of the source has only recently become apparent. Indeed Iron Age use of the site was merely hinted at by the Celtic name of the goddess, Sulis, and by the presence of a few native coins. In early Roman times a temple was constructed, embellished with a strikingly carved pediment showing a male

5.   G. Webster, *The British Celts and their Gods under Rome* (London, 1986).

6.   For Hayling Island and Uley see respectively R. Downey, A. King and G. Soffe, 'The Hayling Island Temple and Religious Connections across the Channel', and A. Ellison, 'Natives, Romans and Christians on West Hill, Uley: An interim report on the excavation of a ritual complex in the first millenium A.D.', in Rodwell, op. cit. (note 1), 289–304 and 305–28; for Wanborough, an interim booklet published by the Surrey Archaeological Society, *The Roman Temple at Wanborough* (Guildford, 1988); a full report has appeared on Harlow, N.E. France and B.M. Gobel, *The Romano-British Temple at Harlow* (West Essex Archaeological Group, 1985), but further work is in progress, cf. R. Bartlett, 'Excavations at Harlow Temple 1985–87', *Essex Journ.* 23 no.i (Spring, 1988), 9–13. Recently Professor Richard Bradley in 'Stages in the chronological development of hoards and votive deposits', *PPS* liii (1987), 361 has posited that developed Iron Age Society may have been moving towards the Roman concept of contractual votive offering.

7.   L. Sellwood, 'The Celtic Coins', in B. Cunliffe (ed.), *The Temple of Sulis Minerva at Bath 2. The Finds from the Sacred Spring* Oxford Univ. Comm. Arch. Monograph No.16 (1988), 279–80.

8.   D. Fishwick, 'Templum Divo Claudio Constitutum', *Britannia* iii (1972), 164–81.

9.   *RIB* 91.

10. The style of masonry which survives at the entrance porch may be compared with that of the Fishbourne Palace, see Downey, King and Soffe, op. cit. (note 6), 297.

11. B. Cunliffe and P. Davenport, *The Temple of Sulis Minerva at Bath 1. The Site* Oxford Univ. Comm. Arch. Monograph No. 7 (1985) and Cunliffe, op. cit. (note 7).

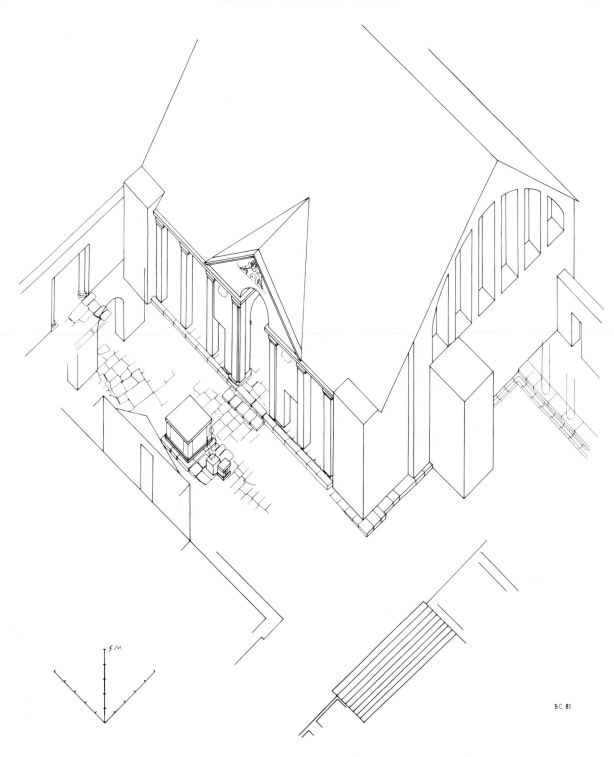

FIG. 1   Precinct of the temple of Sulis Minerva at Bath. (B. Cunliffe)

water-deity conflated with the gorgon appropriate to Minerva. There was also an altar, where animals were sacrificed. The sanctuary accommodated other buildings, baths, a *tholos* and probably a theatre. Not everything was built at once, but virtually all the elements were present by the middle of the second century.

By British standards, epigraphic evidence is good for Bath. Unfortunately not much of the dedicatory inscription remains, but we can speculate that major patronage would have come from local landowners, *negotiatores*, army officers and the like. I have speculated that as in Chichester, Cogidubnus may have played a part. His writ may have run quite widely in southern

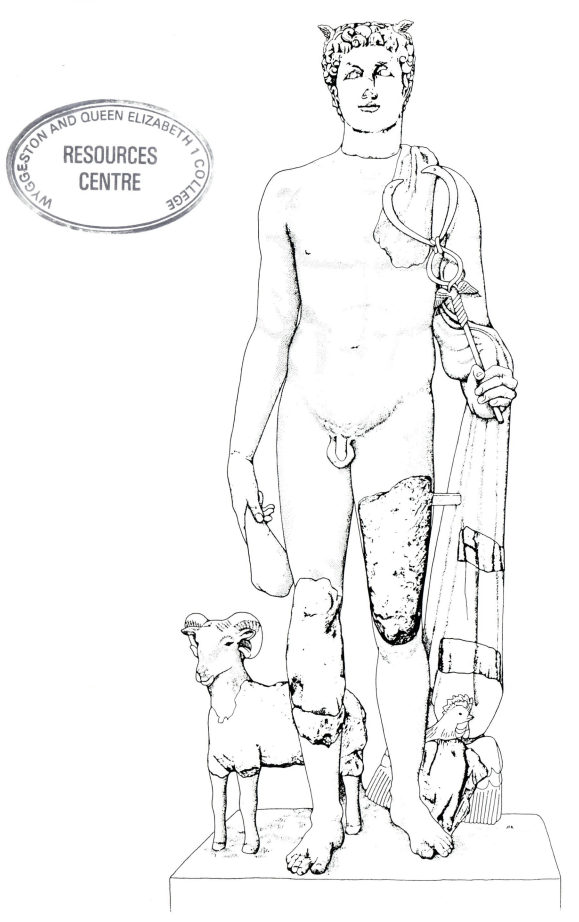

FIG. 2   Reconstruction of statue of Mercury from Uley, Gloucestershire. (Joanna Richards)

Britain, especially if he had established his loyalty during the Boudiccan revolt, and the pediment's apparent allusion to a Neptune-like deity as well as to Minerva is a plausible link with the Chichester cult.

The *romanitas* of the cult at Bath is emphasised by the statue-base found by Professor Cunliffe beside the great altar; it was dedicated by Lucius Marcius Memor who describes himself as a *haruspex*.[12] In the most recent report, it is suggested that he might have been a diviner attached to a legion: this seems unnecessary in a great international sanctuary run on Roman lines and whose rites we might have expected would include the examination and interpretation of entrails. That Sulis catered for native Britons, even of quite humble status, as well has now been made abundantly clear from the recovery of a large number of inscribed lead tablets invoking the aid of Sulis to recover stolen property and to punish malefactors.[13]

The majority of sanctuaries were much less architecturally sophisticated than that at Bath, although Gosbecks near Colchester was provided with a theatre and Frilford with a structure described as an amphitheatre.[14] The typical Romano-Celtic temple found here with central cella and surrounding ambulatory functioned in a virtually identical manner to the temple of Classical type. This is clear from a number of recent or recently published excavations at West Hill, Uley,[15] Nettleton Shrub,[16] Lamyatt Beacon,[17] Harlow,[18] and Springhead (a *Tempelbezirk* with at least four of these temples within the sacred enclosure).[19] The most prominent feature within the cella is likely to have been a cult image of the deity who, whatever the local epithet, was portrayed in Roman guise. At Uley parts of the main statue of Mercury (including its head) were recovered (Fig. 2), and at Harlow the head of Minerva may likewise have belonged to the cult image.[20] Comparison may be made with the famous gilt-bronze head from the temple of Sulis at Bath. Votive altars and statuary have been recovered from these more local sites as they have at Bath; at Nettleton to Apollo *Cunomaglus* (the name means 'hound-prince', and the god here was presumably invoked as a huntsman); to Mercury at Uley; an assortment of sculpture at Lamyatt Beacon includes Mars whose presence is also attested by two of the bronze figurines found there and by iron votive spears.

Iron spears have also been found at Uley and this is but one indication that the transformation of the local godling who presided on West Hill was not a simple process. Mars was primarily a protective deity who looked after the land, his functions overlapping with those of Mercury, master of flocks and herds as well as a god of commerce and of prosperity in general. Model *caducei* (the herald's staff carried by Mercury was called a *caduceus*) of silver, bronze and iron have also been found here.

Most of the smaller votives found at temples were objects of daily use; coins *par excellence* as items of at least nominal value. It may be suspected that a high percentage of the money offered at shrines was used to support the cult or embellish the building and this is emphasised by an inscription on a mosaic at the temple of Nodens, Lydney laid *ex stipibus*, out of offerings.[21] The coin lists from Hayling Island, Harlow and Wanborough show that the practice goes back to

12.   Cunliffe and Davenport, op. cit. (note 11), 36, 129–30 and 181.

13.   R.S.O. Tomlin, 'The curse tablets', in Cunliffe, op. cit. (note 7), 59–277 abbreviated as *Tab. Sulis*.

14.   P. Crummy, 'The Temples of Roman Colchester', in Rodwell, op. cit. (note 1), 258–64; R. Hingley, 'Recent Discoveries of the Roman Period at the Noah's Ark Inn, Frilford, South Oxfordshire', *Britannia* xiii (1982), 305–9.

15.   Ellison, op. cit. (note 6) and monograph forthcoming. A. Woodward and P. Leach, *The Uley Shrines: Excavation of a Ritual Complex on West Hill, Uley, Gloucestershire, 1977–9*.

16.   W.J. Wedlake, *The Excavation of the Shrine of Apollo at Nettleton, Wiltshire, 1956–1971* Rep. Res. Comm. Soc. Antiq. London XL (1982).

17.   R. Leech, 'The Excavation of a Romano-Celtic Temple and a later Cemetery on Lamyatt Beacon, Somerset', *Britannia* xvii (1986), 259–328.

18.   France and Gobel, and also Bartlett (both op. cit. (note 6)).

19.   For a summary cf. S. Harker, 'Springhead, a brief re-appraisal', in Rodwell, op. cit. (note 1), 285–8.

20.   M. Henig in Ellison, op. cit. (note 6), 321–3, fig. 15.5; Bartlett, op. cit. (note 6), fig. 7.

21.   cf. R.P. Wright, 'A revised restoration of the inscription on the mosaic pavement found in the temple at Lydney Park, Gloucestershire', *Britannia* xvi (1985), 248–9.

before the Conquest.[22] Very large numbers of coins have been recovered recently from the sacred spring at Bath and these can be compared with the coins taken from Coventina's Well at Carrawburgh in the nineteenth century but only recently properly published.[23]

In addition to coins jewellery was often given. Clearly wealthy patrons gave items of precious metal, but almost all of the bracelets, rings and brooches recovered from the excavation of Romano-Celtic temples consist of trinkets; they attest a simple piety.

Sometimes bracelets seem to have been deliberately broken, which could represent the 'killing' of the object in order to sacrifice it to the deity; but Dr Graham Webster has made the interesting suggestion that such actions and sometimes the crude refashioning of the fragment into a ring could represent the breaking of a matrimonial tie and the formation of a new one.[24] There is no way of testing such an hypothesis, but it must be pointed out that it accords well with the suggestion that at one level temples existed to give divine sanction to the resolution of conflicts for which litigation was either inappropriate or too expensive.

The most important finds from temples have been until recently the most neglected or they have been studied simply as indicators of the Romano-British economy. These are the animal bones, for sacrifice was central to virtually all ancient religion. At Uley goats and cockerels were selected (known to be the cult animals of Mercury). Sheep and pig only were sacrificed at Hayling, most of the bones at Harlow were of young sheep, while at Bath there was a preponderance of heifer bones.[25] The reasons for such selectivity are not always clear though sometimes as at Uley it is certain enough, and there may have been taboos against offering other species. The heifers at Bath may be explained by the general Roman custom of offering male animals to gods and females to goddesses.

The procedure of offering followed the Roman law of contract. The *solutio* (fulfilment of a vow) leaves the most obvious archaeological traces in the many votive altars inscribed *v(otum) s(olvit) l(ibens) m(erito)*, offerings and sacrifices. It was preceded by the *nuncupatio* (announcement) in which the votary asked for the aid of a deity, specifying the gifts which would be given to the god if he performed what was asked of him. The most exciting evidence of cult in action recovered in recent years from Roman Britain consists of such requests scratched on sheets of lead, most notably at Bath (addressed to Sulis)[26] and at Uley (to Mercury) though important examples have been found elsewhere for example from the river Tas at Caistor St Edmund and from the Thames at London addressed to Neptune.[27] Such tablets are frequently known as *defixiones*, curse tablets, and there are certainly examples of simple cursing, but the name is unsatisfactory with regard to the majority that call for a religious response. The names recorded on the tablets seem for the most part to belong to the lower orders of society but the process with its strong legal overtones belongs to the literate, Roman sphere of things. The explanation seems to be that visitors to shrines were given appropriate texts to copy out, just as the wise testator (now as in the past) will follow the form and language suggested by his legal adviser in making a will.

22.   It has been suggested that the Wanborough coins constitute a hoard, Surrey Archaeological Society booklet, op. cit. (note 6), 17, but I am strongly of the opinion that these coins comprise a deposit of the same kind as those from the other two sites mentioned.

23.   D.R. Walker, 'The Roman Coins', in Cunliffe, op. cit. (note 7), 281–358; L. Allason-Jones and B. McKay, *Coventina's Well, a shrine on Hadrian's Wall* (Chesters Museum, 1985), 50–76.

24.   G. Webster, 'What the Britons required from the gods as seen through the pairing of Roman and Celtic deities and the character of votive offerings', in M. Henig and A. King, *Pagan Gods and Shrines of the Roman Empire* Oxford Univ. Comm. Arch. monograph No. 8 (1986), 57–64 and Webster, op. cit. (note 5), 131–4.

25.   Downey, King and Soffe, op. cit. (note 6), 294; Ellison, op. cit. (note 6), 312; A.J. Legge and E.J. Dorrington in France and Gobel, op. cit. (note 6), 122–33; A. Grant in Cunliffe and Davenport, op. cit. (note 11), 164–72 but not considering the possibility of a religious explanation here.

26.   *Tab. Sulis*, op. cit. (note 13).

27.   The decipherment of these tablets largely by Tomlin but with the assistance of M.W.C. Hassall proceeds year by year in the pages of *Britannia*. See, for the sites mentioned, *Britannia* x (1979), 341–5, nos. 2–4 and xix (1988), 485–7 (Uley); xiii (1982), 408–9, no.9 (Caistor St. Edmund); xviii (1987), 360–3, no.1 (London).

Almost all the new evidence for religious practice has come from southern Britain, perhaps in part because the threats to archaeological sites have been greater in this part of the province. In the upland areas, lack of evidence for built temples may imply far simpler structures like the little rock shelter and carving of a warrior-god at Yardhope in Northumberland.[28] There were important shrines in the vicinity of forts such as Coventina's Well at Carrawburgh and, although this was excavated a century ago, the fine new report on the site by Lindsay Allason-Jones and Bruce McKay is an important work of consolidation.[29] Northern Britain is relatively rich in inscriptions and in sculpture. Eric Birley has provided what will remain the standard survey of the epigraphic evidence for religion, in a paper entitled 'The deities of Roman Britain'; although southern Britain is included in the title it has far less to offer than the Pennines, the Wall region and even southern Scotland.[30] Little new evidence relating to the religious practices of the Imperial army has been recovered in Britain: what there is is largely epigraphic and will be found in Birley's thorough survey.

Excavations in the vicinity of forts and in the large cities have not uncovered any new mithraeum in the past twenty years, although the previous two decades saw the recovery and description of the important mithraea at London, Caernarvon and at Carrawburgh and the publication of the Housesteads sculptures. These were spectacular discoveries, noteworthy in mithraic studies in general, and it is not surprising that mithraism takes almost a half of the book on Oriental Cults by Eve and John Harris published in 1965.[31]

Mithraic studies continue to make progress as is illustrated by numerous publications including a short lived *Journal of Mithraic Studies*. In one paper R.L. Gordon demonstrates that there are good grounds for believing not only that every mithraeum celebrates the sacrifice of the primeval bull but also that these temples and their various parts could symbolise the cosmos on the night of creation; the arrangement of the zodiac around the Walbrook tauroctony is cited here in support of the argument.[32] For scholars wishing to study the London mithraeum, the full publication of the art objects by the late Jocelyn Toynbee has been an important event, and although no full excavation report has yet appeared it is clear that the life of the temple as a mithraeum was largely confined to the third century.[33]

The cult of Isis also flourished in London; previously attested by a graffito on a pot from Southwark and by figurines of Isis and Harpocrates, the discovery of an altar re-used in the foundations of the late Roman riverside wall at Blackfriars is a major event. It shows a mid-third-century governor of Upper Britain restoring a temple to Isis, though whether or not this is the temple recorded on the Southwark flagon is uncertain. The high standing of the dedicator and the good quality of the altar's workmanship are expressive of the high status of the cult at this time.[34]

Still in London, but more controversial, is what may be interpreted as new evidence for the cult of Attis. Twenty years ago a small statuette from Bevis Marks showing a huntsman holding a bow and wearing a Phrygian cap was identified with confidence as Attis, although the attributes of the god are typically those of a shepherd rather than a hunter (Fig. 3). A large statue of the same type, showing 'Attis' accompanied by a hound and a stag was found some years ago with other sculptures in excavations beneath Southwark Cathedral. Ralph Merrifield has added to these a relief upon a small altar from the Goldsmiths' Hall in the west of the City, previously

28. D.B. Charlton and M.M. Mitcheson, 'Yardhope. A shrine to Cocidius?', *Britannia* xiv (1983), 143–53.
29. Allason-Jones and McKay, op. cit. (note 23).
30. E. Birley, 'The deities of Roman Britain', *Aufstieg und Niedergang der Römischen Welt* 18.1 (Berlin & New York, 1986), 3– 112.
31. E. Harris and J.R. Harris, *The Oriental Cults in Roman Britain* (Leiden, 1965).
32. R.L. Gordon, 'The sacred geography of a mithraeum: the example of Sette Sfere', *Journal of Mithraic Studies* I.2 (1976), 119–65, esp. 141.
33. J.M.C. Toynbee, *The Roman Art Treasures from the Temple of Mithras* London and Middlesex Arch. Soc. Special Paper no.7 (1986).
34. M. Hassall in C. Hill, M. Millett and T. Blagg, *The Roman Riverside Wall and Monumental Arch in London* London and Middlesex Arch. Soc. Special Paper no.3 (1980), 196–8.

FIG. 3   Sculpture of Attis (?) from Southwark, London. (Museum of London; Statue in Cuming Museum)

thought to be Diana.[35] Other appearances of a Phrygian-hatted deity in Gloucestershire have led Merrifield to see here a Romano-British deity perhaps identified with Apollo, though he accepts that an Oriental element is probably present. The writer of this paper notes that the Southwark findspot, on a road leading out of London is the sort of site favoured for temples of Attis and of Cybele; also the close association of 'religious' and 'funerary' sculpture at Southwark is suggestive of the guild of *dendrophori*, closely involved in the rites of Attis as well as acting as a *collegium* concerned with funerals. There were certainly *dendrophori* at Verulamium (whose head-quarters may have been the triangular temples excavated by Wheeler), attested by an inscription on a pot from a cemetery at Dunstable.[36]

35.   R. Merrifield, 'The London Hunter-God', in Henig and King, op. cit. (note 24), 85–92.
36.   cf. M. Henig, '*Ita intellexit numine inductus tuo*: some personal interpretations of deity in Roman religion', in ibid., 161 citing *Britannia* xiii (1980), 406–7, no.7.

Of all the Eastern religions, the most distinctive and – in the long term – the most important was Christianity. Here our understanding has been deepened by new discoveries as well as by the re-assessment of old finds, notably by Professor Charles Thomas in a substantial and magisterial monograph.[37] Christianity became established in Britain during the third century, as the martyrdoms of Alban at Verulamium and of Julius and Aaron at Caerleon attest,[38] and survived through the following century and into the 'Dark Ages'. Indeed, it provides a tenuous link between Roman Britain and Medieval and Modern times.

Amongst the new discoveries, the Water Newton treasure, which seems to be the earliest set of Eucharistic plate known from anywhere in the Empire, is of prime importance.[39] It includes two goblets given in one case by Innocentia and Viventia (Fig. 4) and in the other by Publianus as well as a large dish and a wine-strainer. All these items are embellished with the Chi-Rho. Such gifts of plate fall within a tradition of Christian donation which we know to have been widespread and is attested for example in the sixth-century *Liber Pontificalis*. The unexpected element lies in the presence of votive silver-gilt leaves or feathers likewise marked with the Christogram (Fig. 5), revealing a link with pagan custom, for similar 'leaves' dedicated to various deities are known from temple sites.[40] One of the Water Newton leaves carries the formula '*Ianicilla votum quod promisit conplevit*' which echoes a dedication to Nodens at Lydney Park.[41]

Churches were of three basic kinds. In Christian tradition the earliest was the house-church, best represented in Britain by the example at Lullingstone, Kent which, however, dates to late in the fourth century.[42] The site was excavated in the early 1950s but the definitive publication has only just appeared. Recent work on the fragmentary wall-plaster has shown that the decoration consisted not only of friezes of Orantes and Chi-Rhos but also of biblical scenes though, alas, these are too incomplete to identify. It is tempting to interpret the mosaic from Hinton St Mary as the floor of another house-church, because of its prominent central bust flanked by pomegranates and backed by a Chi-Rho.[43] It was uncovered over a quarter of a century ago but, as with Lullingstone, discussion of it has not stopped. Most significantly the hounds chasing deer in side lunettes as well as on each side of Bellerophon in the narthex have come to be seen as symbolising the pains of a Christian's life rather than as Paradise.[44] The Bellerophon myth has been seen as straight Christian allegory, and its appearance on other mosaics at Frampton (where there is also a Chi-Rho) and on a mosaic at Lullingstone has been seen as confirmation of this. However, the Lullingstone mosaic appears to be earlier than the house-church while the rich pagan imagery at Frampton is not consistent with an orthodox Christian explanation.[45] In the Empire at large the myth of Bellerophon and the Chimaera was not a common Christian allegory, and its appearance at Hinton St Mary can be seen either as the conscious choice of a learned Christian owner from the rich mythological repertoire of the Dorchester mosaic *officina*, or as a hint of some rather heterodox ideas.

Christianity set great store on burial, for the sleeping dead would one day be resurrected. Rites such as orientation (East–West burial) and encasing the body in gypsum to preserve it, both of which may be noted at the important Poundbury Cemetery outside Dorchester, Dorset were

37. C. Thomas, *Christianity in Roman Britain to AD 500* (London, 1981).
38. ibid., 47–50.
39. K.S. Painter, *The Water Newton Early Christian Silver* (London, 1977).
40. J. Toynbee, 'A Londinium Votive Leaf or Feather and its fellows', in J. Bird, H. Chapman and J. Clark, *Collectanea Londiniensia Studies in London archaeology and history presented to Ralph Merrifield* London and Middlesex Arch. Soc. Special Paper no.2, 128–47.
41. Thomas, op. cit. (note 87), 116–7.
42. G.W. Meates, *The Roman Villa at Lullingstone, Kent. I The Site* Kent Arch. Soc. Monograph no.1 (Maidstone, 1979); *II The Wall Paintings and Finds* Kent. Arch. Soc. Monograph No.III (Maidstone, 1987).
43. J.M.C. Toynbee, 'A new Roman mosaic found in Dorset', *JRS* liv (1964), 7–14.
44. R.T. Eriksen, 'Syncretistic symbolism and the Christian Roman mosaic at Hinton St Mary: A closer reading', *Proc. Dorset. Nat. Hist. and Arch. Soc.* cii (1980), 43–8.
45. Henig, op. cit. (note 36), esp. 163–4.

FIG. 4 Inscribed silver beaker from the Water Newton treasure. (British Museum)

probably not Christian in origin but they were certainly adopted by Christians.[46] If possible, Christians liked to be buried in close proximity to what Professor Peter Brown has called 'the very special dead': all dead Christians were important but cult was offered to martyrs and confessors. There are indications that this is what happened outside Verulamium where St. Albans Abbey lies on the site of a Roman Cemetery. The first Christian church here was probably a *cella memoria* on the martyr's grave.[47] A Roman *cella memoria* has been found at Wells,

46. C. Green, 'The significance of plaster burials for the recognition of Christian Cemeteries', in R. Reece (ed.), *Burial in the Roman World* CBA Res. Rep. 22 (London, 1977), 46–53, cf. also Thomas, op. cit. (note 37), 128, 237–8 (gypsum burials) and 231–4 (Orientation).
47. See Brown, *Cult of the Saints*, op. cit. (note 3), 69–85 for background to the practice and *Britannia* xvi (1985), 293 for the excavation conducted by Professor and Mrs Martin Biddle on part of the St. Albans cemetery apparently containing pagan graves. Also cf. G.R. Stephens, 'A note on the martydom of St. Alban', *Herts. Arch.* ix (1983–6), 20–21 on the third-century dating of the event.

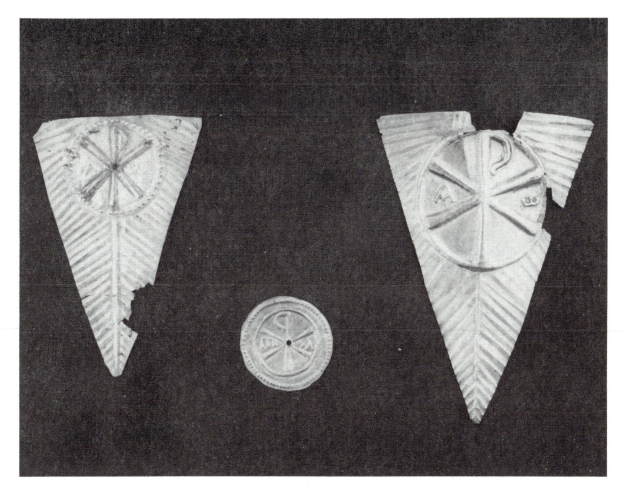

FIG. 5   Silver plaques, with gilding, from the Water Newton treasure. (British Museum)

while others which did not develop into full-scale churches have been excavated at Poundbury.[48] Probable cemetery churches have been recognised at Verulamium and Colchester; St. Martin's, Canterbury has always been a strong candidate for such a church continuing from Roman times, perhaps with a short break in the pagan Saxon period. Excavation has not revealed a Roman cemetery here, and despite the evidence of Bede the case remains unproven.[49]

Finally, there were intra-mural churches, which as the Church became powerful and established in the fourth century, came to be needed as the seats of bishops. The 'church' at Silchester has long been claimed as an example though serious doubts as to this identification have been expressed by Anthony King and at best the case here is non-proven.[50] The building could have been the meeting place of a *collegium*, a club with religious connexions and as ubiquitous in the Roman town as the guild was in the medieval. If so, Bacchus or some other pagan deity may have been worshipped here.[51] The earliest phase of the church of St. Paul in the Bail at Lincoln has been claimed as fourth-century; this is a stronger candidate as Lincoln is known to have been a bishopric.[52] The only certain case is what must be regarded as a

48.   *Britannia* xii (1980), 357–8; Thomas, op. cit. (note 37), 238.
49.   ibid., 170–80.
50.   A. King, 'The Roman Church at Silchester reconsidered', *OJA* ii (1983), 225–37.
51.   The importance of Bacchus to the people of Roman Britain, and especially to those of higher social rank, has only recently come to be realised. It is persuasively demonstrated by V.J. Hutchinson, *Bacchus in Roman Britain: The evidence for his cult* BAR Brit. ser. 151 (Oxford, 1986).
52.   M.J. Jones, 'Archaeology in Lincoln', in *Medieval Art and Architecture at Lincoln Cathedral*, The British Archaeological Association Conference Transactions for the year 1982 (1986), 4–5.

garrison-chapel at Richborough, Kent. Slight remains were uncovered by Bushe-Fox earlier in this century and destroyed in further excavation. The font of a baptistery remained, but was only identified as such in the early 1970s when Mr P.D.C. Brown recognised the structure for what it was and cited continental parallels.[53]

It is abundantly clear that even in the fourth century, Christianity did not oust more traditional forms of religion. The startling formula *'seu gentilis seu Christianus'* scratched on a lead tablet from Bath illustrates a world in which beliefs and expectations were mixed.[54] Sulis or Christ – which would work? The owner of a gold ring, lost at Silchester, had it engraved with the formula *'Seniciane vivas in De(o)'*. Does he live in the Christian God, or some other? Is it a goddess (*Dea*) for the bust on the bezel is labelled 'Venus'?[55] If the uneducated were simply confused, educated Christians and Pagans could think in fairly subtle ways as is revealed by mosaic floors; I have suggested that the Chi-Rho on the chord of the apse in the main hall at Frampton could imply Pagan use of the name of Christ for the themes of the Frampton mosaic as a whole concern the realms of Neptune and of Bacchus, especially the saving power of the latter.[56]

Late, intellectual 'paganism' (if we must use a term derived from the Latin for a back-woodsman), drew its inspiration both from traditional cult and from neoplatonism. There have been two important discoveries in recent years which enable us to see the aristocracy of Late Roman Britain as the cultural equals of those of Gaul and Italy. The first is a remarkable cache of gold jewellery and silver spoons recovered by treasure-hunters on the site of a putative Roman temple at Thetford, Norfolk. Many of the spoons were dedicated to Faunus, otherwise not attested in Britain or, for that matter, anywhere else in the Western provinces, but widely known from the Latin poets as a local Latian god. At Thetford he is given Celtic epithets such as Medugenus (mead-begotten) and Ausecus (prick-eared). Other spoons carry the names of votaries, or rather their *signa*, nick-names used for purposes of the cult such as Persevera (she who has persevered) and Silviola (derived from *silva*, a wood). A fine gold buckle depicts a figure wearing a nebris and holding a pedum and a bunch of grapes who would normally be identified as a satyr but is presumably Faunus himself. One of the rings has supporting woodpeckers on the shoulders, referring thus to Picus (the woodpecker), father of Faunus (Fig. 6). Here the prized possessions of a *collegium* meeting late in the fourth century make allusion to the very origins of Rome and demonstrate the antiquity of the Roman religious tradition.[57]

A mosaic in Trier shows the members of such a *collegium* identified by similar *signa*, meeting for ceremonial feasts.[58] Although not so obviously explicit, the mosaic at Littlecote, Berkshire seems to me of equal importance (Fig. 7). The floor was, in fact, originally discovered in 1730 but it was thought to have been destroyed until it was rediscovered much damaged but *in situ* in 1978. Its imagery is complex and controversial. Jocelyn Toynbee saw the central figure as Apollo with the figures around him representing the seasons and interpreted the chamber as a summer *triclinium*.[59] She has been followed in this comparatively secular interpretation by a number of scholars, amongst them Roger Ling and Roger Wilson.[60] The excavator, Bryn Walters, has established a date for the mosaic as about the reign of Julian. He has explained the symbolism of the mosaic by reference to Orpheus (the central figure is accompanied by a hound as Orpheus always is on British Orpheus floors), but Apollo is assuredly present in the sun-bursts which fill the three apses. The dominant presence is, however, Bacchus, in the two confronted panthers,

53. P.D.C. Brown, 'The Church at Richborough', *Britannia* ii (1971), 225–31.
54. *Tab. Sulis* (note 13), 232–4, no. 98.
55. cf. Henig, op. cit. (note 36), 164, but I do not there entertain the real possibility that the ring is pagan, simply making use of a Christian-influenced formula.
56. loc. cit.
57. C. Johns and T. Potter, *The Thetford Treasure. Roman Jewellery and Silver* (London, 1983); also C. Johns, 'Faunus at Thetford: An early Latian deity in Late Roman Britain', in Henig and King, op. cit. (note 24).
58. J. Moreau, *Das Trierer Kornmarktmosaik* (Cologne, 1960).
59. J.M.C. Toynbee, 'Apollo, Beasts and Seasons: some thoughts on the Littlecote mosaic', *Britannia* xii (1981), 1–5.
60. *Current Arch.* no. 82 (May 1982) for Ling; R.J.A. Wilson, *A Guide to the Roman Remains in Britain* (3rd. edn., London, 1988), 377.

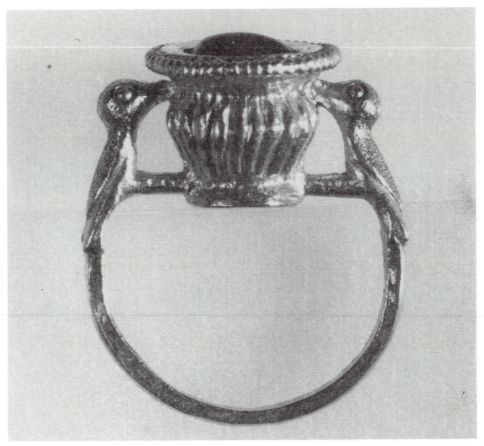

FIG. 6   Silver ring with woodpecker shoulders from the Thetford treasure. (British Museum)

FIG. 7   Littlecote (Wiltshire) shrine and mosaic. (Roman Research Trust)

the panther masks from which the sun-bursts emerge and in the animals around Orpheus which represent the transformations of the god when he was fleeing from the Titans; subsequently he was torn to pieces and reborn as Zagraeus. This detailed syncretism finds support in the writings of fourth-century intellectuals, including the emperor Julian, himself, and Macrobius. The building is placed in a low-lying situation beside the river Kennet, reminiscent of the placing of Frampton by the Frome. It is not a very suitable situation for a summer *triclinium*, and while it would have been almost inevitable that a *collegium* would meet to dine, the religious explanation seemed from the first the stronger hypothesis.[61] The discovery and publication of two Bacchic bronzes from the site, the better of them showing Bacchus Zagraeus with the features of Antinous, greatly strengthens the probability of this being a religious site.[62] The idea of Britain as a backward province dies hard and a recent review of a volume of essays on Roman religion which I co-edited took several contributors to task for suggesting such ideas in what was a backward Celtic province.[63]

For a fine scholar and acute observer of the Roman religious scene in general to have fallen out of touch with the higher reaches of religion in Britain is a tribute to the liveliness of such studies in the province. MacMullen is assuredly right that there cannot have been a great many people in Britain who understood such esoteric doctrines. The villa-owning aristocracy was spread very thin and the upheavals of the later fourth and early fifth century put an end to their society and their speculations.

What happens to Roman religion after this is mysterious. Pagan practices did not die out, but we hear of nothing as organised as the cults of which Gregory of Tours writes in sixth-century Gaul. Gildas, alludes to abandoned Romano-British statuary. Doubtless springs continued to be frequented and life continued at Bath. It has been thought to be secular but the fifth-century heifer bones to which allusion has been made above could argue the continuation of sacrifice, albeit in a crumbling sanctuary. As early as the mid-fourth century the edicts of Christian rulers have been thought to have weighed heavily on pagan practices but archaeology does not fully bear this out. If the burial of the head of the cult statue at Uley can be explained as a Christian attempt to rid the site of an unwelcome demon, this is not the only possible explanation; a piece of bronze sheeting from the same temple carefully folded to 'kill' it and send it through to the divine world originally graced a Christian casket bearing scenes of the Sacrifice of Isaac, Jonah, Christ and the centurion and Christ and the blind man[64] (Fig. 8).

Paganism was not crushed in Britain by the coercion of the Roman state; ironically except at the lower levels of popular superstition,[65] it may have fallen victim to the crumbling of that authority. Only the Church offered an organisation and an assurance of Victory over barbarism and whether in the guise of Pelagianism, emphasising Man's free-will, or in the Catholic stress on Justification through Faith it provided a focus for the descendants of the Romano-British provincials. In the writings of Patrick, of Gildas and of the Pelagian writers and in the story of St. Germanus's visit to Britain to combat the Pelagians, literature helps to flesh-out the story, though few would be as bold as the late John Morris in constructing a coherent narrative.[66]

A discussion such as this is bound to be selective. It has not dwelt on the architecture of temples

61. B. Walters, 'The 'Orpheus' mosaic in Littlecote Park, England', in R. Farioli Campanati (ed.), *Atti del III Colloquio Internaxionale sul Mosaico Antico* (Ravenna, 1984), 433–42.
62. B. Walters and M. Henig, 'Two busts from Littlecote', *Britannia* xix (1988), 407–10.
63. *AJA* xcii no.3 (July 1988), 454–5. (Ramsey Macmullen).
64. This will be published in Ellison's final report on the Uley site.
65. During the fourth century there may have been sporadic interference with pagan practice by the Christian state from time to time, cf. G. Webster, 'The possible effects on Britain of the fall of Magnentius', in B. Hartley and J. Wacher, *Rome and her Northern Provinces Papers presented to Sheppard Frere in honour of his retirement from the Chair of the Archaeology of the Roman Empire, University of Oxford, 1983* (Gloucester, 1983), 240–54, esp. 247–52. For popular superstition and its continuity see now the superb study by Ralph Merrifield, *The Archaeology of Ritual and Magic* (London, 1987), esp. 83–106.
66. John Morris, *The Age of Arthur* (London, 1973), cf. Thomas, op. cit. (note 37), 240–74.

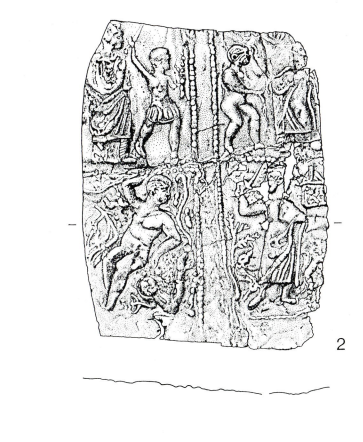

FIG. 8   Decorated Christian casket from Uley (Gloucestershire). (Joanna Richards)

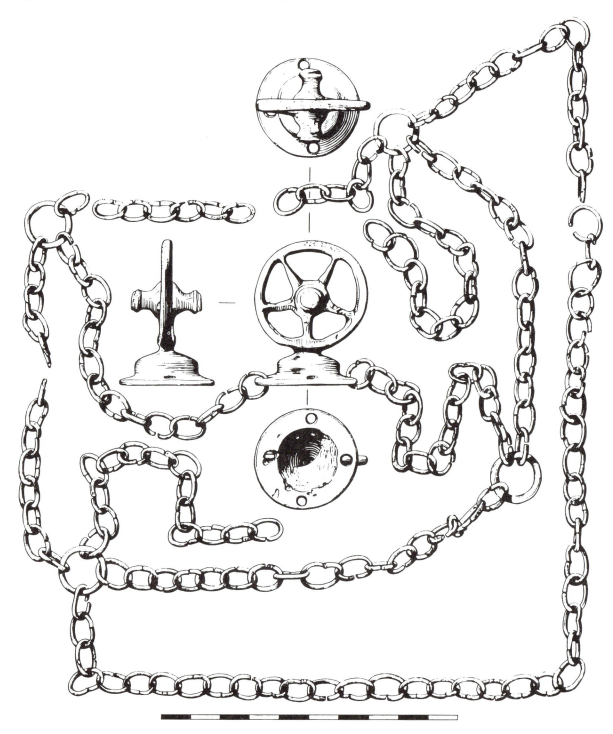

FIG. 9 Priestly regalia from the temple at Wanborough (Surrey). (D.W. Williams)

or on their placing in the landscape which have been the subject of excellent papers;[67] nor has it said much about burials[68] or domestic cult[69] or priestly regalia (Fig. 9) which have also been studied. Future research is bound to enrich our understanding and bring us closer to the very thoughts and prayers of the people of Roman Britain.

67. For the siting of temples see T. Blagg, 'Roman religious sites in the British landscape', *Landscape History* viii (1986), 15–25.
68. For useful assemblies of data see J.P. Alcock, 'Classical religious belief and burial practice in Roman Britain', *Arch. Journ.* cxxxvii (1980), 50–85 and E.W. Black, 'Romano-British burial customs and religious beliefs in south-west England', in ibid, cxliii (1986), 201–39.
69. G. Boon, 'Some Romano-British domestic shrines and their inhabitants', in Hartley and Wacher, op. cit. (note 65), 33–55.

CONSTANTINE I TO CONSTANTINE III

By Simon Esmonde Cleary

The study of the fourth century in Roman Britain has long presented us with a paradox. On the one hand there is a wealth of archaeological data; on the other hand it is poorly understood. How has such a mis-match between evidence and interpretation come about, and how may it be rectified? With such an aim in mind, and remembering that the fourth century was one quarter of the whole Roman period in Britain, it is impossible here to do justice to all facets of the subject. Instead, we shall examine how the study of late Roman Britain has developed, some of its more notable findings, and how it may be expected to develop in the foreseeable future.

Much of the answer lies in the wider field of Roman studies and in the way the discipline has developed over the last century and more. For most of this time, the periods of Roman history deemed most worthy of study were those in which the authors considered the most accomplished stylists and commentators had worked. Thus the world of Cicero and Catullus was extensively anatomised, while that of Ammianus and Ausonius was viewed as degenerate, the literary style bordering on the pastiche and the political system on the oriental. Mercifully, this has been changing and continues to change. For the English-speaking world of scholarship the watershed was the publication in 1964 of A.H.M. Jones' *Later Roman Empire*, from it flowed a huge and exciting literature (one thinks in particular of scholars such as Peter Brown) which has utterly changed the place of the study of the late Empire on the scale of academic respectability.

But the *damnosa haereditas* of the late development of the discipline is still with us; with the archaeology in particular. Briefly stated, the problem is that we lack the coherent and inter-related series of problems and questions whose elucidation can give work on the period a structure. The choice of papers in this volume makes the point neatly. For the Principate there is a range of papers covering the British aspects of such generalising themes as 'The Army' or 'Romanisation'. By contrast the Dominate is not seen as having such clearly-defined topics needing separate treatment. Indeed, the traditional method of analysis of the late Roman period in Britain has often taken the form of a compare-and-contrast exercise with the norms of the early period. Clearly the study of change through time is vital, but such an approach does run the risk of discussing fourth-century Britain in categories more appropriate to the earlier centuries.

Two other problems which have beset the study of late Roman Britain should be mentioned here. The first is the reaction of many students of Roman archaeology to the developments over the last two decades or so referred to (or reviled) as the 'New Archaeology'. To many it has appeared to substitute jargon or mathematics for thought, and it must be admitted that its forays into the Roman period have often been over-simple in their attempts to explain a complex world. But with its emphasis on the social and economic structures of societies, on the identification and explanation of processes of change, and on the presentation of these through quantified data rather than by intuitive deduction, it should be a powerful tool for those seeking to study by archaeological means many of the problems which have now been identified as central to our understanding of the late Roman world. In return, because of the range of sources for the study of that world, any general models or techniques generated through such study should be innately more robust, since they will already have had to prove themselves compatible with tests from a variety of angles. The second problem is that one of the chief dynamics for the study of late

Roman Britain has been the period which succeeded it and saw the establishment of the Anglo-Saxon kingdoms. To what extent did developments in late Roman Britain prefigure features of Anglo-Saxon England, and can relict features of the Roman way be recognised in early England? Unfortunately this has all-too-often in practice meant that features of the archaeology of the fourth century have been studied out of context and in categories more appropriate to the later centuries.

So far, so negative. But it does help explain the poverty of our overall understanding of fourth-century Britain. How, then, should we move forward? We may build on the achievements of those who have studied the late Empire principally from a historical standpoint, and see if some of the general themes which they have identified may help us propose the sorts of inter-related categories of study which characterise and facilitate the study of the early Empire. Here I would propose that we study a series of relationships. By studying relationships rather than single categories of site or artefact one must necessarily seek to integrate different types of evidence. It is also necessary to propose hypotheses and to ask questions. These hypotheses, or models, may be derived from a number of sources: from empirical observation, from parallels elsewhere in the Roman world, from systems of human behaviour observed in the anthropological record. These must then be tested against the available evidence, and in so doing one imposes order on what might otherwise be an inchoate mass of data. Here I propose to look at three very broad series of relationships; the relationship of the state with its subjects; economic relationships, particularly how one may define levels of economic interaction; social relationships, particularly matters of hierarchy – again picking up the theme of the influence of the state. All of these will be seen to interact, and they all involve addressing change through time. They are also all questions which can be addressed through archaeological evidence and which are susceptible of approach through the now generally-accepted basic procedures of the 'New Archaeology', in particular quantification which allows objective testing of models. Clearly in a paper of this size it will not be possible to cover all aspects of late Roman Britain, nor to explore arguments *in extenso*, but I hope that there will be space to indicate major areas of current research and how they may be changing our perception of the period and the place.

By the fourth century the central concern of the Roman state was its own survival. Severely shaken by the military and political crises of the third century, the rulers of the Empire realised that its continuing existence was not a foregone conclusion; it had to be fought for. In literal terms this meant the maintenance of a large standing army and its installations and infrastructure. This meant enormous expenditure with the taxpayer footing the ever-increasing bill. To this end the level of day-to-day supervision of the populace at large was unlike anything in the early Empire. Large civil and financial bureaucracies, dependent respectively from the Praetorian Prefects and the *Comes Sacrarum Largitionum*, reached far down into the localities. The principal purpose of these was to extract the taxation in kind and in precious metal which went to pay the army. An impression of the change in attitude from the early to the late Empire may perhaps be gained by juxtaposing the letters of Trajan to the younger Pliny in Bithynia in the early second century A.D. with the fourth-century imperial rescripts preserved in the *Codex Theodosianus*; the former relaxed and largely *laissez-faire*, the latter insistent and minatory.

For Britain this meant the subdivision of the island into four provinces, each responsible to the *vicarius* of the Diocese of the Britains at London. We have no written and little archaeological evidence for the state of the administration in the various *civitates*, but the councils there would have had as their prime duty the rendering of the tax-assessment, and if they were unable to perform this duty they could be expected to be supplanted by a government *corrector*. In London also was to be found the *Rationalis Summarum per Britannias* and the *Praepositus Thesauri*, responsible to the *Comes Sacrarum Largitionum* for the collection of taxes and the payment of state servants, principally the army. To this end, London occasionally functioned as a mint.

Since the army was the single largest recipient of imperial expenditure in Britain and numerically the largest of the organs of the state in Britain, it is appropriate to examine it here.[1]

---

1. cf. S. James, 'Britain and the late Roman army', in T.F.C. Blagg and A. King (eds.), *Military and Civilian in Roman Britain* BAR 126 (1984), 161–86.

The third and fourth centuries saw extensive changes in the structure of the army in Britain, both in its overall composition and in that of its individual units. Under Constantine I the Roman army had been reorganised along lines of function rather than of a legal status which since 212 had anyway been a dead letter. Round the frontiers of the Empire were now the *limitanei*,[2] the frontier forces charged with holding the barbarians out of imperial territory. In the interior of the empire were the *comitatenses*, a mobile field army, under Constantine I in direct attendance upon the emperor, but later also to be found permanently stationed near frontiers under threat. These troops could be used in a passive sense simply to throw out invaders who had breached the defences of the *limitanei*. They could also be used actively to promote the external wars which the Empire still fought, or for and against usurpers. Fourth-century Britain had two *limitaneus* commands; in the north the *Dux Britanniarum* whose troops on Hadrian's Wall and its outpost and hinterland forts watched the powerful and hostile new confederacies in Scotland, such as the Picts. Round the south-eastern coasts of the island were the forts under the command of the *Comes Litoris Saxonici per Britannias* – the Saxon Shore. The great, early-fifth-century list of late Roman civil and military officers, the *Notitia Dignitatum*,[3] also lists comitatensian troops in Britain under the *comes Britanniarum*, but we do not know at what date they were assigned to the Diocese.

Because of the dearth of literary and epigraphic evidence relating to the island in the fourth century,[4] our knowledge of the army at this date has had to depend on the results of archaeology, and this is a field in which the evidence from Britain has a wider significance. Britain had escaped the military disasters which had afflicted many other frontiers of the Empire in the third century. Because of the relatively minor threat to the northern frontier, Britain's large army was one which could safely be siphoned of troops, whilst leaving sufficient to safeguard the island. This process of 'vexillating', common in the third century, is attested epigraphically, with troops from Britain in *Germania Superior* in 255 (*CIL* xiii 6780), and soon after in the Balkans (*CIL* iii 3228). The depletion of troops is mirrored in the reduced accommodation attested for the third century at two of the British legionary fortresses, Caerleon[5] and Chester[6] (on this as on almost all else about Roman York we are still appallingly ignorant). By the end of the fourth century *Legio II Augusta* which had once filled the fifty acres of Caerleon was now housed in eight-acre Richborough.[7] Excavations on Wall forts such as Housesteads and Wallsend[8] have made clear that at these also there had been a considerable reduction in the amount of accommodation, with barracks for second-century centuries of eighty men being demolished, and some only being replaced by a smaller number of new buildings. These new buildings – 'chalets' – housed an unknown number of men; estimates have ranged from the eight of a second-century *contubernium*, to one soldier and his family. Either way the reduction is marked. The very incomplete evidence from the Saxon Shore forts also speaks of something less substantial than was the norm in the second century. This archaeological evidence from Britain corroborates the picture being gained from the literary and archaeological evidence for the Empire as a whole for the units of the fourth century being much smaller than their earlier counterparts.

Though we know an increasing amount about the installations of the late army in Britain, we are very ill-informed about its arms and equipment, basically since very little of it has been found

2. A.M.H. Jones, *The Later Roman Empire, 284–602* (Oxford, 1964), 649–54; R.S.O. Tomlin, 'The Army of the Late Empire', in J.S. Wacher (ed.), *The Roman World* (London, 1987), 107–34. B. Isaac, 'The Meaning of the Terms *Limes* and *Limitanei*,' *JRS* lxxviii (1988), 125–47.
3. R. Goodburn and P. Bartholomew, *Aspects of the Notitia Dignitatum* BAR Int. Ser. 15 (1976).
4. cf. S. Ireland, *Roman Britain; a sourcebook* (London, 1986); J. Wilkes, 'The Saxon Shore – British anonymity in the Later Empire,' in D.E. Johnston (ed.), *The Saxon Shore* CBA Res. Rep. 18 (London, 1977), 76–80.
5. G.C. Boon, *Isca* (Cardiff, 1972).
6. T.J. Strickland, 'Third century Chester' in A.C. King and M. Henig (eds.), *The Roman West in the Third Century* BAR Int. Ser. 109 (1981), 415–44.
7. *Notitia Dignitatum*, Occ.XXVIII.
8. C.M. Daniels, 'Excavations at Wallsend and the fourth-century barracks on Hadrian's Wall,' in W.S. Hanson and L.J.F. Keppie (eds.), *Roman Frontier Studies 1979* BAR Int. Ser. 71 (1980), 173–93.

or published. It is perhaps worth knocking on the head again (for it refuses to lie down) the notion that certain types of belt-fitting decorated with stylised dolphin's heads, and other associated metalwork is indicative of the presence of Germanic troops in fourth-century Britain. When first advanced[9] this was a reasonable hypothesis. But more recent work[10] has shown that it was a misapprehension. The metalwork in question was associated with the *cingulum militare*, the official belt and mark of status issued to all state servants, whether civil or military and irrespective of ethnic origin.

If the nature of the army had changed, so also had the economic effects of its upkeep on the Empire, and here also we see a change in the relationship between rulers and ruled. Contemporaries such as the anonymous author of the *De Rebus Bellicis*[11] and the *Comes Sacrarum Largitionum* Ursulus[12] all recognised that the revenue needed to pay for the army was the single largest call on the Empire's resources and thus the single largest motor of the economy. Our limited evidence suggests that the levels of taxation ranged from the harsh to the extortionate. This must have affected the lives of nearly all the Empire's inhabitants. Unwittingly the Empire was sowing one of the seeds of its own dissolution; in the fifth century people discovered that under barbarian rulers decline in some areas of life was compensated for by the atrophy of the tax system.[13]

The effects of tax on the urban and rural archaeology of fourth-century Britain will be further considered below, but here we may draw attention to its implications for one of the most commonly found class of artefacts on sites of this date; coins. The Roman Empire, in common with other early societies, minted coins as an aid to the discharge by the state of its duties, principally the payment of its servants. Coins might also have a secondary, commercial use, but the primary purpose of the coinage must be borne in mind when examining the patterning of coin-finds. Troops and other state servants were paid partly in kind (the responsibility of the Praetorian Prefects and their underlings) and partly in gold and silver (the responsibility of the *Comes Sacrarum Largitionum* and his minions). Thus, a certain proportion of tax had to be rendered in gold and silver coin or bullion. Bronze coinage was struck in large part to enable the state to buy in precious metals. So gold and silver acquired a premium above their intrinsic or face values. In archaeological terms this is visible in the extreme scarcity of such coins as site finds. They do, though, occur in hoards, showing that they were in general circulation. Fourth-century Britain has also produced a number of spectacular precious-metal hoards such as those from Mildenhall[14] and Thetford,[15] indicating that at the top of the social hierarchy there were some very wealthy people indeed. Bronze coins, on the other hand, are very common as site finds. In part this must be because many of them were small and of very low value, so the loss of one would mean far less than that of a large second-century bronze coin (it would also be physically far easier). But they also occur on a far wider range of sites, particularly rural sites, than had second-century coins, suggesting that they were far more commonly available and used. Their abundance at towns supports the contention that the urban economy was to a considerable extent monetised. So also does the existence of spates of counterfeiting, for the coin-supply from the imperial mints to Britain was by no means regular and consistent, as has been shown in the pages of *Britannia*.[16] When there was a period of inadequate imperial coin supply, the provincials in Britain responded by issuing their own copies of imperial issues. The irregular imperial supply means that the peaks and troughs in the quantities of coin on a particular site should normally be explained in terms of fluctuation of that supply rather than in terms of fluctuation in the demographic or economic fortunes of that site.

---

9. S.C. Hawkes and G.C. Dunning, 'Soldiers and Settlers in Britain, fourth to fifth century: with a catalogue of animal-ornamented buckles and related belt-fittings', *Medieval Archaeology* v (1961), 1–70.
10. cf. C.J. Simpson, 'Belt-Buckles and Strap-Ends of the later Roman Empire; a preliminary Survey of several new groups', *Britannia* vii (1976), 192–223.
11. cf. E.A. Thompson, *A Roman Reformer and Inventor* (Oxford, 1952).
12. Ammianus Marcellinus XX.11.5.
13. C.J. Wickham, 'The Other Transition: from the Ancient World to Feudalism,' *Past and Present* ciii (1986), 3–36.
14. K.S. Painter, *The Mildenhall Treasure* (London, 1977).
15. C. Johns and T. Potter, *The Thetford Treasure; Roman Jewellery and Silver* (London, 1983).
16. R.M. Reece, 'A short Survey of the Roman Coins found on Fourteen Sites in Britain', *Britannia* iii (1972), 169–76.

So in the changes instituted by the new imperial order of things we may already see that some of the assumptions and questions proper to the study of the first and second centuries are no longer appropriate here. Instead we may see a new range of questions about the rôle and nature of the state and its organs in relation to the life of the Empire in general and the Diocese of the Britains in particular.

To turn now to the question of how economic relationships were conducted at this period. This is an area in which archaeology has a great deal to offer, since much of what it studies, especially artefacts and their distributions, can yield economic information. Clearly there is overlap here with what we have just been considering, for the evidence is that the demands of the state were the single largest economic activity in the late Roman Empire. The state raised only part of what it needed in tax. Over and above that it bought in supplies and finished goods as and when it needed, on a large scale. Our literary evidence[17] suggests that this took place principally at forts and towns. Moreover, the state required much of its revenue and purchases to be transported over considerable distances. Thus the towns would be focal points in the taxation system, and in state purchasing. The citizen would need to obtain gold and silver coin to pay tax at the towns, and it would also be there that this could be obtained, either from the state by its purchasing (the state giveth, the state taketh away), or from money-changers (e.g. the *nummularii* of the law-codes).

This brings us on to the nature and rôle of towns in fourth-century Britain, and to one of the major debates about an aspect of the late Roman period in the island. This debate arose from a paper by Richard Reece,[19] in which he argued, among other things, that the towns of late Roman Britain were but shadows of their second-century selves, 'administrative villages' huddled in the centre of what had been prosperous and expansive classical-style towns. In his view this had happened by the end of the third century. In part this was argument by analogy, for this is what had apparently happened in other areas of the late Empire, for instance Gaul. In part it was an argument from the evidence as he saw it, for instance the precipitate decline of London at the end of the second century, and the number of urban sites where the coin-dated stratigraphy suggested abandonment during the fourth century. This work has attracted a range of responses from 'seminal' to 'rubbish', but at least it has posed questions and stimulated thought in a way rare for the fourth century. Personally I believe it to be untenable, for the following reasons. First, the argument by analogy (an analogy which, it should be noted, only goes one way; Britain must be like the Continent or North Africa, but not *vice versa*). This implies a uniformity over the huge geographical extent of the Roman Empire which nobody has ever tried to sustain; indeed, regional diversity is one of the recurring themes in the study of the Empire at all periods. Nor is the nature of the late towns on the Continent fully understood; research has concentrated too much on the defences and too little on what it was that was being defended. Second, the evidence from urban sites in Britain. London was an unfortunate exemplar, since more recent thought inclines to the view that it has a peculiar developmental history.[20] Even so, it was always difficult to find sites to support the contention that Romano-British towns had shrunk to being administrative villages by the end of the third century. The examples Reece quoted[21] were of sites which did not survive until the end of the fourth century. Ironically, the new excavations at Caerwent[22] have shown that it was in the second and third centuries that it resembled an administrative village, only developing to its full extent in the fourth century. The generality of excavated evidence is for continued occupation of the towns, though that occupation need not have been the same as in the second century, as we shall see. A third problem which Reece did not tackle was the evidence that Romano-British urban cemeteries were at their most extensive in the fourth century. Despite the difficulties which remain in assessing how they relate to the

17.   op. cit, (notes 11, 12).
18.   cf. M. Hendy, *Studies in the Byzantine Monetary Economy: c. 300–1450* (Cambridge, 1986).
19.   R.M. Reece, 'Town and country: the end of Roman Britain', *World Archaeology* xii (1980), 77–92.
20.   cf. R. Merrifield, *London: City of the Romans* (London, 1983).
21.   op. cit. (note 19), 82–3.
22.   R.J. Brewer, *Caerwent 1987: Forum-Basilica and Roman Shop* (Cardiff, 1988).

earlier urban cemeteries, there is nonetheless the point that they were far more extensive than those of any other type of fourth-century settlement, suggesting that the towns were of a different demographic order. The growth in the excavation of cemeteries and the realisation of the importance of such material for the study of demography, disease, religion and society is one of the most noticeable advances in the last twenty years.[24]

Merely to indicate shortcomings in Reece's analysis does not solve the problem he raised: were the towns of fourth-century Britain just a version of the towns of the second century, or were they something else? In the last paragraph but one we noted that towns had an important part to play in the economic activities of the state. This must have provided an important economic underpinning. Also related to their place in the imperial scheme of things there was their rôle as administrative centres. Taking their lead from repeated imperial fulminations against backsliding *curiales* in the *Codex Theodosianus*, historians and archaeologists have tended to look for evidence of the dereliction of civic duties and buildings. In Britain some civic buildings such as the forum at Wroxeter[23] or the basilica at Silchester[25] had either been burnt down and not replaced, or turned over to industrial use. But other fora, such as those at Caistor-by-Norwich or Caerwent,[26] had been rebuilt after fire or simply maintained. Other 'public' buildings such as baths tended also to be maintained. Even if one can make out a case for decline in what has been termed the 'public' town[27] does this affect the life of the town any more than a twentieth-century Town Hall being turned over to bingo or symphony concerts? What of the 'private' town, the buildings of the citizens? Here Professor Frere's remarks[28] on the contrast between Verulamium in the second and the fourth centuries are worth pondering. Working from the evidence of the building-types he characterised mid-second-century Verulamium as being essentially a mercantile settlement, with artisans and traders being far more in evidence than the landed proprietors who were only just beginning to invest in town-houses, their principal residences remaining in the country. By contrast, in the fourth century the dominant building-type in terms both of numbers and of the area of the town's superficially occupied was the town-house. The two towns of which we have the most complete plans, Caerwent and Silchester, suffer from problems of dating due to the early date of the excavations there, but recent re-excavation along with re-analysis of the old records suggests that the familiar plans show essentially the state of affairs in the fourth century.[29] If so, then they agree with Frere's comments for Verulamium, with large areas given over to spacious and gracious housing, with the mercantile activity concentrating along the main through-road, the 'high street'. A similar situation has been suggested for towns such as Cirencester[30] and Chichester.[31] These, then, would be the residences of the living whose bodies were in due course inhumed in the extensive cemeteries. It suggests that the urban population at these larger towns was a mixture of landed proprietors, perhaps resident seasonally to discharge their public duties, and artisans and merchants manufacturing or marketing goods to other town-dwellers and, more important, the local rural populace. This picture has been derived essentially from the 'large' towns, the bigger towns with important administrative functions. For the 'small' towns, the local market towns, these seem to have remained as they had

23. D. Atkinson, *Report on the Excavations at Wroxeter (the Roman City of Viroconium) in the County of Salop 1923–1927* (Oxford, 1942).
24. G.N. Clarke, *The Roman Cemetery at Lankhills*, in M. Biddle (ed.), *Winchester Studies III: pre-Roman and Roman Winchester: Part II* (Oxford, 1979). C.J.S. Green, 'The Cemetery of a Romano-British Community at Poundbury, Dorchester, Dorset', in S.M. Pearce (ed.), *The Early Church in Western Britain and Ireland* BAR 102 (1982), 61–76.
25. M. Fulford, 'Excavations on the Sites of the Amphitheatre and Forum-Basilica at Silchester, Hampshire: an Interim Report', *Antiq. Journ.* lxv (1985), 39–81.
26. S.S. Frere, 'The Forum and Baths of Caistor by Norwich', *Britannia* ii (1971), 1–26. op. cit. (note 22).
27. J.Evans, 'Towns and the End of Roman Britain in Northern England,' *Scottish Arch. Review* ii.2 (1983), 144–9.
28. S.S. Frere, *Verulamium Excavations: Volume II* (London, 1983), 1–25.
29. Pers. comm. R.J. Brewer and M. Fulford.
30. A.D. McWhirr, 'Cirencester 1973–6: Tenth Interim Report', *Antiq. Journ.* lviii (1978), 61–80.
31. A. Down, *Chichester Excavations* 3 (Chichester, 1978).

always been, essentially artisan-based, lacking the larger houses of the landed aristocracy, which were attracted by the administrative functions and public facilities of the 'large' towns.

Two of the most commonly encountered classes of artefact on Romano-British urban sites are coins and pottery. Coins we have already considered, but it is worth repeating that the bronze coinage seems to have been in everyday use in the towns, presumably as small change. When imperial supply was on a down-swing the want of coin was felt, to judge by the bouts of counterfeiting. The existence of an urban economy that was at least partially monetised will have had both economic and social effects, with goods being redistributed not by barter or as a result of social interaction and obligations as is usual in pre-coin-using societies, but to anyone who had the wherewithal to pay. This saw the beginnings of what the economic anthropologists term a 'disembedded' economy. The effect of the three levels of economic activity which have been mentioned can perhaps be discerned in the distribution of pottery in fourth-century Britain; the imperial, the market and the social.

Pottery is abundant on fourth-century sites, and consequently the industry has received a great deal of attention, never more so than over the past twenty years. It has long been recognised that there were three main grades of producer. Most widespread were the products of a small number of major industries, which achieved a regional or supra-regional coverage. These include centres such as the Alice Holt[32] and New Forest[33] and Oxfordshire[34] in the South, and Crambeck/ Malton[35] in the North. Other centres such as Swanpool, Lincoln[36] supplied a smaller regional or sub-regional market. Very poorly understood are a wealth of very local producers perhaps serving no more than one or two market sites, whose products come in abundance from consuming sites, but whose locations of production are scarcely known.[37]

The dominance of the giant, fine-ware producers is often explained in terms of good market penetration by a superior product, aggressively marketed. To an extent this is undoubtedly the case. But here again the influence of imperial on local economics may be discerned. It is now generally accepted that the explanation for the Mediterranean-wide distribution of African Red Slip Ware is that it rode pick-a-back on the transport of grain and olive oil from North Africa for the *annona* of the City of Rome and for other imperial supply commitments.[38] The same may well have happened on a smaller scale in Britain. It is, for instance, noticeable that the distribution area of Oxfordshire products includes a number of Saxon Shore forts which must have been in receipt of state supplies. Alongside this there may be discerned in the fine-ware distribution a clear preference for marketing through towns,[39] suggesting that the towns still had a central economic as well as administrative rôle. Because of our ignorance of the places of production of the bulk of the day-to-day coarse wares it is very difficult to say anything definite about their mode of distribution. Some undoubtedly went to the towns and their markets. But there are indications that some may have been distributed by other means, perhaps reflecting social rather than economic factors.[40]

Another way in which the pottery industry has stood as a paradigm for other, less-well-known, Romano-British industries is in the actual organisation of the industry. The great range

32.   M.A.B. Lyne and R.S. Jefferies, *The Alice Holt/Farnham Roman Pottery* CBA Res. Rep. 30 (London, 1979).

33.   M. Fulford, *New Forest Roman Pottery* BAR 17 (1975).

34.   C.J. Young, *Oxfordshire Roman Pottery* BAR 43, (1977).

35.   J. Evans, *Aspects of Later Roman Pottery Assemblages in Northern England*, unpub. Ph.D. thesis, University of Bradford (1985).

36.   cf. M. Darling, *A Group of Late Roman Pottery from Lincoln* Lincoln Archaeological Trust Monograph Series XVI–1 (London, 1977).

37.   V.G. Swan, *The Pottery Kilns of Roman Britain* (London, 1984).

38.   A. Giardina (ed.), *Società Romana e Impero Tardoantico: III: Le Merci Gli Insediamenti.* cf. review article by C.J. Wickham, *JRS* lxxviii (1988), 183–93.

39.   I. Hodder, 'Some marketing models for Romano-British coarse pottery,' *Britannia* v (1974), 340–59.

40.   op. cit. (note 39), fig. 9. J. Evans, 'All Yorkshire is divided into three parts: social aspects of later Roman pottery distribution in Yorkshire,' in J. Price and P.R. Wilson (eds.), *Recent Research in Roman Yorkshire* BAR 193 (1988), 323–37.

of products and their wide distribution from industries such as Oxfordshire appears from the archaeology not to reflect a very centralised manufacture like that of samian,[41] but the aggregate of a great number of individual workshops. From some of these[42] there is evidence that the industry may have been closely tied in with the annual agricultural cycle rather than a year-round craft specialisation. Thus pottery may have been a form of cash crop. Such hypotheses now need testing for other industries.[43] Such evidence would show a more complex relationship between agriculture and industry and the towns, one more in line with the documented situation in later periods and with modern ethnoarchaeological research.

So, economic relationships and organisation may be seen to overlap with social relationships, and it is to these that we must turn last. In the last two decades research into prehistoric archaeology has largely been concerned with the proposition that, agricultural subsistence apart, the chief dynamic in human affairs at the time was social. The arrangement of settlements, the types of buildings and the distributions of artefacts have increasingly been interpreted as reflections of social relationships, particularly the getting and maintaining of status. This approach can be extended to cover religion, seeing this too as a social artefact and mediator. Such thinking has as yet made little headway in the world of Roman archaeology. In a way this is strange, since the patron-client relationship and the reciprocal obligations this entailed have long been recognised as central to the political and social organisation of the Roman world, early and late. In archaeology such effort as has gone into this question has tended to be expended on the recognition of hierarchy rather than on the analysis of how that hierarchy came about and was maintained or altered. The most fruitful field for the examination of social relationships must be in the countryside, since that is where the bulk of the population lived, and where there is the greatest diversity of settlement types and variation in the artefact and environmental assemblages.

Study of the Romano-British countryside has traditionally been site-based, either the single excavated site or, more recently, the multiplicity of sites to be recognised by aerial and ground survey. (above, p. 115) A broad division has been established between the 'villa', a site whose buildings demonstrate Romanisation in form and building materials, and the 'farmstead', a site whose layout and architecture show little change from those of the pre-Roman Iron Age. Along with this categorisation on essentially morphological grounds have gone others. The structural division is assumed to reflect a social division. This is reinforced by the literary sources for the period which distinguish between the *potentiores* and *honestiores* on the one hand, and the *humiliores* and *coloni* on the other. The division can also be seen to be economic, with the villas more closely aligned with the 'Romanised' economy, and thus able to obtain and maintain the physical trappings of Roman style. The dynamic of the relationship is often thought of as basically exploitative, with the villas deriving income and/or labour from the farmsteads, giving little in return.[44] Two features of this approach must increasingly give concern. The first is the assumption of a dichotomy bordering on an opposition. The second is that it is a largely descriptive approach, which does not seek to analyse how the relationships worked, and how the archaeological material may be interrogated about them.

Equally, there are two developments which are starting to broaden and deepen our understanding. The first is an increasing attention to the agricultural basics (above, pp. 127–34). This has shown that in many important respects the agricultural régime of Roman Britain was part of a millennium-long continuum which came into being in the earlier Iron Age.[45] The

41.   D.P.S. Peacock, *Pottery in the Roman World: an ethnoarchaeological approach* (London, 1982), Chapter 7.
42.   cf. C.J. Young, 'Excavations at the Churchill Hospital, 1973; Interim Report', *Oxoniensia* xxxix (1974), 1–11.
43.   M. Millett and P. Halkon, 'Landscape and economy: recent excavation and fieldwork around Holme-on-Spalding Moor,' in J. Price and P.R. Wilson (eds.), *Recent Research in Roman Yorkshire* BAR 193 (1988), 37–47.
44.   R. Hingley, 'Roman Britain: The Structure of Roman Imperialism and the Consequences of Imperialism on the Development of a Peripheral Province,' in D. Miles (ed.), *The Romano-British Countryside: Studies in Rural Settlement and Economy*, BAR 103 (1982), 17–52.
45.   M. Jones, 'The development of crop husbandry,' in M. Jones and G. Dimbleby (eds.), *The Environment of Man: the Iron Age to the Anglo-Saxon Period* BAR 87 (1981), 95–127. M. Maltby, 'Iron-Age, Romano-British and Anglo-Saxon Animal Husbandry: A Review of the Evidence,' in ibid., 151–203.

developments which may be specifically assigned to the Roman period are few in number, though some such as the intensification of use of marginal land may be related to such stimuli as the imperial taxation system as much as possible population increase. More work is now needed to ascertain whether these innovations are more usually to be found at sites which also display other signs of Roman influence, or whether they are a general phenomenon. This leads us on to the more general question of whether an agricultural difference may be observed between the types of site which are usually placed in a morphological hierarchy. Are villas more 'Romanised' than farmsteads?. Or are villas and farmsteads complementary? Why does the relative frequency of the two gross types vary so much across the country? The second advance has been in the greater amount of attention paid to the farmsteads. This is particularly so in the Midlands and the South, in the North the lack of villas has meant that such studies have always held sway. As yet the results are patchy, for the excavation of such sites is often tedious and unrewarding. But as more are excavated and published, we may begin to realise their potential. Allied to this development has been the parallel increase in the emphasis placed on the agricultural buildings and dependencies and field-systems at the villas, as opposed to the long-standing concern with the dwelling-house, its mosaics and other indicators of Romanisation.

To try to build up a more sensitive picture of the countryside, and most especially of how the various types of site inter-related, there are at least three major levels of study which need to be undertaken. The first is the extensive and intensive field survey of areas of landscape combined with excavation of a range of sites selected because they appear to be representative of different morphological or functional types. The second is the analysis of as many aspects of the structural, artefactual and environmental data as possible, in an intra- and inter-site basis. The third is the devising and testing of models which seek to explain the observed variability within and between sites and in both time and space. Projects of this type have been initiated in areas such as the upper Thames Valley,[47] the middle Nene Valley (the Stanwick Project)[48] and North Humberside,[49] but they need an enormous investment of money and commitment of time and labour.

If we can turn our attention and resources to such problems and approaches then we should be able not only to build up a larger data-base, but one which is more varied. This will enormously enhance our ability to ask new questions of these data, and to try to test hypotheses by bringing to bear quantified data from a number of sites where comparable levels of excavation and research have been carried out. Thus we shall be able to analyse relationships between sites, which will inevitably lead us on to consideration of the relationships between the people the archaeology represents, and how these changed through time. 'Social' and 'processual' archaeology to use the jargon: 'archaeology is people' to use Wheeler's dictum.

In a short paper it is impossible to cover all topics, let alone do justice to those that are included. Some important topics have been omitted; religion is one obvious one, but at least that has recently been excellently treated by far better authorities[50] than this author (above, pp. 219–34). It has been my concern, rather, to consider the three main areas referred to in the opening paragraph. The first has been how the study of late Roman Britain has developed, and how this has influenced the way we still study and see the period. The second has been to point up some of the more important advances in the study of the island in the fourth century in recent years, including some which have a wider relevance than just to Britain itself. The third has been to try to see where we might profitably go next, with the needs and potentialities of archaeology

46. cf. the papers in D. Miles (ed.), *The Romano-British Countryside: Studies in Rural Settlement and Economy* BAR 103 (1982).

47. D. Miles, 'Romano-British Settlements in the Gloucestershire Thames Valley,' in A. Saville (ed.), *Archaeology in Gloucestershire* (Cheltenham, 1984).

48. D. Neal, 'Stanwick', *Current Arch.* 106 (1987), 334–5; *Britannia* xx (1989) (forthcoming).

49. op. cit. (note 43). One can only contrast the work in Britain with the utterly different scale and concept of work in Holland. cf. W.J.H. Willems, *Romans and Batavians. A Regional Study in the Dutch Eastern River Area* (Amersfoort, 1986).

50. M. Henig, *Religion in Roman Britain,* (London, 1984). C. Thomas, *Christianity in Roman Britain to AD 500* (London, 1981).

very much to the fore. A useful result of a better understanding of the fourth century will lie in having a firmer base from which to identify and study the changes which were to come about in the fifth century.

The twenty years since the publication of the first volume of *Britannia* have seen the late Roman period in Britain start to command our attention as a period in its own right, not just as a tailpiece to the early Roman period.[51] If there is a comparable collection of papers to this in twenty years time, then that late Roman period will need to have equal billing with the early.

Whether any of the branches of study that this paper has outlined will have borne fruit it will be fascinating to see, but what is certain is that our study and understanding of late Roman Britain are now set for vigorous growth.

51.   A fuller discussion of late Roman Britain will be found in the author's *The Ending of Roman Britain* (Batsford in press).

A PROSPECT OF ROMAN BRITAIN

By J.J. Wilkes

The Society for the Promotion of Roman Studies chose to mark its Jubilee year 1960–1 by an exhibition of art in Roman Britain. The choice of this theme was intended to honour the memory of Francis Haverfield, founder of the Society and pioneer of the study of Roman Britain. We have recently been reminded of Haverfield's achievement by the published version of a lecture by Sheppard Frere on the occasion of his own retirement from the Professorship of the Archaeology of the Roman Empire, Oxford University, in 1983, to which he had been appointed following the death of Ian Richmond, its first holder, in 1965. The death of Haverfield in 1919, a few weeks before his sixtieth birthday, is said to have been hastened by distress at the loss of several of his pupils in the Great War, notably Leonard Cheesman. The task of editing a revision of the Inscriptions of Roman Britain, which he had been invited to undertake by Theodor Mommsen at the age of twenty-eight, was inherited by R.G. Collingwood. Though in the first instance a philosopher, Collingwood devoted his vacations to Roman Britain and in term taught a succession of distinguished pupils who were to carry on the tradition which Haverfield had established.

The Jubilee exhibition was a notable success. During four weeks in the summer of 1961 eleven thousand visitors came to the Goldsmiths' Hall in the City of London. The catalogue prepared by Professor Jocelyn Toynbee, published for the Society by Phaidon Press with superb photographs by Otto Fein of the Warburg Institute, retains today a prominent place in the literature on Roman Britain. All the well-known pieces were on display, the bronze of Claudius from the river Alde, the Bath Minerva, one of the Lullingstone heads, the sculptures from the Walbrook Mithraeum, the Corbridge Lanx, the Mildenhall Treasure, sculptures and altars from Hadrian's Wall, the Bridgeness panel from the Antonine Wall, helmets from Ribchester and Newstead and pieces from Traprain Law. The richness and variety of this display came as a surprise to many, especially as many lesser known objects were brought to a wider notice for the first time. The exhibition and its highly favourable reception aroused a new interest in the study of Roman Britain. Moreover, the Society's Jubilee can now, in retrospect, be seen to have been a turning-point in the course of field archaeology, as the hasty salvage of the post-war years was superseded by planned schemes of rescue and research excavations in several major settlements of the Roman province.

The Society celebrated its Jubilee under the Presidency of Ian Richmond, doyen of Romano-British Studies. In 1960, during his excavation of the Agricolan legionary base at Inchtuthil on the river Tay, he made one of the most remarkable discoveries of all from Roman Britain. In a sealed pit within a *fabrica* was found a huge hoard of ironwork, including nine iron tyres over 3.5 feet in diameter and nearly ten tons of mainly unused iron nails, of which 875,428 could be identified and classified by size and head-type into six groups. The find demonstrated the supreme efficiency of the imperial Roman army in the matter of supplies and building materials, on which Richmond himself had placed so much emphasis during his working life.

In the 51st volume of the *Journal of Roman Studies* which appeared in 1961, Richmond surveyed the progress of studies in Roman Britain during the previous fifty years. That paper still repays study not only for the wealth of information that it contains but also for an account of the manner in which knowledge had increased and for the definition of the problems yet to be tackled. The years preceding the First World War, it was observed, were marked by advances in the study of military and rural remains but systematic work on urban sites had hardly begun. On the northern frontier the campaigns of excavation at Corbridge proved a great disappointment and interest flagged until F.G. Simpson initiated a strategy of selective excavation devised to establish once and for all the principal historical phases of the Wall.

The Twenties and Thirties were dominated by the work of Wheeler and his followers, advocating strictly controlled methods of excavation paying, special attention to stratigraphy and the recording of finds. Their methods remain the basis of the modern methods of excavation and the reports produced at the time of work in Wales and later at Verulamium and Maiden Castle still repay study. As Richmond observed, these new methods appeared to offer the prospect of solving historical problems by means of excavation, for example the date, nature and manner of construction of town walls, although it was this aspect of his work which drew most criticism from contemporaries.

In the military zone, Wales and the North, the impact of increased archaeological work appears to have had the opposite effect. If the main historical sequence of Hadrian's Wall now seemed to have been defined, and by the end of the Twenties most agreed that it was, new work on sites in the north and in Wales seemed to undermine an historical interpretation that had once appeared simple and clear. In retrospect that process of blurring and complicating can now be seen as beneficial, principally because it demonstrated the value of new work that revealed how much remained to be done. In the matter of Roman Wales, Richmond's diagnosis has surely been proved correct. 'It is a tangled story of pacification and precautions, maintained in some areas and relaxed in others at moments often to be more precisely determined, and finally intensified against sea raiders in a fashion of which too little is yet known. All this is enacted against a background of civilian penetration, especially in south Wales. History becomes as vividly regional a matter as in the Middle Ages, despite the far stricter central control.' Similarly in the north, apart that is from Hadrian's Wall, 'an air of uncertainty also broods over Brigantia'.

In the civil province the heart of the matter was the nature and condition of the native cities of Britannia at different periods in the history of the province. 'Among the chief surprises in the archaeological information about these has been the complication apparent in their history as illustrated by the development of their defences. Silchester, Verulamium and Cirencester have produced evidence of drastic changes in the type of their defensive circuits, representing both expansion and contraction. To weigh these in terms of social development, official status and relations with the provincial government is among the most interesting tasks that lie ahead.'

Nearly thirty years have passed since Richmond took stock of Roman Britain. How the subject and those who study it have changed during that time may be gauged from the fact that now the task of reviewing the state of Roman Britain requires a volume of 80,000 words with more than a dozen contributors. Richmond's death in October 1965, a few days after the end of his final season at Inchtuthil, was a great loss to Romano-British Studies, only mitigated by the passing of his mantle to Sheppard Frere. As Wheeler's successor at the Institute of Archaeology in London and then at Oxford in the place of Richmond he has led the discipline by personal example in the field, in the study and, as the spirit of the age demands, in the committee room. The appearance of this volume can serve as no more than a token of acknowledgement of Frere's achievement.

Each year sees a healthy increment to the bibliography of Roman Britain. This includes the presentation of the primary evidence from the discovery and exploration of sites, major works of reference and works of synthesis of every possible variety and quality. Probably the most significant of all these has been the first volume of the *Roman Inscriptions of Britain*, containing inscriptions of stone, brought to completion in 1965 by R.P. Wright, collaborator and successor of R.G. Collingwood. Sadly it was to be only in 1983 that the full utility of that work could be exploited by the publication of full indices. We still await the rest of the corpus, including stamps, graffiti, and the rest of the Instrumenta. Moreover, since Volume I contains only those inscriptions recorded to the end of 1954, a supplementary volume, the third in the sequence, has now become a matter of urgency. The Map of Roman Britain compiled by the Ordnance Survey reached a fourth edition, in two sheets, in 1978. The same body had earlier published maps of

Hadrian's Wall (1964), the Antonine Wall (1969), and more recently a map and guide to Roman London (1981). Under the guidance of A.L.F. Rivet the British Academy has sponsored the publication of the British contribution to the international project of mapping the Roman Empire to the scale of 1:1.000,000, the *Tabula Imperii Romani*. The two maps, 'Condate-Glevum-Londinium-Lutetia' (1983) and 'Britannia Septentrionalis' (1987), follow the now established format of the series in that they are accompanied by fully documented gazetteers of sites. Along with these admirable compilations students of Roman Britain have an easy recourse to the ancient sources on the topography of the province in *The Place-Names of Roman Britain* (1979), by Rivet and C. Smith.

Studies cannot proceed without these and other works of reference. At the same time it is a distinguishing feature of Roman Britain that each year brings new discoveries that must be interpreted and added to the existing record. In 1913 Haverfield began the reporting of new discoveries by an annual summary, published as a Supplementary paper of the British Academy, itself barely a decade old, that would cover the archaeological, epigraphic and literary output of the year. This ambitious scheme perished in the First World War but the archaeological and epigraphic harvest was registered annually from 1921 in the *Journal of Roman Studies*. These summaries remain the starting point for much of the study of Roman Britain, not least because some finds of major importance were, for accidental or other reasons, not destined to be accorded full and definitive publication. The lack of an annual bibliography of Roman Britain is regrettable, though this function has been in part fulfilled by the excellent publications of the *Society of Antiquaries* and the *Council for British Archaeology*. Moreover, the range and diversity of publications that now impinge upon the study of Britain in the Roman era make the task of isolating the relevant items a near impossibility, and one which would be unlikely to repay the effort.

The annual summary was published in the *Journal* of the following year, until that for the year 1969 and succeeding years was transferred to *Britannia*, a journal of Romano-British and kindred studies founded by the Society in 1970, though not, it should be recalled, without some opposition. The venture proved a success and the most recent issue, Volume XIX for 1988, contains thirteen Papers, seven Notes, twenty-three Reviews, along with the Annual Summary 'Roman Britain in 1987', in a total of 549 pages. The first ten issues were edited by Sheppard Frere and next year (1990) Dr J.P. Wild will take charge as the fourth editor, in succession to the writer and Professor M. Todd. The archaeological section of the annual summary, 'Sites Explored', was for many years compiled at Oxford by Miss M.V. Taylor, once secretary to Haverfield, who was to edit the *Journal* for forty years and was elected President of the Society in the years 1955–58. By the time of her death in December 1963 the task of compiling the summary had fallen to D.R. Wilson, by then Research Assistant to Professor Richmond, who continued in this vital role until 1975 after more than fifteen years' service. During the Seventies and early Eighties the task of compiling the summaries was undertaken successively by Roger Goodburn, Francis Grew and Boris Rankov. The last five Summaries (1983–7) have been compiled by Sheppard Frere.

No one can dispute that the past thirty years have witnessed a significant increase of the database for Roman Britain. In the past two decades this increase has been even greater because of the increase in public funds available to rescue archaeology in all its forms. How to register or measure this growth of information in any way that is valid is not a simple matter but the accompanying Table is an attempt to do just that, albeit in a form that is both crude and superficial. Here the total numbers of individual site-entries, where new discoveries or the results of excavations are reported, are listed by the twenty-seven years from 1961 to 1987 by the nine regional divisions of the Roman province employed throughout the period. Attempts have been made to adjust the totals to compensate for the changes in local boundaries inflicted on the nation in the Seventies but doubtless some errors remain. In addition it must be emphasised that the unit of 'site' on which the Table is based varies enormously in scale, from the chance find of coins or pottery by a roadworker at or in the vicinity of a known Roman site up to the great cities of the province, including the City of London, where the period is notable for a sustained effort of large-scale excavation. Nevertheless the regional and provincial totals for the years do convey the

TABLE SHOWING NUMBERS OF 'SITES EXPLORED' IN ANNUAL SUMMARIES OF ROMAN BRITAIN 1961–1987

YEAR	61	62	63	64	65	66	67	68	69	70	71	72	73	74	75	76	77	78	79	80	81	82	83	84	85	86	87
WALES	5	9	3	6	11	10	9	11	11	10	8	6	12	9	12	8	20	14	15	11	15	14	22	16	14	12	16
SCOTLAND	8	6	12	6	9	8	11	9	7	8	13	10	15	16	17	15	25	15	10	15	18	17	18	17	12	9	15
HADRIAN'S WALL	4	4	2	2	0	2	6	5	8	8	8	8	13	4	18	14	17	8	8	10	10	4	7	8	9	7	10
NORTH	11	10	14	19	20	22	22	25	23	27	31	30	35	34	53	38	43	40	25	40	25	26	22	29	29	17	24
MIDLANDS	24	23	18	26	27	26	37	32	22	41	40	34	51	39	39	32	45	33	25	38	30	8	28	20	21	20	31
EAST ANGLIA	9	7	6	9	13	9	10	9	6	16	17	16	16	14	15	19	23	16	22	28	20	10	25	22	31	42	36
LONDON	2	3	2	1	2	1	3	2	3	5	6	4	4	9	7	7	2	7	5	5	5	3	2	3	3	3	3
SOUTHWEST	9	9	6	9	11	10	13	22	22	15	23	18	11	9	13	11	13	15	12	16	18	15	15	28	22	24	33
SOUTH	15	24	17	21	21	24	30	36	38	38	26	37	34	25	43	36	34	25	36	32	25	24	32	27	37	37	48
TOTAL	87	95	80	99	114	112	141	151	140	168	172	163	207	159	217	180	222	173	158	195	166	121	171	170	178	171	216

impression of a steady increase of activity during the Sixties, followed by some high levels of activity during the Seventies, with a slight falling-off in the Eighties. It must also be emphasised that there can be no real comparison for the level of activity at any specific site over the years. Again the City of London furnishes a good example. Here the Sixties saw some desperate attempts at salvage on major sites, most undertaken at a level of ludicrous impoverishment, whereas the Seventies and Eighties have seen one of the largest programmes of urban excavation to take place anywhere in the world, conducted by the Museum of London's Department of Urban Archaeology.

Before we take leave of this statistical digression it may prove of interest to look briefly at the recorded pattern of site finds and exploration in one of the nine regions on the Table, chosen at random. In the Northern Counties (the traditional counties Cumberland, Westmorland, Durham, Yorkshire, Lancashire, Derbyshire and Lincolnshire) a total of 835 site entries is recorded for the period 1961–87. If we follow the more precise definition of 'Roman' adopted by the gazetteers of the Ordnance Survey Map and the *Tabula Imperii Romani* the total of sites recorded is reduced to 471 entries. These may be listed by the following general categories, though some belong under more than one heading, along with (in parenthesis) the years for which discovery or excavation is recorded for each case.

LEGIONARY FORTRESS Chester, Cheshire (61–72, 74–8, 80–7)

MILITARY DEPOT Walton-le-Dale, Lancs. (81–3); Brompton-on-Swale?, N. Yorks. (68, 70–5, 83)

FORTS Ambleside, Cumbria (63, 76, 81–2); Binchester, Durham (71–2, 76– 80, 86); Blenner-hasset, Cumbria (84); Bowes, Durham (67, 77, 80); Brough-by-Bainbridge, N. Yorks. (61, 64, 68–9); Brough on Noe, Derbys. (65–6, 68–9, 83–4, 86); Brough under Stainmore, Cumbria (72); Brougham, Cumbria (66–7); Burghwallis, S. Yorks. (71–3); Castleford, W. Yorks. (66, 74, 77–8, 80–2, 84–5); Castleshaw, Gt. Manchester (63, 70, 77, 85, 87); Chesterfield, Derbys. (75–8, 84), Chester-le-Street, Durham (63–4, 68, 70, 77–9, 83); Doncaster, S. Yorks. (67, 70–2, 75–8); Ebchester, Durham (64, 72); Greta Bridge, N. Yorks. (73–4); Hardknot, Cumbria (64, 68); Hayton, N. Humberside (75); Ilkley, W. Yorks. (62, 65, 77, 82); Kirkby Thore, Cumbria (61, 78); Kirmington, Humberside (61, 85); Lancaster, Lancs. (70–2, 74–5, 77–8, 80, 83, 87); Lease Rigg, N. Yorks. (76, 78–80); Little Chester (Derby), Derbys. (62, 66, 68–9, 72–3, 79–80, 86–7); Low Burrow Bridge, Cumbria (76); Malton, N. Yorks. (70); Manchester, Gt. Manchester (65, 72, 75, 78–9, 81, 85, 87); Maryport, Cumbria (66); Melandra Castle, Derbys. (66, 69, 73–8, 80, 82, 84); Moresby, Cumbria (78); Newton Kyme, N. Yorks. (67); Newton-on-Trent, Lincs. (81, 84); Northwich, Cheshire (67–70, 72, 74, 82, 85, 87); Old Penrith, Cumbria (77); Papcastle, Cumbria, (62, 84); Piercebridge, Durham (64, 73–6, 80–2); Ravenglass, Cumbria (76); Ribchester, Lancs. (65, 69–70, 72, 74, 76–80); Slack, W. Yorks. (68–70).

FORTLET Apperley Dene, Northumb. (probably native settlement: 74–5).

SIGNAL STATION Stainmore Pass, N. Yorks. (75).

CAMP Brackenrigg, Cumbria (84); Malham, N. Yorks. (67); Plumpton Head, Cumbria (74).

CITY Aldborough, N. Yorks. (61, 64–7, 73–4); Brough on Humber, Humberside (61, 77–8, 85); Lincoln, Lincs. (61–87); York (fortress and colony), N. Yorks. (62–3, 65–9, 71–9, 80–7).

TOWN Ancaster, Lincs. (62–70, 73, 75); Caistor, Lincs. (66, 86); Catterick, N. Yorks. (75, 79, 84); Heronbridge, Cheshire (66); Horncastle, Lincs. (66, 68, 78, 85); Shiptonthorpe, Humberside (84–7); Wilderspool, Cheshire (66–7, 69, 74, 76).

SPA Buxton, Derbys. (74–5).

MINOR SETTLEMENT or POSTING STATION Bainesse Farm, N. Yorks. (82); Burgh-le-Marsh, Lincs. (75–80); Carsington, Derbys. (80, 83–4); Dragonby, Humberside (63–8, 70, 72); Hibaldstow, Humberside (75–7, 79); Middlewich, Cheshire (66, 68–72, 74–5); Navenby, Lincs. (65, 78); Owmby, Lincs. (78); Saltersford, Lincs. (79–80, 82); Sapperton, Lincs. (73, 75– 8, 80, 85–7); Sleaford, Lincs. (63, 79, 85); Tadcaster, N. Yorks. (85); Tilston, Cheshire (79–80, 82); Wetwang, Humberside (71–2, 76, 80); Winteringham, Humberside (64–5, 82).

VILLA Beadlam, N. Yorks. (66, 69, 72, 76); Barholm, Lincs. (65); Barrow-on-Humber, Humberside (82); Brantingham, Humberside (62); Collingham (Dalton Parlours), W. Yorks. (76–8, 80); Eaton-by-Tarporley, Cheshire (80–1); Holme House, N. Yorks. (70–2); Kirk Sink,

N. Yorks. (68, 73–5); Kirmond-le-Mire, Lincs. (75–6); Long Bennington, Lincs. (75–6); Rudston, Humberside (62–6, 70–1); Scampton, Lincs. (73); Walesby, Lincs. (77); Welton Wold, Humberside (71–6, 85, 87); Wharram Grange, N. Yorks. (80); Wharram-le-Street, N. Yorks. (78–9); Wharram Percy, N. Yorks. (71, 74, 76– 7, 80–4, 87); Winterton, Humberside (61, 63, 65, 67–76, 78–85).

TEMPLE or SHRINE Yardhope, Northumb. (76).

INDUSTRIAL SITE (Kilns, etc.) Barnetby Top, Humberside (75); Cantley, S. Yorks. (73); Claxby, Lincs. (73); Crambeck, N. Yorks. (64); Heckington, Lincs. (77); Heighington, Lincs. (76); Holbrook, Derbys. (62); Holme-upon-Spalding Moor, Humberside (67, 70–1, 84–6); Knaith, Lincs. (68); Lea, Lincs. (84–5); Market Rasen, Lincs. (65); Norton, N. Yorks. (63, 67, 75); Quernmore, Lancs. (70–2); Ropsley, Lincs. (79); Scalesceugh, Cumbria (70– 1); Shottlegate, Derbys. (70–1); Swanpool, Lincs. (63).

Of the 364 remaining entries relating to sites in the Northern Counties, a sizeable proportion relates to chance finds which have no obvious relation to any known site or to reports on the precise course of a known Roman road. Nevertheless more than half denote sites, some quite substantial, for which no formal definition is available in the categories currently employed. Perhaps the main task that lies ahead is to ensure that full care and attention is given to such sites, most likely to be farms or homesteads datable to the Roman era from a few finds but with no definitive Roman features. Some of these places, in material terms at least, lie on or beyond the margins of Roman Britain but for any real understanding of how the Roman social and economic order was constituted they can be of cardinal importance. Their exploitation and interpretation is now a major question confronting the archaeologists of Roman Britain and is likely to remain so for many years to come.

SELECT BIBLIOGRAPHY
(1960–88)

GENERAL

A.A. Barrett,	The literary classics in Roman Britain, *Britannia* ix (1978), 307–13
A. Birley,	*Life in Roman Britain* (London 1964)
A. Birley,	*The people of Roman Britain* (London 1979)
A. Birley,	*The fasti of Roman Britain* (Oxford 1981)
E. Birley,	The adherence of Britain to Hadrian, *Britannia* ix (1978), 243–5
T.F.C. Blagg & A.C. King (eds.),	*Military and civilian in Roman Britain* BAR 130 (1984)
G.C. Boon (ed.),	*Monographs and collections I Roman sites* (Cardiff 1978)
A.K. Bowman & J.D. Thomas,	*Vindolanda: the Latin writing tablets.* Britannia Monograph 4 (London 1983)
A.K. Bowman & J.D. Thomas,	New texts from Vindolanda, *Britannia* xviii (1987), 125–42
K. Branigan (ed.),	*Rome and the Brigantes* (Sheffield 1980)
D.C. Braund,	*Rome and the friendly king* (London 1984)
B. Burnham & H. Johnson,	*Invasion and response: the case of Roman Britain* BAR 73 (1979)
R.M. Butler (ed.),	*Soldier and civilian in Roman Yorkshire* (Leicester 1971)
J. Casey & R. Reece,	*Coins and the archaeologist* BAR 4 (1974)
R.G. Collingwood & I.A. Richmond,	*The archaeology of Roman Britain* (2nd.ed. London 1969)
R.G. Collingwood & R.P. Wright,	*The Roman inscriptions of Britain I* (Oxford 1965)
B. Cunliffe,	*The Regni* (London 1973)
W. Davies,	*An early Welsh microcosm* (London 1978)
A. Detsicas,	*The Cantiaci* (Gloucester 1983)
B. Dobson & J.C. Mann,	The Roman army in Britain and Britons in the Roman army. *Britannia* iv (1973), 191–205
R. Dunnett,	*The Trinovantes* (London 1975)
K.T. Erim,	A new relief showing Claudius and Britannia from Aphrodisias, *Britannia* xiii (1982), 277–87
H.P.R. Finberg, (ed.)	*The agrarian history of England and Wales I.11. Roman Britain* (by S. Applebaum: Cambridge 1972)
S.S. Frere,	*Britannia: a history of Roman Britain* (London 1967: 1972: 1987)
S.S. Frere & J.K. St. Joseph,	*Roman Britain from the air* (Cambridge 1983)
E.P. Hamp,	Social gradience in British spoken Latin, *Britannia* vi (1975), 150–62
W.S. Hanson & D.B. Campbell,	The Brigantes: from clientage to conquest, *Britannia* xvii (1986), 73–89
B.R. Hartley & L. Fitts,	*The Brigantes* (Gloucester 1988)
N. Higham & B. Jones,	*The Carvetii* (Gloucester 1985)

251

J.G.F. Hind,   The "Genounian" part of Britain, *Britannia* viii (1977), 229–34

P.A. Holder,   *The Roman army in Britain* (London 1982)
M.G. Jarrett & J.C. Mann,   The tribes of Wales, *Welsh Hist. Rev.* iv (1968), 161–71
M.J. Jones,   *Roman fort defences to AD 117* BAR 21 (1975)
J.C. Mann,   Spoken Latin in Britain as evidenced in the inscriptions, *Britannia* ii (1971), 218–24

I.D. Margary,   *Roman roads in Britain* (3rd. ed. London 1973)
D.J.P. Mason,   Prata legionis in Britain, *Britannia* xix (1988), 163–88
G.S. Maxwell & D.R. Wilson,   Air reconnaissance in Roman Britain, 1977–84, *Britannia* xviii (1987)

F. Millar,   Emperors, frontiers and foreign relations, 31 BC to AD 378, *Britannia* xiii (1982), 1–23

R.M. Ogilvie & I.A. Richmond,   *Cornelii Taciti de vita Agricolae* (Oxford 1967)
Ordnance Survey,   *The Antonine Wall* (1969)
Ordnance Survey,   *Hadrian's Wall* (2nd. ed. 1975)
Ordnance Survey,   *Roman Britain* (4th. ed. 1978)
H. Ramm,   *The Parisi* (London 1978)
R. Reece,   Roman coinage in Britain and the western Empire, *Britannia* iv (1973), 227–51

I.A. Richmond,   *Roman art and archaeology* (London 1969)
D.N. Riley,   Aerial reconnaissance of the West Riding magnesian limestone country, *Yorks. Arch. Journ.* xlv (1973), 210–14

A.L.F. Rivet,   *Town and country in Roman Britain* (2nd. ed. London 1964)
A.L.F. Rivet,   The British section of the Antonine Itinerary, *Britannia* i (1970), 34–82

A.L.F. Rivet,   Celtic names and Roman places, *Britannia* xi (1980), 1–19
A.L.F. Rivet & C. Smith,   *The place-names of Roman Britain* (London 1979)
A. Ross,   *Pagan Celtic Britain* (London 1967)
J.K. St. Joseph,   Air reconnaissance in Britain 1965–8, *JRS* lix (1969), 104–28
J.K. St. Joseph,   Air reconnaissance in Roman Britain, 1969–72, *JRS* lxiii (1973), 214–46

J.K. St. Joseph,   Air Reconnaissance in Roman Britain, 1973–6, *JRS* lxvii (1977), 125–61

P. Salway,   *Roman Britain* (Oxford 1981)
G. Simpson,   *Britons and the Roman army* (London 1964)
F.H. Thompson,   *Roman Cheshire* (Chester 1965)
M. Todd,   *The Coritani* (London 1973)
M. Todd,   *Roman Britain* (London 1981)
R.S.O. Tomlin,   Was ancient British Celtic ever a written language? Two texts from Roman Bath, *BBCS* xxxiv (1987), 18–25

VCH Essex III,   *Roman Essex* (London 1963)
J.S. Wacher,   *Roman Britain* (London 1978)
G. Webster,   *The Cornovii* (London 1975)
G. Webster,   *The Roman invasion of Britain* (London 1980)
G. Webster,   *Rome against Caratacus* (London 1981)
G. Webster (ed.),   *Fortress into city* (London 1988)
J.B. Whitwell,   *Roman Lincolnshire* (Lincoln 1972)
P.R. Wilson, R.F.J. Jones &   *Settlement and society in the Roman North* (Bradford 1984)
D.M. Evans (eds.),

EARLY MILITARY OCCUPATION

J.W. Brailsford,	*Hod Hill I. Antiquities from Hod Hill in the Durden Collection* (London 1962)
D. Braund,	Observations on Cartimandua, *Britannia* xv (1984), 1–6
G.B. Dannell & J.P. Wild,	*Longthorpe II: the military works depot* Britannia Monograph 8 (London 1987)
S.S. Frere,	Brandon Camp, Herefordshire, *Britannia* xviii (1987), 49–92
S.S. Frere & J.K. St. Joseph,	The Roman fortress of Longthorpe, *Britannia* v (1974), 1–129
A. Fox & W. Ravenhill,	Early Roman outposts on the north Devon coast, Old Burrow and Martinhoe, *Procs. Devon Arch. Soc.* xxiv (1966), 3–39
A. Fox & W. Ravenhill,	The Roman fort at Nanstallon, Cornwall, *Britannia* iii (1972), 56–111
K. Greene,	*Report on the excavations at Usk, 1965–76: the pre-Flavian fine wares* (Cardiff 1979)
W.S. Hanson,	*Agricola and the conquest of the North* (London 1987)
B. Hobley,	A Neronian-Vespasianic military site at "The Lunt", Baginton, Warwickshire, *Trans. Birmingham Arch. Soc.* lxxxiii (1969), 65–129
B. Hobley,	Excavation at "The Lunt" Roman military site, Baginton, Warwickshire, *Trans. Birmingham Arch. Soc.* lxxxv (1972), 7–92
B. Hobley,	Excavations at "The Lunt" Roman fort, Baginton, Warwickshire: final report, *Trans. Birmingham Arch. Soc.* lxxxvii (1975), 1–50
H.R. Hurst,	*Kingsholm* (Gloucester 1985)
G.D.B. Jones,	The Roman camps at Y Pigwn, *BBCS* xxii (1968), 100–103
W.H. Manning,	*Usk. The fortress excavations, 1968–71* (Cardiff 1981)
V.A. Maxfield,	Pre-Flavian forts and their garrisons, *Britannia* xvii (1986), 59–72
I.A. Richmond,	*Hod Hill. Excavations carried out between 1951 and 1958* (London 1968)
D.N. Riley,	Two new Roman military stations in mid-Nottinghamshire, *Britannia* xi (1980), 330–35
W. Rodwell,	The Roman fort at Great Chesterford, Essex, *Britannia* iii (1972), 290–93
M. Todd (ed.),	*The Roman fort at Great Casterton, Rutland* (Oxford 1968)
M. Todd,	Excavations at Hembury, Devon, 1980–83: a summary report, *Antiq. Journ.* lxiv (1984), 251–68
M. Todd,	The early Roman phase at Maiden Castle, *Britannia* xv (1984), 254–5
M. Todd,	The Roman fort at Bury Barton, Devonshire, *Britannia* xvi (1985), 49–56
M. Todd,	Oppida and the Roman army. A review of recent evidence, *Oxford Journ. Archaeology* iv (1985), 187–99
J.S. Wacher & A. MacWhirr,	*Early Roman occupation at Cirencester* (Cirencester 1982)
G. Webster,	The military situations in Britain between AD 43 and 71, *Britannia* i (1970), 179–97
G. Webster,	*Boudica* (London 1978)
G. Webster,	Final report on the excavations of the Roman fort at Waddon Hill, Stoke Abbott, 1963–69, *Procs. Dorset Nat. Hist. & Arch. Soc.* ci (1981), 51–90
D.R. Wilson,	A first century fort near Gosbecks, *Britannia* viii (1977), 185–8

THE ARMY AND THE FRONTIERS

L. Allason-Jones & M.C. Bishop,   *Excavations at Roman Corbridge. The hoard* HBMC Arch.
                                   Report 7 (London 1988)
D. Baatz,   *Kastell Hesselbach* (Berlin 1973)
R.L. Bellhouse &   The Trajanic fort at Kirkbride: the terminus of the Stanegate
G.G.S. Richardson,   frontier, *CW* lxxxii (1982), 35–50
P.T. Bidwell,   *The Roman fort at Vindolanda* HBMC Arch. Report 1 (London
                                   1985)
A.R. Birley,   Petillius Cerealis and the conquest of Brigantia, *Britannia* iv
                                   (1973), 179–90
A.R. Birley,   Virius Lupus, *Arch. Ael.*4 (1973), 179–89
E. Birley,   *Research on Hadrian's Wall* (Kendal 1961)
R. Birley,   Housesteads Vicus, *Arch. Ael.*4 xl (1962), 117–34
R. Birley,   Excavation of the Roman fortress at Carpow, Perthshire,
                                   1961–2, *PSAS* xcvi (1962–3), 184–207
R. Birley,   Excavations at Chesterholm-Vindolanda, *Arch. Ael.*4 xlviii
                                   (1970), 97–155
R. Birley,   *Vindolanda: a Roman frontier post on Hadrian's Wall* (London
                                   1977)
D.J. Breeze,   The Roman fortlet at Barburgh Mill, Dumfriesshire, *Bri-
                                   tannia* v (1974), 145–7
D.J. Breeze,   The abandonment of the Antonine Wall: its date and impli-
                                   cations, *Scottish Arch. Forum* vii (1975), 67–80
D.J. Breeze,   *The northern frontiers of Roman Britain* (London 1982)
D.J. Breeze, J. Close-Brooks &   Soldiers' burials at Camelon, Stirlingshire, 1922 and 1975,
J.N.G. Ritchie,   *Britannia* vii (1976), 73–95
D.J. Breeze & B. Dobson,   Fort types on Hadrian's Wall, *Arch. Ael.*4 xlvii (1969), 15–32
D.J. Breeze & B. Dobson,   Roman military deployment in north Britain, *Britannia* xvi
                                   (1985), 1–19
D.J. Breeze & B. Dobson,   *Hadrian's Wall* (3rd. edition London 1987)
G. Brodribb & H. Cleere,   The Classis Britannica bath-house at Beauport Park, East
                                   Sussex, *Britannia* xix (1988), 217–74
W.E. Boyd,   Palaeobotanical evidence from Mollins, *Britannia* xvi (1985),
                                   37–48
W. Bulmer,   The provisioning of Roman forts: a reappraisal of ration
                                   storage, *Arch. Ael.*4 xlvii (1969), 7–13
P.J. Casey,   Excavations at Brecon Gaer, 1970, *Arch. Camb.* cxx (1971),
                                   91–101
P.J. Casey & M. Savage,   The coins from the excavations at High Rochester in 1852
                                   and 1855, *Arch. Ael.*5 viii (1980), 75–87
D. Charlesworth,   The commandant's house, Housesteads, *Arch. Ael.*5 iii
                                   (1975), 17–42
D. Charlesworth,   The hospital, Housesteads, *Arch. Ael.*5 iv (1976), 17–30
D. Charlesworth,   Roman Carlisle, *Arch. Journ.* cxxxv (1978), 115–37
R.W. Davies,   Roman Wales and Roman military practice-camps, *Arch.
                                   Camb.* cxvii (1968), 103–20
R.W. Davies,   The Roman military diet, *Britannia* ii (1971), 122–42
R.W. Davies,   Singulares and Roman Britain, *Britannia* vii (1976), 134–44
C.M. Daniels (ed.),   *Handbook to the Roman Wall* (13th. edition Newcastle 1978)
C. Daniels & G.D.B. Jones,   The Roman camps on Llandrindod Common, *Arch. Camb.*
                                   (1969), 124–33
B. Dobson,   Roman Durham, *Trans. Arch. & Architect. Soc. Durham &
                                   Northumberland* i–ii (1968–70), 31–43

B. Dobson,   The function of Hadrian's Wall, *Arch. Ael.*5 xiv (1986), 1–30
G.H. Donaldson,   Roman military signalling on the North British frontiers, *Arch.Ael.*5 xiii (1986), 19–24
G.H. Donaldson,   Signalling communications and the Roman Imperial army, *Britannia* xix (1988), 349–56
J.N. Dore & J.P. Gillam,   *The Roman fort at South Shields* (Newcastle 1979)
D.P. Dymond,   Roman bridges on Dere Street, County Durham, *Arch. Journ.* cxviii (1961), 136–46
W. Eck,   Zum Ende der legio IX Hispana, *Chiron* ii (1972), 459–62
B.J.N. Edwards & P.V. Webster,   *Ribchester excavations Part I: excavations within the fort* (Cardiff 1985)
S.S. Frere,   The Flavian frontier in Scotland, *Scottish Arch. Forum* xii (1980), 89–97
A.P. Gentry,   *Roman military stone-built granaries in Britain*, BAR 32 (1976)
J.P. Gillam,   The frontier after Hadrian – a history of the problem, *Arch. Ael.*5 ii (1974), 1–15
J.P. Gillam,   Possible changes in plan in the course of construction of the Antonine Wall, *Scottish Arch. Forum* vii (1975), 51–6
J.P. Gillam,   *The Roman forts at Corbridge*, Arch. Ael.5 v (1977), 47–74
J.P. Gillam & J.C. Mann,   The northern British frontier from Antoninus Pius to Caracalla, *Arch. Ael.*4 xlviii (1970), 1–44
W.S. Hanson,   Roman campaigns north of the Forth-Clyde isthmus, *PSAS* cix (1977–8), 140–50
W.S. Hanson,   The organization of the Roman military timber supply, *Britannia* ix (1978), 293–305
W.S. Hanson, C.M. Daniels,   The Agricolan supply-base at Red House, Corbridge, *Arch.
J.N., Dore & J.P. Gillam,   Ael.*5 vii (1979), 1–97
W.S. Hanson & G.S. Maxwell,   An Agricolan praesidium on the Forth-Clyde isthmus (Mollins, Strathclyde), *Britannia* xi (1980), 43–7
W.S. Hanson & G.S. Maxwell,   *Rome's North-West frontier* (Edinburgh 1983)
W.S. Hanson & G.S. Maxwell,   Minor enclosures on the Antonine Wall at Wilderness Plantation, *Britannia* xiv (1983), 227–43
B.R. Hartley,   The Roman fort at Bainbridge, *Procs. Leeds Phil. & Lit. Soc.* xi (1960), 107–31
B.R. Hartley,   The Roman fort at Ilkley, *Procs. Leeds Phil. & Lit. Soc.* xiii (1966), 23–72
B.R. Hartley,   The Roman occupation of Scotland: the evidence of the samian ware, *Britannia* iii (1972), 1–55
A.H.A. Hogg,   Pen Llystyn: a Roman fort and other remains, *Arch. Journ.* cxxv (1968), 101–92
R. Hunneysett,   The milecastles of Hadrian's Wall: an alternative identification, *Arch. Ael.*5 viii (1980), 95–108
M.G. Jarrett,   Legio II Augusta in Britain, *Arch. Camb.* cxiii (1964), 47–63
M.G. Jarrett,   Early Roman campaigns in Wales, *Arch. Journ.* cxxi (1965), 23– 39
M.G. Jarrett,   Legio XX Valeria Victrix in Britain, *Arch. Camb.* cxvii (1968), 77–91
M.G. Jarrett,   *Maryport, Cumbria: a Roman fort and its garrison* (Kendal 1976)
M.G. Jarrett & J.C. Mann,   Britain from Agricola to Gallienus, *Bonner Jahrbücher* clxx (1970), 178–210
I. Jobey,   Housesteads ware: a Frisian tradition on Hadrian's Wall, *Arch. Ael.*5 vii (1979), 127–44
S. Johnson,   Excavations at Hayton Roman fort, 1975, *Britannia* ix (1978), 57–114

G.D.B. Jones,	The western extension of Hadrian's Wall: Bowness to Cardurnock, *Britannia* vii (1976), 236–43
G.D.B. Jones,	The Solway frontier; interim report 1976–81, *Britannia* xiii (1982), 283–5
G.D.B. Jones & S. Grealey,	*Roman Manchester* (Manchester 1974)
G.D.B. Jones & D.C.A. Shotter,	*Roman Lancaster* (Manchester 1988)
L.J.F. Keppie,	The building of the Antonine Wall: archaeological and epigraphic evidence, *PSAS* cv (1972–4), 151–65
L.J.F. Keppie,	*Roman distance slabs from the Antonine Wall* (Glasgow 1979)
L.J.F. Keppie,	The Antonine Wall 1960–80, *Britannia* xiii (1982), 91–111
L.J.F. Keppie & J.J. Walker,	Fortlets on the Antonine Wall at Seabegs Wood, Kinneil and Cleddans, *Britannia* xii (1981), 143–62
L.J.F. Keppie & J.J. Walker,	Auchendavy Roman fort and settlement, *Britannia* xvi (1985), 29–35
W.H. Manning,	Roman military timber granaries in Britain, *Saalburg Jahrbuch* xxxii (1975), 105–29
W.H. Manning & I.R. Scott,	Roman timber military gateways in Britain and on the German frontier, *Britannia* x (1979), 19–62
V.A. Maxfield,	The Flavian fort at Camelon, *Scottish Arch. Forum* xii (1980), 69–78
G.S. Maxwell,	Excavations at the Roman fort at Crawford, Lanarkshire, *PSAS* civ (1971–2), 147–200
G.S. Maxwell,	Excavation at the Roman fort of Bothwellhaugh, 1967–8, *Britannia* vi (1975), 20–35
G.S. Maxwell,	A Roman timber tower at Beattock Summit, *Britannia* vii (1976), 33–8
G.S. Maxwell,	Agricola's campaigns: the evidence of the temporary camps, *Scottish Arch. Forum* xii (1980), 25–54
G.S. Maxwell,	New frontiers: the Roman fort at Doune and its possible significance, *Britannia* xv (1984), 217–23
G.S. Maxwell,	Fortlets and distance slabs on the Antonine Wall, *Britannia* xvi (1985), 25–8
R. Miket,	*The Roman fort at South Shields: excavation of the defences, 1977–81* (Newcastle 1983)
L. Murray Threipland,	Excavations at Caerleon, 1966. Barracks in the north corner, *Arch. Camb.* cxvi (1967), 23–56
V.E. Nash-Williams,	*The Roman frontier in Wales* (2nd. edition by M.G. Jarrett Cardiff 1969)
B. Philp,	*The excavation of the Roman forts at Dover, 1970–77* (Dover 1981)
L.F. Pitts & J.K. St. Joseph,	*Inchtuthil: the Roman legionary fortress.* Britannia Monograph 6 (London 1985)
T.W. Potter,	The Biglands milefortlet and the Cumberland coast defences, *Britannia* viii (1977), 149–83
T.W. Potter,	*The Romans in North-West England: excavations at the Roman forts of Ravenglass, Watercrook and Bowness on Solway* (Kendal 1979)
A. & V. Rae,	The Roman fort at Cramond, Edinburgh, *Britannia* v (1974), 163–224
N.B. Rankov,	M. Oclatinius Adventus in Britain, *Britannia* xviii (1987), 243–9
N.J. Reed,	The fifth year of Agricola's campaigns, *Britannia* ii (1971), 143–8

N.J. Reed,	The Scottish campaigns of Septimius Severus, *PSAS* cvii (1975– 6), 92–102
A.S. Robertson,	*The Roman fort at Castledykes* (Edinburgh 1964)
A.S. Robertson,	Roman finds from non-Roman sites in Scotland, *Britannia* i (1970)̸, 198–226
A.S. Robertson,	Roman "signal stations" on the Gask Ridge, *Trans. Perthshire Soc. Nat. Sci.* (1974), 14–29
A.S. Robertson,	*Birrens (Blatobulgium)* (Edinburgh 1975)
A.S. Robertson,	Roman coins found in Scotland, 1971–82, *PSAS* cxiii (1983), 424–6
A.S. Robertson, M. Scott & L. Keppie,	*Bar Hill, a Roman fort and its finds* BAR 16 (1975)
J.K. St. Joseph,	The camps at Ardoch, Stracathro and Ythan Wells: recent excavations, *Britannia* i (1970), 163–78
J.K. St. Joseph,	The camp at Durno, Aberdeenshire, and the site of Mons Graupius, *Britannia* ix (1978), 271–87
P. Salway,	*The frontier people of Roman Britain* (Cambridge 1965)
D.C.A. Shotter,	The Roman occupation of north-west England: the coin evidence, *CW* lxxx (1980), 1–15
F.G. Simpson,	*Watermills and military works on Hadrian's Wall: excavations in Northumberland 1907–13* (Kendal 1977)
G. Simpson,	The close of period IA on Hadrian's Wall and some Gaulish potters, *Arch. Ael.*4 xlix (1971), 109–18
G. Simpson,	Haltwhistle Burn, Corstopitum and the Antonine Wall: a reconsideration, *Britannia* v (1974), 317–39
M.P. Speidel,	The Chattan war, the Brigantian revolt and the loss of the Antonine Wall, *Britannia* xviii (1987), 233–7
K.A. Steer,	Excavations at Mumrills Roman fort, *PSAS* xciv (1960–1), 97–9
G.R. Stephens,	Military aqueducts in Roman Britain, *Arch. Journ.* cxlii (1985), 216–36
C.F. Stevens,	*The building of Hadrian's Wall* (Kendal 1966)
F.H. Thompson,	The excavation of the Roman amphitheatre at Chester, *Archaeologia* cv (1975), 127–239
M. Todd,	The Falkirk hoard of denarii: trade or subsidy? *PSAS* cxv (1985), 229–32
C.V. Walthew,	Possible standard units of measurement in Roman military planning, *Britannia* xii (1981), 15–35
D.A. Welsby,	*The Roman military defence of the British provinces in its later phases* BAR ci (1982)
D.R. Wilson,	Defensive outworks of Roman forts in Britain, *Britannia* xv (1984), 51–61
R.P. Wright,	Carpow and Caracalla, *Britannia* v (1974), 289–92
J.D. Zienkiewicz,	*The legionary fortress baths at Caerleon* (Cardiff 1986)

TOWNS AND CITIES

A. Baker,	Viroconium. A study of the defences from aerial reconnaissance, *Trans. Shropshire Arch. Soc.* lviii (1971), 197–202
P.A. Barker,	Excavations of the Baths Basilica at Wroxeter, *Britannia* vi (1975), 106–17
P. Bennett, S.S. Frere & S. Stow,	*Excavations at Canterbury Castle. The Archaeology of Canterbury* (Maidstone 1982)

P.T. Bidwell,	*The legionary bath-house and basilica and forum at Exeter* (Exeter 1979)
G.C. Boon,	Belgic and Roman Silchester: the excavations of 1954–8, *Archaeologia* cii (1969), 1–82
G.C. Boon,	*Silchester: the Roman town of Calleva* (Newton Abbot 1974)
G.C. Clarke,	*Pre-Roman and Roman Winchester: the Roman cemetery at Lankhills* (Oxford 1976)
P. Corder, (ed.),	*The Roman town and villa at Great Casterton, Rutland. Third Report* (Nottingham 1961)
P. Crummy,	Colchester, the Roman fortress and the development of the colonia, *Britannia* viii (1977), 65–105
P. Crummy,	The origins of some major Romano-British towns, *Britannia* xiii (1982), 125–34
P. Crummy,	*Excavations at Lion Walk, Balkerne Lane and Middleborough, Colchester* (Colchester 1984)
B.W. Cunliffe,	*Roman Bath*. Research Report of the Society of Antiquaries 24 (Oxford 1969)
B. Cunliffe,	*Excavations at Fishbourne, 1961–69*. Research Report of the Society of Antiquaries 26 (London 1971)
M.J. Darling & M.J. Jones,	Early settlement at Lincoln, *Britannia* xix (1988), 1–58
B. Dix & S. Taylor,	Excavations at Bannaventa (Whilton Lodge, Northants.), *Britannia* xix (1988), 299–339
P.J. Drury,	The temple of Claudius at Colchester reconsidered, *Britannia* xv (1984), 7–50
A. Down & M. Rule,	*Chichester excavations I* (Chichester 1971)
A. Down,	*Chichester excavations II* (Chichester 1974)
A. Down,	*Chichester excavations III* (Chichester 1978)
R.P. Duncan-Jones,	Length-units in Roman town-planning, *Britannia* xi (1980), 127–33
R. Dunnett,	The excavation of the Roman theatre at Gosbecks, *Britannia* ii (1971), 27–47
S. Esmonde-Cleary,	*Extra-mural areas of Romano-British towns*, BAR 169 (1987)
D. Fishwick,	Templum Divum Claudium Constitutum, *Britannia* iii, (1972), 164–81
S.S. Frere,	The excavations at Dorchester-on-Thames, 1962, *Arch. Journ.* cxix (1962), 114–49
S.S. Frere,	The Roman theatre at Canterbury, *Britannia* i (1970), 83–113
S.S. Frere,	The forum and baths at Caistor by Norwich, *Britannia* ii (1971), 1–26
S.S. Frere & S. Stow,	*Excavations on the Roman and medieval defences of Canterbury. The Archaeology of Canterbury II* (Maidstone 1982)
S.S. Frere,	*Verulamium excavations I*. Research Report of the Society of Antiquaries 28 (London 1972), II (London 1983)
S.S. Frere,	Excavations at Dorchester on Thames, 1963, *Arch. Journ.* cxli (1984), 91–174
S.S. Frere,	British urban defences in earthwork, *Britannia* xv (1984), 63–74
M.G. Fulford,	*Silchester defences, 1974–80*. Britannia Monograph 5 (London 1984)
F. Grew & B. Hobley (eds.).	*Roman urban topography in Britain and the western Empire*, CBA Research Report 59 (London 1985)
W.F. Grimes,	*The excavation of Roman and medieval London* (London 1968)
M. Hebditch & J.E. Mellor,	The forum and basilica of Roman Leicester, *Britannia* iv (1973), 1–83

H.R. Hurst,   *Gloucester. The Roman and later defences* (Gloucester 1986)
G.D.B. Jones,   Excavations at Northwich, *Arch. Journ.* cxxviii (1972), 31–77
M.J. Jones,   *The defences of the upper enclosure (Lincoln). The archaeology of Lincoln* (London 1980)
M.J. Jones & B.J. Gilmour,   Lincoln, principia and forum, *Britannia* xi (1980), 61–72
A. MacWhirr, L. Viner &   *Romano-British Cemeteries at Cirencester* (Cirencester 1982)
C. Wells,
A. MacWhirr,   *Houses in Roman Cirencester* (Cirencester 1982)
J. Maloney & B. Hobley, (eds.), *Roman urban defences in the West.* CBA Research Report 51 (London 1983)
P.R.V. Marsden,   *A Roman ship from Blackfriars, London* (London 1965)
P. Marsden,   *Roman London* (London 1980)
P. Marsden,   *The Roman forum site in London* (London 1987)
R. Merrifield,   *The Roman city of London* (London 1965)
R. Merrifield,   *London. City of the Romans* (London 1983)
L. Miller, J. Schofield &   *The Roman quay at St. Magnus House, London* (London 1986)
M. Rhodes,
G. Milne,   *The port of Roman London* (London 1985)
R. Niblett,   *Sheepen: an early Roman industrial site at Camulodunum* CBA Research Report 57 (London 1985)
F.A. Pritchard,   Ornamental stonework from Roman London, *Britannia* xvii (1986), 169–89
W. Rodwell & T. Rowley (eds.), *The small towns of Roman Britain* BAR 15 (1975)
R.F. Smith,   *Roadside settlements in lowland Roman Britain* BAR 157 (1987)
S. Sommer,   *The military vici in Roman Britain* BAR 129 (1984)
G.R. Stephens,   Civic aqueducts in Britain, *Britannia* xvi (1985), 197–208
F.H. Thompson & J.B. Whitwell, The gates of Roman Lincoln, *Archaeologia* civ (1973), 129–207
M. Todd,   The small towns of Roman Britain, *Britannia* i (1970), 114–30
J.S. Wacher,   *Excavations at Brough-on-Humber*, Research Report of the Society of Antiquaries 25 (London 1969)
J.S. Wacher,   *The towns of Roman Britain* (London 1975)
C.V. Walthew,   The town house and the villa house in Roman Britain, *Britannia* vi (1975), 189–205
C.V. Walthew,   Houses, defences and status: the towns of Roman Britain in the second half of the second century AD, *Oxford Journ. Archaeology* ii (1983), 213–24
L.P. Wenham,   *The Romano-British cemetery at Trentholme Drive, York* (London 1968)

RURAL SETTLEMENT

J.R.L. Allen & M.G. Fulford,   The Wentlooge Level: a Romano-British saltmarsh reclamation in south-east Wales, *Britannia* xvii (1986), 91–117
O. Bedwin,   Excavations at Chanctonbury Ring, *Britannia* xi (1980), 173–222
E.W. Black,   The Roman villa at Darenth, *Arch. Cant.* xcvii (1981), 159–83
E.W. Black,   *The Roman villa in South-East England* BAR 171 (1987)
K. Branigan,   *Latimer* (Dorchester 1971)
K. Branigan,   *Gatcombe Roman villa* BAR (1977)
A.C.C Brodribb, A.R. Hands &   *Excavations at Shakenoak Farm, near Wilcote, Oxfordshire I* (1968); *II*(1969); *III*(1970); *IV*(1973); *V*(1978)
D.R. Walker,
R.A. Brown,   The Iron Age and Romano-British settlement at Woodcock Hall, Saham Toney, Norfolk, *Britannia* xvii (1986), 1–58

J.C. Chapman & H. Mytum (eds.),	*Settlement in north Britain 1000 BC to AD 1000* BAR 112 (1983)
B. Clarke,	Calidon and the Caledonian forest, *BBCS* xxiii (1969), 191–201
G. Clarke,	The Roman villa at Woodchester, *Britannia* xiii (1982), 197–228
S.S. Frere,	The Bignor villa, *Britannia* xiii (1982), 135–96
R. Goodburn,	*The Roman villa. Chedworth* (London 1972)
T. Gregory & D. Gurney,	*Excavations at Thornham, Warham, Wighton and Caistor, Norfolk*, East Anglian Archaeology Monograph 30 (Norwich 1986)
D. Gurney,	*Settlement, religion and industry on the Fen-edge; three Romano-British sites in Norfolk.* East Anglian Archaeology Monograph 31 (Norwich 1986)
W.S. Hanson &	Forests, forts and fields: a discussion, *Scottish Arch. Forum* xii (1980), 98–113
N.J. Higham & G.D.B. Jones,	Frontiers, forts and farmers, Cumbrian aerial survey 1974, *Arch. Journ.* cxxxii (1975), 16–53
N.J. Higham & G.D.B. Jones,	The excavation of two Romano-British farm sites in North Cumbria, *Britannia* xiv (1983), 45–72
A.H.A. Hogg,	The Llantwit Major villa: a reconsideration of the evidence, *Britannia* v (1974), 225–50
D.A. Jackson & T.M. Ambrose,	Excavations at Wakerley, *Britannia* ix (1978), 115–242
M.G. Jarrett & S. Wrathmell,	*Whitton. An Iron Age and Roman farmstead in South Glamorgan* (Cardiff 1981)
G. Jobey,	Hillforts and settlements in Northumberland, *Arch. Ael.*4 xliii (1965), 21–64
R. Leech,	The excavation of a Romano-British farmstead and cemetery at Bradley Hill, Somerton, Somerset, *Britannia* xii (1981), 177–252
M. Lloyd-Jones,	*Society and settlement in Wales and the Marches* BAR 121 (1984)
L. Macinnes,	Brochs and the Roman occupation of lowland Scotland, *PSAS* cxiv (1984), 235–49
D.F. Mackreth,	Excavation of an Iron Age and Roman enclosure at Werrington, Cambridgeshire, *Britannia* xix (1988), 59–151
G.W. Meates,	*The Roman villa at Lullingstone, I The site* (Chichester 1979); *II* (Maidstone 1988)
D. Miles (ed.),	*The Romano-British countryside* BAR 103 (1982)
J.H. Money,	The Iron Age hill-fort and Romano-British iron-working settlement at Garden Hill, Sussex: interim report on excavations, 1968–76, *Britannia* viii (1977), 339–50
D.S. Neal,	*The excavation of the Roman villa in Gadebridge Park, Hemel Hempstead, 1963–8.* Research Report of the Society of Antiquaries 31 (London 1974)
D.S. Neal,	Northchurch, Boxmoor and Hemel Hempstead Station: the excavation of three Roman buildings in the Bulbourne valley, *Herts. Arch.* iv (1976), 1–135
A.J. Parker,	The birds of Roman Britain, *Oxford Journ. Archaeology* vii (1988), 197–226
J. Percival,	*The Roman villa* (London 1976)
C.W. Phillips (ed.),	*The Fenland in Roman times* (London 1970)
B.J. Philp,	*Excavations at Faversham, 1965* (Crawley 1968)
B.J. Philp,	*Excavations in West Kent, 1960–70* (Dover 1973)

T.W. Potter,	The Roman occupation of the central Fenland, *Britannia* xii (1981), 79–133
P.A. Rahtz & E. Greenfield,	*Excavations at Chew Valley Lake* (London 1977)
A.L.F. Rivet (ed.),	*The Roman villa in Britain* (London 1969)
W.J. & K.A. Rodwell,	*Rivenhall: investigations of a villa, church and village, 1950–77.* CBA Research Report 55 (London 1986)
RCHM (England),	West Park Roman villa, Rockbourne, Hampshire, *Arch. Journ.* cxl (1983), 129–50
B.B. Simmons,	The Lincolnshire Car Dyke, *Britannia* x (1979), 183–96
J.T. Smith,	Romano-British aisled houses, *Arch. Journ.* cxx (1963), 1–30
I.M. Stead,	*Excavations at Winterton Roman villa and other Roman sites in North Lincolnshire* (London 1976)
C. Thomas (ed.),	*Rural settlement in Roman Britain.* CBA Research Report 7 (London 1966)
M. Todd, (ed.),	*Studies in the Romano-British villa* (Leicester 1978)
J. Turner,	The environment of north-east England during Roman times as shown by pollen analysis, *Journ. Arch. Sci.* vi (1979), 285–90
G.J. Wainwright,	The excavation of a fortified settlement at Walesland Rath, Pembrokeshire, *Britannia* ii (1971), 48–108
J.P. Wild,	Roman settlement in the lower Nene valley, *Arch. Journ.* cxxxi (1974), 140–70
T. Williamson,	The Roman countryside: settlement and agriculture in N.E. Essex, *Britannia* xv (1984), 225–30
D. Williams,	Viticulture in Roman Britain, *Britannia* viii (1977), 327–34
D.R. Wilson,	Romano-British villas from the air, *Britannia* v (1974), 251–61

INDUSTRIES AND CRAFTS

A.C. & A.S. Anderson,	*Roman pottery research in Britain and North-West Europe* BAR S 123 (1981)
T.F.C. Blagg,	Tools and techniques of the Roman stonemason in Britain, *Britannia* vii (1976), 15–72
T.F.C. Blagg,	Roman civil and military architecture in the province of Britain. Aspects of patronage, influence and craft organisation, *World Arch.* xii (1980), 27–42
P.C. Buckland, J.R. Magilton & M.J. Dolby,	The Roman pottery industries of South Yorkshire, *Britannia* xi (1980), 145–64
D. Charlesworth & J.H. Thornton,	Leather found in Mediobogdum, the Roman fort of Hardknott, *Britannia* iv (1973), 141–52
H. Cleere,	The Roman iron industry of the Weald and its connexions with the Classis Britannica, *Arch. Journ.* cxxxi (1974), 171–99
H. Cleere & D.W. Crossley,	*The iron industry of the Weald* (Leicester 1985)
H.E.M. Cool,	A Romano-British gold workshop of the second century, *Britannia* xvii (1986), 231–7
N. Crummy,	Bone-working at Colchester, *Britannia* xii (1981), 277–85
A. Detsicas (ed.),	*Current research in Romano-British coarse pottery.* CBA Research Report 10 (London 1973)
M.G. Fulford,	*New Forest Roman pottery* BAR 17 (1975)
M. Fulford & J. Bird,	Imported pottery from Germany in the late Roman period, *Britannia* vi (1975), 171–81
C.M. Guido,	*Prehistoric and Roman glass beads in Britain and Ireland* Research Report of the Society of Antiquaries 35 (London 1978)

M.R. Hull,	*The Roman potters' kilns of Colchester.* Research Report of the Society of Antiquaries 21 (Oxford 1963)
D.A. Jackson, L. Biek & B.F. Dix,	A Roman lime kiln at Weekley, Northants., *Britannia* iv (1973), 128–40
A.J. Lawson,	Shale and jet objects from Silchester, *Archaeologia* cv (1976), 241–75
M. MacGregor,	*Early Celtic art in north Britain: a study of decorative metalwork from the third century BC to the third century AD* (Leicester 1976)
W.H. Manning,	Ironwork hoards in Iron Age and Roman Britain, *Britannia* iii (1972), 224–50
W.H. Manning,	*Catalogue of Romano-British ironwork in the Museum of Antiquities, Newcastle upon Tyne* (Newcastle upon Tyne 1976)
K.S. Painter,	Two Roman silver ingots from Kent, *Arch. Cant.* xcvii (1981), 201–7
D.P.S. Peacock,	*Pottery in the Roman world* (London 1982)
D.P.S. Peacock & D.F. Williams,	*Amphorae in the Roman economy* (London 1986)
E.J. Phillips,	A workshop of Roman sculptors at Carlisle, *Britannia* vii (1976), 101–8
S. Rees,	*Agricultural implements in prehistoric and Roman Britain* BAR 69 (1979)
M.J. Rhodes,	Inscriptions on leather waste from Roman London, *Britannia* xviii (1987), 173–81
B. Richardson & P.A. Tyers,	North Gaulish pottery in Britain, *Britannia* xv (1984), 133–41
R.B.K. Stevenson,	Romano-British glass bangles, *Glasgow Arch. Journ.* iv (1976), 45–54
N. Sunter & P.J. Woodward,	*Romano-British industries in Purbeck* (Dorchester 1987)
V.G. Swan,	Oare reconsidered and the origins of Savernake ware in Wiltshire, *Britannia* vi (1975), 37–61
V.G. Swan,	*The pottery kilns of Roman Britain* (London 1984)
P.V. Webster,	More British samian ware by the Aldgate-Pulborough potter, *Britannia* vi (1975), 163–70
P.V. Webster,	Severn valley ware: a preliminary study, *TBGAS* xciv (1976), 18–46
D.A. Welsby,	Pottery production at Muncaster, Eskdale, in the second century AD, *Britannia* xvi (1985), 127–40
G.C. Whittick,	Roman lead-mining on Mendip and in North Wales, *Britannia* xiii (1982), 113–23
J.H. Williams,	Roman building materials in south-east England, *Britannia* ii (1971), 166–95
P.J. Woods,	Types of late Belgic and early Romano-British pottery-kilns in the Nene valley, *Britannia* v (1974), 262–81
C.J. Young,	*Oxfordshire Roman pottery* BAR 43 (1977)

RELIGION AND ART

J.P. Alcock,	Celtic water cults in Roman Britain, *Arch. Journ.* cxxii (1965), 1–12
J.P. Alcock,	Classical religious belief and burial practice in Roman Britain, *Arch. Journ.* cxxxvii (1980), 50–85
A. Apsimon,	The Roman temple on Brean Down, Somerset, *Procs. Univ. Bristol Speleological Soc.* x (1965), 195–216
S. Barnard,	The matres of Roman Britain, *Arch. Journ.* cxlii (1985), 237–45

G.C. Boon,	A temple of Mithras at Caernarvon-Segontium, *Arch. Camb.* cix (1960), 136–72
G.C. Boon,	Sarapis and Tutela: a Silchester coincidence, *Britannia* iv (1973), 107–14
P.D.C. Brown,	The church at Richborough, *Britannia* ii (1971), 225–31
D.B. Charlton & M.M. Mitcheson,	Yardhope. A shrine to Cocidius? *Britannia* xiv (1983), 143–53
N.E. France & B.M. Gobel,	*The Romano-British temple at Harlow* (Gloucester 1985)
S.S. Frere,	The Silchester church: the excavation by Sir Ian Richmond in 1961, *Archaeologia* cv (1975), 277–302
C.J. Guy,	Roman circular lead tanks in Britain, *Britannia* xii (1981), 271–6
E. & J.R. Harris,	*The oriental cults in Roman Britain* (Leiden 1963)
M. Henig,	*A corpus of Roman engraved gemstones from British sites*, BAR 8 (1974)
M. Henig,	*Religion in Roman Britain* (London 1984)
R.F. Jessup,	Roman barrows in Britain, *Latomus* lviii (1962), 853–67
C. Johns & T. Potter,	*The Thetford treasure: Roman jewellery and coins* (London 1983)
G.M. Knocker,	Excavation in Colleyweston Great Wood, Northants, *Arch. Journ.* cxxii (1965), 52–72
R. Leech,	The excavation of a Romano-Celtic temple and later cemetery on Lamyatt Beacon, Somerset, *Britannia* xvii (1986), 259–328
M.J.T. Lewis,	*Temples in Roman Britain* (Cambridge 1966)
R. Ling, N. Davey,	*Wall-painting in Roman Britain* Britannia Monograph 3 (London 1981)
R. Ling,	The Seasons in Romano-British mosaic pavements, *Britannia* xiv (1983), 13–22
K.W. Muckelroy,	Enclosed ambulatories in Romano-Celtic temples in Britain, *Britannia* vii (1976), 173–91
J. Munby & M. Henig (eds.),	*Roman life and art in Britain* BAR 41 (1977)
D.S. Neal,	*Roman mosaics in Roman Britain* (Britannia Monograph 1 London 1981)
D.S. Neal,	A sanctuary at Wood Lane End, Hemel Hempstead, *Britannia* xv (1984), 193–215
A. Rainey,	*Mosaics in Roman Britain* (Newton Abbot 1973)
M.J. Rhodes,	Wall paintings from Fenchurch Street, City of London, *Britannia* xviii (1987), 169–72
W.J. Rodwell (ed.),	*Temples, churches and religion in Roman Britain* BAR 77 (1980)
A. Ross,	The horned god of the Brigantes, *Arch. Ael.*4 xxxix (1961), 59–85
D.J. Smith,	Three fourth century schools of mosaic in Roman Britain, in *La mosaique greco-romaine* (eds. G. Picard & H. Stern Paris 1965), 95–114
D.J. Smith,	Roman mosaics in Britain before the fourth century, in *La mosaique greco-romaine ii* (eds. H. Stern & M. Le Glay Paris 1975), 269–89
D.J. Smith,	*The Roman mosaics from Rudston, Brantingham and Horkstow* (Hull 1976)
E.J. Swain & R. Ling,	The Kingscote wall-paintings, *Britannia* xii (1981), 167–75
C. Thomas,	*Christianity in Roman Britain* (London 1981)
J.M.C. Toynbee,	*Art in Roman Britain* (London 1961)
J.M.C. Toynbee,	*A silver casket and strainer from the Walbrook mithraeum in the City of London* (Leiden 1963)

J.M.C. Toynbee,	*Art in Britain under the Romans* (Oxford 1964)
J.M.C. Toynbee,	A new Roman mosaic pavement found in Dorset, *JRS* liv (1964), 7–14
W.J. Wedlake,	*The excavation of the shrine of Apollo at Nettleton, Wiltshire, 1956–71.* Research Reports of the Society of Antiquaries 40 (London 1982)

LATER ROMAN BRITAIN

P. Bartholomew,	Fifth century facts, *Britannia* xiii (1982), 261–70
P. Bartholomew,	Fourth century Saxons, *Britannia* xv (1984), 169–85
R.J. Brickstock,	*Copies of the Fel Temp Reparatio coinage in Britain*, BAR 176 (1987)
G. Brodribb,	Stamped tiles of the Classis Britannica, *Sussex Arch. Collns.* cvii (1969), 102–35
A. Burnett,	Clipped siliquae and the end of Roman Britain, *Britannia* xv (1984), 163–8
R.A.G. Carson,	Gold and silver coin hoards and the end of Roman Britain, in *The Classical Tradition. British Museum Yearbook I* (London 1976), 67–82
P.J. Casey,	Carausius and Allectus – rulers in Gaul? *Britannia* viii (1977), 283–301
B.W. Cunliffe,	*Excavations at Portchester I.* Research Report of the Society of Antiquaries 32 (Oxford 1975)
B.W. Cunliffe,	Excavations at the Roman fort at Lympne, *Britannia* xi (1980), 227–88
D. Dumville,	Sub-Roman Britain: history and legend, *History* lxii (1977), 173–92
R. Goodburn & P. Bartholomew,	*Aspects of the Notitia Dignitatum* BAR 12 (1976)
S.C. Hawkes & G.C. Dunning,	Soldiers and settlers in Britain, fourth to fifth century, *Med. Arch.* v (1961), 1–41
J. Hinchliffe & C. Sparey Green,	*Excavations at Brancaster, 1974 and 1977.* East Anglian Archaeology, Monograph 23 (Norwich 1985)
J.S. Johnson,	The date of the construction of the Saxon Shore fort at Richborough, *Britannia* i (1970), 240–8
J.S. Johnson,	*The Roman forts of the Saxon Shore* (London 1976)
S. Johnson,	A late Roman helmet from Burgh Castle, *Britannia* xi (1980), 303–12
S. Johnson,	*Burgh Castle: excavations by Charles Green 1958–61.* East Anglian Archaeology. Monograph 20 (Norwich 1983)
D.E. Johnston (ed.),	*The Saxon Shore* CBA Research Report 18 (London 1977)
M.E. Jones & P.J. Casey,	The Gallic Chronicle restored: a chronology for the Anglo-Saxon invasions and the end of Roman Britain, *Britannia* xix (1988), 367–98
J.C. Mann,	The northern frontier after AD 369, *Glasgow Arch. Journ.* iii (1974), 34–42
M. Miller,	Stilicho's Pictish war, *Britannia* vi (1975), 141–5
B.J. Philp,	The Roman fort at Reculver, *Arch. Journ.* cxxvi (1969), 223–5
A. Ravetz,	Fourth century inflation and Romano-British coin-finds, *Num. Chron.*7 iv (1964), 201–12
S.E. Rigold,	The Roman haven of Dover, *Arch. Journ.* cxxvi (1969), 78–100
N.S. Ryan,	*Fourth century coin-finds from Roman Britain: a computer analysis* BAR 183 (1987)

N. Shiel, *The episode of Carausius and Allectus* BAR 40 (1977)

E.A. Thompson, Britain, AD 406–410, *Britannia* viii (1977), 303–18

E.A. Thompson, Gildas and the History of Britain, *Britannia* x (1979), 203–26

E.A. Thompson, *St. Germanus of Auxerre and the end of Roman Britain* (Woodbridge 1984)

M. Todd, Famosa pestis and fifth century Britain, *Britannia* viii (1977), 319–25

R.S.O. Tomlin, The date of the "Barbarian Conspiracy", *Britannia* v (1974), 303–9

M.G Welch, Late Romans and Saxons in Sussex, *Britannia* ii (1971), 232–7

J.J. Wilkes, Early fourth century rebuilding in Hadrian's Wall forts, in *Britain and Rome* (eds. M.G. Jarrett & B. Dobson, Kendal 1966), 114–38

I. Wood, The fall of the western Empire and the end of Roman Britain, *Britannia* xviii (1987), 251–62

INDEX

NAMES

Adminius, 83
Agricola, Gn. Iulius, 32, 61, 63, 66, 72, 181
Almonsbury, 5
Amiens, 87, 88
Antoninus Pius, 52
Ardoch, 50
Ashville, 4, 127
Attis, 226
Augustus, 16, 18
Aulus Plautius, 26, 61

Bagendon, 86
Baldock, 210
Barburgh Mill, 51
Bar Hill, 50
Barton Court Farm, 4, 123, 126, 132, 142
Bath, 86–7, 88, 89, 185, 188, 208, 211, 220, 221, 224, 231
Bavay, 88
Beauport Park, 211
Belgae, 13
Bewcastle, 44
Birdoswald, 43, 44
Birrens, 44
Boudicca, 21, 76, 180
Bowness, 41
Brandon Camp, 25–6
Brantingham, 206
Braughing, 10, 11
Brittones, 67
Brough-on-Humber, 204
Burnswark, 67
Butser Hill, 8

Caerleon, 21, 22, 111, 211, 237
Caerwent, 87, 97, 108–11, 239, 240
  basilica, 97
  curia, 97
  defences, 92
  forum, 92
  houses, 108–10
Caesar, Julius, 13, 16, 19, 25, 176, 177
Caistor-by-Norwich, 92, 97, 240
Caledones, 62, 71
Caledonia, 62, 69
Calpurnius Agricola, 53
Camelon, 50
Canterbury, 10, 12, 84–5, 87, 88, 91, 96, 103, 209
  baths, 85

  forum, 85, 96
  Iron Age settlement, 84
  imported stone, 88
  street-grid, 84, 103
  temple-precinct, 85, 96
  theatre, 85, 96
Caracalla, 54, 61
Carausius, 193
Carlisle, 43, 57, 131, 208
Carpow, 54
Carriden, 69
Cartimandua, 27, 28, 31
Cassivellaunus, 16
Castledykes, 69
Castor, 171
Cerealis, Petillius, 31, 32
Chester, 211, 237
Chesterholm (*Vindolanda*), 41, 44, 56–7, 58
  writing tablets, 44, 70
Chesters, 43
Chichester, 27, 83, 89, 220, 223, 240
  collegium, 83
  forum, 83
  Jupiter column, 83
  inscriptions, 83
  Iron Age settlement, 83
  military occupation, 83
  temple, 83, 89
Cirencester, 86, 88, 91, 94, 102, 107, 111, 199, 204, 215, 240, 246
  amphitheatre, 102
  basilica, 86
  cemetery, 107–8
  defences, 102
  forum, 86, 94
  fort, 86
  houses, 111
  planning, 86
Claudius, 26, 61, 76
Claydon Pike, 123
Clodius Albinus, 94
Cocidius, 58
Cogidubnus, 27, 81, 83, 221
Colchester, 10, 11, 19, 20, 21, 23, 24, 25, 28, 75, 76–7, 89, 91, 102, 131, 180, 200, 220
  defences, 77, 102
  forum, 76
  gates, 77

267

SUBJECTS